COMING OUT OF COMMUNISM

Coming Out of Communism

The Emergence of LGBT Activism
in Eastern Europe

Conor O'Dwyer

NEW YORK UNIVERSITY PRESS
New York

NEW YORK UNIVERSITY PRESS
New York
www.nyupress.org

References to Internet websites (URLs) were accurate at the time of writing. Neither the author nor New York University Press is responsible for URLs that may have expired or changed since the manuscript was prepared.

Library of Congress Cataloging-in-Publication Data
Names: O'Dwyer, Conor, 1972– author.
Title: Coming out of communism : the emergence of LGBT activism in Eastern Europe / Conor O'Dwyer.
Description: New York : New York University, [2018] | Includes bibliographical references and index.
Identifiers: LCCN 2017060993 | ISBN 9781479876631 (cl : alk. paper) | ISBN 9781479851485 (pb : alk. paper)
Subjects: LCSH: Gay liberation movement—Europe, Eastern. | Sexual minorities— Political activity—Europe, Eastern. | Homosexuality—Europe, Eastern.
Classification: LCC HQ76.5 .O29 2018 | DDC 306.76/60947—dc23
LC record available at https://lccn.loc.gov/2017060993

New York University Press books are printed on acid-free paper, and their binding materials are chosen for strength and durability. We strive to use environmentally responsible suppliers and materials to the greatest extent possible in publishing our books.

Manufactured in the United States of America

10 9 8 7 6 5 4 3 2 1

Also available as an ebook

In years to come, maybe in the distant future, entry into the European Union, and not 1989, may come to be seen as the moment when a new kind of national direction was initiated that did, in fact, bring Eastern Europe into Europe.
—Gale Stokes, historian

Be nice to the devil until you have crossed the bridge.
—Romanian proverb

CONTENTS

LIST OF FIGURES AND TABLES

ACRONYMS

AOF: Alliance of Families (Alianța Familiilor)

CNCD: National Council for Combatting Discrimination (Consiliul Național pentru Combaterea Discriminării)

COC: Cultuur-en Ontspanningscentrum

COE: Council of Europe

ČSL: Czechoslovak People's Party (Československá strana lidová)

ČSSD: Czech Social Democratic Party (Česká strana sociálně demokratická)

ENP: European Neighborhood Policy

EP: European Parliament

GI: Gay Initiative (Gay iniciativa)

G-LIGA: G-League

GLL: Gay and Lesbian League (Gay a lesbická liga)

HOS: Movement for Civic Freedom (Hnutí za občanskou svobodu)

HRHO: Movement for Equality of Homosexual Citizens (Hnutí za rovnoprávnost homosexuálních občanů)

HZDS: Movement for a Democratic Slovakia (Hnutie za demokratické Slovensko)

ICSE: International Committee for Sexual Equality

IGCLN-POLAND: International Lesbian and Gay Culture Network in Poland

ILGA: International Lesbian, Gay, Bisexual, Trans and Intersex Association

JOBBIK: Movement for a Better Hungary (Jobbik Magyarországért Mozgalom)

KDH: Christian Democratic Movement (Kresťanskodemokratické hnutie)

KDNP: Christian Democrats (Kereszténydemokrata Néppárt)

KDU-ČSL: Christian Democratic Union–Czechoslovak People's Party (Křesťanská a demokratická unie–Československá strana lidová)

KPH: Campaign Against Homophobia (Kampania Przeciw Homofobii)

LGBT: lesbian, gay, bisexual, and transsexual

LPR: League of Polish Families (Liga Polskich Rodzin)

MDF: Hungarian Democratic Forum (Magyar Demokrata Fórum)

MCF: MCF Roma Alliance Party (MCF Roma összefogás)

MIÉP: Hungarian Justice and Life Party (Magyar Igazság és Élet Pártja)

MONAR: Youth Movement against Drug Addiction (Młodzieżowy Ruch na Rzecz Przeciwdziałania Narkomanii)

MP: Member of Parliament

MSZP: Hungarian Socialist Party (Magyar Szocialista Párt)

MW: All-Poland Youth (Młodzież Wszechpolska)

NGO: nongovernmental organization

ODS: Civic Democratic Party (Občanská demokratická strana)

OI: Otherness Initiative (Iniciatíva Inakosť)

PDSR: Party of Social Democracy of Romania (Partidul Democrației Sociale din România)

PIS: Law and Justice (Prawo i Sprawiedliwość)

PO: Civic Platform (Platforma Obywatelska)

POS: political opportunity structure

PM: prime minister

PRM: Greater Romania Party (Partidul România Mare)

PROUD: Platform for Equality, Recognition, and Diversity (Platforma pro rovnoprávnost, uznání a diverzitu)

PSNS: Real Slovak National Party (Pravá slovenská národná strana)

PUNR: Romanian National Unity Party (Partidul Unității Naționale a Românilor)

QLF: Queer Leaders Forum

ROP: Movement to Rebuild Poland (Ruch Odbudowy Polski)

SDK: Slovak Democratic Coalition (Slovenská demokratická koalícia)

SDL: Party of the Democratic Left (Strana demokratickej ľavice)

SLD: Democratic Left Alliance (Sojusz Lewicy Demokratycznej)

SMO: social movement organization

SNS: Slovak National Party (Slovenská národná strana)

SO: Self-Defense (Samoobrona)

SOHO: Organization of Associations of Homosexual Citizens (Sdružení organizací homosexuálních občanů)

SPR-RSČ: Association for the Republic–Republican Party of
Czechoslovakia (Sdružení pro Republiku–Republikánská strana
Československa)

SZDSZ: Alliance of Free Democrats–Hungarian Liberal Party (Szabad
Demokraták Szövetsége–a Magyar Liberális Párt)

TR: Your Movement (Twój Ruch)

WVS: World Values Survey

1

The Benefits of Backlash

The Divergent Trajectories of LGBT-Rights Activism after Communism

Not that long ago, the term "postcommunist LGBT-rights movement" might have been dismissed as a double oxymoron.[1] After all, are not the societies of the former Eastern bloc deeply conservative when it comes to homosexuality? They were so before communism, and they remained so under it. Moreover, had not civil society and its close cousin political activism been pronounced, if not dead, at least in critical condition after the fall of communism?[2] As even a cursory survey reveals, however, the politics of homosexuality has become not only dramatically more salient in postcommunist Europe but also far more complex. Let us consider a few cases to illustrate.

Romania makes a good starting point. Homosexuality was criminalized there until 2001, punishable under the infamous Article 200 by up to five years in prison. In 1993, when the Romanian government applied to join the Council of Europe, it was granted membership in return for the promise to repeal Article 200 within six months. Six years later the promise was still unfulfilled, leading one observer to note that "Romania has a playful attitude toward international commitments."[3] By 2006, however, Romania's legal framework for lesbian, gay, bisexual, and transsexual (LGBT) people had undergone a transformation, and the country was one of five named by Human Rights Watch for exemplary progress on LGBT rights.[4] Today, Romania has more expansive antidiscrimination protections—notably in the area of transgender persons—than most of its neighbors and many West European countries.

Poland presents an example of rapid social and political change, though not (yet) legal change. In 2004, just two months after joining the European Union, the country earned international notoriety by banning Pride parades in Warsaw and several other cities. Radically antigay political parties were elected to government, antigay youth groups were attacking Prides, and a stridently homophobic political rhetoric was being employed by national political leaders. Yet, by 2011, the tide had turned dramatically. The most vociferously antigay party had imploded, Warsaw had become the first postcommunist city to host the EuroPride festival, and strongly organized, highly professional, well-funded gay-rights nongovernmental organizations (NGOs) had built national activist networks. Several prominent LGBT-rights candidates had been elected to the national parliament, having campaigned with an anticlerical party that listed legalization of same-sex unions as one of its core goals. A highly visible campaign for registered partnerships with major party backing was soon under way.

As a final example of the divergent politics of homosexuality evident a generation after 1989, consider the Czech Republic. During the 1990s, Czech activists built one of the best-organized and most influential LGBT-rights movements in the region. In 1999, the activist and analyst Scott Long called SOHO, then the main Czech group, "the only genuinely national gay and lesbian network in the former Soviet bloc—and, arguably, one of the best organized in Europe."[5] In 2006, Czech activists achieved their long-held goal of enacting same-sex registered partnerships, becoming the first country in the region to do so. As important as the legislation was, especially symbolically, it was incomplete, and prominent rights advocates vowed to campaign to correct its shortcomings and further the goal of equality. Within a year, however, all of the major Czech LGBT-rights organizations had disbanded, and the movement became one of the region's weakest—despite the country's better than average gay-rights framework. Thus, the Czech example is one of pioneering legal change but social movement decay.

In sum, the reality on the ground is not only varied, it is often surprising, and changing quickly. Explanations of why this is so have not kept up. But one may ask: Why look for an underlying theoretical explanation for this divergence? Why even group these countries together? Aside from the fact that, in all of them, communism created an extremely repressive environment for homosexuality, should we not expect that things would be different some two decades later?

The similarities among the region's political systems, however, did not end with communism's collapse. Almost immediately after that transformational event, they embarked together on joining the EU—a project that would also prove transformational. As the exit from communism happened in the course of just one year, the annus mirabilis of 1989, so too entry into the EU was a process characterized by simultaneity—with common timetables, common conditions, and common requirements for accession.[6] Yet, though the EU accession process emphasized common requirements and timetables, *how* those conditions interacted with communist legacies and domestic politics was far from straightforward. The result has been that EU accession has shaped the domestic politics of homosexuality in ways that are systematic and patterned but also surprising and poorly understood.

* * *

This book is about social movements after communism, in particular those mobilizing around LGBT rights. It argues that much of the region is experiencing a trajectory of increasingly organized and influential activism. LGBT-rights activism in postcommunist Europe deserves the attention of students of comparative politics, LGBT politics, and transnational norm diffusion, first, because until recently it would have seemed so unlikely; second, because it offers a new and dramatic perspective into the transnational dynamics of social movement development; and third, because it offers a strong test of the robustness of liberal democratic values and the possibility of deeper social change in new democracies. Most centrally from this book's perspective, however, postcommunist LGBT activism deserves our attention for the insights it affords into the consequences of domestic backlash against transnational norms.

There is a striking puzzle at the heart of the region's LGBT-rights politics: Why is the most organized activism often found in societies where attitudes toward homosexuality are least tolerant? As this book will show, the transformation of homosexuality from "moral" taboo to political issue in Eastern Europe coincided precisely with the first round of postcommunist countries joining the EU. In a number of the EU applicant-states, this politicization of homosexuality initially took the form of strongly antigay rhetoric and policies. The irony was hard to miss: though homosexuality had long been taboo and though LGBT persons had long experienced discrimination, overt political backlash occurred precisely at the moment that these states had passed the democratic litmus test of EU accession. Analysts and activists alike decried the postaccession backlash, but with time it has become increasingly clear that some rights movements have emerged from this backlash stronger than ever. Poland is the clearest example, as we will see.

Poland's example underlines a clear but little-noted aspect of LGBT activism since 1989, namely the breadth of variation both cross-nationally and over time in how such activism has been organized. There are surprising differences regarding *when* and *how* collective action crosses three important thresholds: that between uncoordinated localism and national organization, that between informal social movement communities and formally established, institutionally complex social movement organizations (SMOs), and that between constituent-oriented service provision and political, even electoral mobilization. After communism's collapse, activism had not crossed any of these thresholds: it was local, informal, and apolitical—comprised of friendship networks oriented toward self-help and services. By 2011, we find considerable variation among the region's rights movements vis-à-vis these thresholds, and even examples that have crossed all three.

Explaining this variation offers broader insights into backlash's role as a catalyst of social movement development, especially in contexts with unfavorable political opportunity structures (POS) and scarce resources for collective action. As this book argues, when LGBT movements face threatening opposition, it allows them to solve several collective action problems at once, and with minimal resources. Coming under attack generates solidarity. Specifically, backlash threatens to disrupt the quotidian expectations and arrangements of the movement's constituents. Social movement scholars have ascribed great importance to these expectations, taken-for-granted routines, informal arrangements, and "routinized patterns of making do" that individuals use to negotiate daily life—naming them, in one memorable formulation, "the immediate protective surround."[7] When individuals feel that their immediate protective surround is threatened, they become more willing to contribute to collective action and riskier, more political forms of action. Second, by triggering framing contests around homosexuality and transnational norms, backlash increases the visibility and resonance of homosexuality as a rights issue. Finally, this framing contest attracts allies that might not otherwise find common cause with the movement.

Applying this argument to postcommunist Europe, here in brief are the conditions that have catalyzed organized and politically oriented LGBT activism in *some* parts of the region. States seeking EU membership are (simultaneously) exposed to unusually intense external leverage—through both conditionality mandating legal changes protecting LGBT persons from discrimination and exposure to transnational EU advocacy networks. Where this leverage sparks strong backlash from hard-right political groups, it also helps LGBT-rights activists overcome the above challenges to collective action: solidarity, resonance, and allies. Where transnational leverage does *not* spark backlash, rights activists continue to face these challenges unaided, challenges that are particularly acute in new democracies with less than robust traditions of civil society.

To build this argument, this book focuses primarily on Poland and the Czech Republic from 1989 through 2012, cases with contrasting trajectories and counterintuitive outcomes. Both emerged from communism as societies in which gays and lesbians faced official and unofficial discrimination across a range of areas, including employment, public services, policing, and, of course, family policy. In Poland, this discrimination was undergirded by lower tolerance and a politically influential Catholic Church. Today, Poland, a society seemingly inhospitable to gay rights, has a highly organized, politically mobilized movement, whereas in the Czech Republic, the region's most LGBT-tolerant society, a once-promising movement has deinstitutionalized and depoliticized itself.[8] The empirical analysis probes this variation between otherwise similarly situated countries, drawing on histories of LGBT activism,[9] fieldwork conducted between 2007 and 2011, and content analysis of two national newspapers. A separate chapter explores further variations on the argument by extending it to the additional cases of Hungary, Romania, and Slovakia.

This argument can contribute to three literatures: the legacy of communism on civil society; transnational norm diffusion and its subfield, Europeanization; and the comparative politics of homosexuality. Analyzing the organization of postcommunist LGBT activism extends these literatures to still underexplored contexts while also addressing conundrums each is ill-equipped to handle on its own. For example, the variation in activism in a region noted for communism's uniformly demobilizing legacy on civil society is puzzling. Likewise, for scholars of diffusion it is puzzling that the embodiment of EU minority-rights norms in increasingly organized domestic social movements has occurred when EU leverage was weakest (i.e., after accession) and where the "fit" between EU and domestic norms was lowest.

Finally, this argument builds on a growing comparative scholarship on the politics of homosexuality "on the periphery."[10] Typically, however, this scholarship has sought to explain policy change or attitudinal trends. An excellent example is Phillip Ayoub's recent book on the diffusion of LGBT-rights norms in Europe, including postcommunist Europe.[11] Ayoub captures norm diffusion through policy change and individual attitudes toward sexual minorities, arguing that change in both has been primarily driven by the ways in which EU enlargement built connections between transnational networks and domestic rights advocates. Like this book, Ayoub is also deeply appreciative of the indirect dynamics by which domestic backlash against transnational norms may advantage domestic activists.[12] What separates our approaches is my focus on the organization of activism as the outcome of interest: this book process traces cycles of mobilization and countermobilization over a more than 20-year span. This approach allows us to focus more closely on the pivotal role of LGBT-rights *opponents* in the framing of homosexuality in the public sphere. Norm visibility is an important catalyst of political and attitudinal change, as Ayoub shows, but norm visibility is as much a product of *opposition* to transnational norms as it is of the choices of transnational advocacy networks and their domestic NGO partners. This insight becomes especially clear when looking, as this book does, at societies equally exposed to transnational norms and networks but not to hard-right backlash. Here, the Czech Republic stands out as a country with as deep connections to West European networks as any of its neighbors, comparatively tolerant attitudes toward homosexuality, and relatively accommodating state authorities; yet its LGBT-rights movement has traced an arc of decline since the late 1990s.

This book's focus on the organization of activism also gives a better picture of the range of difficulties faced by LGBT-rights movements "in the periphery."[13] Insufficient support from transnational networks or opposition by social conservatives are not the only hurdles faced by social movements in contexts where extant mobilizing structures are weak, nor even the most daunting ones. Sustaining collective action also requires overcoming apathy within the movement's constituencies; managing conflict among the movement's leaders over goals and strategies; and adjusting to shifts in the priorities of domestic authorities, especially regarding the availability of funding and other resources. Surprising as it may seem, even policy success can create its own challenges for social movements: after achieving policy goals, there is a temptation to declare victory and demobilize. The Czech movement furnishes a good example. Focusing on movement organization over longer time spans offers us greater analytical traction on these dimensions of activism, on which deeper social change depends.

A third advantage of this book's long-term process-tracing approach is to look closely at who participates and how. By focusing on movement organization, we can capture major shifts in "sexual citizenship" even where policies and attitudes are lagging, as they generally are in postcommunist Europe. In this way, we may think of the region's LGBT activism in terms of what Jeffrey Weeks has described as "the long process of the democratization of everyday life."[14] This democratization is about the expansion of "sexual or intimate citizenship," that is, about acknowledging "the ways in which minorities and deviants have been excluded from the rights and obligations of full citizenship."[15] While the winning of policy changes like registered partnerships, protections from labor discrimination, and equal access to social services are central to this revolution, the practice of sexual citizenship is broader and more participatory. As Judith Butler writes, "[W]hen we struggle for rights we are not simply struggling for rights that attach to my person, but we are struggling *to be conceived as persons.*"[16]

Expanding the boundaries of such citizenship was the first task of modern LGBT activism in Western Europe and the United States, paving the way for recent policy gains like same-sex marriage. Focusing on sexual citizenship, the organization of activism, and also the role of backlash offers a way to read postcommunist developments in a broader comparative context. As Weeks argues, backlash was a driving force behind sexual citizenship in the West. For example, the enactment of same-sex partnerships in Britain in 2005 was preceded by a period of New Right mobilization, as embodied in Prime Minister Margaret Thatcher's "New Victorianism." The passage of Section 28 in 1986, which banned the promotion of homosexuality in British schools, was a highpoint of such backlash. Section 28 sought to exclude homosexuality from the public sphere and had a chilling effect on activism, at least initially. Ultimately, as Weeks describes, Section 28 helped the British movement:

> For what it did above all was to mobilize a lesbian and gay community that had been badly battered by the HIV/AIDS crisis. It is from this date that a new energy for coming out, community-building and working towards legitimization, fuelled by anger at the neglect of lesbian and gay issues in the early epidemic, came to the fore, with incalculable effects. It also rescued the reputation of the offending local authorities [whose sex education curricula had been the impetus for passing Section 28]. The rather haphazard efforts by a number of left-wing controlled local governments to introduce equal rights policies were floundering under the weight of media attacks and financial crises. Suddenly these were legitimized, and a certain nostalgia arose for their courage.[17]

The larger arc of Britain's LGBT movement was, Weeks argues, the accretion of this two-steps-forward-one-step-back organizing. This book's focus on backlash builds on this literature, which, in analyzing activism in terms of citizenship (as opposed to policy-oriented collective action), highlights its affective, emotional, and framing aspects.[18]

Of course, as instructive as it is to "read forward" the parallels of first-wave LGBT movements in the United States and Western Europe in analyzing sexual citizenship in postcommunist Europe, we should also be cautious about extending the defining features of postcommunist movements back to first-wave ones. Yes, on the one hand, in the US the transition from the "underground" homophile movement to the politically organized and highly visible gay liberation movement was birthed by the 1969 Stonewall Riot.[19] Decades later, Polish activists would label their own defiance of state bans on Pride parades "Polish Stonewall." However, important differences between these contexts abound. As John D'Emilio shows, the American gay liberation movement was built on a preexisting network of homophile organizations. Moreover, the movement was pushed forward by primarily domestic factors, notably the example of the civil rights movement and broad cultural shifts about sexuality in the 1960s. Thus, though moments like Stonewall—in which the gay community felt a heightened threat to its immediate protective surround, and mobilized against it—were critical, much of the American movement's success was based on society becoming more open.[20] The same point can also be made about prominent first-wave LGBT movements in Western Europe. As M. V. Lee Badgett argues, the Dutch LGBT movement's pioneering enactment of same-sex partnerships was dependent on Dutch society's unusually open attitude toward homosexuality.[21]

Starting conditions on the "LGBT-rights periphery" of postcommunist Europe are different: society is in general comparatively closed, and the legacy of communism means there are no preexisting mobilizing structures comparable to those enjoyed by Western predecessors. On the plus side, second-wave LGBT movements benefit from the existence of a highly developed transnational advocacy network, which can both promote the example of gains made in the LGBT-rights core and shape the POS faced by movements and their opponents. These new circumstances give postcommunist LGBT movements their distinctive, transnational developmental trajectories.

This introductory chapter presents a comparative framework that can identify the conditions and explain the causal mechanisms by which transnational pressure may boost the organization and influence of LGBT activism "on the periphery," where, typically, the resources for such activism are few. The chapter first describes the wide variation in the politics of homosexuality in Eastern Europe since communism's collapse. It then reviews possible explanations for this variation in the extant literature, drawing on what might be termed the two "grand narratives" of postcommunist political development: the domestic narrative of weak civil society and the transnational narrative of norm diffusion through EU accession. This book proposes a social movement framework that knits together the insights of both narratives by highlighting the critical role of hard-right backlash in organizing activism and the conditions under which it does so. The chapter's final sections discuss the research design, data, and country cases that will be used to illustrate and test the theory.

As a last prefatory note, a word regarding terminology is necessary. As mentioned earlier, scholars recognize a wide set of identities and orientations under the umbrella terms "LGBT" and "sexual minorities." Speaking broadly, gays and lesbians were the most visible elements of the movement as it emerged in the West in the 1960s, and these activists tended to conceive of sexual identity in terms of a fixed orientation.[22] Over time, bisexual, trans, and queer movements emerged, whose constituents envisaged sexuality more as a constructed identity; queer politics, in particular, espoused a subversive, anti-institutional, and radical view of sexual freedom. In Eastern Europe, communism suppressed the articulation of nonheteronormative orientations and identities until relatively recently, and this legacy has complicated conceptions of identity, and their respective visibility within the movement.[23] The term "LGBT," though now widely used in postcommunist countries, was not always in common usage. In the early 1990s, activists favored the term "homosexual" in naming organizations. Later, the preferred usage became "gay" or "lesbian." More recently, the identity "queer" has been embraced by some activists, though not all. Other identities remain distinctly underrepresented, notably transgender and bisexual, not to mention intersex. Indeed, as Joanna Mizielińska has noted, often there are inconsistencies in activists' self-presentation: for example, the English-language website of Poland's Campaign Against Homophobia used the term "LGBT," while its Polish-language version used only the terms "lesbian," "gay," and "homosexual."[24]

In practice, the lion's share of groups described in this book are concerned with sexual orientation rather than gender identity: the emphasis is on gay and lesbian rather than bisexual, trans, and queer. In order to mark broad shifts in the self-understandings of activists over time, the case-study narratives will note moments when the language of self-identity shifted and when various identities within the movement came into tension with each other. For ease of exposition, however, I will follow the scholarly convention of using the umbrella terms "LGBT" and "sexual minorities" to refer to the movement, its members, and its goals. Likewise, I will use "LGBT rights" to cover the gamut of policies and goals from ensuring basic civil rights to more ambitious (for the region) goals such as same-sex marriage.

Finally, I use the terms "homophobic" and "antigay" synonymously to include all forms of prejudice based on sexual orientation and gender identity. "Antigay politics" and "political homophobia" refer to the set of stigmatizing discourses and strategies purposefully deployed by states, political elites, and social movement actors against LGBT persons, which, as Michael Bosia and Michelle Weiss note, is occurring in an increasingly modular and transnational fashion.[25] As they write, "Today's homophobic political strategies range from straightforward or seemingly 'rational' processes of marginalization—of branding gay rights, like so often women's or ethnic minorities' rights, as either 'special interests' and thus not a priority, or as a threat to the nation—to often violent vilification and abuse."[26]

Social Attitudes, Legal Rights, and the Organization of Activism

The first step in understanding the rapidly changing field in which the region's LGBT movements mobilize is to break it down into three related but conceptually distinct components: social attitudes; policy and legal rights; and how activism is organized. The last of these is the primary focus of this book. The second step is to recognize that these components develop at different speeds, and sometimes even move in different directions.

The first component is social attitudes. How is homosexuality perceived by the broader society? The second component concerns legislation, public policy, and court rulings. Both of these are relatively straightforward to tap empirically because there exist ready-made indices allowing them to be compared cross-nationally: in particular, the World Values Survey (WVS) for attitudes and the ILGA–Europe Rainbow Index for legal rights. The final component, how activism is organized, concerns the conceptual distinction between politics as officially codified and politics as it is lived, that is, sexual citizenship. Are minority rights exercised, or do they simply exist on paper? Do minorities participate on equal terms in political life and the public sphere? Is rights activism structured in terms of social movements, political parties, or rather as local and informally organized communities, such as self-help groups? How do activists frame homosexuality as an issue?

How activism is organized is the most difficult of the three dimensions to compare systematically across countries. Unlike social attitudes or legal rights, there are no cross-national indices to consult. Also, one thing that becomes clear in any careful study of homosexuality in formerly communist societies is that activism and group consciousness of some sort have always existed, taking form as hidden subcultures. It would be erroneous to write off these precursors to social movement mobilization. Indeed, there is a long tradition in social movement theory showing that informal networks of solidarity become assets in the building of formal organizational networks later. How, then, do "social movement communities" become "social movement organizations"?[27] The following empirical chapters present one of the first in-depth comparative studies of how LGBT activism in this region has developed over the broad span of the postcommunist period.

Comparing across these three elements in postcommunist Europe reveals not just that they may develop at different speeds, but that progress on one dimension may be accompanied by backsliding on another. I argue that this kind of uneven development results from the *interaction* of domestic politics and transnational pressures: more specifically, the interaction of the communist legacy with the transnational pressures of EU integration.

The relevance of the communist legacy is evident in a comparison of social attitudes and legal frameworks East and West. Figure 1.1 draws on cross-national public opinion data collected in the World Values Survey to compare attitudes toward homosexuality in both regions.[28] As Figure 1.1 shows, there is a clear difference between postcommunist countries and the rest of Europe regarding attitudes toward homosexuality. Only the Czech Republic exceeds the European average. This chasm in attitudes persists if we probe it across different survey questions regarding homosexuality (e.g., "How would you feel if your neighbor was gay?"). The enduring relevance of the communist legacy is also apparent when comparing Eastern and Western European countries in terms of rights, as in Figure 1.2. Here, I draw on a cross-national index of rights for lesbian, gay, and bisexual people constructed by the Brussels-based NGO ILGA-Europe (International Lesbian, Gay, Bisexual, Trans and Intersex Association in Europe). The index, based on data from 2010, ranges from a minimum score of -4 to a maximum of 10; each country's score reflects state policy on such issues as same-sex partnerships and marriage, parenting rights, and provisions preventing discrimination on the basis of sexual orientation.[29] The similarity to Figure 1.1 is striking and serves as another strong indicator of the communist legacy. Even a cursory inspection of the scores indicates an East-West divide.[30] Postcommunist countries as a whole score lower in terms of legal rights—1.3 on average compared with 4.3 for the rest of Europe.[31]

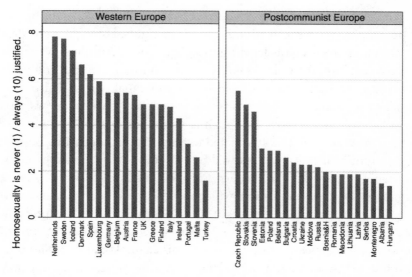

Figure 1.1. Attitudes toward Homosexuality in Western Europe and Postcommunist Europe Compared (circa 2000)

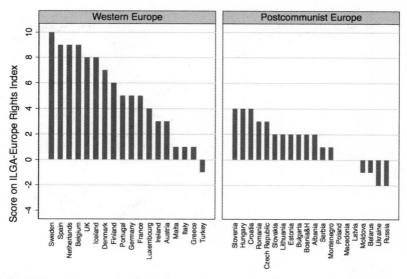

Figure 1.2. Rights of Gays, Lesbians, and Bisexuals in Western and Eastern Europe Compared (2010)

The picture becomes more complex, however, if we consider the relationship between social attitudes and legal rights. Using the same data as above, Figure 1.3 plots legal rights against social attitudes. We might assume without, it would seem, being too controversial that countries with more tolerant attitudes regarding homosexuality would also have more progressive LGBT-rights frameworks. As Figure 1.3 shows, this is in fact true in Western Europe. It is *not* the case in Eastern Europe, where the relationship is attenuated to nonexistent. Something besides the communist legacy, as captured by attitudes toward homosexuality, is shaping legal rights in Eastern Europe. That something, this book argues, is the European Union, which incentivizes countries like Romania or Croatia to adopt legal rights for LGBT people far beyond what the prevailing social attitudes would otherwise support. (Chapter 2 will return to and develop this argument.) This example illustrates how attitudes, rights, and activism may move at different speeds. They may also move in different directions, as becomes evident when we turn to how activism is organized.

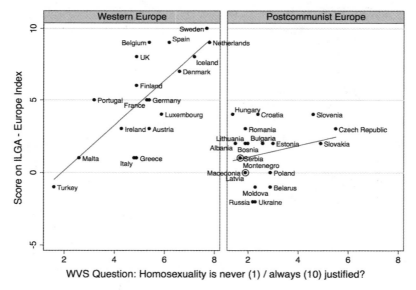

Figure 1.3. Social Attitudes (circa 2000) vs. LGBT Rights (2010) in Western and Eastern Europe

When comparing the organization of LGBT activism and the practice of sexual citizenship, there are no cross-national indices to draw on. This is the reason for the comparative case studies and process tracing in the empirical chapters of this book. For now, however, to present a stylized but not inaccurate picture, let us consider one indicator of activism: Pride parades. These are largely a symbolic form of activism. They do not change social practices, at least not immediately. They do not end with the enactment of new policies or legislation. They do not, at least not directly, lead to the election of political candidates. But they are nonetheless immensely important to LGBT-rights activism as a social movement. They are the visible manifestation of sexual citizenship, of LGBT persons exercising their civil liberties in the public sphere. They help define the movement both to itself and to the broader society: they attract attention to the cause; they generate discussion; and they articulate identities and represent interests. To quote from one activist in Poland:

> [T]here are [only a few] situations where there is no difficulty in coming together, for example, the Equality Parade. . . .[32] This year it was a big success because 3,500 people came and even though some organizations were quarreling with each other—because that's the way it is, sometimes they quarrel—it was clear that this is the Equality Parade, that we're all there, and that we all march together. . . . And as far as it goes about things like the Equality Parade, there will always be solidarity because the goals are shared; in that moment we are not divided.[33]

In demonstrating proof of the movement's solidarity and its numbers, Prides are, of course, also tests of movement strength. If turnout is disappointing, they indicate weakness. By increasing visibility, they inevitably also expose the leadership to attacks from the outside. In Poland, for example, the Cracow parade was denounced as a "demonstration of sin" by the local Catholic bishop.[34] They are also a test of the movement's logistical and organizational capacity because they require permits, security measures, and management of the participants. If any or all of these elements of hosting Prides seem problematic for a given movement's leadership, they may choose not to host them.

Hosting a Pride parade is not a perfect indicator of movement strength, but clearly it *is* an indicator. It is striking, therefore, that Warsaw

Prides have been held since 2001 and, moreover, that they have grown in size and significance even as they have faced political bans and a barrage of public criticism. Not only did the Polish movement continue to hold Prides in the face of hard-right backlash, they mounted legal challenges to parade bans in national and international courts. By contrast, Prague, the center of Czech LGBT-rights activism, did not hold a Pride parade until 2011—despite the fact that Czech society is generally more tolerant of homosexuality and the Czech parliament enacted same-sex registered partnerships.[35] As described in the following chapters, the lack of Prague Prides was a deliberate choice on the part of Czech activists not to politicize gay rights out of fear that it might turn public opinion against them. This contrast between Czech and Polish activism speaks to the possibility that "closed societies"—those characterized by intolerant attitudes toward homosexuality—may spur LGBT groups to stronger organization and activism.

Organized, visible, and influential activism matters because social movements are not just a civic good in themselves. They have positive and noticeable impacts on the lives of LGBT persons. Recent scholarship has shown how the implosion of the women's movement in Russia in the 1990s facilitated the rise of a misogynistic political discourse and escalated discrimination against both women and LGBT people under the Vladimir Putin regime.[36] Comparative work by Andrew Reynolds has shown that the election of even one LGBT parliamentarian is strongly linked to legal breakthroughs for sexual minorities in that particular country.[37] Poland has now elected two such MPs. In 2011, it elected the first transgender MP in Europe, and it also elected the former head of the country's largest LGBT-rights group, the Campaign Against Homophobia (KPH). In the highly visible arena of Warsaw city politics, it elected an openly gay candidate and rights activist, Kristian Legierski, in 2010. Activists also note a growing number of openly gay candidates over time, from around 10 in 2011 to over 30 in 2014.[38]

Having laid out the contours of this region's rapidly changing politics of homosexuality and LGBT activism, let us now return to the larger theoretical question that these politics pose: How can we explain that the most organized and influential activism is found where attitudes toward homosexuality are least tolerant? The next sections lay out a comparative framework to make sense of this puzzle. This framework is grounded in

the civil-societal and transnational diffusion paradigms that have dominated scholarship since 1989, but it also highlights those paradigms'
shortcomings and seeks to resolve them using social movement theory.

Backlash: The Link between the Domestic and Transnational Determinants of Activism

The communist-legacies and Europeanization literatures rightly highlight both the scant resources for collective action and the extraordinary
impact of EU pressures on the region's changing politics of homosexuality. Lacking, however, is a framework theorizing *how* and *when*
transnational pressures interact with domestic factors to boost social
movement mobilization. The core concepts of social movement theory—
POS, mobilizing structures, and framing—can be used to build such a
framework. Shifts in EU leverage alter the domestic POS and *may* spark
framing contests between domestic and transnational norms, which in
turn catalyze the rapid organizational development of activism.

Scholarship on postcommunist activism is dominated by the thesis
that civil society is depressed across the board. Because of communism's
legacy of forced participation in a state-defined public sphere, a lack
of trust in and unwillingness to join voluntary organizations enfeebles
activism. Compared against established and postauthoritarian democracies, citizens of postcommunist democracies have significantly lower
rates of participation in voluntary organizations.[39] Case research has
shown this legacy's negative consequences for the organization of activism, which is seen as dominated by informal networks and elite networks funded by international donors.[40]

Even today, this narrative forms the starting point for studying activism in the region.[41] There is, however, an implicit assumption across this
scholarship of viewing civil society in a political vacuum, that is, in the
absence of an opposition. Tsveta Petrova and Sidney Tarrow identify this
assumption when they critique the literature's focus on "the magnitude
of individual participation" and inattention to the "relational dimensions
of participation."[42] Yet even their notion of "transactional activism"—
defined as "lateral ties among civil society groups and vertical ties between these groups and public officials"—is based on brokering, not on
the clash of polarized forces.[43] Postcommunist LGBT movements are

also resource-poor, but this lack can be compensated for by one asset they often do have—a threatening opposition. Even where formal rights are weak, LGBT persons fashion a whole set of informal arrangements— clubs, tacit "don't ask don't tell" agreements in the workplace, and so forth—to negotiate daily life. As noted earlier, these taken-for-granted routines form what some scholars have termed the "immediate protective surround." Research in contexts as varied as homeless activism and NIMBY (Not in My Backyard) movements has shown that threats to this protective surround are powerfully generative of collective action, even if mobilizing structures are weak.[44] This finding is based on a key argument from prospect theory that "individuals are especially averse to loss and therefore will endure considerably more risk in order to preserve what they already have than they will in order to gain something new."[45] As James Jasper has argued, such threats are perceived emotionally, as a kind of "'moral shock'. . . . [that] raises such a sense of outrage in a person that she becomes inclined toward political action, *with or without the network of personal contacts emphasized in mobilization and process theories.*"[46]

The EU's promotion of LGBT-rights norms in applicant-states provoked varying degrees of hard-right backlash, which in turn disrupted this "protective surround." As Chapter 2 will describe, the EU's identification with these norms built over time. The 1991 European Agreements made respect for minority rights a membership requirement, even if the initial emphasis was on ethnic minorities. In 1997, the Treaty of Amsterdam extended antidiscrimination principles to sexual orientation, and an Intergroup on LGBT Rights was established in the European Parliament (EP). Directive 2000/78 banned discrimination on the basis of sexual orientation, and the 2000 European Charter of Human Rights gave the principle of nondiscrimination constitutional status.[47] These norms became nonnegotiable for applicant states.

Theorizing the impact of this kind of transnational norm on domestic politics has spawned a broad literature on diffusion and Europeanization.[48] It highlights two mechanisms by which transnational norms penetrate domestic politics: external incentives and social learning. External incentives depend on an instrumental logic of consequences, in which external actors use both leverage and their capacity to reshape the distribution of resources among domestic actors to promote norms.

By imposing obligations on states in areas directly relevant to LGBT activists, conditionality amplifies these activists' political significance. They can serve as brokers between the EU-level institutions and states, especially in monitoring implementation.[49] Social learning, by contrast, relies on a logic of appropriateness: norms diffuse through persuasion, exposure to new arguments, and the reshaping of identities. As Kelly Kollman argues, social learning deepens and organizes advocacy networks around EU norms.[50] Scholars posit that such learning depends on "norm fit," the extent to which transnational norms fit within a society's values, culture, and political operating procedures.[51]

This framework has been successfully applied to the spread of same-sex unions in Western Europe,[52] but its application to gay-rights advocacy in the new member-states of postcommunist Europe raises conundrums. Regarding external incentives, how can we explain that the greatest growth in the organization of Poland's gay-rights movement has occurred *after* Poland joined the EU, when external leverage was at its nadir? To be clear, this is not to argue that hard-right backlash generated the Polish movement out of nothing. As Chapters 4–5 will show, a fledgling movement already existed in the 1990s; it had begun to become more organized before Poland joined the EU, as evidenced by SMOs like KPH, Campaign Against Homophobia. This much would not surprise Europeanization scholars. What is surprising from a Europeanization perspective is what fueled the movement *after* accession, pushing it from fledgling to exemplary for the region. Tackling this question responds to recent calls for more attention to the pull of external incentives after accession, as analysts have noted a range of cases where "external influence is more enduring than predicted."[53] Further, if social learning is unlikely in the absence of "norm fit," what accounts for the upward trajectory of LGBT activism in Poland, given its strong identification of Polishness with Catholicism?

Both conundrums resonate with debates in the diffusion literature itself. Norm fit has been critiqued as crude and overly static, especially regarding culture and framing.[54] Margaret Keck and Kathryn Sikkink's "boomerang model" offers one of the richer theorizations of domestic-international linkage, one that can be applied even in contexts where transnational and domestic norms clash. They argue that activists can "go around" opponents by reaching out to international allies to put pressure on domestic authorities.[55] Ayoub's work on "the ways in which—and the degree to which—marginalized groups make governments and societies see and interact with their ideas" extends this argument to LGBT rights.[56] In both cases, however, the conditions underpinning "boomerang effects" depend primarily on the characteristics of norm *advocates*, not opponents—for example, strong international leverage and agenda-setting power for Keck and Sikkink and openness to international norms and the embeddedness of domestic interest groups in transnational networks for Ayoub.[57] Clifford Bob has argued, however, that such approaches neglect the pivotal role played by conservative opposition—itself often transnationally organized—to transnational progressive norms; Bob sees norm diffusion less as a persuasion process and more as a pitched battle whose outcome is often policy deadlock.[58]

This book's argument synthesizes the insights of both approaches. Like Keck and Sikkink and Ayoub, it argues that visibility is a critical resource for building social movement organization, but, like Bob, it finds that visibility is the product of sharp framing contests between norm opponents and advocates. This dynamic jumps out when comparing social movement trajectories among societies equally exposed to transnational norms and networks but not to hard-right backlash. The role of norm *opponents* is generally undertheorized in the diffusion literature, but it allows for a richer understanding of transnational-domestic linkage and norm fit. One of the book's critical contributions, therefore, is to theorize the conditions under which backlash builds movements and how.

Social movement theory offers a way to enrich the diffusion and Europeanization literatures. External incentives can usefully be conceptualized in terms of how their use, especially the threat of sanction, shapes the POS, that is, the established power relations in which social movements are embedded. Analytically, this move focuses attention on conditionality's impact on the relative openness of domestic political institutions; the stability of elite alignments; the presence of elite allies; and the state's propensity for repression.[59] In states with a history of repressing homosexuality, it does not require active state participation for further repression of a social movement to occur.[60] It is sufficient that the state not rein in threatening groups. Will, for example, participants in a Pride parade be safe from counterdemonstrators? If EU leverage raises the costs of even passive repression, it opens the POS. If leverage upsets prevailing political alignments—by strengthening either the Euroskeptic hard-right or pro-European forces—it alters the POS. Last, if leverage divides elites, making some available as movement allies, it likewise reshapes political opportunities. As mentioned above, the EU's engagement with LGBT rights varied over time. Before 1997, its engagement with LGBT rights through the accession process was minimal. After 1997, when some states were formally recognized as candidates, EU leverage escalated. When states became EU members, leverage evaporated. Thus, the movements' trajectories can be divided into three periods: 1989–1997, 1998–2004, and 2004–2012.

Social movement theory also offers the concepts of framing and framing contests, which provide a key linkage between external leverage and domestic social movement mobilization. Ultimately, collective action is made possible when activists construct frames that resonate, that is, when they negotiate a "shared understanding of some problematic condition or situation they define as in need of change, make attributions regarding who or what is to blame, articulate an alternative set of arrangements, and urge others to act in concert to affect change."[61] Finding resonant frames often involves "framing contests," in which different framings of an issue are deployed, often against each other. Identifying when framing contests resonate has spawned a wide literature, but two conditions are relevant here: frame credibility and salience.[62] The former refers to the "apparent fit between the framings and events in the world."[63] If activists frame homosexuality as a rights question, this frame will gain in credibility if rights and the "immediate protective surround" actually appear threatened. If opponents and advocates both portray homosexuality in terms of EU rights—albeit as an anathema for the former—it likewise enhances the credibility of the rights framing. Second, framing contests resonate when they increase the frame's salience, that is, its visibility and centrality. Where backlash sparks resonant framing contests, it reinforces credibility and heightens salience, helping overcome a challenge faced by any social movement but especially postcommunist ones: gaining resources to mobilize.

Since the breakdown of communism, homosexuality has been subject to multiple framings and, since the onset of EU accession, framing contests.[64] In the 1990s, homosexuality was invisible politically and, when considered at all, tended to be framed either in terms of morality or therapy. In Poland the former prevailed, allowing for a limited charity-based activism. In the Czech Republic, early activism's links to psychologists provided a therapeutic frame. With EU accession, a new framing emerged, that of rights and protections against discrimination—which were made concrete by the requirement that applicants amend their labor codes to include them. In itself this new framing was not sufficient to generate the resources of resonance, solidarity, and allies. When, however, it was countered by a fourth framing of homosexuality—as a threat to national identity and moral codes—it sparked a framing contest that could generate these things.

These mechanisms' effects are visible in the organization of activism, which may be compared along three dimensions: formal vs. informal organization; local-scale decentralized networks vs. national-scale centralized ones; and apolitical vs. political orientation. Friendship networks, professional associations, memory communities, self-help groups, clubs, and service providers are all examples of mobilizing structures—similar in helping overcome obstacles to collective action but differing in "their degree of organizational formalization and centralization as well as their formal dedication to social change goals."[65] While all such mobilizing structures are legitimate means for recruiting participants and directing their efforts, social movement theorists caution that "for the movement to survive, insurgents must be able to create a more enduring organizational structure to sustain collective action. Efforts to do so usually entail the creation of the[se] kinds of formal social movement organizations."[66]

This is not to say that SMOs are the sole marker of movement success, or that their emergence need crowd out less formalized or politically oriented activism. Resource mobilization scholars are highly cognizant of how SMOs themselves draw on informal networks for recruitment and cooperate with service organizations to address constituents.[67] The contention is rather that, for a robust social movement to push for political change, an institutionalized and integrated layer of activism must also exist. Otherwise, it will develop in other directions than political mobilization—for example, toward "commercialization" if service-provider groups become dominant or "involution" if self-help groups and clubs become dominant.[68] The experience of postcommunist LGBT activism bears out the centrality of developing formally institutionalized, centralized and territorially integrated, politically oriented activist groups. Because homosexuality was so stigmatized under communism, apolitical activism was common, but it was generally acknowledged by activists as a cover allowing them to work with, for example, HIV/AIDS sufferers. Likewise, even where a developed network of self-help and service-oriented groups exists, if SMOs are absent progress on policy tends to stall.

Scope Conditions: When Does Backlash Organize Activism?

Transnational pressures boost gay-rights activism when the hard right becomes politically pivotal in a comparatively closed society. In this context, EU leverage shifts the POS while also producing resonant framing contests, or backlash. These contests generate the mobilizing resources of visibility, solidarity, and domestic allies. Where these conditions do not obtain, social movement development remains a domestic affair, for better or (in postcommunist countries) for worse. Two conditions determine where and when framing contests have this kind of resonance: (1) the degree to which hard-right political parties and affiliated groups are pivotal in national politics, and (2) how open a society's political culture is to claims for equal political status by nontraditional and minority groups. While the former can and does vary over the period studied, societal openness is considered fixed in the short- to medium term. Figure 1.4 depicts the permutations of possible outcomes.

The horizontal axis captures society's openness to minority groups and perspectives. Ronald Inglehart and Christian Welzel's postmaterialism index empirically gauges openness, allowing for cross-national comparison.[69] In postmaterialist societies political and social life are governed by (1) secular-rational as opposed to traditional values and religiosity, and (2) values of self-expression as opposed to "survival values" (see Figure 1.5). The index reveals a divide between postcommunist countries and the rest of Europe on both dimensions. Generally, postcommunist societies are defined by survival values and relatively high secularization. Only the Czech Republic and East Germany attain West European levels of postmaterialism. By comparison, Polish society is closed. It is *both* more traditional than secular and more survival- than self-expression oriented: its closest neighbors on the index are Turkey,

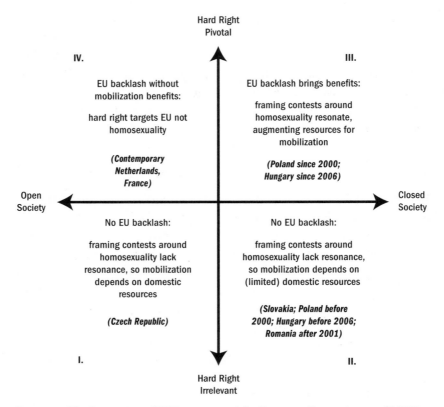

Figure 1.4. The Interaction of EU Leverage and the Domestic Determinants of LGBT Movement Mobilization

Malaysia, and India.[70] In order to substantiate the argument's logic in a broader set of cases, Chapter 7 will trace the trajectory of LGBT-rights activism in three other postcommunist new EU member-states besides Poland and the Czech Republic, namely Hungary, Romania, and Slovakia. As Figure 1.5 shows, these are generally representative of the closed variant of postcommunist society. Hungary and Slovakia exemplify the type of closure characteristic of postcommunism, that is, secular-leaning societies in which survival values strongly predominate over those of self-expression. Romania also exhibits strong survival values, but, like Poland, it is also characterized by traditionalism and high religiosity.

Returning to Figure 1.4, the vertical axis captures the political relevance of the "hard right," a category consisting of parties actively and

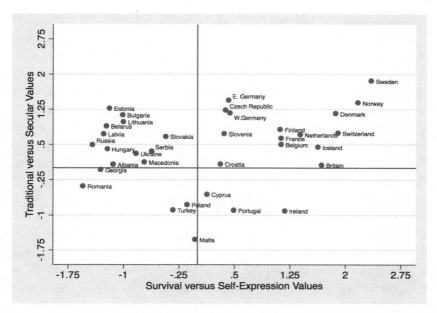

Figure 1.5. Situating the Country Cases by Societal Openness (circa 2000)

publicly opposed to homosexuality. Aside from parties that Cas Mudde labels the "populist radical right," for most parties of the right homosexuality occupies contested territory: some strongly oppose it, while others are indifferent, even tolerant.[71] Thus, this analysis defines the hard right as Mudde's "populist radical right" parties plus those conservative or Christian Democratic parties willing to form alliances with them. When the latter ally with populist radicals, they endorse intolerance and become accomplices in antigay politics. We may say that the hard right becomes politically pivotal when this kind of alliance makes an electoral breakthrough and becomes a credible candidate for shaping government policy. At such moments, framing contests around homosexuality gain unusual resonance. Such breakthroughs also raise legitimate fears on the part of LGBT persons that their "immediate protective surround" is threatened, triggering the galvanizing consequences for activism described above. To be clear, this framework focuses on the effect of hard-right breakthroughs, not their causes. Nor does it assume that closed societies necessarily have a strong right; as Poland illustrates, the hard right's fortunes may vary widely over time.

The threshold at which a hard-right alliance becomes a credible candidate for government will vary by electoral- and party-system size. Because European politics mostly consists of parliamentary systems with proportional representation electoral rules, multiparty governments are the rule, and hard-right political backlash is typically best understood in terms of coalitions between parties. Theoretically—and as Chapter 7 will show empirically—it is possible that hard-right breakthrough may occur without a formal coalition between the populist radical right and either the conservatives or the Christian Democrats. Hungary illustrates this rare scenario: in 2010 the conservative Fidesz party was elected with an absolute majority, which allowed it to form a government without its former ally, the populist radical right Jobbik party. Further, Fidesz's rise was preceded by what might be called an extraparliamentary breakthrough, a systematic and sustained escalation in antigay violence that began after the country's 2006 elections and culminated in the 2010 landslide. Hungary, therefore, cues us to the possibility of alternative indicators of threat to the "protective surround" such as recurring and organized attacks on Prides or the staging of referenda against LGBT rights. These may be useful in extending this framework to nonparliamentary or nondemocratic settings.

Figure 1.4 organizes the interaction of EU pressure and communist legacy on social movement development in terms of four ideal-typical scenarios. The figure also summarizes our expectations about the trajectories of activism in the Czech Republic, Poland, Hungary, Slovakia, and Romania between 1989 and 2012, which will be analyzed in Chapters 4–7. (For simplicity, Figure 1.4 does not attempt to capture the preaccession, accession, and postaccession periodization described above. It does, however, indicate the approximate dates when movement-building trends shifted in various countries. Chapters 4–7 develop more precise chronologies.) In Quadrants I and II, we do not expect EU pressure to trigger resonant framing contests because hard-right parties are politically irrelevant. Even if such parties demonize homosexuality to mobilize supporters (as in Quadrant II), it will not bring greater salience to the issue because they occupy the fringe. Slovakia exemplifies this scenario; it is relatively closed according to the postmaterialism index, but the escalation of EU conditionality was not accompanied by a hard-right breakthrough. Through the period here, its LGBT movement was much less organized than those of its neighbors. It also describes Poland and Hungary before the onset of EU accession politics. In Romania, the 2001 decriminalization of homosexuality coincided with the marginalization of the hitherto pivotal hard right; as Chapter 7 argues, this prevented the country's LGBT-rights movement from expanding beyond a narrow focus on policy lobbying. In Quadrant I, not only are hard-right parties irrelevant, society is more open—which describes the Czech Republic. In neither Quadrants I nor II would we expect framing contests around homosexuality and EU norms to resonate: cycles of social movement mobilization should be determined by domestic, not transnational, factors. Domestic factors may be more favorable in Quadrant I than II because of greater societal openness, but movements in both should face the headwinds of communism's demobilizing effects on activism.

In Quadrants III and IV, hard-right parties are pivotal. In Quadrant III—which captures Poland during and after accession and Hungary after its hard right's 2006 extraparliamentary breakthrough—we expect a highly resonant framing contest in which EU norms clash with intolerant attitudes. The resultant backlash is expected to bring the movement high visibility, increase solidarity, and win allies among pro-Europe elites outside of the movement. In Quadrant IV hard-right parties become pivotal in comparatively open societies. Since we find no postcommunist examples, subsequent chapters will not explore this scenario; however, in Western Europe, the category has more potential. Holland offers the clearest example: here, where tolerance of homosexuality could be considered a point of national pride, populist radical right parties from the now-defunct Pim Fortuyn List through its successor, the Party for Freedom of Geert Wilders, have justified intolerance toward Muslim immigrants *because* of Islam's alleged homophobia.[72] Though not as open a political culture as Holland, France offers another example of a populist radical right (here the National Front) that has moved from the fringe to within striking distance of government by combining anti-EU, anti-Muslim, and anti-immigrant policies with largely tolerant views toward LGBT issues.[73] This paradoxical amalgam of intolerant tolerance sits uneasily on the left-right spectrum. In terms of its effect on building LGBT activism, we would expect a net drag: rather than allying LGBT rights with the EU, this framing allies them with its critics and is less attractive to pro-EU allies.

Research Design and Plan of the Book

The argument laid out above poses a special set of challenges when it comes to applying and testing it empirically. First, there are the difficulties of measuring and comparing how activism is organized across countries and over time. The organization of activism is a complex variable, involving resources, framing, and networks. Second, because of the role of backlash, activism develops through an unfolding process of mobilization and countermobilization by rights advocates and their opponents. Only careful process tracing and structured case-study comparisons can hope to untangle complex causal dynamics such as these. Other aspects of my argument—such as the visibility of homosexuality as an issue and changes in legal rights frameworks (as opposed to the organization of activism)—are, however, more amenable to large-N application of the comparative method. Thus, the following empirical chapters employ a multimethod research design. Where suitable cross-national data are available and where the logic of the particular causal mechanism under discussion allows, I employ statistical analysis. For example, Chapter 2 makes use of ILGA-Europe data on the strength of LGBT-rights protections across Europe to statistically analyze the impact of EU conditionality on rights frameworks in postcommunist countries, controlling for other factors such as socioeconomic development, religiosity, and national religious tradition.

Where either the lack of cross-national data or the endogenous character of backlash-driven mobilization strains the assumptions necessary for statistical techniques, the analysis employs close process tracing of a smaller number of case-study comparisons. These offer an alternative means of inferring causality, tracing the response/counterresponse nature of activist mobilization over time.[74] To maximize the leverage of the comparative case studies, we need cases that allow us to compare changes in activism over time while allowing variation in the two critical causal factors laid out in this chapter: the openness of society and the relevance of the hard right in national politics. To take full advantage of the leverage offered by process tracing, we should look for country cases that vary on both dimensions. Such cases allow us to home in on the mobilizing effects of backlash (where it occurs), while holding constant the effects of Europeanizing conditionality, which, thanks to the timing and implementation of the accession process, applies to all countries in equal measure.

Poland and the Czech Republic, which form the central paired comparison of the book, offer two cases with contrasting trajectories and counterintuitive outcomes. These countries offer maximal contrast regarding the key independent variables while sharing broad similarities on a number of other variables. The case-study method is, of course, a limiting research design if the goal is generalization. When, however, dramatic political change highlights the need to revisit widely held theoretical beliefs—here about the effect of communist legacy and transnational pressure on civil society development—then the case study is an ideally suited approach. It allows us to trace social processes over time, measure complex variables like framing and the organization of activism, refine and rebuild theory, and explore its plausibility.

To gather the data for the comparative case studies of Poland, the Czech Republic, Hungary, Slovakia, and Romania, I engaged in multiple rounds of fieldwork, drawing on interviews, participant observation, archival work, and analysis of domestic media.[75] The Polish case study is based on fieldwork in Warsaw and Cracow over four trips between 2007 and 2011.[76] The Czech fieldwork was concentrated over a four-month period in the summer and early fall of 2011 and was spread across Prague, Brno, and Olomouc. In all countries, I conducted in-depth, semistructured interviews with rights activists; representatives of NGOs and political parties; state officials; representatives of European agencies such as the EU delegation, the Council of Europe, Helsinki Foundation for Human Rights, and ILGA-Europe; and domestic academics and policy experts. The fieldwork in Hungary, Romania, and Slovakia was conducted in 2011; this research consisted of interviews and participant observation of Pride parades, and is presented in Chapter 7.[77] In all, the fieldwork comprised over 100 interviews. In many cases, I was able to reinterview the same respondents over time, allowing me to capture the changing dynamics of LGBT-rights politics. Second, I undertook participant observation of activist-organized public events, most notably the Warsaw Equality March in 2007 and 2009, the EuroPride festival in Warsaw in 2010, an LGBT-themed art exhibition at the Warsaw National Gallery in 2010,[78] and a political rally for registered partnerships at the Polish parliament in July 2011. During these events, activist groups such as KPH organized discussion forums, presentations, and debates on LGBT issues in Poland and Europe. In both countries, I gathered expert analyses and public reports and, through archival research, articles from the Polish and Czech press. Last, I draw on the growing academic literature on Czech LGBT history and politics, much of it associated with the Gender Studies Department at Charles University in Prague.

To orient the reader regarding the layout of the book, the bulk of the study is centered around an in-depth paired comparison of Poland and the Czech Republic, which comprises Chapters 3 through 6. First, however, Chapter 2 offers a building block for the argument, reviewing the EU's use of leverage through the enlargement process. It first describes the EU's own path to embracing LGBT equality and how the evolution of that commitment affected the strength of EU leverage over time in the first-wave postcommunist applicant-states. It then reviews and extends empirical research on variation in *policy protections* for LGBT persons in Europe, establishing that in postcommunist countries EU leverage had a significant impact on the quality of legal frameworks for sexual minorities even after controlling for domestic factors. Thus, Chapter 2 helps us understand why hard-right backlash against EU gay-rights norms occurred, setting the stage for Chapter 3. That chapter focuses on the mobilization of the hard-right against the EU's exercise of leverage to promote minority-rights norms. It does so through an analysis of the discourse both of political parties and the media. Chapters 4, 5, and 6 then trace the evolving organization of each country's rights movement through the different stages of the EU accession process: preaccession (late 1980s-1997), accession (1998–2004), and postaccession (since 2004). Chapter 7 expands the set of comparative case studies to three additional "new" postcommunist EU member-states: Hungary, Slovakia, and Romania. On the one hand, the addition of these cases builds confidence in the analytical framework summarized in Figure 1.4 by showing that other movements follow the expected trajectories given their combination of societal openness and hard-right backlash. On the other hand, these cases also allow us to explore variations in related causal elements in the argument. Romania, for example, offers an unusual case of antigay backlash *before* the onset of EU leverage; thus, it underlines the importance of external leverage in setting a ceiling on the scope of repression, without which the "benefits of backlash" are diminished.[79] Hungary offers a good example of an extraparliamentary route to hard-right breakthrough. Finally, Slovakia, where the potential elements of hard-right alliance never managed to cooperate, underlines that societal closure is a necessary but not sufficient condition for the benefits of backlash. Chapter 8 concludes by discussing the wider implications of this argument: especially, its lessons for other countries on the "LGBT-rights periphery" beyond the reach of EU leverage, the nature of visibility as a resource for other kinds of social movements, and what constitutes social movement "success."

Conclusion

Go to observe the counterprotestors at a Pride event anywhere in the region, and you will find placards denouncing "Euro-Sodom" and cultural imperialism from Brussels. At first glance, therefore, LGBT rights would seem to be an area of political life largely untouched by the otherwise deep changes wrought by Eastern Europe's democratic transition and integration into the EU. It is easy to conclude that deeply rooted taboos about homosexuality—which predated but were then amplified under communist rule—still hold unquestioned sway, and that LGBT rights remain off limits in the public sphere. One might fix the blame not just on old taboos but also on the EU's role in inflaming them.

Against the background of such antigay episodes, however, this book makes the argument, first, that the broader picture in the region is actually one of increasing rights and better-organized, more influential gay-rights movements. Second, it argues that the antigay rhetoric of hard-right politicians in Eastern Europe and their attempts to ban Prides and drive the "homosexual agenda" from the public sphere not only indicate this broader change, but in fact help to drive it. This explains why now, some two decades after the fall of communism, we can find some of the region's most organized and influential rights movements in societies with "closed" political cultures, that is, ones characterized by comparatively high levels of religiosity and lower tolerance of self-expressive values. Moreover, by looking closely at the politics of LGBT-rights activism in this region, we have much to learn about the dynamics of such activism more broadly, especially in other societies whose political cultures are relatively closed and whose traditions of civil society are weak. As homosexuality becomes more politicized in parts of Africa, Latin America, and Asia, the experience of postcommunist Europe has many lessons to offer.

This chapter has presented an analytical framework that draws on the insights of social movement theory to outline a broadly framed argument identifying the conditions under which transnational pressure for expanded legal rights may also lead to deeper change in sexual citizenship through the building of organized and influential LGBT-rights movements. Specifically, it has argued that transnational pressures boost the organizational development of LGBT activism when the hard right becomes politically pivotal in a comparatively closed society. In this context, transnational pressure produces polarizing framing contests. These contests generate the mobilizing resources of issue visibility, solidarity among activists, and allies outside the movement. Where these conditions do not obtain, social movement development remains a domestic affair, for better or (in new democracies with weakly developed civil society) for worse.

2

EU Enlargement and LGBT Rights

"Returning to Europe" and Discovering a New World

Between June and December 1989, Communist parties across Eastern Europe were forced out of power in a cascade of popular protest that swept across borders and unmade the Cold War division of Europe. Almost precisely at the midpoint of this process, a much smaller event occurred in Copenhagen's city hall that highlighted a political-cultural fault line between Europe's now reuniting halves. On October 1, 11 gay couples participated in a civil ceremony in which the Dutch state legally recognized their relationships, the first time any state had done so. As Kelly Kollman writes, this ceremony "sparked a revolution in how western democracies recognize and regulate the relationships of same-sex couples who live within their borders."[1] Over the next decade, many West European states and eventually the EU itself became increasingly committed to promoting LGBT equality, not only in their own societies but also in those of EU-aspirants. Just as postcommunist societies began their "return to Europe"—which took concrete political form in the goal of EU membership—the nature of EU citizenship, and in particular sexual citizenship, was changing.

This chapter describes how the EU came to embrace policies furthering LGBT equality and then promoted them transnationally through the enlargement process. It addresses three main questions. First, what was the EU's own path to these policies? Second, how have scholars conceptualized EU leverage in diffusing these policies, and what are the findings in extant empirical analyses of this diffusion in Western Europe and first-wave postcommunist EU applicant-states?[2] Third, if we extend the geographic scope to include not just first-wave postcommunist EU applicant-states but all of postcommunist Europe, can EU leverage still be shown to significantly influence states' adoption of LGBT-friendly policies? To be clear, the dependent variable in this chapter is policy, not the organization of activism. Further, in focusing on policy, this analysis makes no claims about policy *implementation*. Even if clear EU norms about antidiscrimination policy have emerged, their implementation is in the hands of states, as applicants and then as members.

Even with these caveats, policy change is inherently important, which is why comparative studies of LGBT politics typically take it as the dependent variable.[3] However, this chapter's focus on policy is undertaken for more instrumental reasons, that is, as an indicator of EU leverage. Showing that leverage was a significant factor driving the adoption of LGBT-friendly policies in postcommunist states helps us understand why hard-right backlash (against such EU intervention) occurred. Thus, this chapter furnishes a building block for the subsequent chapters' analysis of how, via backlash, EU leverage indirectly shaped the organization of LGBT activism. Insofar as inadequate policy implementation reflected backlash, the implementation gap only illustrates the book's argument.

The first part of the chapter reviews how the EU developed antidiscrimination provisions regarding sexual orientation through its labor market competencies and then incorporated them as broader rights through jurisprudence, the European Social Charter, and the sponsorship of transnational advocacy networks such as ILGA-Europe. This review of the EU's own path to LGBT rights shows that its application of leverage in the postcommunist applicant-states, far from being a constant, was itself an evolving force. This insight sets up the periodization used to structure the comparative case studies in Chapters 3–7, which is based on the strength of EU leverage over applicant-states at different stages in time: preaccession, accession, and postaccession.

The chapter's second part describes the mechanisms by which EU leverage brought about significant changes in the legal frameworks of postcommunist applicant-states. Besides describing how such leverage has been conceptualized, it reviews extant empirical research on the relative causal impact of EU leverage vis-à-vis domestic factors in explaining policy variation. After all, a host of domestic factors also shape the policy framework in a given country. To play devil's advocate against the Europeanization literature, one might argue that variation in the sensitivity of European states' legal frameworks to LGBT rights is primarily determined by these domestic factors, that the "EU effect" is more "EU artifact." The record of scholarship shows, however, that in this issue area EU leverage was a strong driver of policy change in first-wave postcommunist EU member-states—much stronger, in fact, than it was in the "old" member-states of Western Europe.

The chapter's final section builds on this extant research by extending the analysis beyond first-wave postcommunist member-states to all of postcommunist Europe, that is, to countries that share the same negative legacies regarding homosexuality but vary more widely in their degree of exposure to EU leverage. To preview the results, I find that, where EU leverage is highest, policy frameworks for sexual minorities are better than domestic factors would predict; however, this finding does not hold for the first-wave postcommunist member-states since their accession, reflecting their weaker exposure to EU leverage after that point.

The EU's Path to LGBT Rights and Their Role in EU Enlargement

A broader European LGBT advocacy network can trace its origins at least as far back as the 1950s, when the Dutch group COC (Cultuur-en Ontspanningscentrum) established the International Committee for Sexual Equality (ICSE), but the EU itself came only much later to the field, in the 1990s.[4] If we have in mind the exercise of "hard leverage," the EU's embrace of LGBT equality was later still—well into the process of Eastern enlargement. That said, the intertwining of a transnational European advocacy network with European-level institutions, both in the EU and the Council of Europe (CoE), was a long-running process.[5] Thus, by the time the EU did exercise hard leverage in support of LGBT rights in the postcommunist applicant-states, it did so in concert with an advocacy network that could offer extensive organizational support to domestic activists. Hard leverage and the soft power of transnational advocacy were difficult to separate in practice. From the perspective of domestic hard-right coalitions, the EU's extension of antidiscrimination norms to LGBT people resembled the leading edge of an expansive agenda.[6]

When the ICSE was established as an umbrella organization for nationally based "homophile" groups in the 1950s, homosexuality was still taboo even in Western Europe, limiting such groups' influence on mainstream politics. There were additional, more radically oriented attempts to set up transnational networks in the 1970s, but the first sustained advocacy group—the International Lesbian, Gay, Bisexual, Trans and Intersex Association (ILGA)—was not established until 1978.[7] Global in ambition, ILGA was primarily European in practice. From early on, the group saw the institutions driving European integration as allies in lobbying domestic governments for rights.[8] In 1981, ILGA supported a resolution in the Assembly of the CoE addressing employment discrimination; in 1984, it worked with the European Parliament's Committee on Social Affairs to produce the Squarcialupi Report, which made recommendations to establish equal rights for gays and lesbian in all member-states.[9] In 1994, this collaboration with the EP led to the Roth Report, which was followed by a "Resolution on equal rights for homosexuals and lesbians in the EC": though nonbinding, it elevated LGBT rights to new prominence in the EU's policy agenda.[10] The EP became one of ILGA's biggest allies, especially with the establishment of the Intergroup on LGBT Rights in 1997, but ILGA had also built links with the European Commission by the early 1990s.[11]

As the EU became increasingly committed to LGBT rights, ILGA's organizational development closely tracked milestones in the EU's own developmental trajectory. In 1996, in the midst of negotiations over the Treaty of Amsterdam, ILGA-Europe was established as a regional branch of ILGA-World "in order to take advantage of emerging European opportunities."[12] One year later, the Treaty entered into force, and Article 13 formally granted the EU competence to "take action to combat discrimination based on sex, racial, or ethnic origin, religion or belief, disability, age, or sexual orientation."[13] To emphasize its commitment to enforcing this norm, in 1998 the EP warned that it would block the accession of any country that "through its legislation or policies violates the human rights of lesbians and gay men."[14] In 2000, the norm was codified as the Employment Framework Directive (2000/78/EC), which mandated legal change in member-states and applicant-states to bring their labor codes into compliance. As one assessment put it, "Given the number of countries and the population affected, the Employment Directive is arguably the most important single legislative initiative in the history of European lesbian, gay, and bisexual rights."[15] During this same period, the EU adopted the European Union Charter of Fundamental Rights, which also included explicit nondiscrimination protections covering sexual orientation (Article 21). Joke Swiebel notes that the EU's are the only internationally binding legal protections for LGBT people.[16]

Alongside this formalization of minority protection norms, the EU supported the continued development of a transnational advocacy network centered around ILGA-Europe. In 2001, ILGA-Europe became an official partner of the European Commission, which, from that year, has also provided the lion's share of its funding.[17] Over time, ILGA-Europe made associates of some 359 organizations located in 44 European countries.[18] Included among them are other associations with transnational reach, such as the European Pride Organizers Forum, the Network of European LGBT Families Associations, and the European Forum of LGBT Christian Groups. To this already-rich field, one must also count multi-issue NGOs that have become strongly engaged with LGBT rights, for example, the Open Society Foundations, Amnesty International, and the Helsinki Foundation for Human Rights.

Looking to politics outside the LGBT advocacy network and the institutions with which it is directly engaged, there are numerous indications of the growing salience of LGBT rights in EU politics. They have come to play a role in the EU's own high politics. Take the example of Rocco Buttiglione, an Italian Christian Democrat who was nominated as EU commissioner for justice, freedom, and security in 2004. The EP rejected the nomination because of Buttiglione's views on homosexuality, which he had publicly declared a sin.[19] Beyond its implications for LGBT-rights advocates, this episode had institutional significance as the first instance in which the EP exercised its veto power over the composition of the Commission.[20] The issue's salience can also be seen in national-level politics in Western Europe, most conspicuously in the wave of national legislation and referenda enacting some form of same-sex unions, even with the support, in some cases, of conservative parties like Britain's Tories and Germany's Christian Democrats.[21] Allies can be found at the highest levels of national politics: in 2009, for example, British prime minister Gordon Brown vowed to expand same-sex partnerships to Eastern Europe:

> I'm fighting to get all the countries in Europe to recognize civil partnerships carried out in Britain. . . . We want countries where that hasn't been the case—especially in Eastern Europe—to recognise them. . . . [I]f we

could show Eastern Europe[,] as well as Western Europe, that this respect for gay people is due, that would be really important.[22]

Corroboration, albeit in the form of condemnation, can be found among social conservatives in Eastern Europe and the former Soviet Union; as the chairman of the Russian parliament's Foreign Affairs Committee recently claimed, the expansion of gay culture "has now turned into the official policy of the EU."[23]

Of course, one should be careful not to overstate the ascendancy of LGBT rights in EU politics, as the variation in legal rights even among West European countries attests (see Figure 1.2). This was true during the EU's first Eastern enlargement and remains true today: in ILGA-Europe's 2017 survey of LGBT policies across Europe, Italy and Greece received comparable rankings to most states in postcommunist East Central Europe—and far below the rest of Western Europe.[24] There are differences among West European member-states regarding adoption by same-sex couples, the legal definition of same-sex relationships (marriage versus partnerships), and social welfare rights.[25] Given this diversity, we should not assume convergence to some common EU policy model in the future, nor should we be surprised by the imperfect implementation of policies adopted as a requirement for accession once membership has been gained.

That said, by 2000 a clear norm of support for sexual minorities had become entwined in the EU's sense of its identity and policy mission. Meanwhile, the EU was deeply engaged with another defining mission, enlargement into postcommunist Europe. Reviewing the chronology of the relationship between Eastern Europe's new democracies and the EU, in 1991 the first "European Agreements" were signed. These set membership as a goal, but they were vague on basic terms such as timelines, requirements, and assistance. At a time when the Cold War division of Germany was ending, optimism for a rapid "return to Europe" reigned. Between 1993 and 1995, the relationship deepened considerably when European Council summits in Copenhagen and Madrid laid out three so-called Copenhagen criteria for applicant-states: (1) stable democratic institutions, (2) a functioning market economy, and (3) the capacity to take on the obligations of membership, including the entire corpus of accumulated EU legislation and regulation known as the *acquis communautaire.* Implicitly, these bore on the rights of sexual minorities, first, because the European Council's first criterion mandated that each candidate country achieve "stability of institutions guaranteeing democracy, the rule of law, *human rights and respect for and protection of minorities.*"[26] Second, by mandating harmonization with the *acquis*, the criteria locked applicant-states into the expanding antidiscrimination provisions in the EU's labor regulation. Given the still implicit nature of norms pertaining to sexual orientation, however, EU influence was less about leverage and more about leading by example.

In 1998, the year in which the EU opened accession negotiations with the Czech Republic, Hungary, Poland, Estonia, and Cyprus, the accession process became formalized and began to entail real adjustments by applicant-states—just as EU norms about sexuality were gaining legal force and the European advocacy network was strengthening. Where the will for adjustment to EU norms was weak, the Commission used conditionality to force them. Indeed the label "negotiations" was something of a misnomer, as the asymmetric power balance between applicant- and member-states allowed the latter to dictate terms to the former, demanding stricter policy adjustments than in any earlier enlargement.[27] As Andrew Moravcsik and Milada Vachudova write, the negotiations were better described as a "process of checking that the candidates have adopted EU law, chapter by chapter and page by page. The requirements are massive, nonnegotiable, uniformly applied, and closely enforced."[28] (Of course, after accession was a different story.) The opening of negotiations was delayed by two years in a second wave of states with a weaker record of democratic reform, comprising Romania, Slovakia, Bulgaria, Latvia, Lithuania, and Malta. This delay only amplified the EU's leverage, as it signaled possible exclusion from the EU club. During this period, compliance with the Copenhagen Criteria was monitored by the European Commission, which had formidable resources for information gathering, including delegations in each applicant-state. The Commission's annual reports on "Progress Toward Accession" publicly scolded applicants for norm violations.[29]

On May 1, 2004, all the above states but Romania and Bulgaria gained EU membership. (Romania and Bulgaria joined in 2007.) At this point, the leverage of EU institutions over member-states weakened drastically. There was no comparable monitoring of compliance with EU norms to that employed before membership, and formal sanction for noncompliance would now be a lengthy and demanding process.

Leverage and Policy Diffusion in Western Europe and the First-Wave Postcommunist EU Applicants

As European integration has deepened and widened, an extensive literature has theorized the channels by which EU policies and norms diffuse to the national level.[30] This section reviews this literature and summarizes some of its notable empirical findings. Following the rationalist and constructivist traditions in international relations theory, this literature has emphasized two main channels of transnational influence. The first is "external incentives," which holds that states adopt EU norms for instrumentally rational reasons—if the payoffs of adoption outweigh the costs.[31] The EU influences this calculation both directly, through the use of conditionality, and indirectly, by creating new opportunities and constraints for domestic actors to pursue their interests.[32] Specifically, this calculation is shaped by the clarity of EU norms, the magnitude of the reward for compliance, the credibility of the promise of reward, and the leverage of domestic veto players.[33] As we have seen above, regarding LGBT rights, these factors had shifted strongly in favor of at least minimal adoption of EU norms by the late 1990s. The EU's expanding engagement with the issue was increasingly formalized, and the stringency of policy harmonization, especially compared to earlier rounds of EU enlargement, increased the credibility of the promise of membership.[34] Finally, the magnitude of accession's rewards—access to the single market, to investment, to the Structural Funds, to name just a few—maximized the leverage of domestic NGOs and other rights advocates in accession negotiations. These groups could act as policy brokers between national governments and the EU.[35] The European Commission sought out their input and formally included them in consultation over policy harmonization. Since states had reputational incentives to signal their commitment to EU norms by "overfulfilling" in symbolically important areas like minority rights, this granted rights advocates extra leverage.[36] As described in Chapter 1, Romania adopted a far more progressive antidiscrimination framework than the *acquis communautaire* required. This eagerness was motivated, we can safely assume, by the

country's poor record of compliance in many other areas, which ultimately delayed its membership by three years.

The second channel of EU influence, "social learning," theorizes
norm diffusion through a constructivist-oriented logic of appropriateness.[37] States become persuaded of the appropriateness of EU norms, a
process that is complementary to, and even concurrent with, external incentives.[38] Such persuasion occurs through the participation of national-
level policy makers and other political elites in EU networks. It also
occurs as accession and membership expose countries to transnational
networks of domestic and European actors.[39] Not only can these networks offer financial support to domestic advocacy groups, they also
can help legitimate these groups among otherwise indifferent domestic
groups.[40] Such transnational support is especially important in postcommunist countries since domestic groups have comparatively fewer
resources.[41] A recent survey of LGBT organizations in the East European EU-12 and West European EU-15 states found that at least part of
the organizational budget came from international sources in 83 percent
of the former, compared with 32 percent of the latter. The *majority* of
the budget came from international sources in 56 percent of the East
European groups, compared with only 5 percent of the West European
groups.[42]

In recent empirical work, Ayoub offers a pathbreaking comparison
of transnational leverage's role in the adoption of LGBT rights in the
"old" member-states of Western Europe (EU-15) and the "new" members included in the first wave of (mostly) postcommunist applicant-
states (EU-12).[43] Using cross-national data on the membership of
domestic LGBT-oriented NGOs in European-level advocacy networks
and controlling for the effects of domestic and broader international
determinants of rights frameworks, Ayoub finds that the dynamics of
rights adoption differ significantly between the "first mover" states of
Western Europe and Eastern Europe's "new adopters." In the former,
the emergence of homosexuality as a political issue was a gradual, primarily bottom-up process; whereas, in the latter, the LGBT-rights issues
emerged comparatively recently, largely through the EU accession process. Ayoub's central finding is that in first-mover states, rights adoption
has been driven primarily by domestic factors, especially levels of economic development, and has only marginally been affected by ties with

European-level advocacy networks and other transnational channels. New-adopter states present almost the reverse image: they are primarily "dependent on international resources for making new issues visible and are more inclined to see policy adoption as a means to gain external legitimacy and improve reputation." In short, they "display greater dependence on transnational actors and are more influenced by international channels."[44] Though Ayoub finds weak evidence for the more direct pressure of conditionality, stronger links between European-level advocacy networks, domestic LGBT groups, and states are found to increase the probability that the latter will adopt higher levels of rights.[45]

Ayoub's findings strongly confirm the "disruptive" effect of EU accession on the politics of homosexuality in postcommunist societies. For much of society this top-down legal change came as something of a shock. From their perspective, it reflected national politicians responding to incentives from Brussels in consultation with NGO representatives of a historically marginal, even invisible, minority. During the accession negotiations, these NGOs benefited from an unprecedented influx of resources and recognition from abroad, allowing them outsized influence compared with their actual "ground organization," for example, their grassroots presence, their territorial reach, and their links with domestic allies. As others have noted, a similar narrative could be found across a variety of other areas affected by accession.[46] It should not have been a surprise that shortly *after* the EU's 2004 enlargement a hard-right backlash was one of the first results and that, where societies were more closed, homosexuality quickly became politically salient and LGBT rights came under attack. Looking comparatively across postcommunist Europe, the next chapters explore the different ways in which the right responded to this EU leverage, again *after* gaining membership. Where a hard-right coalition mobilized successfully and resorted to antigay policies, it catalyzed a counterresponse by rights activists that led to the now-evident differences in activism across the region.

Extending the Analysis to All of Postcommunist Europe

Before turning to backlash's effect on the organization of LGBT activism, however, this chapter's final section further probes the significance of EU leverage on the diffusion of LGBT-friendly policies. It seeks to build on the extant empirical work by expanding the boundaries beyond the first-wave postcommunist EU applicant-states. To do so, it draws on ILGA-Europe's Rainbow Index of lesbian, gay, and bisexual policy frameworks, which covers all postcommunist Europe (as well as Western Europe) from 2009 through 2013. Using multivariate analysis, I assess the relative weight of domestic factors and EU leverage in explaining variation in policy protections for sexual minorities.

One gap in Ayoub's analysis is that it only includes postcommunist countries that became EU members in the first wave of enlargement (2004–2007). It excludes the rest of the region, which comprises states with widely divergent degrees of exposure to EU leverage. These states may be divided into four groups: EU members,[47] candidates and "potential candidates" for membership, participants in the so-called European Neighborhood Policy (ENP), and countries without formal arrangements for deeper integration of any kind. The candidates for membership—Croatia, the former Yugoslav republic of Macedonia, and Turkey—have all opened formal accession negotiations with the Commission. Serbia, Montenegro, Bosnia and Herzegovina, and Albania comprise the "potential candidates" and, like Croatia and Macedonia, are working toward membership through the Stabilization and Accession Process. The ENP offers a measure of integration without a commitment from the EU about future membership and encompasses Armenia, Azerbaijan, Belarus, Georgia, Moldova, and Ukraine. With no such formal agreements with the EU, Russia might be considered a "permanent outsider," the state at the greatest remove from European integration.

Generally, these additional categories contain states considered "reform laggards" across a host of policy areas, including rights frameworks for sexual minorities. Excluding them from the analysis potentially understates the effect of EU leverage on rights adoption since the truncated sample consists of states that, as was evident even in the 1990s, enjoyed the highest odds of EU membership and, therefore, had less to gain in terms of reputation from adopting legislation benefiting sexual minorities. It makes sense to compare the original new adopters (EU-12) not only against the first-movers (EU-15) but also against later applicants, potential applicants, ENP states, and "outsiders." Doing so allows us to probe a fuller range of variation in external incentives and social learning as drivers of rights adoption; additionally, it allows us to include a wider range of variation on domestic factors such as economic modernization, since the first-wave applicant-states comprised the more economically developed tier of postcommunist countries. As an important caveat, the Rainbow Index can expand the geographic range of our analysis, but since its time frame is limited (beginning only in 2009), it cannot tell us about the impact of leverage in the first-wave postcommunist applicant-states (the EU 12) *before* they became member-states. That said, it can offer insights about policy improvements in these states after membership.

For the purpose of this analysis, I emphasize the complementarity of external incentives and social learning as components of EU leverage, which is in keeping with the literature but is also necessitated by the absence of comparative data on transnational linkages between EU-level rights groups and domestic ones across postcommunist Europe.[48] To capture EU leverage (as the combined sum of external incentives and social learning pressures), I employ a proxy variable "EU proximity," which categorizes states into the four groups described above. To describe the theoretical expectations regarding EU proximity's effect on the quality of rights frameworks across groups, consider first the "outsiders." Such states effectively have no possibility of accession, which eliminates external incentives to adopt EU norms. Similarly, we would expect little role for social learning. EU-level advocacy networks are unlikely to invest resources where they see little hope of rights gains. There is no role for NGOs as brokers in the absence of any formal integration process between the state and the EU. Last, domestic rights groups cannot effectively shame the authorities for failure to live up to EU norms that they never committed to, even nominally. From both external incentives and social learning perspectives, then, we expect minimal EU leverage.

At the other end of the spectrum, maximal leverage may be expected in applicant- and potential applicant-states. Among these the "payoff" for compliance (full membership) is much higher than for the other categories, as is the credibility of the EU's promise of membership itself. For reputational reasons, states may "overfulfil" regarding rights for sexual minorities in order to signal the seriousness of their overall commitment to EU norms. Likewise, we expect the strongest impact of transnational social learning channels in this group: EU-level advocacy networks should invest most heavily in linkages with domestic rights groups where external incentives maximize those groups' leverage as brokers. Additionally, the prospect of full and equal membership in the EU amplifies the credibility of these NGOs in linking rights with EU principles.

Turning now to the ENP states and the member-states (both postcommunist and West European), here we expect EU leverage to be moderate at best. In ENP states both the potential payoff for rights adoption (less than full membership) and the credibility of the EU's promise is weaker than it is in applicants and potential applicants.[49] Likewise, we expect less robust linkages between EU- and domestic-level advocacy groups because, by the same logic as above, the comparatively weaker effect of external incentives undercuts the position of domestic NGOs as brokers and lowers the return to transnational groups of investing resources in them. Additionally, we would expect the promise of "second-class membership" to offer weaker footing for advocacy groups attempting to shame states for failure to live up to EU principles. Last, relative to applicants and potential applicants, we should also expect a weaker effect of transnational pressures in EU member-states themselves. This is, after all, the finding in Ayoub's analysis of rights frameworks in the established member-states of the EU-15. Leverage should also be weaker in the first-wave member-states of postcommunist Europe—that is, after accession. Because the data in the Rainbow Index begin in 2009, however, we can only analyze their policy ratings after accession. Certainly, before joining they faced strong pressures to achieve at least minimum compliance with EU labor market directives. However, the external incentive structure shifts radically after accession: there are no comparable instrumental reasons for additional rights adoption. Further, there is a tendency for transnational advocacy networks to shift attention and resources to the next batch of transition states after the previous ones join the EU.[50]

The Dependent Variable

The dependent variable in my analysis is ILGA-Europe's Rainbow Index, which compares the *legal* situation of gays, lesbians, and bisexual (LGB) people. Constructed by a team of legal and regional experts, the composite index rates 47 European states in terms of their legislation regarding the rights of LGB people and, to a more limited extent, their practice toward them.[51] Each state receives a score between -4 and 10. Points are given to countries recognizing same-sex partnerships, parenting rights, and homophobia in hate speech/crime legislation. Points are subtracted if states ban same-sex acts, specify unequal age of consent, or if they have violated the rights of LGB people regarding peaceful assembly and freedom of association.

While clearly a great advance for researchers, the ILGA-Europe index is not without its limitations. First, because it began in 2009, its coverage is limited. My analysis includes the data from 2009 through 2013 since this overlaps most closely with the period covered in the following chapters. Second, the index does not incorporate policies covering transgender people before 2012: it addresses the rights environment for gay, lesbian, and bisexuals only.[52] This makes comparisons between earlier years, when the index contained fewer components, and later years difficult. To allow for such comparisons, I used the coding criteria for the 2010 index to back-code the subsequent years. As a final shortcoming, measures such as ILGA-Europe's, which attempt to tap multifaceted concepts across different political-cultural contexts, risk flattening complexity and missing important nuances. To take one analogue, the Freedom House's rankings of democracy are invariably subjected to this critique. Yet democratization scholars continually return to Freedom House data for want of a better substitute and because failing to learn from differences among countries is a loss of its own. The same defense is offered here. By presenting a broad comparison between postcommunist countries at various degrees of proximity to EU leverage, even the purely cross-sectional comparisons in the ILGA-Europe index offer the opportunity to disentangle domestic and transnational effects.

As a first cut at the relationship between EU leverage and the quality of legal frameworks for sexual minorities, Table 2.1 presents a comparison of means across the various categories of members, candidates and potential candidates, ENP states, and "outsiders." It shows that, overall, there is a statistically significant difference in rights between countries depending on their proximity to EU accession.[53] The main difference appears to be between potential and actual members, on the one hand,

TABLE 2.1. Comparison of Subgroup Means by Proximity to the EU

	Mean Score on ILGA-Europe Index		
	All Countries	Western Europe	Postcommunist Only
EU PROXIMITY			
• Member-states	4	5.1	2.2
• Candidates and "potential" candidates	2.4	3.5	2
• European Neighborhood Policy (ENP)	−0.3	—	−0.3
• EU "outsiders"	2.3	2.9	−2
F-test (H0=all groups' means are equal)	Reject H0 with 95% confidence	Cannot reject H0	Reject H0 with 99% confidence

and neighbors and "outsiders," on the other. Among postcommunist countries, the difference in means between actual and potential members is only 0.2 points and is statistically insignificant.

Independent Variables

As described above, EU leverage is captured through the variable "EU proximity," which categorizes states into members, candidates and potential candidates, ENP states, and outsiders. A purely domestic model of rights frameworks would trace differences among European countries to just a few major factors that have been identified in the literature on the politics of homosexuality: communism's legacy, religion's role in society (both national religious tradition and overall religiosity), and the level of economic development.[54] All of these factors relate closely to a more proximate variable, *attitudes about homosexuality* in society. Because of its close causal proximity to the outcome of legal change, the variable social attitudes is less theoretically satisfying as an explanation; however, I use social attitudes as a proxy indicator of domestic context in the statistical analysis to check the robustness of the results. To measure social attitudes toward homosexuality, I draw on the WVS question asking respondents to place themselves on a 10-point scale whether "Homosexuality is never (1) / always (10) justified."[55] My variable is the mean value of responses by country. A word of caution regarding these data and the religiosity data, which are based on the same source: because the WVS has been conducted over several waves with a changing cast of countries in each wave, it was necessary to combine data from two separate survey waves to construct these variables.[56] For each country I used the most recent data on attitudes toward homosexuality (and religiosity) from before the construction of the ILGA-Europe rights index: these were WVS waves 4 and 5, conducted around 2000 and 2006, respectively. It would have been better to have data from one point in time, but I judged this alternative an acceptable indicator of how countries varied on this deeper political-cultural dimension, especially given the range of variation.[57]

Ronald Inglehart's celebrated postmaterialism thesis posits that, as *economic development* raises living standards, it reduces the political salience of bread-and-butter economic issues.[58] Increasingly, it predicts, citizens in wealthy societies will turn their political engagement to "values issues" such as environmentalism, multiculturalism, gender equality, and tolerance of homosexuality. The last of these is often seen as the paradigmatic postmaterialist issue.[59] Cross-national studies have consistently confirmed the posited relationship between economic development and attitudes toward homosexuality, including in postcommunist countries.[60] The path of economic development under communism and the subsequent shock of postcommunist transition tended to foster "survival values," which promote intolerance.[61] Though my dependent variable is the quality of rights, not attitudes, my expectation is that intolerant attitudes are not conducive to expansive minority rights frameworks. Following the literature, I measure economic development through per capita GDP (in 2008 US dollars).[62] In line with standard practice for countries at very different levels of economic development, I use the logged value of GDP.

Because there are reasons to suspect that communist legacies also affect attitudes toward homosexuality through channels other than economic development, a postcommunist dummy variable is included. The expectation is that postcommunist countries will have worse rights frameworks than the West European countries in the sample, even when controlling for other differences among them. As illustrated in Figures 1.1 and 1.2, postcommunist countries stand out both for their consistently lower legal freedoms and less tolerant attitudes regarding sexual minorities. This situation reflects *communism's legacy* of de jure

and de facto repression of homosexuality. Many communist governments criminalized homosexuality at some period during their tenure.
Some, notably the Soviet Union and Romania, maintained this policy
until after communism fell. Even in regimes that decriminalized homosexuality before 1989, communism's legal legacy was one that did not
recognize sexual orientation as a category and that lacked a concept of
protections against discrimination.

Even if, however, there was some variation in the legal status of homosexuality by the late 1980s, the unofficial sphere of daily practice looked
rather similar across countries. Since Stalin, communist governments
across the Eastern bloc were socially very conservative, overlaying a
"neo-Victorianism" on societies already predominantly traditionalist in
their cultural norms.[63] Gays and lesbians faced pervasive discrimination
both from the state authorities and the broader society. As one illustration, though homosexuality was never criminalized in Poland, its secret
police used the threat of disclosing sexual orientation to blackmail and
recruit informants. From 1985 to 1988, Poland's secret police pursued
a crackdown on gay men, "Operation Hyacinth," which implicated
some 11,000 people.[64] The memory of this everyday repression still
drives many sexual minorities to hide their orientation and, consequently, not push for greater rights. According to regional activists,
this tendency is still quite noticeable today: most LGBT people prefer
to develop their own "underground" networks and clubs rather than
publicly fight for acceptance. They prefer that activists *not* draw attention to LGBT rights, reasoning that making public claims will upset
these tacit accommodations with society at large.

Since LGBT rights touch on core doctrinal issues of the major religious faiths in Europe, my domestic model of rights adoption also
includes a variable for a country's *predominant religious tradition*:
Protestant, Catholic, Orthodox, or Muslim. Even in secularized societies, national religious traditions are institutional templates with wide-
ranging effects and long-lasting consequences, especially for legal and
political institutions.[65] Pippa Norris and Ronald Inglehart, for example,
write that these traditions "imprint themselves" on society "via the
major channels of cultural transmission and socialization."[66] Even for
the nonreligious in a given society, attitudes toward issues like sexual
liberation will be shaped by national religious traditions. To categorize

predominant national religious traditions across Europe, I draw on the research of Norris and Inglehart, who divide the continent into Catholic, Protestant, Orthodox, and Islamic traditions based on the plurality religion.[67] In the statistical analysis, this becomes a categorical variable.

National religious traditions shape society's attitudes and political values in an institutional, path-dependent way that endures even after secularization has gained hold. By contrast, *religiosity* captures differences in the degree to which a society's political values are influenced by religious belief. Secularization is an erosion of religiosity, regardless of national religious tradition. It is generally seen as a component of the shift to a postmaterialist society.[68] In secular societies, people are less attentive to spiritual matters and find religious teachings about sexuality less compelling. Following Norris and Inglehart, I measure religiosity using the WVS question "How important is God in your life?"[69] As with the question on tolerance of homosexuality, possible answers range on a scale from 0 (not important) to 10 (very important). My expectation is that countries with high levels of religiosity will, all things being equal, have weaker legal rights frameworks than countries with low religiosity.

Analysis and Results

This final section presents the results of a multivariate regression analysis of the hypothesis that EU leverage—which is greatest when states are applying, or expect to apply, to become EU members—leads to improvements in national-level LGB rights frameworks. As described earlier, this analysis does not attempt to distinguish between external incentives and social learning mechanisms but considers their effects on the quality of rights to be complementary. The dataset includes 47 states from Western and Eastern Europe, and the dependent variable is each country's score on the Rainbow Index for each of the five years from 2009 through 2013. EU leverage is captured primarily cross-sectionally (as differences among states at different removes from EU accession) rather than longitudinally (as states move through the stages of accession). (For technical details on the regression analysis, see the Appendix.) The baseline for comparison is states that have no intention of pursuing EU membership, which includes both postcommunist and West European states. To lead with the main conclusion, I find evidence that where EU leverage was strongest (i.e., among applicant- and potential applicant-states) rights frameworks were of higher quality than we would expect based on domestic determinants such as level of economic development, communist legacy, national religious tradition, religiosity, and attitudes toward homosexuality.

Table 2.2 presents the results of random effects models of various theoretical specifications. *Model 1* is the bare-bones EU leverage framework, without any control variables to capture domestic context other than a postcommunist dummy variable to account for the fact that the categories "outsider" and "EU member" include both postcommunist and West European cases. Model 1 shows that potential member and member-states have significantly higher scores on the Rainbow Index than the baseline nonaspirant states. Everything else being equal, this boost is, however, not enough to overcome the strongly negative effect of having a communist legacy, the effect of which is roughly double that of EU incentives. This model does not find a statistically significant difference between nonaspirant and ENP states.

Model 2 presents a strictly domestic account of LGB-rights frameworks, using variables highlighted in the extant literature: economic modernization, communist legacy, national religious tradition, and religiosity. Not surprisingly, these factors show a high degree of explanatory power. As expected, greater religiosity is associated with weaker LGB-rights frameworks. Further, countries with Protestant national religious traditions have better rights frameworks than the baseline Orthodox countries; in this model, the effects of Muslim and Catholic religious traditions are indistinguishable from those of Orthodoxy. Also as expected, economic modernization exercises a positive effect on the rights framework. Last, the effect of the communist legacy remains substantively strong and statistically significant even after controlling for the deeper structural features of the societal context just mentioned.

Model 3 brings together the domestic and EU variables. The substantive effect of the domestic variables remains essentially unchanged. This suggests that, generally speaking, the domestic side of the story matters more for the level of rights comparatively. That said, Model 3 does affirm that, in the situation where we would expect Europeanizing pressures to be most powerful—namely, for candidate and potential candidate states—there is a substantively and statistically significant boost to LGB

TABLE 2.2. The Transnational and Domestic Determinants of Legal Rights Frameworks for Gays, Lesbians, and Bisexuals in Europe (2009–2013)

Random effects GLS regression, DV: country score on ILGA Europe Rainbow Index

	"EU Effect" Model (I)	Domestic Factors Model (II)	Domestic Factors + "EU Effect" (III)	Public Attitudes Model (IV)	Public Attitudes + "EU Effect" (V)	Everything (VI)
Tolerance of homosexuality				1.126*** (0.156)	0.956*** (0.190)	0.528** (0.247)
Religiosity		−0.610** (0.281)	−0.690** (0.282)			−0.336 (0.319)
Predominant National Religion (excluded category = Orthodox):						
• Catholic		1.448 (0.985)	1.676 (1.034)			1.719* (0.981)
• Muslim		0.796 (1.426)	0.574 (1.520)			1.205 (1.478)
• Protestant		2.171* (1.314)	2.242* (1.307)			2.245* (1.236)
GDP per capita (log of)		0.764** (0.382)	0.922** (0.393)			0.802** (0.395)
Post-communist	−2.996*** (0.859)	−1.784** (0.885)	−1.859** (0.867)		−1.402* (0.832)	−0.881 (0.969)
EU Proximity (excluded category = "EU outsider"):						
• ENP	−0.783 (1.818)		2.006 (1.612)		0.313 (1.480)	2.095 (1.535)
• potential member	1.290** (0.643)		1.185* (0.634)		1.300** (0.643)	1.226* (0.629)
• member	1.404* (0.742)		0.305 (0.774)		1.116 (0.735)	0.478 (0.759)
Constant	3.578*** (0.750)	−0.714 (4.885)	−2.392 (4.958)	−1.489* (0.767)	−1.022 (1.363)	−6.400 (5.284)
R^2	0.32	0.62	.65	0.55	0.61	0.69
# of observations	233	205	205	210	210	205

Standard errors in parentheses; *p<0.10, **p<0.05, ***p<0.01

rights beyond what we would expect based on domestic factors alone. For EU member-states, however, this effect washes out after controlling for domestic determinants—a result in line with previous scholarship.[70] In other words, EU membership was not associated with rights levels beyond what we would expect based on domestic factors alone. Among West European member-states, we can interpret this result as reflecting the earlier exposure of these societies to LGB rights contemporaneously with the global movement's founding and development since the 1970s; consequently, they differ little from West European nonmember-states. Among the postcommunist states that joined in 2004–2007, we can interpret it as indicating a strategy of "minimum-necessary" legal change before accession and little additional change in the period covered in the dataset.[71] As before, among ENP states, which faced weaker and less credible incentives to burnish their rights reputation, we find no significant boost for rights beyond what domestic factors would predict.

Models 4, 5, and 6 are included as a means of validating the analysis above. Instead of using domestic measures of society's "deep structure" (e.g., religious tradition and economic development), I use a more proximal indicator of societal openness to LGB rights: attitudes toward homosexuality. The logic is intuitive: where public attitudes about homosexuality are tolerant, we expect more developed legal frameworks for sexual minorities. Like Model 2, Model 4 is a domestic-only look at LGB rights; not surprisingly, it confirms the intuition just described. Model 5 adds our proxies for EU leverage (cf. Model 3). Interestingly, this model reaffirms a statistically significant rights boost for the category of candidate and potential candidate states; furthermore, this boost is substantively equal to the negative effect of the communist legacy. For this class of states, then, EU leverage can "overcome" communism's negative legacy regarding sexual minorities' rights. With regard to the other categories of EU proximity, however, gains in the quality of rights are not statistically significant when controlling for domestic factors.

Last, Model 6 draws together all the variables from the previous models. As one would expect, including both the proximate and deeper indicators of societal openness washes out much of the statistical significance of some of the domestic variables, though the general direction of the coefficients remains unaffected. For example, attitudes toward homosexuality pick up much of the effect of religiosity. Likewise, the effect of communism's legacy is attenuated here. It is, thus, all the more striking that the substantive and statistical significance of EU leverage for the category of candidate and potential candidate states is unshaken in Model 6.

To summarize, this analysis shows support for the positive effect of EU leverage on legal frameworks regarding sexual orientation in postcommunist Europe. More specifically, it shows that the quality of rights in states facing the greatest leverage (i.e., applicants and potential applicants) is higher than we would expect it to be based on domestic factors alone. In line with previous scholarship, however, my analysis cannot discern a corresponding effect for other categories of EU proximity with a high level of confidence. Put differently, the promise of membership has a stronger effect on the quality of rights frameworks than being a member does. Moreover, if the promise lacks credibility, as in the ENP states, its effect on rights is also hard to discern relative to domestic factors.

As an important caveat, these findings should not be taken as evidence that EU pressures did not force important legal changes in the first round of postcommunist applicant-states, who had become members by the time period covered in this analysis. As a matter of law, they had to make major, often highly controversial, changes to their labor code to prevent discrimination on the basis of sexual orientation. To put this in context, the United States still lacks such federal-level protections, even after the legalization of same-sex marriage. Thus, even the "minimum necessary" changes enacted by the first postcommunist entrants were deeply significant *politically*. It was common in interviews with Polish rights activists that, even as they expressed frustration that the EU's effect was not bigger, they declared that the whole of Poland's legal framework for LGBT people was the result of EU pressure.[72] That EU leverage could have a positive influence on a controversial issue like this is heartening, at least to rights advocates. To opponents, it only confirms their suspicion that European integration threatens national identity, the conception of the family, and traditional values.

Conclusion: Beyond Policy Change, after Accession

As this chapter has shown, EU leverage had a significant impact on the adoption of policies benefiting sexual minorities through the accession process, but it also confirmed that such characteristic features of closed society as high religiosity and lagging economic development also depress such policies. Given these results, EU membership itself was bound to unleash a host of questions about these new policies and the activist groups that had lobbied for them, especially in the comparatively closed societies of Poland, Romania, Slovakia, and Hungary. (For the comparatively open Czech Republic, this chapter's findings do not suggest any obstacles to rights gains after accession.) First, there was the question of implementation: Would these rights and the principles of antidiscrimination on which they were based be exercised? Would sexual minorities be able to participate on an equal footing in the public sphere? Given this region's long history of feigned compliance with the agenda of larger powers—which was abundantly clear under communism but also under imperial rule prior to World War I—there were abundant grounds for skepticism.[73] It is precisely this tension between the minority-rights commitments that countries made as EU applicants and how some of them behaved as EU members that is captured in the book's opening epigraphs. Second, what would become of the activist organizations that had benefited from the accession process? Here, too, were grounds for concern: the loss of the role of broker, the tendency of transnational advocacy networks to move on to "needier cases" after states graduate to the EU club, and the background constant of low levels of civic participation in postcommunist societies. Finally, what would be the response of LGBT-rights opponents, especially as EU leverage weakened? Here, this chapter's findings that the EU's positive effects on rights are visible primarily when its leverage is maximal (i.e., in *potential* member states) foreshadowed postaccession turbulence in Hungary and Poland—closed societies where hard-right breakthrough coincided with weakening EU leverage.

As Chapter 1 argued, the catalyst for Poland's renewed mobilization was the onset of hard-right backlash in the postaccession environment. This backlash reflected the logic of EU leverage (or rather the diminution of such leverage) and so can be understood in terms of how external incentives reshape the domestic POS. Beyond this insight, however, more work is needed by Europeanization scholars to explain contentious politics and activist organization after membership.[74] Scholars of the transnational diffusion of LGBT rights such as Ayoub have noted the linkage between new rights and new forms of contention: "Even if this international visibility [for gay rights] is at first negatively received and domestically contested, it can still be politically effectual by virtue of creating a legitimizing discourse."[75] The following chapters push this insight further: domestic movements become more organized not "even if" international visibility produces backlash but "especially if."

How the Hard Right "Europeanized" Homosexuality

An Analysis of Party Rhetoric and Media Discourse

Lesbians and faggots are ideal citizens of the European Union.
—Slogan yelled by hecklers at the 2004 March of Equality in
Poznan, Poland

The phenomenon that we have observed in Poland had been
growing for years, and the 2005 election results were just an
example of a dramatic acceleration, an escalation of a rebel-
lion against modernity.
—Aleksander Smolar, political scientist

Chapter 1 introduced the concept of hard-right backlash, which
occurred in some but not all postcommunist countries acceding to the
EU.[1] This chapter applies this concept, comparing cycles of hard-right
mobilization in Poland and the Czech Republic. Backlashes are crucial because they create framing contests with wide resonance in the
public sphere. This occurs in two ways. First, backlash brings unprecedented media attention to an issue that had previously languished in
the obscurity of taboo; it increases the issue's visibility and centrality,
that is, its salience. Second, by politicizing homosexuality—even if by
casting LGBT rights as part of a threatening foreign agenda—hard-right
backlash transforms how homosexuality is framed, enhancing the credibility of activists' framing of it as a rights issue, as opposed to a morality
or therapy one. As discussed earlier, frames are shared understandings
through which social movements "make attributions regarding who
or what is to blame, articulate an alternative set of arrangements, and
urge others to act in concert to affect change."[2] Thus, framing is critical to recruiting and mobilizing constituents and to attracting allies
from outside the movement. Just because a frame exists does not mean,

however, that it is effective in these tasks. It must also resonate: that is, it must be salient and credible.[3] Framing contests can be critical in generating resonance, especially if other social movement resources are scarce. Hard-right backlashes enhance the credibility and salience of the gay-rights frame by threatening the minority's protective surround and marking the issue as symbolic of wider EU principles.

In postcommunist Europe, at least three framings of homosexuality are available for rights advocates and their opponents to draw on. First, there are the legacy framings, those understandings of homosexuality formed before 1989 that continued to define prevailing social attitudes in the 1990s. These legacy framings were shaped, on the one hand, by the state's policies toward gays and lesbians under communism, which varied across countries, and, on the other hand, by the advent of the HIV/AIDS epidemic in the 1980s. The key features of the legacy frame in Poland and the Czech Republic were as follows. In Poland, this framing portrayed homosexuality in terms of religious teaching, as an individual moral failing. HIV/AIDS added a more public policy dimension, but it was also addressed in terms of morality and charity.[4] In the Czech Republic, the legacy framing was socio-therapeutic, informed by the fields of sexology and psychology. The advent of HIV/AIDS only reinforced this "medicalized" frame. In neither country was homosexuality framed in political terms. As the previous chapter described, the EU's growing engagement with problems of discrimination brought another possible framing of homosexuality into view beginning in the late 1990s—that of rights, of sexual orientation as just another kind of minority status with equal claims to political inclusion and protections against discrimination. While attractive to LGBT advocates in postcommunist countries, on its own this rights framing was not sufficiently resonant to generate the organizational resources of visibility, solidarity, and allies. It would take a framing conflict for that—which brings us to the last relevant framing and the focus of this chapter, the hard-right framing. Here homosexuality is cast as a threat to national identity and, critically, as something imposed by the EU. As Ayoub has dubbed it, this is the "defend-the-nation frame."[5]

This chapter develops two main analytical claims. First, and to put the point somewhat provocatively, in closed postcommunist societies it was the hard right that "discovered" homosexuality as a salient issue in the mainstream political discourse, displacing the largely apolitical legacy framings that had predominated after 1989. Of course, LGBT activists already understood the political dimensions of homosexuality, but their perspective had not penetrated the broader public discourse. Second, the link between homosexuality and the EU in the public sphere was likewise forged chiefly by the hard right as part of this larger framing contest. The hard right used the EU's purported "homosexual agenda" as a symbol of liberal, secular transnationalism's broader threat to national and religious identity. This counterframing enhanced the credibility of the movement's own framing of LGBT rights in EU terms: the hard right and the movement did not agree on much, but they agreed that acceptance of LGBT rights was a signifier of acceptance of EU norms more broadly. There was, of course, an irony that the EU's tools for promoting protections for LGBT people in postcommunist countries were actually rather limited, but perception was more important than reality.[6] From the hard right's perspective, this "Europeanization of homosexuality" ultimately backfired because it did less to tarnish the EU's image than it did to present them, the hard right, as enemies of what was in the first years after accession the increasingly popular project of European integration. Thus, while invoking the LGBT threat may have helped the hard right mobilize its Euroskeptic base, by the same token it helped turn Euro-advocates into movement allies as a way of demonstrating support for EU integration.

To gauge how EU accession influences the saliency and credibility of homosexuality as a rights issue—as opposed to one of morality or therapy—this chapter compares two very different contexts, Poland and the Czech Republic. As described in Chapter 1, the former is a comparatively closed society in which the hard right became politically pivotal over the course of the accession process, and the latter is a comparatively open society in which the hard right dwindled into insignificance. Framing contests raged over homosexuality in Poland, whereas in the Czech Republic the issue received relatively little attention, despite the country's more tolerant social attitudes. Since framing contests are dynamic processes in which both the salience and character of frames evolve over time, they are best analyzed through process tracing, qualitative data, and content analysis. This chapter employs all three. In the first part, I focus on the composition and character of hard-right political parties over time, tracing their origins, path to power (or irrelevance), and how through their counterframing they forged a link between homosexuality and the EU that (inadvertently) enhanced the "apparent fit" between activists' own EU rights frame "and events in the world," that is, that frame's credibility.[7] The chapter's second part analyzes the salience and visibility of this framing contest in the broader public discourse. Here I use content analysis to compare the Polish and Czech print media.

Counterframing and Credibility: Hard-Right Mobilization and Rhetoric in Poland and the Czech Republic

Chapter 1 laid out the following criterion for identifying the hard right in postcommunist political systems: namely, the hard right consists of two kinds of parties, the "populist radical right" and those conservative or Christian Democratic parties willing to form alliances with them. This section's first task is to describe which parties fit this criterion, what they believe, and with what degree of success they have been able to mobilize voters. The second task is to understand how and to what degree the hard right links the EU with homosexuality in their rhetoric and public statements. We should recall at the outset that the trajectories of the Polish and Czech hard right have diverged sharply since 1989 (see Figure 3.1). The Polish hard right's ascendance coincided with the intensification of EU leverage. Meanwhile, its Czech counterpart slid into oblivion. In Poland, this timing enhanced the credibility of the EU rights frame because the rhetoric of the populist radical right League of Polish Families (LPR) and the conservative Law and Justice Party (PiS) relentlessly linked LGBT rights with EU overreach. The Czech hard right's irrelevance prevented any such association.

"Poland A" versus "Poland B"

To orient our examination of the hard right's "discovery" of homosexuality in Poland, a few general observations about the development of its party system are in order. First, it has been very turbulent: parties are born and die with a rapidity that is unsurpassed in the region.[8] This matters for the politics of homosexuality because it means that the system

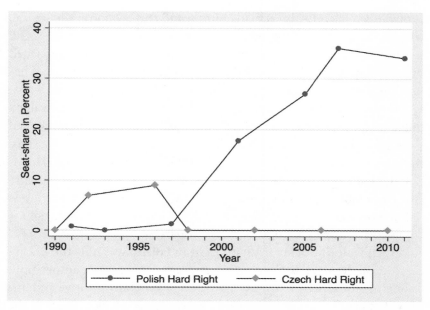

Figure 3.1. Hard-Right Seat Share in National Parliamentary Elections (Poland and the Czech Republic)

is more open to new parties, including those with extreme views, than would be a more institutionalized party system.

It is also true, however, that beneath the changing party labels and electoral fortunes there remains a basic division born in the twilight years of communism, that between the successors of the Solidarity movement and those of the Communist Party. The churn of parties is greatest among the former, which may loosely be identified as the "right." This term must be used cautiously, however, because the Polish "right" is divided both by attitudes toward the market *and* toward national identity. On the one hand, the post-Solidarity "right" contains both economically liberal parties and those critical of the economic reforms associated with Poland's "shock therapy" in the 1990s. The latter parties call instead for a mix of statist and redistributive economic policies more typically associated with social democracy.[9] On the other hand, the "right" also contains both religious-nationalist parties and secular-Europhile ones.[10] Instead of the familiar left/right terminology, Poles often describe this party system with the terms "Poland A" and

"Poland B." Poland A is secular, "European," and economically liberal, while Poland B is religious, nationalist, and favors an economy of "social solidarity."[11] It is also Euroskeptic, reflecting a nativist strain described by one scholar as a "deeply, culturally ingrained perception of social belonging, and of the foundations of the polity, in which the social whole is considered prior to the individual, and in which local culture is valued differently from Western culture."[12] As we will see, this understanding of national identity has its roots in Poland's interwar politics. In sum, since the traditional left-right spectrum is bisected by issues of national identity, the Polish party system offers populists and the hard right greater space to mobilize than in a system in which the left-right spectrum is defined primarily by economic issues.[13] As a result, the Polish right is comparatively open to populist, outsider parties.

A final factor favoring the hard right in Poland was how the EU accession process acted to weaken programmatic party competition. Though Poles' attitudes toward the EU were generally positive and improving over the 2000s, there were pockets of deep ambivalence in the electorate as well, especially in the late 1990s and early 2000s. The hard right's rise and dominance from 2005 to 2007 was made possible by this period of growing Euroskepticism—or at least strong ambivalence about EU membership—before accession. Since all the mainstream parties took EU membership as their stated foreign-policy priority, they faced a difficult balancing act between not jeopardizing Poland's prospects for membership and responding to outsider parties' fearmongering about what membership would mean for voters personally. As Anna Grzymała-Busse and Abby Innes write, "The political headache for competing parties, then, has been how to manage governance and this [EU-imposed reform] agenda without destroying their own popularity. The successful competitive strategies have been those of technocracy, populism, and nationalism—the last two tending to be combined."[14] In other words, parties competed not over policy differences but over support for (or opposition to) the EU as a whole.[15] As Grzymała-Busse and Innes further note, in Poland "a fourth of the seats in the fall 2001 election [were] claimed by anti-Union parties, who range[d] from the merely skeptical to the outright antagonistic." Ironically, results such as these were typical for countries "in the forefront of EU candidacies—and precisely because they have done the most to hew to the EU line and accept EU demands, they have been least able to debate the future of their state."[16]

During the 1990s, when EU membership still appeared as a fuzzily defined and distant prospect, the Polish hard right was a fringe phenomenon. Populist radical right parties did exist, but they were not considered credible partners by other parties.[17] Surprisingly, Poland lacked a successful self-identified Christian Democratic party. Parties of the right certainly made frequent use of religious and nationalist themes in their programs, but neither theme was particularly useful for distinguishing among these parties.[18] The best organized Christian-oriented party, the Christian National Union, was allied with the center-right.[19] Finally, all mainstream parties officially favored EU membership.[20] The conditions were not yet in place for a hard-right coalition bringing together the populist radical right with either a conservative or Christian Democratic party. Not only was "Poland B" not yet radicalized, it was still partnered with the more liberal elements of the post-Solidarity camp.[21] By the time of Poland's 2005 elections, however, growing Euroskepticism coupled with weak policy differentiation among parties and a fractured "right" allowed an opening for "Poland B" to break through electorally. PiS and LPR entered government, and the mainstream parties, which had competed on their EU-technocratic credentials, suffered disappointing to catastrophic results.[22]

LPR and PiS were newly established hard-right parties that took unprecedentedly nationalist and Euroskeptic positions. LPR espoused a "Poland for the Poles" nationalist ideology so extreme that most observers classified it as populist radical right (or even far-right).[23] PiS was the larger of the two and would become the senior coalition partner in the PiS-LPR-SO government. It was conservative by origin,[24] though as it competed with LPR for the support of the Polish Catholic Church's doctrinaire wing, nativism and populism came to define it more than conservatism.[25] Both parties portrayed EU accession—and the host of economic, political, and antidiscrimination reforms associated with it—as an elite project supported by a network of ex-nomenklatura insiders of dubious Polishness. Both called for domestic regime change, the installation of a so-called Fourth Republic. This was understood as a moral and patriotic renewal with echoes hearkening back to the program of interwar Poland's illiberal demagogue Roman Dmowski, who espoused a nativist vision of an ethnically pure, Catholic Poland.[26] Of central interest to our focus here, both parties fomented an increasingly strident antigay rhetoric linking homosexuality with European integration and presenting themselves as defenders of Polish values against this threat.[27] In 2001, PiS and LPR took 9.5 and 7.9 percent of the vote, respectively, just a few points less than the largest right party, Civic Platform (PO). In 2005, PiS increased its vote to 27 percent and LPR received 8 percent. Together with another newcomer to the party system, the agrarian-populist Self-Defense (SO) party,[28] they formed a coalition government that lasted until fall 2007.[29] This government represented the height of Poland's hard-right backlash.

Having described the Polish hard right's origins and path to power, we turn now to their rhetoric around homosexuality and the EU from 2001 through 2007.

The League of Polish Families: The Hard-Right's Extremist Core

LPR was founded in May 2001 by a group of politicians associated with earlier, and less successful, attempts to politically mobilize the far right in Poland.[30] As described in the most comprehensive study of the LPR to date, the party "regarded the politics conducted in post-1989 Polish society as [an] anti-Polish conspiracy agreed upon by the participants of the Round Table Talks [acting in collaboration with] international forces based in the European Union, Jews and masonry."[31] Its program combined seemingly all possible elements of a closed society: extreme conservatism on issues of gender and family; nationalism, antisemitism, and xenophobia; a populist call to cleanse corrupt elites (especially former communists); and autarchic economic policies.[32] None of these themes were new in postcommunist Polish politics, but combining them to achieve an electoral breakthrough was. LPR's success where predecessors failed was, to quote one scholar, "best understood in light of the emergence of the EU as a political issue, which was the direct consequence of the immanent accession of Poland to the EU."[33] LPR was the only party in 2001 that opposed accession outright.

A critical factor in LPR's electoral success was the support of Radio Maryja, a radio network founded by the Catholic priest Tadeusz Rydzyk in 1991 that, by the early 2000s, had become an influential media empire. Radio Maryja counted a listenership on the order of 2–3 percent of Polish radio, and it was especially popular among "the elderly and those with minimal education."[34] Rydzyk was known for his antipathy to the EU; he campaigned against Poland's accession because "it would impose a moral behavior on the country."[35] The term "moral behavior" was not meant in a complimentary sense. It was meant as secular-liberal moral behavior, hence incompatible with Poland's moral order. Instead, Radio Maryja emphasized the need to expand the influence of Catholicism—a deeply conservative brand of Catholicism, it should be noted—in Polish politics and society.[36]

Besides Radio Maryja, LPR's rise was abetted by an extraparliamentary youth organization, the All-Poland Youth (Młodzież Wszechpolska, MW), which was originally founded in the interwar period and later reestablished by Roman Giertych in December 1989.[37] While LPR denounced its opponents in parliament, MW intimidated them physically in public places—a strategy that political analyst Rafał Pankowski has compared with that of fascist movements in the 1930s.[38] MW activists were particularly intent on shutting down, or at least disrupting, Pride parades. As the following chapters will describe, they physically attacked Pride marchers on a number of occasions. They also staged numerous street demonstrations against EU membership.[39] A number of MW leaders involved in these incidents later became LPR politicians.[40]

LPR's rhetoric toward the EU was extreme—"more Euro-reject than Euroskeptic" as one observer put it—and of a piece with its antiliberal and nativist views.[41] Polish political scientist Krzysztof Jasiewicz, in his analysis of LPR's 2005 election manifesto, summarized the party's position as "an all-out assault on the establishment consensus regarding Poland's accession to the European Union and on the institution itself. The EU is presented as a mortal threat to Polish national identity, to the very existence of a Polish sovereign state, to the well-being of the Polish economy, and to the core values of European Christianity. The EU assumes the place here of the Other."[42] Besides LGBT persons, LPR's imagining of the EU Other also included Germans, Jews, and Freemasons, but the official manifesto was more cautious regarding race and nationality. There was, however, one "group they dared to cast openly in the role of Other: homosexuals."[43]

To offer a particularly raw example of the virulence of LPR's rhetoric and the way in which it conflated homosexuality and the EU as foreign threats to Polish values, let us consider an article by LPR parliamentarian Wojciech Wierzejski published in the party-affiliated paper *Myśl Polska* on April 15, 2001.[44] The article is entitled "Euro-Faggots on the Offensive." In it Wierzejski identifies the EU as a propagator of homosexuality, promoter of same-sex partnerships, corrupter of the traditional family, and foe to the Catholic Church. Amsterdam, known for its liberal-secular political culture, is taken as a stand-in for the EU. The terms used to describe LGBT people include deviants (*dewianci*), perverts (*zboczeńcy*), and faggots (*pedały*). Same-sex partnership ("relationship between faggots") is contrasted with "love between men and women." In Wierzejski's view, the EU "exports" homosexuality just like any other good in the common market:

> Because Euro-Union can lately boast neither healthy nor even normal (mad?) cows . . . it decided to give humanity the best thing it has— *deification of sexual deviance, specific preeminence of faggotry* in society and *equality of all the perversions against nature.*[45]

This text comes from 2001, that is, before a majority of referendum voters elected to enter the EU. It should be noted that LPR's message evolved somewhat after Poland entered the EU and the party entered government. Rather than defending Poland from the EU, the party outlined Poland's mission to defend Europe from left-liberal corruption from within the EU. It sought to "work for the 'creation' of a new Europe, free of homosexuals, by the ever pure Polish nation."[46]

The virulence of LPR's antigay rhetoric in the public sphere shows how sharply it departed from liberal-democratic norms. This rhetoric condemned homosexuality as a moral failing and threat to society. It advocated the infringement of LGBT individuals' rights—especially if they made their sexual orientation public—and turned a blind eye to harassment and physical intimidation. Homosexuality was frequently equated with criminality, mental illness, pedophilia, necrophilia, and zoophilia.[47] Among the most vociferous antigay LPR MPs was Wojciech Wierzejski, who posted a note on the door to his office in parliament barring entry to homosexuals.[48] Wierzejski also declared that "persons identified as

active homosexual members should be subjected to a customary, social, and common intolerance so that they could not consciously, openly,
publicly, and fearlessly walk with their heads high in the air showing
their faces."[49] At a 2005 campaign rally, he called for "discrimination
against homosexual activists in all spheres of life," vowing "to ban all gay
organizations 'when the LPR comes to power.'"[50] LPR further proposed
that Poland reintroduce the death penalty for "murderer-pedophiles."[51]
As the party frequently described gays as pedophiles, the latent intimidation here was obvious. In one commercial during the 2005 election
campaign, an LPR supporter declared: "I have the courage to say that
two 'pederasts' [sic] are not man and wife."[52]

This kind of discourse can be found, of course, in many countries,
even democratic ones; however, it is relegated to the fringe of politics, and
most of the time it is invisible. In Poland during this period, antigay and
anti-EU rhetoric entered the political mainstream and was impossible to
overlook, even at the highest levels of state.[53] LPR's founder Roman Giertych was appointed minister of education in 2005, a move that not only
legitimized his well-known views on homosexuality and the EU—not to
mention evolution, feminism, and so on—but also gave him an institutional perch from which to promote them.[54] LPR campaigned to eradi-
cate homosexuality from Polish schools—a "problem" with which it often
seemed obsessed.[55] In 2003, in the midst of the national debate about the
adoption of EU norms prohibiting discrimination against LGBT persons
in the labor market, an LPR MP proposed legislation banning homosexuals from becoming teachers.[56] After Giertych's appointment as education minister, a wave of protests, mostly by university students, occurred
across Poland. Giertych responded by announcing that "left wing and homosexual organizations" were behind the attacks.[57] The LPR's Wierzejski
called the demonstrations "unpardonable attacks on the government and
its ministers." Claiming they had been organized by homosexuals, he demanded a full investigation by the Interior Ministry into "whether and to
what degree these organizations are connected with pedophile networks
and organized crime groups trafficking in narcotics . . . [as well as] how
far the penetration of these organizations extends into Polish schools."[58]

LPR used its power in the Education Ministry to move beyond mere
antigay rhetoric, despite being constrained by EU and even Polish law.
In 2006, Minister Giertych illegally dismissed the head of the national

teacher training center, Mirosław Sielatycki, because the center distributed books "encouraging teachers to organize meetings with LGBT nongovernmental organizations such as Campaign Against Homophobia (KPH) or Lambda."[59] It later turned out that what Giertych had in mind was the Polish translation of a handbook on antidiscrimination policy published by the CoE. The replacement director, who was appointed by Giertych, was quoted as saying that "active homosexuality is contrary to human nature" and that "because the objective of the school is to explain the difference between good and evil, beauty and ugliness. . . . [it] has to explain that homosexual practices lead to drama, emptiness and degeneracy."[60] This episode was later discussed in Poland's parliament, where Giertych justified his firing of Sielatycki for promoting the handbook:

> Is this what we want taught in Polish schools? Must we agree that Polish schools organize such operations at our cost and against the curricula? And that's not just one example, because we've seen in previous years, especially during the governments of the leftist parties, entire campaigns aimed at convincing the Polish educational system to disseminate homosexual propaganda. There were camps for children and youth, during which Mr. Biedroń and the Campaign against Homophobia, which according to the textbook should be invited to meet Polish children and teachers, taught about how gender is a matter of convention, that it can be changed several times in one's lifetime; camps where young people were put in coeducational rooms for the night just to prove that gender doesn't matter; camps where boys were being dressed up as girls and girls as boys, where visits of *German transvestites in Polish nurseries* were organized. This is also what we've dealt with there. A large mighty organization, *in a sense an international one as well*, which was supposed to encourage the Polish educational system to do things they do in the Netherlands or Belgium.[61]

During its tenure in the Education Ministry, LPR also barred the Polish LGBT-rights group KPH from accessing EU educational funds, stating that "the Ministry does not support actions that aim to propagate homosexual behavior and such attitudes among young people."[62] The ministry also rolled out an Internet filter for Polish schools that blocked access to sites mentioning homosexuality, including those of rights NGOs.[63]

As a number of Polish analysts have pointed out, LPR's rhetoric of exclusionary nationalism and scapegoating of minorities tapped directly into political currents from the interwar period, in particular, the "National Democracy" (Endecja) movement. The Endecja was most closely associated with Roman Dmowski, leader of the best organized party of the period, the National Democratic Party (Stronnictwo Narodowo-Demokratyczne). In the ethnically and religiously heterogeneous amalgam that was interwar Poland, Dmowski espoused an exclusionary vision of the state ("Poland for the Poles"). As his theorizing developed, he came to associate Polishness with Catholicism, writing in 1927, "Catholicism is not an appendage to Polishness. . . . it is embedded in its essence, and in a large measure it is its essence. To attempt to dissociate Catholicism from Polishness, and to separate the Polish nation from its religion and the church, means to destroy the very essence of that nation."[64] Non-Catholic minorities, especially Jews and Germans, were seen as morally corrosive to society and a threat to state sovereignty.[65] The Endecja proposed to "make the Polish state the exclusive property of Catholic Poles . . . 'the Catholic state of the Polish nation.'"[66]

As the historian Andrzej Walicki has argued, these ideas continued to inform Polish conceptions of national identity even after the fall of Poland's interwar state and under communism.[67] They found life in the more nationalistic members of the Solidarity movement: recalling Dmowski, these members called themselves "true Poles," language that excluded non-Catholics. In 1999, on the 60th anniversary of Dmowski's death, an overwhelming majority of Poland's parliament voted to commemorate his contributions to independence, omitting reference to his illiberal policies and celebrating his linkage of religion and national identity.[68]

LPR sought to transform the Endecja's ideology for contemporary Poland, adapting its conflation of nationalism and Catholicism to confront two new national enemies, the EU and homosexuals. The EU was cast as German domination in a new guise.[69] Politicized anti-Semitism was recast as politicized homophobia.[70] As the Polish sociologist Adam Ostolski wrote of LPR during this period:

> Prewar anti-Semitic language is currently turning up not only in anti-Semitic declarations: this language and the practices that accompany it

are also (and even above all) being repeated today in contexts which have nothing to do with Jews. The new object of this discourse is homosexuals.[71]

LPR's rhetoric appropriated the Endecja's motif of a "civilizational conflict" between nation and outsider. In both, nation is understood as Catholic and under threat, respectively, from "Talmudism" or the "civilization of death"/"homosexual lobby."[72] Ostolski cites an illustrative passage from a contemporary radical-right affiliated newspaper, *Nasz Dziennik*, which wrote of Poland's LGBT movement in 2004:

> We are dealing with a radical movement, a wide-ranging network of organizations, pressure groups, radical intellectuals and activists, who not only seek to protect their interests but also to change our laws, our customs, our morality, and even our Catholic religion. . . . This is not about the purported struggle for gay rights: it is about the destruction of traditional society based on the primacy of the family. . . . Their main goal is the destruction of society.[73]

There are strong similarities between this text and the comments of LPR MP Wierzejski quoted earlier. LPR politicians echoed this rhetorical device of portraying a small minority as a pervasive national menace in speeches and public statements.

In sum, LPR defined itself against the EU and framed its antigay program within this larger field. As one analyst put it, "In LPR discourse, the topic of gay rights was firmly linked to the EU: the latter was routinely accused of promoting homosexual lifestyles and imposing them on Poland."[74] This interconnectedness was obvious to any observer of a Pride parade during the mid-2000s, at which All-Poland Youth and other counterdemonstrators would shout slogans such as the one serving as this chapter's epigraph or, to take another typical example, "Eurosodom halt!"

Law and Justice: LPR's Ally and Competitor

PiS represents the other, and larger, half of Poland's hard-right tandem. It is, as analysts of Polish politics agree, harder to pin down programmatically than LPR, as it is less extreme than the far right and more extreme than the mainstream conservative parties in the region.[75] I place it in the hard-right category because it is a conservative party that allied with the populist radical right, thereby validating and participating in the latter's antigay, Euroskeptic rhetoric.[76] PiS and LPR were both founded in 2001, and for the better part of the 2000s PiS was in sharp competition with LPR for the "Poland B" electorate. Here, it employed an antigay rhetoric and tactics not out of place with LPR's. Like LPR, PiS evoked historical resonances from interwar Poland, the so-called Second Republic.[77] Namely, it promised a "moral revolution" to install a "Fourth Republic" and purge the lingering political and moral corruption that the 1989 revolution (the starting point of the "Third Republic" in this accounting) had failed to dislodge. Following its electoral breakthrough in 2005, PiS invited LPR into the government, an event that was perceived by the LGBT community as a direct threat to their already precarious position in Polish society. As with LPR, this discussion focuses on how PiS contributed to a discourse around homosexuality and the EU that portrayed both as foreign to the Polish nation.

To focus first on PiS's treatment of homosexuality, the party participated in the trope of portraying homosexuality as a social pathology. A particularly notorious example occurred just before Poznań's 2004 March for Tolerance. Two PiS city councilors protested the planned march in the most derogatory terms. Councilor Przemysław Alexandrowicz declared, "I don't want a march of alternative sexual orientations in Poznań, such as homosexuality, paedophilia, necrophilia, or zoophilia."[78] His colleague, city councilor and president of PiS's Poznań branch Jacek Tomczak, added that "the term 'sexual orientation' suggests that it could also have to do with promoting such propensities as paedophilia, zoophilia or necrophilia."[79] Unwitting confirmation that such comments were *not* those of the political fringe, that they in fact illustrated a broader hard-right discourse about homosexuality, was provided in the context of a subsequent lawsuit that KPH brought against both officials (the case was Lesbian activists versus Alexandrowicz and Tomczak). The court ruled against the plaintiffs for reasons that are worth quoting at length:

> The defendants were allowed to make such statements not only for their own interests but in the interests of society. The Court does not feel they were made in an attempt to degrade the victims. Although homosexuality

is not considered a deviance or illness, it does in some sense differ from the normal order, a behaviour that diverges from accepted norms and against nature and for the Court the linguistic meaning of certain phrases is important. . . . Poles have a phobia towards homosexuality. In this context of Polish feelings towards this occurrence that is homosexuality, *the statements made by the defendants do not take on a degrading character and objectively do not negatively affect the opinions of Poles towards homosexuals in Polish society.*[80]

In clearing the defendants, the court in fact incriminates them: the public statements of the PiS politicians were homophobic, but they did not make an already derogatory public discourse any worse. It is a dubious specimen of legal reasoning, but it brings the pervasiveness of the hard-right backlash about homosexuality, in which PiS played a large role, into sharp focus.

Lest one speculate that the episode cited above was an example of local but not national party tactics, it is only necessary to recall that such comments, especially about Pride parades, could be heard from the party's leaders. Culture Minister Kazimierz Michał Ujazdowski (PiS) warned, "Let's not be misled by the brutal propaganda of homosexuals' postures of tolerance. It is a kind of madness, and for that madness, our rule will indeed be for them a dark night."[81] The new prime minister, Kazimierz Marcinkiewicz (PiS), publicly stated that if "a person tries to infect others with their homosexuality, then the state must intervene in this violation of freedom."[82] In the 2005 parliamentary elections campaign, homosexuality became the dominant issue in defining the religious-secular divide in politics, eclipsing both abortion and religious education, which in one analyst's words "had all but vanished" as issues.[83] PiS and LPR vied to stress their intolerance of homosexuality.[84] Finally, PiS consistently supported the controversial education minister and LPR leader Roman Giertych in his mission to combat homosexuality in Polish schools, as described above. PM Jarosław Kaczyński publicly defended Giertych in 2007, saying:

I assure you that if a man from the PiS were Minister of Education, he would take the same direction as Giertych. . . . I want to say it clearly, I am also against the promotion of homosexuality in school. . . . I don't see any reason to support the fashion for promoting homosexuality.[85]

Beginning in 2004, opposition to Prides became a rallying point, as Chapter 6 will detail.[86] PiS's cofounder, then president of Warsaw, and later president of Poland Lech Kaczyński directly contravened EU norms by banning Warsaw's March of Equality in June 2004, just months after the country joined the EU. Ignoring a cavalcade of EU criticism, Kaczyński presented himself as a defender of decency. In summer 2005, with the prospect of elections that fall, Kaczyński again banned the event, citing disruptions to traffic.[87] Meanwhile, PiS ran television spots with the appeal that "[r]ather than provocative parades of homosexuals, we want state help for Polish families."[88] In the opinion of many political observers, including my interviewees, Kaczyński's stand was decisive in defining the still-new PiS's identity. As Chapter 6 will describe, these bans marked the beginning of a heated battle about Prides that spanned the next several years and extended across Poland.

These actions and this rhetoric were deeply embedded in a PiS narrative about protecting Polish values from liberal Europe. The party's position toward the EU has evolved over time, but during the early 2000s PiS was continually testing the limits of Euroskepticism.[89] The broader context for the party's treatment of the EU was an understanding of Western Europe as hostile to Christian belief. To quote party chief and future PM Jarosław Kaczyński, "In Western Europe they want to ban the Christmas tree and they have criminalized people who criticize homosexuality. In a moment they will go after the churches. . . . It is a question of facts, not opinions." As Kaczyński defined his attitude toward the EU, "We have to tell them: we are us, we have our own rules."[90] Within the relatively short space of PiS's time in government, it managed to undo a number of gender-related policies enacted as conditions for EU membership. After the 2005 election, one of the government's first actions was to abolish the Government Plenipotentiary for the Equal Status of Men and Women, the only state office with an official mandate to deal with issues affecting LGBT persons.[91] It was replaced with a Plenipotentiary for Family Affairs. Even as PiS was exiting power, it rejected the EU Charter of Fundamental Rights because, the government argued, it would mean a "change of the definition of family" and the "acceptance of homosexual marriage."[92] (Neither in fact was necessitated by the Charter.)

In sum, while PiS was never as ideologically extreme as LPR, it partnered with LPR in creating a political discourse that both demonized and "Europeanized" homosexuality in the years from 2001 through 2007. One may argue that PiS's alliance with LPR was more tactical than heartfelt and that the party also contained more moderate voices. Regardless, PiS's encroachment on the hard-right themes of Catholic values, Polish sovereignty, and fighting corruption proved to be successful electorally. It won over LPR's voters in droves in 2007, and the latter failed to reenter parliament.[93] Even if PiS's motives were instrumental, the consequences for the politics of homosexuality in Poland were momentous. First, as the next section shows, this hard-right backlash made homosexuality visible as a political issue in a way that it had never been before. Second, as Chapters 5–6 will show, the backlash also became a catalyst for gay-rights activists, allowing them to recharge a moribund movement in an environment that offered few conventional resources for such activism.

The Czech Hard Right: A Study in Contrasts

The task of analyzing the hard right in Czech party politics is a briefer one because, as depicted in Figure 3.1, this segment of the party system never achieved an electoral breakthrough. Moreover, by the time the Czech Republic entered the EU accession phase, its hard-right parties were dwindling into irrelevance. As with Poland, this analysis begins by considering features of the broader party system that, in this case, helped doom the hard right. The first contrast between the two is the degree of institutionalization.[94] If Poland has been among the region's party systems most open to the entry of new parties, the Czech Republic has been one of the most closed. If electoral volatility has been consistently high in Poland, in the Czech Republic it has been comparatively low. This relative stability raises the bar for sudden shifts in the party system's composition. Unlike Poland—where a religious divide overlaps with both a nationalist and a market-redistributive divide—the Czech party system lacks a religious divide among either parties or voters. The issue of market reform, in further contrast to Poland, is not one that divides the right between nationalist-minded supporters of greater redistribution and Europe-facing economic liberals.[95] As a result there are no Czech A and Czech B camps that become increasingly polarized with the onset of European integration.

With the broader picture of party system development in mind, let us now turn to the handful of Czech hard-right parties since 1990 and analyze both the role of the EU and homosexuality in their rhetoric and the extent to which the two were linked. The main Czech populist radical right party during this period was the Association for the Republic–Republican Party of Czechoslovakia (SPR-RSČ), which achieved "virtual hegemony" over the Czech far right in the 1990s.[96] SPR-RSČ was dominated by its mercurial leader, Miroslav Sládek, whose ideological obsessions centered on the German and Roma "threats."[97] Opposition to homosexuality never became one of the party's themes, as it did for LPR and PiS in Poland. To the extent that the party received media attention, it was for its anti-German positions and the bizarre antics of its leader, such as when he smashed his seat in parliament.[98] In further contrast to the Polish hard right, SPR-RSČ did not define itself in opposition to the EU. In 1992, SPR-RSČ broke through the 5-percent threshold for parliamentary representation, but it was thoroughly isolated in parliament and riven by internal disputes, mostly surrounding Sládek. In 1998's elections, the party failed to receive enough votes to remain in parliament, and in 2000 it was formally disbanded. No other populist radical right alternatives ever achieved anything approaching SPR-RSČ's (limited) success in Czech politics.[99]

With the inexorable decline of the populist radical right over the 1990s, the core for a hard-right bloc was clearly weak in the Czech Republic; however, let us briefly consider the two other potential elements of such a bloc, had it existed: parties of the Christian Democratic and Conservative types. Surprisingly for so secular a country, the Czech Republic has a well-established Christian Democratic party, the Czechoslovak People's Party (ČSL). It has its roots in the interwar period and even under communism remained in existence, albeit as a Communist-controlled satellite party. Since 1989, it has fashioned itself as a kingmaker in the country's tight coalitional politics. It has been a member of both left governments (2002–2006) and right ones (2006–2009). While out of government from 1998 to 2002, it allied itself with liberal parties in the so-called Quad Coalition. Thus, given its need to exploit its coalition potential with both the left and right, ČSL has been ideologically pragmatic. While its program is oriented toward the family and Christian morality, as one would expect, it is not the kind of party seeking to challenge the EU or stoke controversial social issues, like the LPR or PiS in Poland.

Of the other conservative parties, the Civic Democratic Party (ODS) has dominated this part of the political spectrum for the entirety of the period considered here. Founded by economist Václav Klaus, the party modeled itself on Thatcherism: secular-conservative, with liberal principles, and neoliberal on economic issues. According to Vít Hloušek and Lubomír Kopeček's typologization of the region's parties, ODS is classified as "conservative-liberal," together with the Slovenian Democratic Party.[100] Notably, the Polish PiS and the Hungarian Fidesz are classified as "national conservative." The chief difference between these two branches of the conservative family is the latter's emphasis on social conservatism, nationalism, and Catholicism. ODS's choice of coalition partners reveals its considerable ideological flexibility, but never in a direction more conservative than its own. It has governed with liberals (e.g., ODA), Christian Democrats (e.g., ČSL and the Christian Democratic Party [Křesťanskodemokratická strana]), Greens, and even, informally, Social Democrats (ČSSD). It must be acknowledged that the party built a reputation for Euroskepticism, especially under Klaus; however, this dynamic reversed after 2002, when ODS lost national elections, Klaus lost leadership of the party, and the new leader, Mirek Topolánek, moved the party back to the center, especially regarding the EU.[101] As discussed in Chapter 6, Klaus would later play the role of spoiler in the Czech LGBT movement's campaign for same-sex partnerships; however, even over the course of this legislation, ODS never made the issue one of party discipline. Instead, its MPs were free to vote their conscience, and many voted in favor.

Finally, we should consider other Czech social actors sympathetic to hard-right aims. Recall that, in Poland, such actors as the All Polish Youth and Radio Maryja lent strong support to hard-right political parties, amplifying their antigay and Euroskeptic discourse. In the Czech Republic, a number of far-right, primarily neo-Nazi, groups are active outside of party politics, and the Czech "White Power" music scene is known in Europe.[102] One should not be misled by the number of groups, however. It is high because these groups are constantly changing names and reconfiguring organizationally to avoid being shut down by the authorities—not to mention internal disputes. Further, only one of the groups, the National Alliance, included opposition to homosexuality as part of its agenda.[103] The dominant theme overall is anti-Roma racism. Thus, we do not find equivalents here of Poland's Radio Maryja or the All-Poland Youth, extraparty organizations capable of influencing the media discourse about homosexuality and of mobilizing voters to support hard-right parties.

In sum, the Czech hard right was (1) a marginal political force even at its height and (2) was far more animated by anti-German and anti-Roma sentiments than antigay ones. Consequently, homosexuality never became a salient topic in the political discourse in the way that it did in Poland, nor was it linked in the same way to EU integration. To quote one survey of the Czech political spectrum, far-right parties "have always been treated as pariahs at the political level."[104] Moreover, "the reporting of the media is strongly negative, irrespective of whether the media are private or public."[105]

Counterframing and Salience: A Content Analysis of the Czech and Polish Media

Having shown how, through their public statements and actions, the hard right displaced legacy framings of homosexuality with a "defend-the-nation" one and thereby enhanced the credibility of the EU rights frame, the remainder of this chapter gauges the extent to which this framing contest resonated in the broader media discourse. Chapter 1 made the claim that, as a legacy of communism, homosexuality was a taboo, even politically invisible, topic in the public discourse for most of the 1990s. As a result of hard-right mobilization, in the early 2000s this discourse began to change, and by the decade's midpoint a profound shift was under way. "Homosexual propaganda," LGBT rights, homophobia, and same-sex unions all became major topics in the media. The observation that such a shift had occurred surfaced repeatedly in my field interviews and has also been made by regional analysts. This section provides systematic empirical evidence of homosexuality's path from obscurity to salience using content analysis of the leading daily newspapers in Poland and the Czech Republic, respectively *Gazeta Wyborcza* and *Mladá fronta dnes*. This analysis allows us to track the issue's visibility in the domestic media using quantitative data.

My argument that, in closed societies with a politically mobilized hard right, EU accession sparked a framing contest that gave unprecedented salience to homosexuality in the media sphere builds on insights of scholars who have examined the discourse around homosexuality in postcommunist Europe.[106] For instance, in a compelling study of the Polish media from spring 2002 to summer 2005, sociologist Agnieszka Graff discovered a dramatic upswing in the number of articles dealing with gender roles and sexuality, including homosexuality.[107] In the three years leading up to accession, she found that some 11 percent of cover stories in the center-right *Wprost* concerned what she termed "gender talk." In the year before accession alone, this number rose to 50 percent. More telling perhaps than the article counts were the article titles themselves. *Wprost* ran covers with such titles as "The Dictatorship of Equality" (June 2004), which was accompanied by photos of people with mouths taped shut like hostages while a rainbow flag hung in the background. The accompanying article described how "sexual minorities and feminists 'terrorize' the 'normal' majority."[108] In August 2003, center-left *Polityka* devoted its cover to "Homo-Condemnation." Its tone was sympathetic, drawing attention to the surge of intolerance toward gays and lesbians in Poland.[109] The contrast between these two cover articles—one representing the hard-right framing of homosexuality as a moral threat and the other the liberal, pro-EU framing of homosexuality as a question of political rights—encapsulated the framing contest that was reshaping this issue's salience in Polish society. As Graff writes, "In the more nationalistic forms of this discourse, Poland's submission to and adjustment to EU norms as a condition of admission was portrayed as a threat to masculinity."[110] Graff's characterization of such gender talk closely echoes the "defend-the-nation" framing of homosexuality in hard-right parties' rhetoric, as described in the preceding sections:

> A highly formulaic narrative emerges from the mass of articles I have examined. The master story unfolds as follows: Things used to be "normal" and "natural," men and women used to know who they are, but sex roles in Poland—indeed worldwide—are in crisis today, so that the future looks bleak. Nonetheless, the natural order (i.e., male domination) will soon be restored.[111]

Wprost's cover in the week following Poland's EU accession encapsulated this script: it was titled "The Return of the Real Male."[112]

Graff's insights about the connection between EU accession and the salience and character of the public discourse around sexuality are incisive and strongly align with my own argument. However, her study also suffers from methodological constraints that limit its causal claims. First, it covers a relatively brief period in time, from 2002 to 2005. Though this represented the height of EU leverage, the absence of data over a longer time span makes it impossible to assess just how exceptional this period's "gender talk" was: the absence of a baseline unnecessarily limits her claim. Second, Graff's study is limited to Poland. To appreciate just how exceptional the EU's impact on "gender talk" was in a relatively closed society like Poland, it would be helpful to have a comparison with a more open society, such as the Czech Republic.

The final section, therefore, undertakes an analysis of the place of homosexuality in the Czech and Polish public discourses from the 1990s through 2012 through a content analysis of two of the countries' largest and most comparable daily newspapers. In addition to resolving the methodological constraints mentioned above, this analysis also narrows the broader focus on "gender talk" to the more specific issue of homosexuality. The goals of the analysis are, first, to gauge changes in the issue's salience and, second, to pinpoint critical turning points in any such changes, especially in relation to hard-right mobilization. Using the digitized archives of *Gazeta Wyborcza* and *Mladá fronta dnes* I count the number of articles containing key words related to homosexuality. Thus, the number of articles serves as the measure of salience. A small number of articles indicates low salience. As is clear from my field interviews and from the extant literature, the baseline salience in both countries (i.e., the starting point of the early 1990s) was nil, or, as one respondent described this period, the "regime of silence."

To begin, a brief word about each paper's history and place in its country's media landscape. *Gazeta Wyborcza* is Poland's most influential news daily.[113] It began as an underground paper during Poland's transition to democracy in the late 1980s. After 1989, *Gazeta Wyborcza* quickly became Poland's largest newspaper and remained so during the period analyzed here.[114] Its politics are generally considered left-of-center and secular. The paper's full digital archive is available going back to 1989. *Mladá fronta dnes* occupies a similar space in the Czech print media market, though its politics are generally considered center-right.

As its name, which translates as "Youth Front Today," indicates, it was a Communist-aligned paper before 1989; however, it shed its Communist ownership and editorial line immediately after the Velvet Revolution and quickly became among the largest and most influential papers.[115] At the time of this analysis, its circulation was in the 200,000–300,000 range, about the same size as *Gazeta Wyborcza*'s. Like its Polish counterpart, it is generally seen as tolerant of homosexuality and secular in orientation. While it would have been ideal to compare two center-left (or center-right) dailies, my analysis was constrained by data availability: only these two dailies had digital archives extending back to the 1990s.

Figure 3.2 presents a yearly count of the number of articles containing at least one instance of the term "homosexual" in its adjectival form.[116] In both languages, it is a foreign borrowing; therefore, its meaning is unambiguous and need not raise concern about counting articles referencing some other concept.[117] Neither do we undercount articles since the term is the preferred usage in both languages. The figure confirms that in both countries homosexuality as an issue has risen in salience. In Poland

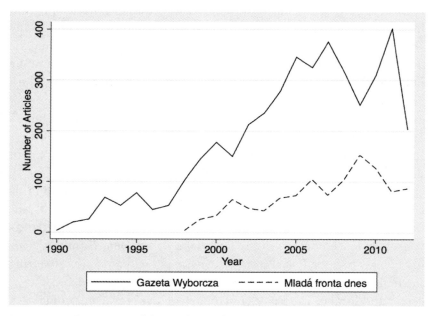

Figure 3.2. A Comparison of the Incidence of Articles Containing the Term "Homosexual" in *Gazeta Wyborcza* and *Mladá fronta dnes* (1990–2012)

it confirms the near absence of homosexuality from the discourse in the 1990s. In the Czech Republic, homosexuality's rise in salience is not nearly as dramatic. Unfortunately, *Mladá fronta dnes*'s archive does not extend back beyond 1998: however, as a practical matter, this truncation is not problematic because both my interviewees and extant histories indicate that homosexuality was not politically salient in the 1990s.[118] The Czech plot shows a gradual increase in visibility—with a noticeable spike around 2007–2008—while the Polish plot shows sudden spikes and drop-offs. The timing of these spikes supports the argument that homosexuality's politicization tracked the shift from preaccession to accession politics. The number of articles mentioning homosexuality rose sharply around 2004 through PiS and LPR's time in government. Afterward, the number of articles fell.

These cycles of salience are highly suggestive, but to probe the timing more closely Figure 3.3 charts the incidence of the term "homophobia" (in Polish *homofobia*, in Czech *homofobie*).[119] If increasing salience resulted from a hard-right backlash against "homosexual propaganda"

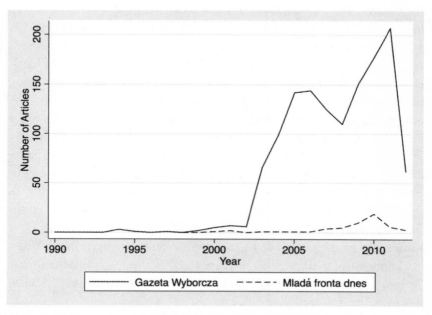

Figure 3.3. A Comparison of the Incidence of Articles Containing the Term "Homophobia" in *Gazeta Wyborcza* and *Mladá fronta dnes* (1990–2012)

and other forms of baleful outside influence, we would expect these two terms to track each other. During the 1990s, the term was absent from the media in both.[120] After 2000, the contrast between the Czech and Polish plots is obvious. In Poland, the number of stories mentioning homophobia skyrockets, closely tracking the plot for "homosexual" in Figure 3.2. In the Czech Republic, the term homophobia remains all but absent from public discourse until 2010, when there is a slight uptick. Together with Figure 3.2, these data provide strong evidence that, in Poland, the hard right's rise corresponded with an antigay shift in the discourse. As a side effect, though, homosexuality gained unprecedented salience.[121] The Czech Republic experienced no such discursive shift, but nor was there a matching increase in homosexuality's salience.

Conclusion

This chapter has compared the effects of hard-right backlash on the framing of homosexuality in Poland and the Czech Republic. This comparison looked first at the mobilization of and the discourse employed by the hard right during and after the EU accession process. It then moved to analyze the salience of homosexuality in the broader public discourse, as reflected in both countries' leading newspapers. In Poland, a closed society by regional standards, EU accession prompted a surge of hard-right parties that through their rhetoric sparked a framing contest that, on the one hand, linked homosexuality with EU integration (thereby enhancing the credibility of the EU rights frame) and that, on the other hand, gave homosexuality unprecedented salience. It is extremely suggestive that, in Poland, the sudden rise in articles about homosexuality exactly coincides with a tenfold increase in articles about homophobia, previously a virtually unknown term in the Polish press. By contrast, in the more open society of the Czech Republic, the hard right never focused its attention on homosexuality, nor did it experience an electoral surge in the period of EU accession. Quite the opposite, it was a declining movement directed primarily against Germans and the Roma. As the content analysis revealed, the issue of homosexuality experienced less visibility in Czech public discourse.

The next three chapters continue this focused comparison of Poland and the Czech Republic, training the lens now on the organization of activism in each country. What were the effects of hard-right backlash on movement development? The narrative line that emerges from this analysis runs as follows. In Poland, hard-right backlash sparked by EU accession led to an increase in homosexuality's salience as a political issue *and* an increase in the organization of LGBT activism. Thus, transnational pressure and domestic polarization combined to enable the Polish movement to overcome the general postcommunist obstacles to social movement development, making it one of the strongest movements in the region. Backlash brought visibility, solidarity, and allies. The Czech movement followed a different path, one in which domestic factors—in particular a more favorable legacy of state engagement with homosexuality under communism—drove movement development. Absent the benefits of backlash, however, the Czech movement struggled mightily against the postcommunist obstacles to activism, and the overall arc of its history shows a movement in decline after the country's accession to the EU.

Activism before EU Leverage

Poland and the Czech Republic, 1980s–1997

First of all, I submit that we decide what our future organization will look like, so that we can finally be legal. On this
point I personally stake all for the future. . . . The establishment of an organization must be our first and main goal.
—Michal Rada, Czech activist, January 1990

Why did the mobilization of Polish gays have such an inci-
dental character? . . . [M]ost Polish gay organizations have
only a few active members. . . . Neither do they command
political power, nor do they possess any protest potential.
—Krzysztof Kliszczyński, Polish activist, surveying the
movement from 1989 to 1999

Accession to the EU was a cherished dream for East European states
through the 1990s, proof positive of putting the communist past behind
them.[1] As Andrew Janos observed, however, the path from "Eastern
empire" (Soviet domination) was also the path to "Western hegemony."[2]
Joining the EU required opening up comparatively closed societies to
norms and practices that had grown significantly more postmodern
since the Iron Curtain had established a divided Europe. EU leverage
pried open areas of social life that had long been politically taboo, perhaps none more obviously than homosexuality. As we have seen, in
some countries this leverage led to hard-right backlash motivated, to
quote the Polish prime minister Jarosław Kaczyński, by the need "to tell
them: we are us, we have our own rules."[3] The next three chapters ask
how these transnational pressures affected the development of LGBT
activism after communism. They explain how activism was organized
from the early 1990s through 2012. Rather than explaining policy change

per se or wider social attitudes toward homosexuality, the goal is to explain how LGBT activists move from social movement communities based on informal local networks to broad-based, formally organized, and politically mobilized SMOs.[4] A full explanation of the mobilization cycle must also address why complex, formalized organizations fall into decline. The next three chapters trace a close comparison of movement development in the Czech Republic and Poland structured by these goals. They draw on a diverse array of sources from fieldwork interviews and participant observation to movement-generated reports and policy papers to the work of scholars in both countries. The goal is careful measurement of organizational change through "thick" process tracing.

The following factors are crucial to this cycle of mobilization: the political opportunity structure, especially the perceived threat of repression, either directly or indirectly; the available resources for mobilization (including preexisting resources from the late-communist era); and how homosexuality is framed. Each of these factors is in part a function of transnational dynamics, which are themselves variable: they depend primarily on the changing leverage of the EU over the course of the accession process.[5] For most of the 1990s, in the area of LGBT issues, transnational pressures were at their weakest—virtually nonexistent when compared with what was to come. The preaccession period offers, then, a view of postcommunist LGBT activism when domestic factors dominate.

The POS was slightly more favorable in the Czech Republic, but to emphasize these differences would be to miss the overwhelming similarity between the two countries, namely, the vast expansion in opportunities for activism occasioned by communism's collapse. As mentioned already, there were, however, strong contrasts in both the preexisting resources for mobilization and how homosexuality was framed. Czech activists had more developed networks and resources to draw on, thanks to the greater engagement of Czech psychologists with homosexuality under communism. The framing of homosexuality—whether in terms of morality or therapy—also differed, and these differences were also rooted in the communist era. In Poland, the morality frame prevailed, allowing for a kind of limited charity-based activism; whereas in the Czech Republic, early activism's links to psychologists provided a therapeutic frame. Because of these differences, Czech activists were quicker to build institutional structures connecting local groups and coordinating them toward political goals. By the late 1990s, Czech activists had crossed the thresholds from uncoordinated local activism to national organization, from informal social movement communities to SMOs, and from constituent-oriented service provision to politically oriented activism. In Poland, they had accomplished none of these.

Political Opportunity Structure, Framing, and Mobilizing Structures Compared

In both countries, the preaccession POS was defined primarily by domestic factors and, in the *absence* of binding EU conditionality, not international ones. Domestically, the fall of communism had cracked open the POS, allowing for political pluralism. Across the issue spectrum, the early 1990s witnessed the explosion of new forms of association, from political parties to interest organizations to social groups. From the perspective of sexual minorities, the end of state censorship, which made possible personal ads and community magazines, was a particularly important feature of this opening. After years of repression, there was pent-up demand for spaces allowing community.

The first dimension of political opportunity is given by the degree of openness of formal political institutions.[6] Here, the Czech Republic and Poland did not differ meaningfully during this period, nor after for that matter.[7] Relatedly, we do not find significant differences in either state's propensity for repressing activism, either directly or indirectly. As we saw in Chapter 3, although the Czech hard right demonstrated a capacity to mobilize electorally in the 1990s, they were shunned by other parties and lacked any influence over the state.[8] Poland's hard right was not electorally mobilized either, and populist radical right parties were a fringe phenomenon. Thus, there were no appreciable differences in the hard right's capacity to threaten the stability of elite arrangements. Finally, because of homosexuality's low salience during this time, we find no significant differences in the availability of elite allies.[9] In sum, communism's collapse opened the POS for activists of all kinds, and since it did so in both countries, it cannot explain differences in the organization of Czech and Poland activism in the 1990s.[10]

If the POS offers little comparative leverage here, two other features of the domestic environment do: how homosexuality was framed and the level of extant mobilizing structures that activists could draw on. Both were strongly determined by the legacy of the old regime, and both were more favorable for Czech activists. This section describes the Polish and Czech authorities' differing approaches to homosexuality during late-stage communism. It was these *domestic* differences, rather than transnational pressures, that explain the relative success of the Czech movement in the preaccession period, as well as the Polish one's failure to transition from informally organized, locally oriented, and apolitical activism.

Before entering into the cases, however, let us briefly revisit the question of which identities and orientations among the movements' constituencies were represented during this period. In both countries, gay men were the most visible constituents, with some representation of lesbian and bisexual orientations. In my research, I did not uncover any significant transgender activism yet; likewise, queer activism was not visible. Both movements were concerned with sexual orientation, not gender identity, as will be clear from the discussion below.

Homosexuality in Late-Communist Czechoslovakia

Czechs entered the postcommunist period with the beginnings of an activist network in place. In communist-era Czechoslovakia, the state had supported a comparatively extensive network of academics and doctors doing research on the psychology and medicine of human reproductive behavior.[11] This work was centered in the Ministry of Health's Institute of Sexology, and research on homosexuality was a core part of this program. When Czechoslovakia decriminalized gay male sex in 1961, it was largely as a result of these researchers' efforts. As Scott Long argues, the "medicalization" of homosexuality in communist Czechoslovakia was, despite the negative connotations of that term, generally a positive development, "engender[ing] an atmosphere where homosexuality could be sympathetically and seriously described in public—even, in the late eighties, by the state newspaper for youth."[12] Through this research network, support groups for gay, lesbian, and bisexual people were formed as early as 1976 and gained further momentum with the onset of the HIV/AIDS epidemic. Funding for these groups—for newsletters, social events, and workshops—came from the state, under the rubric of HIV/AIDS prevention. The sexologists' aim was not to "cure" homosexuality: they did not consider it a disease or a matter of individual choice. The theory was that homosexuality could create psychological problems if gays were unable to come to terms with their orientation, leading them to become socially alienated. The group's purpose was, therefore, to provide a space to be "sociable" and become better integrated into society.[13] As Long writes, "The Institute of Sexology at Charles University in Prague was a territory where gays and lesbians could actually exchange, and reflect on, their experiences—discovering commonalities and contemplating *non-therapeutic* forms of change."[14]

In 1988, sexologists Ivo Procházka and Antonín Brzek established a so-called Socio-Therapeutic Club in Prague, of about 30 gays and lesbians.[15] Besides offering therapy, it was a discussion group and a space to socialize. Some of its members had visited LGBT-rights groups in Britain and elsewhere. Within a short time, another group formed under the name Lambda; it had largely overlapping membership with the Socio-Therapeutic Club but broader aims than self-help counseling. Under the Sexological Institute's auspices, a monthly bulletin, *Lambda*, was published. Distributed for free, it contained articles aimed at HIV/AIDS prevention but also more broadly on issues of community interest. Membership grew steadily, and by the summer it was estimated at around 100 and extended beyond Prague.[16]

In a relatively short time, this group of "patients" came to see their activities more broadly than therapy. They aspired to create greater freedoms for gays and lesbians in Czechoslovak society.[17] One early goal was to lift censorship on same-sex personals ads in newspapers. This campaign met with success: in fall 1989 the newspapers *Mladá fronta dnes* and *Mladý svět* began running personal ads.[18] A second goal was legal recognition for gay and lesbian associations. In March 1989, Lambda submitted an application for legal status. The petition was viewed favorably by the authorities; however, by the time the legal formalities were taken care of, the Velvet Revolution had swept the Communist Party from power. Thus, by the time Lambda's petition to become a registered public association was accepted in February 1990, a new regime was in place. Status as a public association is important because it belies the dominant understanding of postcommunist civil society as based on informalism, personal connections, and apoliticism. Lambda was, in the beginning, largely based on such connections, but it aspired to formalized representation of the interests of gays and lesbians, recognizing that in doing so it was also representing the interests of those who were not public about their sexual orientation.[19] Two other examples indicate Lambda's increasingly political understanding of its mission—even under communism. These were, first, its participation in an international conference in Budapest sponsored by ILGA in summer 1989 and, second, its endorsement of legalizing same-sex partnerships.[20]

These early developments demonstrate the existence of a surprisingly well-developed network of gays, lesbians, and allies even before 1989—especially by regional standards. This network was more institutionalized than a friendship network though less institutionalized than an SMO. Though it lacked formal legal status, the state was aware of its existence and, in fact, helped fund and organize it. Meetings were typically in someone's apartment. The goals were therapy and self-help, not political action. Its members certainly did not call themselves activists. What mattered, though, was that this network constituted SMOs in the making. Many participants in these early groups, both "patients" and doctors, went on to become leading figures in the Czech movement after 1989, notably, the movement's de facto leader Jiří Hromada as well as figures such as Dr. Ivo Procházka. Even if such quasi-formal networks would not be counted as civil society organizations by the accounting of Leninist legacy scholars,[21] from the perspective of social movement theory they exemplify the kind of mobilizing structures and preexisting resources for mobilization on which robust social movements can later be built. Finally, the fact that Czech state officials were willing to recognize and work with gay and lesbian groups even under communism helps account for the less confrontational approach of the Czech movement's main leaders through the present day. As we will see, Polish activists have been sharper critics of their government's policies and sought to apply pressure through public manifestations, while Czech activists have preferred to lobby politicians individually and not to mobilize support though public events like Prides.

The organization of gay and lesbian groups in late-stage communism as self-help groups complemented the issue's framing. Reflecting the perspective of the doctors and psychologists leading these groups, homosexuality was framed in medical terms: it was understood as a biological trait, not a chosen identity. HIV/AIDS prevention was always an implicit subtext of the groups' activities. In their first newsletter, the Socio-Therapeutic Club's founders, Dr. Ivo Procházka and Dr. Antonín Brzek, framed the group's goals as "socio-therapeutic care," which "raises [members'] life satisfaction, enables acceptance of their current health condition, and works preventively against the appearance of possible complications."[22] Some have criticized this framing as the "medicalization of homosexuality" and faulted it for suppressing claims to group identity or "gay culture."[23] Later, this framing was faulted for stifling a gendered— and, more specifically, feminist—perspective on homosexuality.[24]

Even acknowledging these criticisms, a comparison with the prevailing frame for homosexuality in Poland at this time shows the comparatively favorable basis that the therapeutic framing provided for Czech activists after 1989. First, it fit tightly with the movement's organization as self-help groups, and it opened up a connection to state support through the framework of HIV/AIDS prevention. Second, it allowed gays and lesbians to present themselves as "normal" citizens, albeit citizens with different sexual preferences. This is not to claim the absence of prejudice and social taboo about homosexuality in Czech society in the 1980s and early 1990s. There was plenty of prejudice to be sure; moreover, as we saw in the last chapter, in both countries homosexuality was invisible in the larger political arena. But in the absence of a cohesive rationale for homophobia such as the morality frame allowed in Poland (see below), Czech gays and lesbians could even in this early period conceive of activism in terms of political goals. It is striking after all that these self-help clubs had applied for legal status *prior* to the Velvet Revolution. After the revolution, Czech activists could consider their work in terms of emancipation, albeit emancipation from the communist past and its legacies: social taboo, lack of self-confidence, lack of community, and a host of discriminatory provisions in the legal code.[25] These included equalizing the age of consent for heterosexual and homosexual sex, removing homosexuality from the list of psychological disorders, the destruction of communist-era secret police files on homosexuals, and addressing HIV/AIDS.[26]

Homosexuality in Late-Communist Poland

To understand the situation in which the first homosexual organizations formed after 1989, it is necessary to step back to view Poland in the mid-1980s. In the aftermath of martial law, the communist regime was loosening its grip on society, making Poland one of the freer Eastern Bloc countries, particularly in the social and cultural spheres. It was certainly far freer than Czechoslovakia.[27] This relative freedom did not extend to homosexuality, however. In this regard the situation in Czechoslovakia was considerably freer. Poland's homosexual groups, such as they were, were fully underground. The framing of homosexuality also differed in Poland; it was understood in terms of morality, especially Catholic morality. The advent of AIDS/HIV did not fundamentally alter this framing; rather, Catholic morality was adapted so that charity toward those infected with HIV/AIDS became part of the frame. Unlike the therapeutic framing, this one offered little room for political activism, but it offered an easy justification for homophobic ideas.

Descriptions of Poland's homosexual circles during the 1980s are few. One of the most extensive comes from research conducted by the Polish sociologist Ireneusz Krzemiński and his associates.[28] According to this research, the first stirrings of gay and lesbian associational life can be traced to around 1985. At that time, an informal gathering of mostly young people met occasionally in a Warsaw pub near Chełmska Street. As the sociologists note, "This was not an organization in the sense of organized structures. It was not really even possible to call it an organization; rather, it was loose group of acquaintances who were linked by their sexual orientation."[29] Gradually the group grew in size, and "members" were kept informed by word of mouth as to the next meeting time and place, which shifted among private apartments and cafés around Warsaw. Like the early Czech groups, the members were mostly gay men.

As the meetings grew larger, they were sometimes attended by visitors from ILGA, who came from Germany, France, and Austria and shared perspectives about the situation of gays and lesbians in the West.[30] A mimeographed samizdat-style journal *Efebos* appeared and was circulated among acquaintances. Precise numbers are unavailable, but one participant described this milieu as "a couple of hundred people" at its height.[31] On the basis of donations from members and with further financial help from ILGA, there was even an attempt to establish a fund to build the movement, but it failed for lack of money. Unlike the Czech Republic, these underground groups had no institutionalized form and lacked support from state authorities, even in the form of HIV/AIDS prevention efforts. Attempts to register the groups were denied on the grounds of preventing "moral damage to society."[32]

Despite these signs of communal identity and activity, in fact the gay and lesbian scene remained apolitical, underground, and invisible. The term "coming out" had entered the usage of these early members, but "[n]o one 'came out' on the street because they were too afraid."[33] Krzemiński et al.'s respondents also recalled that, insofar as this network could be said to have concrete goals, they were to destigmatize the image of homosexuality in society—to show that "a gay can be a normal man, and a lesbian a normal woman."[34] If some optimistic individuals dreamed of a program of gay and lesbian rights, they acknowledged this as something for the very distant future.[35] Even at their height, which lasted only from 1986 to 1987, these circles never outgrew the status of an extended friendship network.

Without overdrawing the Czech gay and lesbian community at this time, we can nevertheless see significant differences in kind. This community had access to the state; it had a more formalized organization; and even before communism fell, it was in the process of gaining legal status as a public association. In Poland, one cannot speak of anything with a formal character (e.g., statutes, organizational structures), much less an organization in the public sphere. As Krzemiński et al. write of Poland's communist-era community, "It is difficult to describe the supporters or even opponents of the movement, since not many people were aware of its existence."[36]

The framing of homosexuality in late-communist Poland was not shaped by a sympathetic circle of psychologists and sexologists. The analogous Polish academics dealt with homosexuality in the context of research on criminal behavior among the youth.[37] Homosexuals were seen as part of a corrupting subculture that posed a moral threat through ties to prostitution and criminality. The spread of the HIV/AIDS epidemic—it claimed its first Polish cases in 1985—only reinforced this negative framing. Besides being a threat to the youth, homosexuality was now a *medical* threat to the public.[38] Gay men in particular were targeted by the authorities for increased surveillance and repression. The best example was Operation Hyacinth, in which Citizens' Militia members entered schools, universities, and businesses and took suspected gay men to the police, using the threat of HIV/AIDS and this group's purported criminal tendencies as justification.[39] Meanwhile, the state's medical response to the disease was plagued by missteps. Although the state drafted a national public health strategy in 1987 as part of the World Health Organization's Global Program for the Prevention of HIV, it never received funding and never entered into practice.[40] By 1989, the number of HIV-positive persons had risen to 721. The Polish press was now filled with articles on the epidemic, though accurate knowledge of the disease was limited.[41] Anthropologist Jill Owczarzak relates that, in this period, hospitals were known to burn the beds of AIDS patients after they had left.[42] A National Office of AIDS Prevention was not established until 1993. As Owczarzak summarizes the situation under communism, "no institutions based on shared gay identity existed in Poland to take up the fight against AIDS."[43]

This framing of homosexuality as a moral threat was compounded by the outsized role of Catholicism in Polish society. Church teaching portrayed homosexuality in terms of moral failing, individual weakness, and psychological immaturity. Some of the most visible "experts" on homosexuality were priests. Owczarzak mentions Father Józef Augustyn, whose still-widespread theory of homosexuality "argues that the 'problem' with gays is a lack of personal identity that manifests itself in compulsiveness, lack of self-control, and neurotic aggression."[44] These traits were understood in terms of an individual's failure to mature out of homosexual desires during adolescence, and homosexuality itself was seen as an evolutionary anomaly. In short, homosexuals were "childlike" and "disabled."

This morality framing remained predominant through the 1990s, and it reflected the complexities of a deeply Catholic country trying to address the HIV/AIDS epidemic.[45] In 1989, Pope John Paul II addressed AIDS at last, arguing that HIV patients deserved the same care and respect as any other sick persons.[46] However, if AIDS was not a sin, it nonetheless was the result of a "crisis of values" and a "break[down] of moral principles."[47] Portrayed as sufferer-sinners, LGBT people were at the same time unworthy of tolerance and fitting objects of Christian charity, especially HIV/AIDS sufferers. The Church's appeals to minister to AIDS patients characterized them as sufferers deserving help while avoiding discussion about the mode of transmission.[48]

From the perspective of LGBT people, this framing provided no basis for conceiving of homosexuality in terms of political claims. Additionally, since it tended to equate Polish identity with the Church, at a symbolic level this framing excluded LGBT people from full membership in the national community, which only further justified intolerance. It was a sign of their weakness that in the 1990s even the nascent LGBT-rights groups adopted this framing. These activists "saw championing the importance of a Christian ethic as a primary way to win . . . [the public's] support."[49] Unlike the Czech Republic, then, there was little if any connection between homosexuality and political rights. To quote the Polish analyst Agnieszka Graff, "The idea of civil liberties was somehow considered inapplicable to 'matters of sexual preference.'"[50]

To recapitulate the chief points of the comparison so far, Czech activists began the 1990s with two big advantages over their Polish counterparts. First, they had more developed mobilizing structures as a legacy of a network of sexologists and psychologists under communism. These scientists were sympathetic to the situation of gays and lesbians, and a number of them even became part of the movement after 1989. Second, the dominant "morality" framing of homosexuality in Poland imposed significant obstacles to expressing social grievances. Even though the Church became involved in HIV/AIDS care, its understanding of the disease and homosexuality did not allow LGBT people to present their grievances in political terms.

The Organization of Czech Activism: An Auspicious Beginning

Having described the more favorable framing of homosexuality and the more developed associational networks in the Czech Republic even before 1989, this section will trace how LGBT activism unfolded in the 1990s—that is, before EU accession put its imprint on the framing of homosexuality. This period was by all accounts a remarkable one, for activism quickly crossed several important thresholds of social movement development. Gays and lesbians moved (1) from uncoordinated local association to national spanning structures, (2) from informally organized social movement communities to institutionally articulated and officially recognized SMOs, and (3) from constituent-oriented service provision to politically oriented activism. The account below traces these developmental milestones based on a combination of field interviews, documents from movement SMOs, and the available Czech and Polish historical literature.

The Velvet Revolution brought a flurry of organizational genesis as local, typically very informally organized social groups, sports clubs, cultural organizations, support groups, but also political activist circles were established across the Czech Republic. As described above, the first gay and lesbian groups had sprung directly out of the Socio-Therapeutic Club established by the psychologists and sexologists at the Czech Institute of Health. One of these, the Prague-based Lambda, was already working toward official status before the Velvet Revolution. In January 1990, Lambda was granted legal status. By this time a number of other Lambda groups were springing up outside Prague, among them groups in the cities of Brno, Ostrava, Hradec Kralové, Most, and České Budějovice.[51] Thus, when Lambda received legal status, it was as Lambda Union (Svaz Lambda), and it incorporated these various local and regional groups as members. Lambda Union was a "spanning organization" structured on the principle of territorial representation, aggregating and organizing the goals and concerns of gays and lesbians across the country.

Though, as we have seen, both Lambda and the Socio-Therapeutic Club already had a political dimension to their activities, the Velvet Revolution brought an explicitly political understanding of homosexuality to activism. During the revolution's mass protests in November, a Prague student, Jiří Kříž, had distributed flyers advertising a discussion group called the Movement for Tolerance.[52] On December 13, Kříž published an article in the newsletter of Civic Forum, the broad coalition that toppled the Communist Party in the revolution. In it, he called for establishing institutions to represent gays and lesbians and wrote that the Movement for Tolerance "sought wide-ranging collaboration with the public . . . so that the public could gain access to information that to this point has been addressed only to a narrow circle of homosexuals."[53] Several members of Movement for Tolerance had frequented the Socio-Therapeutic Club and Lambda, but their strategy of seeking public visibility and making political claims engendered some criticism from the former organizations' leadership, who feared that Czech society was not ready for political claims by gays and lesbians.[54] Others in the Club/Lambda circles were coming around to a more broadly political orientation, however. This chapter began with an epigraph from one Lambda member, Michal Rada, who in January 1990 voiced the growing belief that it was necessary to establish a national-level, officially recognized, formally organized structure.[55]

A representative from the Movement for Tolerance announced on Czechoslovak TV that there would a public meeting on February 2, 1990 at a restaurant in Prague. The response was far larger than expected. For activists looking back at it later, this meeting marked the turning point when the movement went from the closed circle approach of the Socio-Therapeutic Club to that of a social movement. One participant, Jiří Hromada—an actor who had been involved in organizing protests as part of the Velvet Revolution and who was also involved with Socio-Therapeutic Club/Lambda—was one of the attendees. He recalled, "Everyone spoke of a breakthrough, or rather they were shouting out their hopes, their complexes, and their resolutions."[56] Hromada would become the leader of an emerging network of broad-based, politically oriented gay and lesbian groups.

The first of these was the Movement for the Equality of Homosexual Citizens (HRHO), which was founded at the February 2 meeting. It is worth noting that the very title of the group declared a political goal, equality, and, from that first meeting, its members sought legal status for the organization.[57] On January 25, HRHO organized a demonstration on Prague's Old Town Square, where it publicly presented its demands for rights and at which President Václav Havel gave a speech.[58] HRHO also decided to participate in post-'89 Czechoslovakia's first democratic elections. Hromada, the actor quoted earlier, ran as an independent candidate on the list of the Movement for Civic Freedom (HOS) in the June 1990 federal elections.[59] HRHO's electoral program included (1) abolishing the law punishing consensual activity between adults and (2) equalizing the minimum age for consensual sexual activities for heterosexuals and homosexuals.[60] Hromada's electoral bid proved unsuccessful, as, in fact, did that of the larger HOS list of which he was a part.[61]

HRHO's model of public demonstrations and issuing demands in the public space was unusual not only for Eastern European gay activism but, as it turned out, even for the Czech movement going forward. Its attempt at electoral mobilization had many critics, including within the movement. Drs. Ivo Procházka and Antonín Brzek of the Socio-Therapeutic

Club/Lambda circle were the most prominent of these. As HRHO was launching its campaign, Procházka and Brzek were lobbying behind the scenes with the sitting government for both provisions in HRHO's program. On May 2, a month before the elections, these activities paid off, as the Czech parliament repealed the so-called homosexual paragraph as part of its larger reform of the criminal code.[62] Procházka and Brzek withheld their support from HRHO, and the success of their nonelectoral approach and single-issue focus on gay and lesbian rights, as opposed to building broader alliances beyond the movement, helped define the content and focus of activism to come. Direct popular and electoral mobilization was a path that had not yielded results, while theirs had. The consequences can be seen in the absence of Pride parades in Prague, the epicenter of Czech activism, until 2011. HRHO's January 25 demonstration on Old Town Square was more precocious than its organizers could have realized.

The organizational field was opening up dramatically, as new groups ranging from formal to informal and constituency oriented to politically oriented established themselves in the first years after the Velvet Revolution. Beyond the groups discussed above, there were also Gay Help and the Ganymedes Movement (Hnutie Ganymedes) in Slovakia as well as the commercially oriented LEGA in Hradec Králové.[63] Finally, there was also a wave of locally based groups, the so-called gay clubs (*Gay kluby*), which were direct participation, constituency-oriented groups: discussion circles, counseling centers, film societies, bars, and social spaces, all meant to foster public community. In 1991, a spanning organization, Gay klub ČR, was established to bring together this local network of clubs.[64]

Beyond the divergence in methods among the more cautious Svaz Lambda and the more radical HRHO, not to mention the burgeoning network of *Gay kluby* with their more local concerns, some activists grew concerned that the movement was in danger of fracturing or at least of dissipating its strength.[65] Therefore, on June 24, 1990, a new federal-level umbrella group, the Organization of Associations of Homosexual Citizens in Czechoslovakia (SOHO), was founded in Brno. SOHO effectively incorporated the entire network of LGBT groups, clubs, associations, and press throughout the 1990s, subsuming as well the other bridging associations, Svaz Lambda and Gay klub ČR. The idea was that HRHO would serve as the movement's political representative, Lambda as its social-cultural institution, and SOHO as the coordinator of these and all other branches of the movement.[66] SOHO met four times a year and was tasked with representing all gay and lesbian groups in their dealings with state institutions.[67] Together with its journal *SOHO revue*, it became *the* dominant organizing structure of the movement and remained so for the decade.[68] In the early 1990s, SOHO's main goal was to move its constituents away from the hidden subculture model to one of open integration into society as self-declared gays and lesbians. For example, it actively promoted the establishment of the gay clubs mentioned above, especially outside the bigger cities. With SOHO's support these too began to register as civic associations and banded together in the territorial-representative model. In 1991, they organized themselves in a national, spanning association, Gay Klub.

Given its short gestation, SOHO's institutional structure was remarkably articulated and disciplined. The activist and analyst Scott Long went so far as to compare SOHO to a miniaturized state: "SOHO's 'queer nation' seems built on the belief that the best way to influence the government is to flatter it by imitation."[69] SOHO operated on a formalized model of interest representation organized along territorial lines that mimicked the territorial principle of the Czech political system. It was constituted by elected delegates from the member regional organizations across the republic,[70] which, as mentioned above, met four times a year in regular congresses. At its height SOHO incorporated between 30 and 40 member organizations.[71] The collective number of participants across SOHO's various constituent groups was estimated at 1,000 to 2,000.[72] Like a state, the policies of SOHO's governing presidium were implemented by an executive apparatus of departments organized by function: a foreign affairs section, AIDS prevention section, and an in-house media group. As Long, writing at the end of the 1990s, commented, "SOHO is the only genuinely national gay and lesbian network in the former Soviet bloc—and, arguably, one of the best organized in Europe."[73]

Besides defying the conventional wisdom about the weakness of civil society organizations in postcommunist countries, SOHO challenged the notion that such organizations lack financial resources. While it is true that most of SOHO's constituent groups were volunteer-based and marshaled very modest financial resources, SOHO itself quickly grew to command a rather considerable budget, which drew on an array of sources: regular contributions from its member organizations, grants from domestic and international agencies, and proceeds from the various public events that it organized. Its budget also reflected the strong support of the Czech state, though this support was entirely in terms of HIV/AIDS prevention policy. In 1994, for instance, about 54 percent of SOHO's revenue came from Czech state agencies to combat HIV/AIDS.[74] Figure 4.1 shows the rapid rise in SOHO's budget during this period. At its height in 1997, revenues were 3,922,128 Kč, approximately $200,000. As described below, SOHO was unusual for postcommunist civil society organizations in having a permanent office. As a third peculiarity for a postcommunist civil societal organization, SOHO had a staff of full-time, professional activists. This aspect of SOHO's development is one of the most interesting and draws attention to the extraordinary role of the Czech state in (indirectly) supporting the movement.

As mentioned earlier, SOHO published a magazine called the *SOHO revue*. Besides providing a channel for communicating with the movement's constituency, it also became a financial asset for SOHO. *SOHO*

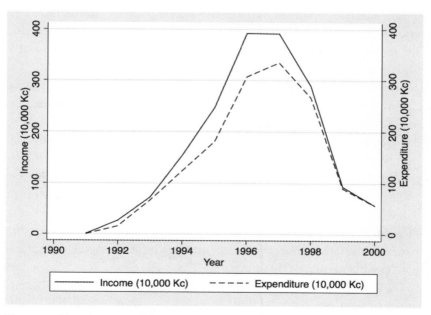

Figure 4.1. SOHO's Financial Resources in Nominal Czech Crowns (Kč)

revue began as a commercial publication presenting the face of the movement to the wider public, including a heterosexual readership. In April 1991, it was launched with a circulation of 15,000, but after a print run of just over a year, sales were insufficient, and production was halted. The magazine was rescued, however, after a leadership change at its publisher, the state-owned Orbis.[75] Publication resumed in early 1993 under the editorship of Hromada, who also served as SOHO's president. Hromada won financial support for the magazine from a state-sponsored agency, the National Center for the Support of Health, arguing that the magazine could effectively promote its public campaign for HIV/AIDS prevention.[76] This backing allowed the journal to publish regularly through 1997, during which time Hromada remained editor-in-chief.

The connection to Orbis extended even further in ways that indirectly benefited the movement. The journal's board was employed as full-time editorial staff for Orbis in its other publications. *SOHO revue* thus fulfilled a critical practical concern, providing a living to full-time activists, including Hromada and four other editors. For the better part of the 1990s, Orbis provided the movement's leaders with steady jobs directly related to their activism while also providing a de facto movement headquarters in the form of the *SOHO revue*'s editorial office. As one interviewee put it, "In essence they were state employees." Beyond stable employment, connections to a publishing house were invaluable for the movement. As Hromada himself noted, "The real center of the gay movement became those two editorial offices of the journal. Thanks to them, SOHO had an office in the middle of Prague, administrative services (including telephones, copiers, office supplies) for free. So, indirectly, the state helped us greatly in our aims."[77] Finally, the connection to Orbis also proved valuable politically. As the preeminent state publishing house, Orbis published the Czech Chamber of Deputies and Senate bulletin. Editing this bulletin also fell under the purview of the *SOHO revue* editorial team. This allowed Hromada and his colleagues to monitor Czech politics closely and develop personal connections with parliamentarians.[78] Over the years Hromada built a network of contacts with politicians across the spectrum.

By 1991, the center of activism had begun shifting toward SOHO and its president Hromada. SOHO's relationship with *SOHO revue* helped cement its dominance, as the journal was the main forum for information throughout the country. In 1992, Svaz Lambda was dissolved, and its various local Lambda organizations were registered individually as public associations; these then joined SOHO. A similar process occurred with Gay klub ČR.[79] Svaz Lambda, which had served as the Czech Republic's representative in ILGA until this time, ceded this role to SOHO in 1992. The Prague chapter of Lambda did not dissolve, but in 1992 it split into male and female groups, M-klub and L-klub. New organizations continued to form over the course of the 1990s, notably the student group STUD at Masaryk University in Brno, but these affiliated themselves with SOHO and its articulation of the movement's goals.[80]

With the dissolution of alternative spanning associations like Svaz Lambda and Gay klub ČR, we can note a change in the structure of activism and the framing of its goals. A distinction emerged that had not previously existed, or that at least had been blurred, during the fluid period after the Velvet Revolution. Namely, a distinction arose between what might be called the "civic association orientation" and the "club orientation." The former, whose essence is captured in this chapter's epigraph, concerned the goal of establishing legally recognized gay and lesbian associations, whose internal organization would offer institutionalized representation. Thus, it was self-consciously political. The club orientation, by contrast, was less movement-like and less political. It was about creating places where sexual minorities could associate. As Jan Seidl writes, "Over the course of the 1990s, there came about a conceptual shift in the understanding of 'gay club' from that of a group of people to that of a place."[81] Coincident with this shift, many local Lambda associations turned their attention to local community and increasingly delegated the "political work" of rights advocacy to SOHO's Prague center, which in practice meant the activists in SOHO revue's editorial office.

Having described the paths and modes by which Czech activism became organized, and even institutionalized from 1990 to 1997, let us conclude with a few notes on the framing that activists employed. First, the therapy framing described earlier remained very much in place—as the above references to the continued prominence of members of the communist-era networks Socio-Therapeutic Club and Lambda would suggest. Much as in a self-help group, the movement saw its mission as creating space for gays and lesbians to be "sociable"—to associate publicly, freely, and without shame. It was necessary, therefore, to create institutional and physical spaces to be sociable and "come out." This framing also informed the activists' approach to HIV/AIDS, which, as we saw earlier, remained an important source of financial resources for SOHO. Because the number of AIDS cases in the Czech Republic remained low in comparison with rates in the United States or Western Europe, the movement's engagement with the epidemic focused more on education to promote safe behavior than it did on service provision to those infected with the virus. Thus, the sociability approach was evident here too. As SOHO's Dr. Ivo Procházka put it in 1995, "[It's impossible] to successfully prevent the spread of the HIV virus as long as the majority of us do not accomplish our successful 'coming out' . . . as long as we fail to address the homosexual-behaving men who remain outside of the gay community."[82]

Significantly, activists did not face a framing contest with opponents of homosexuality—as they already did in Poland, albeit in a small-scale and uncoordinated way (see below). As Seidl's analysis of the *Soho revue* found, the "enemy" against which Czech activists organized in these early years was the legacy of communism.[83] This they equated with hiding one's sexual orientation and with the absence of spaces for public sociability. Of course, as time progressed and the memories of the pre-1989 experience grew more distant, overcoming communism's legacies would become less compelling in framing the movement's goals. Arguably, the therapy framing of homosexuality was inward-looking, limiting the movement's appeal to potential domestic allies. HRHO, as we have seen, was an exception, a group that sought broader political connections and engagement outside the community, but, as we have also seen, it was superseded by SOHO.

Last, what were the concrete goals that the movement set for itself during this period, and what success did it make toward achieving them? With the disappearance of HRHO, political activism shifted from electoral mobilization and political outreach to single-issue lobbying. As mentioned earlier, SOHO's rise coincided with the reconfiguration of other spanning organizations like Svaz Lambda and Gay klub, which became more locally, community, and even commercially oriented. The political side of the movement's agenda was delegated to SOHO. In practice, this meant that lobbying shifted to the Prague-based network of activists around the *SOHO revue*. In the process, the *SOHO revue*'s strongly held views about the most effective strategies for lobbying in the postcommunist context came to dominate political activism. As former SOHO president Hromada recounted in an interview, and as I heard echoed in interviews with other activists, the strategy consisted of pragmatism, flexibility, and behind-the-scenes persuasion. Gay and lesbian rights were presented as a way of joining the social mainstream.[84] Activists, in this view, should promote coming out and public sociability but not accentuate gay identity or difference, which might be construed as threatening to heternormative values.[85] Practically speaking, this strategy meant that Czech activists, in contrast to neighboring countries such as Poland and Hungary, did not organize Pride marches. When public events did occur, they tended to be organized around HIV/AIDS prevention and commemoration.[86] Otherwise, they took the form of community-building and were focused inward rather than outward to the broader public.[87]

SOHO focused on incremental and legal change, concentrating its efforts on the following areas: reform of the Criminal Code, destroying records of police wiretaps on gays conducted before 1989, removing homosexuality from the list of psychiatric disorders, winning the right for gay men to donate blood, and the enactment of registered partnerships for same-sex couples.[88] Evaluations of the policy record are mixed. In interviews and internal reports, leaders such as Hromada and Procházka take a favorable view.[89] Others, notably Seidl and his collaborators, express doubts as to how much credit for changes such as the delisting of homosexuality as a psychiatric disorder (achieved in 1993) could be claimed by the movement.[90] Likewise, reforming the Criminal Code was achieved as early as August 1990, and, as mentioned earlier, owed more to the networking of doctors in the Sexological Institute than to the lobbying of then-active groups like the Movement for Tolerance. Beyond the goals mentioned above, SOHO did not pursue broader antidiscrimination legislation. Already during this period registered-partnership legislation had emerged as the signature issue for SOHO, though its efforts here proved unsuccessful.[91]

Mixed though its lobbying record may have been, by the late 1990s Czech activism had taken the form of a pragmatic, single-issue-oriented movement with a high degree of institutionalization and solid financial footing. It had succeeded in creating institutional as well as physical spaces where gays and lesbians could associate publicly. These developments bore the imprint of the movement's origins in the HIV/AIDS prevention strategies developed before 1989 in the self-help circles housed in the Health Ministry. These origins continued to exercise a major influence over activism, not least through the channel of financing and leadership. As we will now see, the crossing of these thresholds—the building institutionally articulated and officially recognized SMOs, the consolidation of national spanning structures, and the development of politically oriented activism—far outstripped the progress of activists across the border in Poland.

The Organization of Activism in Poland: An Invisible and Inchoate Movement

The network of gay and lesbian groups was much less developed and the framing of homosexuality less favorable in Poland before 1989 than in the Czech Republic. As one Polish activist recalled the situation at the moment of regime change in 1989, "The word 'gay' did not exist in Poland at all—people of homosexual orientation were called scornfully 'faggot'; there was no *legal* gay organization, no gay newspapers, and no clubs."[92] The contrast between the Polish and Czech movements' trajectories from 1990 and 1997 could not be more striking. The Polish movement failed to consolidate formally organized SMOs; its one national spanning institution broke down so that the network reverted to locally based organization; and activism retained a predominantly self-help, constituent-services orientation rather than developing a political one. By the late 1990s, the existence of a broader Polish movement was very much in doubt.

Before 1989 there were underground circles of gays and lesbians in a few larger Polish cities.[93] The fall of communism opened the POS, allowing a new wave of (also very informal, also very small) gay and lesbian groups to form. On February 23, 1990, these banded together to form an umbrella group called the All-Poland Association of Lambda Groups (Ogólnopolskie Stowarzyszenie Grup Lambda).[94] Initially it comprised three groups in Warsaw, Gdańsk, and Wrocław. The timing of the legalization of the first gay and lesbian groups in Poland and the Czech Republic was, therefore, very close; however, the sharply divergent development trajectories of the Czech SOHO and the Polish Lambda Association thereafter highlighted the consequences of Poland's social closure, in particular its religiosity. The framing of homosexuality in terms of morality and charity, together with an unsupportive state and hostile societal attitudes, hobbled the movement. As one telling example, during the 1990s most Polish activists would not allow their names or photographs to be used in newspaper articles.[95]

Initially, however, the period following the founding of the Polish Lambda Association was one of rapid organizational growth. In 1991, a network of local Lambda associations was established throughout Poland. By 1992, the network counted member groups in 15 cities.[96] From the beginning, an emphasis on self-help, HIV/AIDS, and apoliticism was evident. As one movement historian writes, "For the most part, the activists of the Association of Lambda Groups were against public activism, claiming that increased visibility might be harmful to homosexual persons by attracting unwanted attention and fuelling violence."[97] In this atmosphere, growth soon slowed and internal solidarity ebbed. The Polish Lambda Association failed not only to institutionalize but even to draw attendees to its meetings, as one participant recalled:

> At the beginning of 1992, only one new group was established, in Bydgoszcz, and as early as late 1991 a conflict broke out in the Gdańsk [Lambda] group, leading to its fracturing within the next half year. Additionally, especially among groups who wanted at this time to intensively develop their activities, there was a feeling that the centralized structure [of the Polish Lambda Association] was too constraining. The activists who had founded these [local] organizations became disappointed by their low effectiveness.[98]

In the face of financial problems and coordination difficulties among groups, internal conflicts broke out.[99] Among Lambda Association's biggest critics was the gay and lesbian press.[100] In 1994, a number of local Lambda groups suspended their membership, and in 1997 the Polish Lambda Association was dissolved. As one activist recounted,

The reason for this decision was the small number of those willing to cooperate and the high costs of involvement: correspondence, telephones and travel, which members often had to cover out-of-pocket. It was also decided that in place of the previous Lambda Associations they would establish regional associations and informal groups.[101]

Besides scarcity of resources and difficulties of coordination, a perhaps still bigger problem faced by the Polish Lambda Association was the unwillingness of many of its members to publicly declare their sexual orientation.[102] Social taboos against homosexuality in Poland remained strong even by postcommunist standards. For example, in 1991, the vice-minister of health described gays as "perverts" on television.[103] Identifying with, not to mention actually joining, a gay- and lesbian-rights group was risky for someone fearing the consequences of coming out, and this problem hobbled organization-building. Activism's organizational infrastructure, which had numbered 14 associations at its height, was falling apart almost as quickly as it had emerged.[104]

As a social movement with political goals, Polish activism was foundering. Rather than disappear entirely, however, it changed orientation and tactics, focusing on self-help and structuring itself around service provision. After the shuttering of the Polish Lambda Association in 1997, a group of Warsaw activists set up a local group focusing on HIV/AIDS prevention, which was seen as the best means to gain legitimacy given taboos around homosexuality.[105] To evoke a sense of continuity with the past, they called it the Lambda Warsaw Association (Stowarzyszenie Lambda Warszawa, hereafter Lambda Warsaw), but legally speaking it was a new and separate organization from the previous Polish Lambda Association's Warsaw chapter. Lambda Warsaw's primary goals were providing counseling and conducting education programs, and, as part of the latter, promoting a more positive image of homosexuality in society. It was *not* political: in the words of one member, "Above all, we feel a call to provide help to society—be it homosexual, bisexual, or transsexual—but not to engage in lobbying."[106] It organized Poland's first crisis counseling telephone hotline and received money from the UN Development Program to promote safer-sex education among gay men. It also opened a library in its office in Warsaw where it hosted discussion groups.

Unlike its Czech counterpart SOHO, Lambda Warszawa did not easily find state funding in the framework of HIV/AIDS prevention. Its initial request to the municipal government of Warsaw for funding for HIV/AIDS prevention, which came in 1998, was "denied on the grounds that Lambda was a *gay and lesbian* organization, rather than an *HIV prevention* organization."[107] Depending on the composition of the Warsaw government, Lambda Warsaw received sporadic funding for HIV/AIDS prevention over the next several years.[108] The difference in the level of domestic public funding between Poland and the Czech Republic was striking. Recall from Figure 4.1 that the Czech Republic's SOHO alone received something on the order of $100,000 from the state for HIV/AIDs prevention work in the mid-1990s. By comparison, in 2005, the Polish National AIDS Center allocated $15,000 for *all* NGO organizations working in this area throughout the country, to be distributed through public competitions.[109] Lambda Warsaw's apoliticism—its insistence that its work take place "'inside' the gay community, rather than affecting broader social or political change"—was also motivated by the desire not to jeopardize funding possibilities for its activities.

After several years of such activities, Lambda Warsaw broadened its operations to include cultural and recreational ones, such as film festivals and sports clubs. During the first years of its existence, its internal organization was informal and collegial, matching the group's small scale and focus on self-help and services. It did not employ formalized decision-making structures or organizational hierarchies. As its activities began to broaden, such structures and hierarchies became more necessary. However, these developments did not occur during the period in focus here. Before 1998, that is before EU accession began in earnest, the attributes of Lambda Warsaw as a network were local, informal, and institutionally thin. To the extent that personal connections held the organization together, it was vulnerable to conflicts between personalities, not to mention the fraying of personal, even romantic, attachments among members.[110]

Following Polish Lambda Association's implosion, Lambda Warszawa was the only registered LGBT group in Poland until 2001.[111] Outside of this one group, LGBT-related issues were primarily understood within the purview of HIV/AIDS prevention. Even in this area of focus, Lambda Warszawa faced competition from other civil society organizations. Another group that became active in the field of HIV/ AIDS was an older NGO called Youth Movement against Drug Addiction (MONAR). MONAR's network of addiction treatment centers was established in the 1970s. Because of the link between intravenous drug use and HIV, MONAR began in 1990 to include gays with the disease within its purview of service activities.[112] The major actor in the area of HIV/AIDS care was, however, the Polish Catholic Church.[113] As noted above, the Church had begun to engage with the AIDS epidemic in the early 1990s, though on its own terms. A Polish priest, Arkadiusz Nowak, took the lead in promoting Church-run palliative centers, and his efforts resulted in the creation of a state-run National AIDS Center in 1993. Thus, the fledgling network of HIV/AIDS services soon came to be dominated by the Church and, in cooperation with the Church, the state: "The National AIDS Center remains the main coordinating organization for HIV prevention efforts and care for people living with AIDS at the national, regional, local levels."[114]

The Church's framing of its HIV/AIDS outreach—charity for the ill regardless of their sins—reinforced the morality framing of homosexuality discussed earlier. It is important to appreciate the Church's unparalleled political and societal prestige in Poland in the 1990s. At its behest, abortion was banned in 1993, religious instruction in schools reinstated in 1991, a mandate that radio and television respect "Christian values" adopted in 1992, and a Concordat with Rome signed by the government in 1997.[115] The hegemony of the Church's framing of homosexuality was so pervasive that even HIV/AIDS activists adopted it. By and large, gay and lesbian activists either described their service work in terms of charity or explicitly rejected a political framing of their goals in order to prevent public attacks.[116]

Given both the weight of taboo and the security-through-obscurity tactics of the movement, such attacks were few, though not entirely absent. For example, the MONAR centers became a locus of controversy when they opened their doors to AIDS patients. Though they had been operating since the 1970s as drug-rehabilitation centers, the inclusion of AIDS patients sparked protests in the neighborhoods where they were located. From 1990 through 1992, there were public protests demanding the centers be shut down, and in a number of cases violence and attempted arson. The kinds of placards on display at such demonstrations would not have been out of place in those from the 2000s, reading, for example, "Faggots out!"[117] Yet, despite the similar rhetoric, compared to what would come later, antigay mobilization in this period was local, uncoordinated, and lacked ties to political parties. In short, the network of antigay activists looked similar in structure to the movement itself. Finally, the Church's position on the controversy over the MONAR centers was telling: it criticized the attacks, arguing that it was a Christian duty to care for the sick, including AIDS patients. During this period in which the Church put its stamp on a wide range of social issues, it apparently saw little need to combat gay rights as a political issue. They were not yet a threat.

Hamstrung by the tendency to frame its goals apolitically, Poland's movement was falling into decline in the late 1990s. By 1997, the Association of Lambda Groups was defunct, as the network of locally based, grassroots chapters disappeared. My research uncovered only one national-level attempt at political lobbying in this period, during the discussions about rewriting the Polish Constitution. Rights advocates lobbied to include sexual orientation as one of the grounds for discrimination banned constitutionally—a minimal demand that proved unsuccessful.[118]

Conclusion

This chapter has traced the process of movement formation from its origins in the 1980s through the immediate aftermath of the fall of communism to the end of the 1990s. During this period, the pressures of EU integration did not strongly affect domestic political developments, especially not in the area of LGBT activism. In fact, beyond the LGBT population, gay and lesbian issues were not politically visible in either the Czech Republic or Poland. Communist-era attitudes predominated in both and, in Poland, were further amplified by the political ascendancy of the Catholic Church. While, as described in Chapter 3, both countries had their own hard-right nationalist parties, in neither case did such parties concern themselves with homosexuality as a political problem.

Yet despite these similarities between the two countries, a comparison of the nascent LGBT-rights movements in each proves to be a study in contrasts. We find a burgeoning movement in the Czech Republic and a moribund movement in Poland. Czech activists had moved from informal organization to the consolidation of an SMO that could speak for the movement and that aggregated a broad network of local groups into a national-level structure. Finally, the Czech movement had articulated political goals—such as equalizing the age of consent and registered partnerships—and even accomplished some of them. By contrast, the Polish movement had failed to move from local to national organization; informal affiliations still formed the basis of organization; and, motivated by concerns regarding funding and safety, activists were avowedly apolitical in orientation, focusing on service provision rather than social change. These contrasts were the result of differences in how homosexuality was framed and the extent to which networks for gays and lesbians existed in late communism. In Czechoslovakia, a therapy framing of homosexuality prevailed thanks to a network of sympathetic psychologists and sexologists affiliated with the Ministry of Health. This network provided an environment in which gays and lesbians could associate and form links that would serve as the basis for activism after 1989. In Poland, homosexuality was framed in morality terms; while this framing made limited HIV/AIDS outreach possible, it did not offer a basis for gays and lesbians to associate either under communism or afterward. In both countries, homosexuality was visible to the wider public through the prism of HIV/AIDS; however, in the Czech Republic, the epidemic inclined the framing toward the medical establishment, while in Poland it reinforced the morality framing of the Church.

One similarity that this process tracing has revealed is that, despite their many differences, neither the Czech or Polish movements were much affected during this period by EU pressures or opportunities. Success or failure in this period was dependent on domestic factors, namely resources available to the movement and the limits or opportunities presented by the legacy framing of homosexuality. In the next stage of the story, the influence of transnational factors would become much more pronounced.

5

Activism under EU Leverage

Poland and the Czech Republic, 1998–2004

Practically everyone in SOHO realizes that we are reaching the end of an era, and it is necessary now to react to transformations in both society and the [LGBT] minority itself.
—Jiří Hromada, president of SOHO, speaking in 2000

When we acceded to the EU, gays and lesbians were the biggest Euro-enthusiasts. Perhaps we even use the EU too much, because our opponents then accuse us of being cosmopolitans who distance themselves from our culture.
—Tomasz Szypuła of KPH

In 1998, the European Parliament warned that it would block the accession of any country that "through its legislation or policies violates the human rights of lesbians and gay men."[1] Within two years, EU Directive 2000/78 entered into force, mandating the enactment and enforcement of antidiscrimination protections in the labor code, and explicitly including sexual orientation within its ambit. Even in closed societies seeking EU membership, homosexuality ceased to be simply a question of morality or even charity; it was a now a question of EU law and legal rights. Most directly, this law required legal protection from labor-market discrimination, but, as the EP resolution indicates, equal protection presumed political and human rights. These changes held *potentially* transformative consequences for LGBT activism in applicant-states, which, as the last chapter showed, had been a primarily domestic affair in both Poland and the Czech Republic.

The first potentially transformative consequence brought into play by EU leverage was that of catalyzing a framing contest between EU norms and national ones, thereby reframing homosexuality as an EU issue. As we saw in Chapter 3, this is precisely what happened in Poland's closed society. Even before Poland's hard right scored electoral breakthroughs (after EU membership), its relentless attacks on EU overreach and "homosexual propaganda" gave LGBT issues unprecedented visibility and resonance. The more successful LGBT groups were quick to seize on the EU frame, but this frame's credibility was greatly enhanced by the fact that both the supporters *and* opponents of LGBT rights portrayed them in EU terms.

Second, as Chapter 2 argued, the onset of EU leverage opened up a new role for activists, that of broker between national governments and the EU regarding the former's compliance with EU norms. The EU's recognition of activist groups as brokers gave them new legitimacy, and insofar as this association strengthened ties between domestic activists and EU-level counterparts like ILGA-Europe, it exposed them to the latter's policy and organizational experience. The latter was helpful in professionalizing domestic activism, especially since fulfilling the role of broker required a high level of administrative capacity—compiling monitoring reports, working through formal diplomatic channels, and following the EU's bureaucratic protocols. KPH, a Polish NGO founded during this period, maximally exploited the brokerage role.

As *potentially* transformative as both of these EU-related factors were for activism's organization, there were also some limiting factors, also EU-related. First, the logic of external incentives meant that the perception of threat to sexual minorities' "immediate protective surround" was minimal. Even where hard-right rhetoric about homosexuality was increasingly harsh, no applicant-state was going to jeopardize its accession prospects by implementing antigay policies or tacitly allowing organized repression.[2] Recall from Chapter 1 that the threat of disruption to the immediate protective surround is a key element of social movement mobilization, especially where mobilizing structures are nascent or weak. In the absence of a strong sense of threat to the protective surround during the accession period, it remained difficult for gay-rights groups to mobilize their constituents on a large scale, and the urgency of the issue for potential domestic allies was comparatively low. As we will see, hard-right pressure during this period had some beneficial effects on internal solidarity—facilitating cooperation between LGBT groups and preventing schism—but this effect was much greater after accession.

A second factor limiting the EU's impact on the organization of activism was the nature of the EU's funding process. Though the Commission's policy of seeking out NGO partners for monitoring applicant-states' implementation of the *acquis communautaire* opened up brokering roles, and though the EU created new funding possibilities for NGOs, because national governments decided to whom and how this funding would be distributed, it was hard to come by for a controversial topic like LGBT issues.

In Poland, these factors' net effect was positive for activism. During the accession period, a previously moribund movement refounded itself and, especially through KPH, became a broker between the government and the EU. The reluctance of Poland's parliament to adopt EU antidiscrimination policies only heightened the importance of the brokerage role while at the same time feeding the framing contest between EU and national norms described in Chapter 4. By the period's end, KPH was a professionally organized SMO with firm links to EU institutions and advocacy networks, clear political goals, and cooperative relations with other domestic LGBT groups. Departing from preaccession practice, KPH abandoned the morality framing and adopted the EU-rights one. Besides KPH, two other activist groups stood out during this period: Lambda Warsaw, which we encountered in the previous chapter, and IGCLN-Poland, which organized Poland's first Pride parade in 2001. If KPH indicated the Polish movement's future trajectory, the latter two groups illustrated its still transitional character. Lambda Warsaw remained primarily service-oriented, though like KPH it was affiliated with ILGA-Europe. IGCLN-Poland (International Lesbian and Gay Culture Network in Poland), however, looked more like preaccession activism: informal, strictly domestic, and primarily apolitical. Compared with what it would become after accession, even KPH was organizationally underdeveloped: its domestic allies were few and its capacity for grassroots mobilization was weak. To speak in terms of the three thresholds of movement development introduced in the earlier chapters, Poland crossed two of them during this period. First, with KPH, it developed away from informally organized social movement communities into institutionally articulated SMOs. Second, its leading SMOs expanded from constituent-oriented service provision to politically oriented activism, albeit with limited capacity to mobilize the grass roots. The third threshold—moving from a network of local groups to national spanning organizations—remained out of reach during this period, but the building of strong and cooperative SMOs, in Warsaw especially, laid the groundwork for this extension after 2004.

With respect to the orientations and identities constituting the Polish movement, the accession period represented more continuity than rupture with the past. Gays and lesbian represented the most visible interests. That said, queer conceptions of sexuality also began to emerge, as evidenced by the first queer-studies conferences in Polish universities between 2000 and 2004.[3] These were, however, primarily academic affairs and, as Joanna Mizielińska argues, their translation into broader activism was often rather superficial. Thus, queer activism was at most a subcurrent, and trans activism still lacked any organized representation.[4]

In the Czech Republic, the net effect of increased EU leverage was limited by comparison; consequently, activism continued to be shaped primarily by domestic factors, even as these became less favorable. Though the country also faced EU pressure to change its labor code, this demand provoked no heated political controversy. No parliamentary deputy spoke against the change, and it was passed without incident.[5] There was, therefore, less opportunity than in Poland for activists to broker between the EU and national government. Further, as we saw in Chapter 3, no framing contest emerged around homosexuality and, not only did no new political parties with strongly antigay rhetoric emerge, the one party with the most potential for antigay rhetoric, SPR-RSČ, completed its slide into oblivion during this period. Euroskepticism, though evident in Czech politics, never became associated with homosexuality.[6]

In the absence of a framing contest like Poland's, the leading SMOs continued to employ the public-sociability frame, which, as we saw in the previous chapter, had been applied to registered partnerships. As Věra Sokolová notes, the latter became "without competition *the* issue which . . . dominate[d] the discourse on homosexuality in the media."[7] Even though partnerships could be presented in terms of emulating Western Europe's most progressive states, they were *not* a precondition for EU membership and were never part of the accession process. Thus, registered partnerships substituted for an EU framing of LGBT activism, closing it off from potential allies among pro-European elites.

Meanwhile, domestic conditions took a turn for the worse. The primary shock was SOHO's loss of state funding—funding that had been directed toward HIV/AIDS prevention, but which SOHO had also been able to leverage toward movement-building. Dwindling funding fed SOHO's increasing focus on the narrowly defined goal of registered partnerships. This goal allowed them to exploit the political contacts won through Orbis; however, it had two negative consequences. First, it took SOHO away from grassroots constituents, many of whom were uninterested in a limited version of partnerships. Second, it split the activist core between those advocating an elite-oriented and lower cost strategy for a limited registered partnerships law and those preferring a broader conception of same-sex unions. The latter would be harder to pass but in the longer term could build up the movement.[8] This split grew into a divisive *internal* framing contest.[9] By contrast, no such internal framing contest occurred in Poland because the hard right's threatening discourse served to unite the movement. Between 1998 and 2004, the Czech movement experienced slippage on several fronts. First, the broad-based SMOs established in the 1990s declined and then split, sometimes acrimoniously. Thus, the movement experienced a reversion to localism. At the same time, while a part of the movement became more politically engaged than ever, a large part turned inward, that is, toward constituents and away from political goals.

Regarding the orientations and identities visible within the movement, this period marked a decisive shift from the self-identification of homosexual to that of gay, lesbian, and bisexual. This shift was evident in the naming of activist groups. As we will see, SOHO (i.e., the Organization of Associations of *Homosexual* Citizens) was replaced by *Gay* Initiative (GI) and *Gay* and *Lesbian* League (GLL). In movement publications, the terms gay, lesbian, and bisexual (not transgender or queer) predominated. Most activists continued to conceive of sexual minorities in terms of sexual orientation (understood as genetically given) rather than (constructed) identity. That said, at this time the notion of queer identity gained a foothold, being introduced through seminars offered in the Program in Gender Studies at Charles University in 2001–2002.[10] As will be described, such identity-based notions remained controversial among activists, playing a role in the split between GI and GLL.

Poland: A Movement Reborn

For the better part of the 1990s, LGBT (and counteractivism) had comprised local, informal, and low-density networks. Beginning with the hard right's mobilization as a self-styled bulwark against EU imperialism, these networks started to become national, more institutionalized, and denser. As Chapter 4 described, antigay networks first made the jump from local to national, social movement to political organization, and (un)civil society to the political-party sphere. LGBT-rights networks were slower to cross these thresholds.

Between 1997 and 2001, Lambda Warsaw was the only formally recognized civic association in this sphere. Beginning in 2001, however, new groups began to appear, mainly in Warsaw. These new groups were more visible, political in their demands, and, at least in the case of KPH and Lambda Warsaw, professional and SMO-like in their organization. They drew on a broader target audience not limited to HIV/AIDS prevention. ILGCN-Poland organized Poland's first Pride march in 2001 in Warsaw. Lambda Warsaw had initially focused on service provision, but now it underwent something of a shift in its orientation. Besides disseminating information to prevent HIV/AIDS and running a counseling hotline and various public health programs, it expanded to cultural and recreational activities.[11] The basis of its internal organization shifted from friendship network to professionalized SMO.[12] However, the largest and most visible LGBT group founded during this period was KPH. Over time, it became the central, national-level SMO setting the agenda and frame for the broader movement, a Polish analogue to the Czech SOHO. To appreciate the organizational changes that Polish activism underwent during the accession period, KPH is the natural starting place.

The group began in Warsaw, and its founding marked the moment that Polish activism shifted from predominantly self-help-oriented activities to political ones.[13] In its own words, KPH aimed to promote

[p]ublic discussion on gay and lesbian issues and increased social representation for all sexual minorities, as well as, most importantly, political lobbying that would lead to introducing the concept of same-sex partnerships.[14]

Interviews by Ireneusz Krzemiński and his team in 2004 allow for a carefully drawn portrait of KPH in its early years.[15] At its founding, it drew predominantly from students between 20 and 30 years old without former activist experience. It was run very much on a grassroots model, with recruitment built on personal and friendship networks. In practice, leadership was centered in the figure of Robert Biedroń. One of KPH's founders, Biedroń had a taste for politics and a personal history in the center-left SLD party in the 1990s, during which time he was the unofficial party spokesman on LGBT issues.[16] Biedroń helped give KPH its political edge. Its members saw themselves as addressing the absence of self-consciously political activism. Political activism would eventually take the form of policy goals—such as antidiscrimination policy and registered partnerships—but in the first few years it was understood, in Krzemiński's words, as a general "war against homophobia."[17] The name Campaign Against Homophobia captured the frame, not self-help and constituent services but political representation directed outward to society at large. While there was a spectrum of views within KPH about how radical its demands should be, through internal compromise and creativity its members were able to coordinate on projects that married political rights and group identity.[18] The prime example of this was the campaign "Let Them See Us" (Niech nas zobaczą), which is described below.

KPH's internal organization during its early existence was of the informal variety typical for postcommunist Europe. According to one estimate, only 3 percent of Polish NGOs receive funding from international organizations, and a full 75 percent of Polish NGOs lack any financial reserves.[19] Likewise for KPH, financial resources were minimal, and labor was provided exclusively by volunteers. The group had no office of its own, depending instead on various feminist groups in Warsaw for a space to meet.[20] There are no data on finances from before 2004; we can assume this reflects the absence of formalized budgeting procedures.[21] KPH's political orientation made funding even more difficult than the already forbidding norm for Polish civic associations. Typically, such associations relied on project-related grants from relevant national ministries or local governments for funding. This was the strategy used, for example, by Lambda Warsaw, which provided services to high-risk groups in exchange for public funding. Even with its explicit apoliticism, Lambda Warsaw faced high hurdles because of an unwillingness to fund anything regarded as promoting homosexuality.[22] Since KPH was explicitly politically oriented, it did not even attempt to access funding from domestic institutions like the Ministry of Health, as Lambda Warsaw did.[23]

Instead, from its inception KPH cultivated links to transnational, especially EU-level, networks, notably that of ILGA-Europe but also the European Commission and EP. As illustrated by the chapter's epigraph, KPH was eager to exploit opportunities to serve as a broker between the EU and Polish authorities. Its activities had already begun to develop in the direction of professionalized lobbying as accession to the EU drew nearer. KPH monitored government compliance with EU norms, documenting discrimination, analyzing the press, and bringing the antigay rhetoric of politicians to the attention of international observers. It did so both through its affiliation with ILGA-Europe and directly with the Commission and the EP.[24] The entry into this kind of activity was gradual and continued into the third, postaccession stage. In this way, KPH became the standard-bearer for the broader movement, especially in relation to the EU.

To put this role in perspective, most other activist groups lacked such linkage to the EU-level actors during this period. KPH and Lambda Warsaw were the only groups affiliated with ILGA-Europe.[25] In an earlier study, based on interviews with Polish activists and state officials in 2007, recollections of many respondents suggested that interactions with EU actors and networks were minimal.[26] Krzemiński et al. draw similar conclusions based on their interviews with activists, finding that despite their participation in various European conferences on sexual minorities, "close-knit, regular collaboration did not occur."[27]

Over time, KPH proved itself capable of winning funding through EU sources, notably the European Social Fund, but, for most Polish activist groups, accessing funding from EU sources was very difficult.[28] Two main problems presented themselves. First, there was the hurdle of being a new organization, without a track record or experience in winning EU grants. Applying directly for EU funding demands a high level of administrative capacity. Without professional staff and with minimal resources to begin with, Polish gay and lesbian groups were, paradoxically, largely locked out from EU funding to develop precisely those organizational assets.[29] As one activist not affiliated with KPH observed in a 2007 interview, "I've tried to apply for funding . . . and I've come away with almost nothing, so I'm skeptical about the degree of commitment of the EU. . . . It doesn't mean that there's not something available . . . but it's not accessible to small folks like myself."[30] In the context of this quote and others to follow, it should be emphasized that activists' views regarding the EU's impact on LGBT issues can be colored by the group with which they were affiliated. As described above, a group like KPH is more transnationally oriented, and its members are more likely to take a nuanced view of the EU relationship—impotent in some ways, very valuable in others. The skeptical tone of the quote above likely also reflects frustration with how international funding can create a privileged position for certain groups based on language capabilities, grant-writing capacity, and professionalization.[31]

A second problem, at least regarding EU funding, was the structure of such grants, which are implemented by national or regional governments. If domestic politicians view projects as politically controversial, it is safer to fund others instead. Given the plethora of grant seekers, it was not hard for domestic authorities to select alternative proposals from NGOs representing other worthy causes. In my interviews with rights advocates and political elites more generally, most agreed that the EU's financial capacity to nurture advocacy networks was severely constrained.[32] Because international resources were beyond reach, NGOs often turned to local governments—despite the obstacles discussed above. Such was Lambda Warsaw's strategy: it had the cost, however, of preventing the group from being as politically vocal as KPH.[33]

In the judgment of KPH's former president Robert Biedroń, the group's biggest accomplishment in this period was its 2003 campaign "Let Them See Us," the goal of which was to counter the increasingly strident and negative framing of homosexuality coming from hard-right groups like LPR, elements of the Church such as Radio Maryja, and youth organizations like Młodzież Wszechpolska.[34] The campaign consisted of billboards of same-sex couples holding hands, which were posted across Poland. The campaign was revolutionary because it showed photographs of real people openly declaring themselves as gays and lesbians in public; moreover, it did so by posing them in everyday, unsexualized, unsensational settings. The photographs portrayed the couples publicly but also as "normal" Poles. Other than the caption "Let Them See Us," there was no text. The message was political but implicit; gays and lesbians are the same as "us" and, implicitly, should have the same rights. In technique and execution, the campaign had the feel more of art photography than political lobbying; it was based on photographs exhibited as portraits in the "gallery" of public space. In short, it was an artful compromise among the different elements of KPH, politics with culture/identity, lobbying with art-based activism. Despite its neutral tone, "Let Them See Us" provoked a sensation in Poland. Critics denounced it as a series of "depravations and deviations," and it sparked a debate about the participation of gays and lesbians in the public sphere.[35] Most local governments refused to cooperate with KPH in promoting it. In many locales, KPH found that it could not rent space on billboards. Yet, as is often the case with such censorship, these difficulties only heightened media attention, and, according to many of my respondents, this was the first occasion that homosexuality began to be seriously discussed in the public sphere.[36] The campaign offered a good example of how hard-right backlash boosted the movement—even before the onset of political party backlash after EU membership.

Besides KPH and Lambda Warsaw, this period also saw the emergence of more grassroots groups, though these were generally more inward-looking and community-oriented than political. The most prominent of these was the ILGCN-Poland, which organized Poland's first Pride march in 2001 in Warsaw. From a movement-building perspective, Prides are critical events because they generate solidarity, visibility, and provide a venue for allies to publicly endorse gay rights. After Poland joined the EU and the hard right began attacking them, Prides served all of these functions. At the preaccession stage, however, the Warsaw Pride—officially called the March of Equality (Marsz Równości)—was a very different affair. First, its organizer, the newly established ILGCN-Poland, was very informally organized and avowedly apolitical. Until 2004, it served primarily as a space in which one could "come out" publicly, not insignificant in Poland at that time but not a larger political statement. The idea to hold a march came not from any contact with European activist networks but from seeing footage of a Pride abroad on TV.[37] The first parade in 2001 was a small, Warsaw-based affair of about 300 participants. As one commentator observed, given how little visibility the

LGBT community had—even to itself—the march "allowed Warsaw's lesbians and gays to assess their forces."[38] Over the next two years the parade grew in size (to as many as 3,000 participants in 2003) and reach (attracting participants from across Poland), but its character changed little—largely apolitical, informally organized, and inward-looking.[39] What is particularly striking about Warsaw Prides before EU accession was the lack of controversy surrounding them. Organizers did not face administrative obstacles getting permits. Media coverage—to the extent that there was coverage—treated them in a light, if mocking, tone.[40] As ILGCN-Poland's founder Szymon Niemiec observed,

> For [the first] three years . . . the media didn't write about it [the parade]; they treated it like some curious little situation. . . . In 2003, Lech Kaczyński signed the papers for the parade without comment. In 2004, when they [PiS] started to make their election campaign for parliament, he banned the Parade for the first time. . . . [This was] when the All-Polish Youth and other nationalists started to react against it . . . [and when] the media started talking about gay rights as a political issue.[41]

As the next chapter will describe, the character of Prides changed radically after accession, when they became intensely political, much larger, and drew broad participation by domestic and international allies.

The cooperation among the groups comprising the Polish movement during this period is striking, especially compared to the Czech movement, which began to experience internal rifts at this time. From its founding, KPH maintained a division of labor with Lambda Warsaw; it would focus on politics, while Lambda would maintain its orientation toward self-help and counseling. In my interviews, activists recalled that IGCLN-Poland also had its own niche within this cooperative network: it did not do political activism (KPH's domain), and it did not do social services (Lambda Warsaw's turf).[42] As one Lambda Warsaw member described the relationship, "Perhaps the most [fruitful collaboration], as far as other gay organizations goes, is that with KPH. We support each other; each month we have a joint meeting of both governing boards for the sake of information sharing: what we're doing, ideas for joint projects, etc."[43] Moreover, the LGBT and feminist movements cooperated quite closely. There is little evidence of the kind of divisive split between lesbians and gay men that would become manifest in the Czech Republic. As one Polish activist wrote, "In Poland there is a kind of strategic alliance between feminist and LGBT groups."[44] Speaking of the variety of groups making up the Polish movement, one Lambda Warsaw member described a cooperative network of activism:

> These groups are diverse, but they are not conflicting because there is no danger among these organizations of any of them being greedy. For example, with KPH we strive so that they work only and exclusively with the outside (lobbying and so on), and we occupy ourselves with internal activism, i.e.[,] help and counseling.[45]

As this quote suggests, one mechanism employed to prevent rivalry is a division of labor among groups, particularly the separation of political lobbying from other fields of activism. While a certain amount of rivalry about the number of members and the importance of activities inevitably remained, this division of labor prevented such competition from undermining solidarity. As one Lambda member commented about the possibility of competition over members, "That's kind of an artificial problem because it's well known that we [Lambda Warsaw] attract a completely different kind of person than KPH, because it's strictly a political organization."[46] To the extent that intergroup rivalry existed, it primarily concerned financial resources.[47]

The comparison here with contemporaneous developments in Czech activism is illuminating. Around 2000, the Czech movement was experiencing escalating tension between its "political" and "cultural/identity" camps. This tension resulted ultimately in a fracturing of the movement's lobbying wing, GI. Out of this conflict, a new and competing rights organization was founded, GLL. Both groups largely lost touch with the broader network of self-help and support-oriented groups, as the dissolution of SOHO showed. In Poland, by contrast, KPH was able to resolve such tensions without fragmenting and without isolating the political lobbying groups from the others.[48]

Because KPH emerged as the de facto leader of the Polish movement, its successes in terms of professionalization, visibility, and coordinating a growing network of LGBT groups were highly significant for the larger movement. As with the wave of gay and lesbian activism in the 1990s, most groups were still informally organized and resource-poor for most of this period. In contrast to the 1990s, though, a large part of activism was now political, and the different groups were better integrated with each other, governed by specialization in complementary niches. The EU had made available a new language for talking about the movement's goals—one of rights and policy protections rather than morality and charity to the sick—and KPH embraced this new framing.

As noted earlier, however, the real breakthrough in the organization of Polish activism would come later, after accession. For now, the movement still had one glaring weakness: it was unable to mobilize either the broader LGBT community or potential domestic allies in significant numbers. Pride parades, which consisted of only a couple hundred participants and few allies, illustrated this weakness. Likewise, KPH, despite both its lobbying efforts and visibility as a target of hard-right rhetoric, could boast of few political allies. In the 2001 parliamentary election campaign, the social democratic SLD made vague promises about loosening restrictions on abortion and enacting registered partnerships. After winning the elections, however, it turned its attention to shoring up support for the 2003 public referendum on EU accession, quietly dropping its campaign pledges. SLD's lack of seriousness about LGBT issues could be seen in the fate of Maria Szyszkowska, a professor of philosophy at Warsaw University and SLD senator who proposed a registered partnerships bill in 2002. Szyszkowska's proposal won approval in the Senate, but it died in the Sejm, failing to attract support even from her own party. Indeed, her sponsorship of the doomed measure was generally credited with ending her political career.[49] Szyszkowska was, for the moment, KPH's lone political ally. Other parties either fulminated against "homosexual propaganda" (on the hard right) or avoided saying anything for fear of alienating voters (if they appeared too tolerant) or of endangering EU membership (if they appeared too intolerant).[50]

The Czech Republic: A Movement Fractures

If the Polish movement was experiencing rebirth during the accession period, its Czech counterpart experienced a string of shocks that highlighted its fragility and precipitated fracture and deinstitutionalization. Magnifying these shocks was a growing disagreement among activists about framing the movement's goals. These eventually led to organizational schism. Unlike in Poland, EU accession politics offered activists few resources to address these dilemmas. Absent a framing contest with the hard right, the EU frame lacked resonance. Likewise, the Czech parliament's relatively unproblematic harmonization with the EU's labor market *acquis* obviated the need for brokers. Finally, the hard right's irrelevance meant there was no perceived threat to the immediate protective surround. All of these factors contributed to anemic participation by the movement's constituents and indifference by potential liberal and pro-EU allies.

As we saw in Chapter 4, the framing of homosexuality in the Czech Republic was strongly influenced by the legacy of communist-era therapeutic groups and the still-strong influence of their former members. Registered partnerships came to be seen by the movement's leadership as the means for legally establishing the public sociability that these groups had sought. This assimilationist framing informed the style of activism, which was pragmatic, nonconfrontational, and single-issue-oriented: enacting registered partnerships. Radicalism and identity politics were to be avoided. The practical consequences of this style were most obvious when it came to Pride parades, which the leadership opposed. These principles had guided the movement during the 1990s, serving as the rationale behind the methodical building of a national-level SMO like SOHO. Between 1998 and 2004, this framing became less compelling for key constituencies within the movement, most notably lesbian and feminist activists, but also the wave of younger activists coming into the movement. At least some of the latter rejected the biologically determined view of sexual orientation espoused by the older generation of gay activists in favor of a more constructivist and queer-oriented identity politics.[51] For them, public sociability and official recognition in the form of registered partnerships were not enough; challenging broader gender norms should be the central goal. As we will see, the costs of transforming the movement into a single-issue campaign were significant; they included not only loss of potential support from feminist allies and the wider network of informal LGBT groups that emerged in the wake of SOHO's fall but also the schisms within the movement.

The best description of these costs comes from Věra Sokolová, an academic in the gender studies program at Charles University in Prague and a feminist activist. In her analysis of the campaign for registered partnerships, in which she was also a participant, Sokolová argues that its organizers framed their goals in ways that excluded lesbians and feminist allies. The crux of this internal framing contest was the following: Were registered partnerships to be a first step to broader rights, for example, marriage, or were they the final goal? Feminist and lesbian activists argued that issues like the right of adoption were being sacrificed for the sake of registered partnerships.[52] Making adoption a part of the campaign would doom it, argued Hromada and the movement's main, primarily male, leadership, because Czech society would see it as too radical. As Sokolová put it, "[The assimilationists] argue that to accomplish something, they have to be patient, calm, rational, compromising and above all, non-conflicting. . . . Gay and lesbian representatives do not want to appear radical because our society and media do not like radical voices."[53]

The registered partnerships frame drove a wedge between LGBT-rights activists and the women's movement, a natural ally. The leadership of both began disassociating themselves from each other.[54] As a result, the "discourse on homosexuality . . . has had a distinct anti-feminist character."[55] Sokolová illustrates her thesis personally, recounting how after giving a public lecture on homophobia, GI president Hromada commented, "I really enjoyed your talk, but I don't think that feminism has any use for 'us.'"[56] In Hromada's view, feminism's critique of gender relations was radicalism, and in his words, "We don't need radicalism, what we need most is the ability to compromise."[57] No such rupture took place in Poland; KPH even used the offices of feminist groups for its early meetings. Thus, unlike Poland, the movement's defining framing contest took place internally, rather than between the movement and its critics.

The publications of the movement's leading SMOs during this period, first SOHO and then GI, provide a good indicator of the EU's place in how Czech activists framed homosexuality in this period—and how different this was from Poland. Consider a 2003 report published by GI, *Social Discrimination: Lesbians, Gay Men and Bisexuals in the CR.*[58] The report was financed through an EU grant, and, as its authors note, the support of ILGA-Europe was critical in winning this funding.[59] The report's content makes clear that activists are operating with an

EU reference point in mind. There are lots of references to standards in EU member-states and comparisons with other postcommunist countries seeking accession. Yet, while the Czech activists are aware of the EU and receive funding through EU networks, they do not employ the comparison with the EU in the same way as their Polish counter-parts—if we take KPH as representing the Polish movement. For Czech activists, the EU comparison is validating: it shows that the country's path is largely in line with European standards and that the enactment of registered partnerships would bring it even more closely in line. By contrast, as we saw earlier in this chapter, in Poland the comparison with the EU was employed by KPH activists to show Poland's *lack of fit* with EU standards. In reading the Czech report, one is struck by the tone in which Czech activists compare their situation with that in EU coun-tries, as well as that in the rest of Eastern Europe. The report compares the legal situation of gays, lesbians, and bisexuals favorably with that in EU member-states, claiming *greater* progress than in Austria, Greece, Italy, and Great Britain.[60] In comparing other postcommunist EU ap-plicants, the report highlights points of *difference*, noting a "striking difference between the Czech Republic and other candidate countries" regarding individuals' openness about their sexual orientation.[61]

The internal framing contest over partnerships was accompanied by a deinstitutionalization of the activist network, as the leadership diverted its attention from the grass roots to focus on political lobbying.[62] While this enabled the benefits of professionalization, it weakened the overall robustness of the activist network, as the grass roots disengaged from political activism and as its feminist and lesbian allies turned away. De-spite his otherwise strong assessment of SOHO in its heyday, Long fore-shadowed this disengagement:

> Concealed in its [SOHO's] success, though, is a certain thinness to its structure. . . . In SOHO's [organizational] chart, the government is there; but the "citizens" beneath are bound together only by geographic ties. The movement does not yet engage with the range of other identities, experi-ences, needs that people may bring to bear on it. I suspect that a deepen-ing of this "civil society within"—the construction of new intricacies, the recognition of new links and needs—is necessary before SOHO can be fully effective in the larger civil society without.[63]

Long's analysis proved prescient: in 2000, SOHO was dissolved and replaced by GI. In the 2003 GI report entitled *Social Discrimination: Lesbians, Gay Men and Bisexuals in the CR*, SOHO's former leadership presented the change as motivated by the desire to replace the term homosexual (as in the Organization of Associations of Homosexual Citizens, or SOHO) with the more "modern identification" "gay" and "because of the *new economic situation* both in the Czech Republic and *inside the gay movement*."[64] This vague allusion to a "new economic situation in the Czech Republic" referred to a government austerity package in the spring of 1997 that reduced state support for the nonprofit sector across the board. This broad shock to the movement's resources was compounded by a second, more specific one, namely the decision by the Ministry for Local Development to shutter Orbis, the publishing house that put out *SOHO revue* and employed a number of SOHO activists as editors.[65]

The language in the GI report is somewhat vague, but given the steep drop in funding for SOHO depicted in Figure 4.1, the toll of declining support from the state is clear. The report also characterizes the replacement of SOHO by GI as a change in the movement's organizational basis: "from an association of organizations into an association of individuals." The main focus of the newly established GI, in the words of the report, was "to appeal to public opinion and to seek the legalization of registered partnerships." With SOHO's dissolution, its former regional sections became independent and, as the former SOHO leaders acknowledge, subsequently demobilized: "Not all of them succeeded in accepting responsibility, some disappeared, others significantly limited their activities. They are, however, gradually being replaced by newly born, informal activities of young gay men and lesbians."[66] Finally, the movement's leadership detected a liberalizing shift in the broader public discourse about homosexuality. Former SOHO president Hromada publicly noted in 1999 that the "gay community can be satisfied with the progress of media presentation. Media [have] left the *bulvár* trend, which characterized the news about gays in the early '90s."[67] Around this time, Hromada also declared that "in its attitude towards gays and lesbians Czech society belongs among the most tolerant in the world."[68]

Despite the vagueness of the GI report's language, it highlights a process of deinstitutionalization of the movement and a narrowing of its frame. Activism was losing its national reach. SOHO had been notable for its ability to span and coordinate the activities of regional LGBT groups across the country. GI abandoned this function. This decision was not a consequence of the development of subnational organizations strong enough not to require a coordinating center. As the report acknowledges, the subnational groups were typically weaker after SOHO's demise; if they survived, they survived as informal groupings. The territorial restructuring of activism was a retreat to pockets of strength, notably in Prague. Last, the report confirms that the movement's leading SMOs were self-consciously narrowing their goals to policy change, and in particular to the enactment of registered partnerships. Seidl's description of these organizational changes between 1998 and 2006 is worth quoting at length. First, he describes the old model of "regular plenary meetings of organized societies with legal status":

> The functioning of SOHO had since 1990 been based precisely on the principle of formalized membership in organizations. If an individual wanted to influence something through this structure, he had to do so by means of his [representative] organization, which if it identified with his opinion would pursue it in SOHO's parliament.[69]

With time, Seidl continues, "An [alternative] civic associational form arose, which was constituted on the basis of the specific social interests of its members (sport, tourism, theater, and so on) and not necessarily even on the basis of sexual orientation alone."[70] Many constituents also began to find SOHO too constraining of alternative viewpoints. The result was

> [a] [new] situation, in which many gays and lesbians no longer identified with the principle of formalized organization, [which] created space for doubts about [SOHO's] legitimacy for a swath of the community. . . . At the same time, as a result of the changed financial environment in the last three years of the decade and the reduced financial resources that SOHO could distribute directly, the perceived value of SOHO's "spanning" function declined for member organizations, which were forced to seek other financial resources for their activities.[71]

In short, after 2000 both the reorganized core of ex-SOHO activists and the network of organizations that had constituted SOHO were considerably weaker than during the 1990s.

In the process of the movement's organizational redefinition, its associated monthly magazine *SOHO revue* underwent major changes. As described in Chapter 4, *SOHO revue* owed its existence to funding from the Health Ministry as part of its HIV/AIDS prevention efforts. However, it had been far more than a public service bulletin about AIDS; it served as the movement's political-cultural mouthpiece and offered employment as editors to key figures such as Hromada. In 1997, this arrangement ended as the state publishing house Orbis closed and as funding from the Ministry declined. *SOHO revue* was unable to continue. In 1998, its editorial team found a private publisher, and a revamped *SOHO ABSOLUT revue* appeared. It lasted only a year. Through Hromada's efforts, yet another private publisher was found for a renamed *Gayčko* monthly, but it was primarily commercially oriented.[72] Concurrent with these developments was the growing presence of the Internet as a source of news, commentary, and community for LGBT persons.[73] This quick succession of increasingly commercial, less movement-oriented magazines after 1997 illustrated the consequences of declining state support and complemented the trends of movement fragmentation and deinstitutionalization.[74]

As a result of these shifts, the character of activism changed. Decision making was increasingly concentrated in the hands of the GI leadership, who saw themselves as full-time lobbyists for registered partnerships. Their lobbying strategy dictated pragmatism and conciliation over idealism and identity politics. Concretely, this meant an avoidance of tactics that they saw as provocative, such as Pride parades. One cost of these shifts was to create a wedge between full-time activists and the wider group of social movement participants and potential participants, that is, the grass roots. Another cost was to open a rift within the movement between supporters of the pragmatic goal of limited registered partnerships and its critics, who argued that a more far-reaching conception of same-sex rights was called for. At first, this faction of dissenters was organized informally, though it was coherent enough to have a name, G-League (G-Liga).

This growing split reflected tensions within the movement regarding the framing and tactics employed by the "old" leadership, especially those of GI president Jiří Hromada. Hromada's influence in the movement was enormous. Since the early 1990s, he had led the largest activist organizations. His was also the face of the movement; according to Sokolová's analysis of the media's coverage of homosexuality between 1991 and 2004, Hromada appears—"[that is, he] comments, gives an interview, expresses personal or official views, is mentioned, consulted, or cited"—in over 70 percent of all articles.[75] For lesbians, feminists, and activists outside of Prague, however, Hromada was also identified with problems in the Czech movement. He was criticized for advocating a too-limited version of registered partnerships, and for marginalizing feminism. His opposition to Pride parades for fear of offending mainstream opinion was seen as damaging to the movement. All of these positions, his critics charged, were founded in an outdated, communist-era understanding of homosexuality, the socio-therapeutic framing. Some joked that G-League's motto was "Dohromady bez Hromady," a play on words in Czech that translates as "All together without Hromada."[76] This criticism took its toll on Hromada, who wrote in 2000 that he felt worn out "not from the challenging struggle against problems that make sense, but from the mortifying squandering of energy on quenching squabbles, on settling trifles, on clearing away spite and intrigue, and on coming to terms with incomprehension."[77]

In 2003, the divide between G-League and GI became official when a contingent of activists in GI broke off and founded their own advocacy group, the Gay and Lesbian League (Gay a lesbická liga, GLL).[78] GLL was founded as a challenge to GI's claim to speak for the movement. As mentioned earlier, one of its core constituencies was lesbians and feminists, but it also attracted a younger generation of activists, who came of age after the fall of communism.[79] One of GLL's core founders was the student activist group from Brno, STUD. For both feminists and younger activists, the socio-therapeutic framing of homosexuality held little resonance and, indeed, was often the subject of criticism. Like GI, GLL was oriented purely toward lobbying; it did not offer social services or community events. Its goals were public visibility for the movement and, interestingly, the enactment of registered partnerships, though in a more expansive form. Acknowledging the movement's internal rifts, it emphasized equal representation of gays and lesbians, always providing at least two spokespeople for each group in its public statements.[80] Countering the socio-therapeutic model, it viewed homosexuality in terms of culture and gender, seeking thereby to build links with feminists. Finally, it sought to reactivate the movement's base outside of Prague, as could be seen in the participation of activists from Brno. Yet despite these differences, GLL also made the legalization of registered partnerships a goal, at least as a first step to more expansive same-sex unions.[81] GLL's split from GI should be seen as a weakening of the network. While the two groups did work jointly for registered partnerships, they were in many ways competitors and rivals, sometimes at a personal level. They offered differing framings of homosexuality and duplicated rather than complemented each other's efforts. In an environment of scarce resources for activism, such duplication weakens SMOs' effectiveness.[82] This rivalry contrasted the division of labor and cooperation noted in the various Polish activist groups at this time.

To summarize the shifts in the organization of Czech activism between 1998 and 2004, the movement underwent fragmentation and deinstitutionalization. It also became more narrowly oriented, as GI and GLL focused their attention on the campaign for registered partnerships. I characterize these developments as a weakening of activism, and I trace them to a decline in the movement's traditional resource base (i.e., state funding for HIV/AIDS prevention) and an internal framing conflict about registered partnerships. From a broader perspective of civil society after communism, neither should be surprising; they echo scholarship on communism's legacies for how activism is organized— that is, as overly professionalized NGOs without robust grassroots participation.[83] Seen from this perspective, the period from 1998 to 2004 was a case of regression to the mean, from unusually organized activism to something more typical for the neighborhood. These shifts do not, however, capture the whole picture. Outside of political activism, the Czech Republic retained a wide-ranging and comparatively vibrant network of socially oriented LGBT groups. As the authors of a Czech government committee report on minorities noted, "In almost all cases, gay organizations active in the CR engage in organizing leisure time activities such as trips, sporting events or discussions. Almost none of them develop enlightenment or political activity in relation to majority society."[84] Moreover, these groups operated generally free of disruption or harassment by conservative groups.

Not surprisingly, Prague was home to the greatest number of such clubs and social groups, including M-Klub Lambda (a group for seniors); GaLes (a group of university students); Gaysport, Pratety, and Aquamen (sports-based clubs); and Skupina3 (something between a self-help and travel club). In Brno, the country's second biggest city, student-based STUD put on annual film festivals, ran support services, and organized social activities. Brno was also home to GaTe (for gay teens) and Pěšky atd. (for outdoor activities). There were also specifically lesbian groups across the country, which published a journal, *Promluv*, and organized an annual film festival, Apriles. LOGOS, a group of gay Christians, was also active.[85] In the city of České Budějovice, one of the original member associations of SOHO, South Bohemia Lambda, organized recreational activities and provided social services. South Bohemia Lambda was exceptional as one of the few organizations to maintain its legal status as a civic association since the early 1990s. Typically, groups in this period were short-lived and informally organized, in addition of course to being apolitical.

To keep in mind the comparison with Poland, it is worth pausing to note the differing direction of Czech developments: a separation between the political and social aspects of the movement, and a tendency among the latter to turn inward. This difference from Poland was exemplified in the attitude toward Pride parades. Whereas in Poland these parades were beginning, albeit modestly, in the preaccession period, in the Czech Republic the dense network of social and political groups did not organize Pride festivals. The closest equivalent was an annual "Candlelight" parade to commemorate victims of AIDS, organized by SOHO with financial support from the Health Ministry.[86] Hromada and the majority of the SOHO leadership opposed Pride parades as projecting the wrong image of homosexuality, opting instead for this more somber and more narrowly defined march against AIDS.[87] Other SOHO community events had a similar inward-looking character, for example, the annual "Gay Man" pageant (begun in 1996) and the fielding of a team in the international Gay Games in Amsterdam in 1998.[88] Such events were mostly invisible to the broader public.

The Campaign for Registered Partnerships

Having traced Czech activism's organizational trajectory during the accession period, let us close by examining the movement's signature issue during these years: registered partnerships. This campaign offers valuable analytical insights into how the movement operated. Did it approach the issue as a campaign to publicly mobilize its grassroots supporters or as a lobbying effort directed at persuading political elites? Who were its allies—and opponents? To what extent did it exploit the potential leverage offered by EU accession to further its goals? Last, which goals did it choose *not* to pursue in order to focus on partnerships?

To begin with the last question, Czech activists virtually ignored antidiscrimination during this period. It receives only token acknowledgment in the several reports authored by SOHO's policy experts, which were in part funded by the EU.[89] It is not mentioned in Jiří Fanel's 2000 history of the movement, and barely mentioned in Seidl's more recent one. The latter, in fact, notes that "the gay and lesbian representation did not feel the absence of explicit antidiscrimination legislation as a significant problem"[90] This issue is also unmentioned in the critiques of SOHO and its conception of registered partnerships.[91] Czech antidiscrimination protections for sexual minorities were not politically difficult to enact, but as a consequence of their neglect by the movement nor are they particularly robust, a fact noted by the government itself in a 2007 report by its committee on minority rights.[92]

The EU's use of conditionality to mandate that applicant-states adopt antidiscrimination provisions did not provoke the same controversy among political elites that it had in Poland, and consequently the Czech government's attitude toward antidiscrimination policy was minimalist. According to one of the government's own committees, the Working Group for the Issues of Sexual Minorities of the minister for human rights and national minorities, Czech lawmakers amended a number of provisions in the Labor Code to encompass sexual orientation in antidiscrimination protections, but they did not extend these protections beyond the minimum necessary for EU compliance.[93] Preoccupied with the campaign for registered partnerships, GI and GLL did not apply much pressure on the government to extend antidiscrimination protections into areas where, according to earlier research by the same rights groups, sexual minorities faced discrimination, for example, education, housing, health care, and welfare policy.[94] As the government committee's report summarized, "A law that would comprehensively anchor the right to equal treatment and a ban on discrimination based on sexual orientation has not yet been enacted."[95]

Antidiscrimination policy may be considered the "dog that didn't bark," the clue that tells by virtue of its absence: registered partnerships' near total displacement of antidiscrimination policy in the literature generated by and about the Czech movement shows how little EU leverage influenced its strategy. Czech activists did not act as brokers between the EU and the national government: since registered partnerships were not mandated by EU conditionality, there was little room for them to serve in this role. Further, because of the irrelevance of the hard right, antidiscrimination policy passed through parliament without igniting a framing contest between EU values and national ones, as in Poland. Thus, Czech activists were less able to frame their cause within a larger EU rights frame.

The Czech movement's focus on one big project, registered partnerships, can be understood as a cost of limited resources, but in doing so it put all its energy into an issue for which the EU accession process offered little leverage. The EU itself had no common position on the recognition of same-sex partnerships: they were neither part of the Copenhagen Criteria nor the *acquis communautaire*. As Kelly Kollman shows, there was a trend toward growing acceptance of such unions in Western Europe in the early 2000s, but EU countries ran the gamut from acknowledgment of to resistance to such partnerships, and certainly no other postcommunist country had such legislation.[96] To the extent that European norms could be cited by activists, it was only in terms of the models offered by some West European states, not all of them even EU members.[97] Further, given the hard right's irrelevance in Czech politics, framing partnerships in terms of EU norms lacked the credibility offered by a conservative counterframe depicting LGBT rights as another example of EU hegemony. Finally, GI and GLL lacked a model for how to organize such a campaign in a postcommunist setting; they were forced to learn from trial and error. If Czech activists were acting according to Europeanization theory's assumptions—and especially the assumptions of this school's external incentives variant—then partnerships are the last policy area on which they should have trained their efforts. Yet, for the Czech movement, registered partnerships became the defining issue in this period during which EU leverage was greatest. They were the goal toward which all SMOs turned their efforts, and they became the wedge that increasingly divided them in terms of tactics.

The campaign for registered partnerships was, in short, a domestic political story. Its twists and turns are best understood in terms of the parameters of social movement mobilization after communism: scarce resources for collective action and weak mobilizing structures. All of these were laid bare as state support for the nonprofit sector and HIV/AIDS prevention declined. To these more general features of postcommunist social-movement mobilization, the idiosyncratic features of Czech parliamentary and party politics must be added for a full picture of the campaign.

The campaign took place almost entirely within the Czech parliament and was more about lobbying than popular mobilization.[98] In all it took five attempts over seven years before legislation was finally passed in 2006.[99] Yet, as the activist and gender scholar Věra Sokolová put it, the stop-and-go path to eventual legislative victory was a game of parliamentary maneuver and delaying tactics, reflecting more the "inflexibility and conservatism of the Czech parliament than it did the real opinions of Czech society."[100] Proponents of registered partnerships did not face public opposition, and in general the media were strongly sympathetic. Even in parliament, there was no coherent coalition against, and certainly not a hard-right one. The chief cleavages ran within parties, not between them.

Only one party opposed registered partnerships in principle, the Christian Democrats (KDU-ČSL).[101] The Christian Democrats were a small, well-established party in Czech politics; the main reason that the parliamentary deliberations over registered partnerships took as long as they did was due to the Christian Democrats' determined efforts to use parliamentary procedure to stop the bill. It was referred multiple times to a variety of parliamentary committees to prevent a general vote on it.[102] The Christian Democrats' natural partners in opposition, the radical-right populist SPR-RSČ, were in terminal decline and soon to be voted out of parliament. They, however, did not oppose the partnerships in principle. Their reaction was particularly interesting, especially when considered against the homophobic behavior of their closest Polish counterpart, LPR. SPR-RSČ argued against the proposal in parliament but did so using sympathetic rhetoric and offering the rationale that it did not go far enough! Thus, in parliamentary deliberations their MPs detailed the *deficiencies* of the proposal compared to same-sex partnership laws in other countries.[103] The closest parliament's discussion came to the kind of homophobic discourse evident in Poland was in the rhetoric of one Christian Democratic MP, Pavel Tollner, who declared, "This campaign, of which we are all the addressees—understandably the young more than the older—will lead to an unacceptable culmination of homosexual and bisexual behavior as well as other perversions. I wanted to say swinery, but they talked me out of it."[104] Notably, however, this outburst was roundly condemned by the Christian Democrats themselves, who forced him to publicly apologize, declaring that homosexuality "cannot be labeled an abnormality" and emphasizing that their "reservations about the law concerned the adoption of children . . . [and that] otherwise we see no great differences between homosexuals and heterosexuals."[105] In sum, registered partnerships did not catalyze anything that could be characterized as a hard-right backlash.

Given this political environment—in which the public was largely supportive of registered partnerships, and the major parties did not oppose them—the movement adopted the strategy of persuading individual parliamentarians. In this approach, Hromada's wide political contacts assumed particular importance. To win over the persuadable MPs, GI and GLL opted, first, to moderate their demands and, two, not to exert public pressure (i.e., not to publicly shame MPs into supporting the proposal). GI did mount one petition campaign, but tellingly it was aimed at celebrities and public figures: some 400 of whom signed.[106] Otherwise, neither GLL nor GI attempted to mobilize grassroots pressure on politicians through public marches or petitions. The campaigners' willingness to compromise in order to win political support went hand in hand with an unwillingness to mobilize their grassroots supporters for fear of appearing too radical.

The biggest compromise concerned adoption. GI president Jiří Hromada was particularly forceful in keeping adoption rights off the table, even as lesbian activists in the movement pushed for their inclusion. When the Czech press reported in 2000 that "lesbian activists want to open again a discussion about raising children by homosexual couples," Hromada criticized adoption's proponents for being "too aggressive" and stated that "adoptions and the upbringing of children has never been, is not and will not be a part of the Registered Partnership law."[107] Elsewhere he wrote that

> it is completely irresponsible to impose on the public that the Registered Partnership is or could be an alternative [to] marriage. The proposed law . . . [does] not place a legitimate relationship between two people of the same sex on the same level as marriage because it could not do so. By marriage *we* understand man, woman and children, for whom it [such a unit] creates the most appropriate environment for coexistence and [the] upbringing of children.[108]

Statements such as these inflamed cleavages within the movement and alienated potential grassroots participants.

The lobbying campaign stretched from 1998 to 2006. Given the headwinds just described, the persistence of Czech activists was impressive. Even if activism had become single-issue lobbying by a small circle of Prague-based stalwarts, their capacity to draft complex legislative proposals, mount them in the face of repeated defeats, and cultivate allies among the major parties and media all bespoke a highly capable lobbying organization. The first parliamentary proposals came in 1998—after a long gestation within SOHO—and, as described earlier, were cosponsored by individual MPs from across the major political parties. The press was supportive, and no less influential a figure than President Václav Havel publicly endorsed the campaign. Additionally, the issue complemented the governing Social Democrats' efforts to accentuate human rights, and, as part of this push, they established a Government Committee for Human Rights, which included Hromada as a member.[109] Despite these favorable conditions, the parliamentary calculus was tight, and at the end of a two-year process of obstruction by the Christian Democrats, the proposal was defeated in a vote of 88 to 87 on December 2, 1999.[110] It was a huge disappointment for the movement, and helped accelerate the organizational and strategic changes in SOHO described earlier.

In September 2001, a new proposal emerged in parliament, again with the movement's sponsorship (now organized as GI), but this time the bill was submitted by the government itself. This represented a new level of commitment by the governing Social Democrats; however, parliamentary elections were drawing near, and the campaign's leadership accepted the party's decision to postpone a vote until after the elections. This decision, which exacerbated disagreements among activists about the place of adoption in registered partnerships, started the process of internal fragmentation that led to the 2003 founding of a new and competing claimant to the role of representing the LGBT community, GLL. Unfortunately for the movement, the 2002 elections forced the Social Democrats into coalition with the Christian Democrats, who demanded that registered partnerships be removed from the government agenda as a condition of their support. Though the government was forced to oblige to maintain its majority, Justice Minister Pavel Rychetský (ČSSD) began work on a new registered partnerships proposal in the fall of 2003.

This became the last phase of the registered partnerships campaign, but it also laid bare the movement's fragmentation. The diverging camps described above—the "old guard" represented by GI and the "new generation" of G-Liga—formally broke in 2003, as G-Liga became GLL. Each camp claimed to be the true voice of the movement, and the rivalry became very sharp and personalized, as the next chapter will describe. Rychetský's work on registered partnerships seemed to accelerate the split. GI criticized the new proposal as too watered down but nevertheless endorsed it as better than nothing. The rationale was that a strategy of "small changes" would lead to greater progress in the end than holding out for a big breakthrough.[111] GLL criticized GI for accepting such a big compromise as Rychetský proposed, asking, "Where is the line at which a small step is so small that it no longer makes sense?"[112] Despite GI's willingness to settle for small steps, by the time the Czech Republic became an EU member in spring 2004, it still had not enacted registered partnerships. In the following chapter, we will take up the final stage of the campaign, and its repercussions for the movement.

Conclusion

In Poland, EU accession helped reframe homosexuality from a question of individual morality to one of European law and human rights, and led to a reorganization of activist networks both among LGBT-rights advocates and on the hard right. Exploiting the opportunity to broker between the national government and the EU, the network of advocates became more political and professional. It still remained mostly Warsaw-based, however. The network of opponents also changed. What before had been local, ad hoc protests against HIV/AIDS treatment centers now also became a wider, more political network of nationalist political parties. While these changes were evidently at the root of the growing political polarization around homosexuality, this polarization reached its zenith in the next stage, after Poland's membership was formalized in May 2004—at which point conditionality lost its edge. While this period of intense EU pressure to amend Polish discrimination policy constituted undeniable progress, it also set the stage for a populist political backlash from 2004 to 2007.

The Czech Republic offers a stark contrast. Most fundamentally, EU accession hardly touched the politics of homosexuality in this country. It sparked no hard-right backlash and was not taken up by rights activists as a tool of leverage or model for emulation. Consequently, Czech activists devoted almost all of their energies to a project for which the EU accession process offered no leverage, registered partnerships, and largely ignored the area for which it did, antidiscrimination policy. In terms of how activism was organized, the contrast with Poland deepens. In the late 1990s, Czech activists had constructed a highly institutionalized network of functionally delimited but territorially integrated SMOs with strong connections to state institutions and state resources. By the close of this period, there was instead a patchwork of mostly informally organized clubs only loosely tied to a fragmented SMO core that was squabbling over who truly represented the movement.

6

Activism after EU Leverage

Poland and the Czech Republic, 2004–2012

It's great there was this fight, even if it was really brutal. Before, the marches interested only people connected with the movement. Now, the more hate the new government is showing toward gays and lesbians, the more so called normal people are beginning to understand that something is wrong.
—Polish activist recalling the 2004 Poznań Pride March

If someone were now to want to introduce some sort of discriminatory regulations for homosexual persons, all organizations would stand together. Of that I have not even the slightest doubt.
—Activist, Lambda Warsaw

[With] the battle behind us . . . [the goal now] is to maintain what has been achieved.
—Jiří Hromada, GI (Czech Republic)

On May 1, 2004, the EU admitted eight postcommunist states, including Poland and the Czech Republic.[1] The European Commission now lost the leverage of conditionality and the mandate for oversight of policy implementation. As a matter of international law, the legal conditions for entry were still binding, but as a matter of practical implementation and public perception, those conditions now looked much less formidable. Infractions against EU law could be brought before the courts, but as a post hoc and reactive approach, this was a much weaker form of monitoring than before. Criticism of a state's failure to protect minority rights—criticism that typically now came from the European

Parliament—became the main source of external leverage. Finally, even if EU law applied equally to the new member-states, the possibility of passive repression increased as leverage waned. The weakening of leverage opened up the potential for changes to the POS, depending on the hard right's access to political power.

Where the hard right gains access to power, the first consequence of weakening leverage is a significant increase in the threat to the "immediate protective surround." Even in countries where LGBT protections have been modest at best and where social stigma remains high, the empowerment of the hard right threatens sexual minorities' quotidian routines, taken-for-granted rules of everyday life, and potentially even the right to participate in the public sphere.[2] Since the threat of such loss helps activists overcome even very daunting collective action problems, we would expect more grassroots participation and cooperation among activist groups—in short, greater movement solidarity. Much of this mobilization will be driven by emotional dynamics, defending citizenship as opposed to lobbying for concrete policies. The greater the hard-right threat and the more virulent its repression, the greater the visibility, credibility, and resonance of the movement's framing of homosexuality as a *political* issue of European standards and associated liberal norms. As this framing contest gains resonance—extending from the discursive sphere that previously contained it to the political sphere of actual repression—the frame will draw allies for whom LGBT rights become a larger symbol. The availability of such allies will also depend on the magnitude of the hard right's electoral breakthrough, and the extent to which it upsets prevailing alignments among elites.

Polish activists' perceptions of the state's capacity and propensity for repressing the movement increased dramatically immediately after accession, first as Prides came under attack and then as a hard-right government occupied power from 2005 to 2007. During this time, the movement experienced both active and passive repression. The most visible repression involved Pride marches, which faced administrative bans, discriminatory policing, and organized violence. Since Prides had been taking place without incident since 2001, their suppression amounted to a loss of the possibility for full participation in the public sphere. As the following sections will describe, the Pride parade controversy was part of a broader and sustained deterioration of the political environment for sexual minorities between 2004 and 2007.

The EU seemed powerless to improve the situation, despite several attempts. In January 2006, the EP condemned "a series of worrying events, as widely reported by the press and NGOs, ranging from banning gay prides or equality marches to the use by leading politicians and religious leaders of inflammatory, hate or threatening language, police failing to provide adequate protection or even breaking up peaceful demonstrations, violent demonstrations by homophobic groups, and the introduction of changes to constitutions to explicitly prohibit same-sex unions."[3] While no state was mentioned by name, Poland was clearly among the targets of concern.[4] A second resolution in June 2006 rebuked Poland specifically for "an increase in intolerance caused by racism, xenophobia, anti-Semitism, and homophobia."[5] Both resolutions provoked defiant responses: speaker of parliament Marek Jurek (PiS) declared that they "promot[ed] an ideology of homosexual communities."[6] Parliament then passed a resolution dismissing the EP's charges.

In my conversations in Warsaw in summer 2007, there was a strong sense among activists, especially those outside the more transnationally oriented KPH, that the EU was impotent. As Szymon Niemiec, founder of Warsaw's Equality March, observed, "The EP sent a letter to the Polish parliament saying, stop homophobia in Poland. . . . The answer of the Polish parliament was, 'We don't care.'"[7] Yga Kostrzewa of Lambda Warsaw noted: "The EP has criticized us twice now for homophobia. Our politicians said, 'They don't attack our way of thinking, they attack Poland.'"[8] Another activist put it this way, "I don't believe that I have an EU umbrella over me. It doesn't make me feel any more courageous when I walk out on the streets. I didn't believe it back then, and I believe it even less now, since Poland joined the EU." Similar sentiments were voiced by public officials and policy experts. One official involved with the accession process stated, "Accession [to the EU] would be impossible [today] with such policies, such statements, such problems in the area of human rights. . . . There is no system of being a watchdog or a system of monitoring democratic standards in the new member-states. When you are in, you are in, and the line is not to interfere in internal policy."[9]

By contrast, the absence of hard-right backlash in the Czech Republic meant that its LGBT movement experienced no threat to the protective sound. While the waning of leverage opened up the potential for repression, the absence of hard-right mobilization, either socially or politically, removed this as a possibility. No Czech activist that I spoke with ever showed concern about state obstruction—indifference maybe, but not repression or collusion with antigay activists. Indeed, Czech LGBT respondents typically emphasized their comfort being "out."

From these different starting points as new EU members, the contrasts between the two movements grew only more pronounced. Over the next years, Polish activists decisively reversed the trends of the 1990s: by 2012, their movement could boast of large-scale grassroots participation, a coordinated national network of professionalized SMOs with close links to transnational advocacy networks, an increasing number of domestic allies, and, by the 2011 parliamentary elections, LGBT activists in national office. The experience of head-on attack by hard-right nationalists and retrenchment on political rights catalyzed a counteroffensive that carried activism to new heights of mobilization for the region. Meanwhile, the Czech movement continued trends of deinstitutionalization and demobilization that had set in around 2000. After achieving a limited legal victory with same-sex registered partnerships, the two main rights groups dissolved themselves. Activism did not disappear entirely, but it became less social-movement-like and more technocratic: many of the former leaders opted for service on a government committee on human rights, while other forms of community became inward-looking, centered in clubs and service provision.[10]

This chapter concludes the comparative tracing of activism's organization across both countries, drawing on monographs, NGO reports, firsthand accounts, and participant observation of Prides in Warsaw in 2007, 2009, and 2010. To provide thematic focus to an eventful period, the Polish section concentrates on two pivotal moments: the battle over Prides, which marked a turning point in organizational development and solidarity; and the 2011 election campaign, which saw activism push farther across the threshold of political mobilization than in any other postcommunist country. In tracing the Czech movement, the chapter will focus on the conclusion of the campaign for registered partnerships—and the demobilization that followed. It concludes by analyzing efforts in 2011 to reestablish the movement after several years of organizational vacuum.

Poland: A Movement Mobilizes

The greatest organizational development of Poland's LGBT movement has been since 2004. Initially, it appeared quite the opposite—that the movement was fighting for its existence. In 2005–2007, Poland experienced the most nationalist-populist government since 1989, key members of which targeted the so-called homosexual lobby. From the perspective of Europeanization theory, these developments boded ill for EU norm diffusion and for the movement itself. The period between 2005 and 2007 was a turning point for activism, the moment when an already fierce discursive backlash against homosexuality was reinforced by an electoral breakthrough that put the hard right in a position to credibly threaten the immediate protective surround. After enduring intense political attack through 2007, the movement emerged stronger than before. When the hard-right PiS-LPR government collapsed in a corruption scandal in 2007, it was replaced by the liberal, pro-European Civic Platform (PO) party. Under PO-led government, the movement continued to develop rapidly, growing in territorial reach, sophistication, and mobilization capacity. Though the predominant minorities represented under the rubric LGBT remained gays and lesbians, during this period the movement widened its base. The most visible example was transgender people: in 2007, the group Trans-Fuzja was established and in 2011 its head was elected to parliament. Further, the notion of queer sexuality broke from the academic seminar circuit into broader activism, as could be seen in events such as Queer-in-May (first held in Cracow in 2009) and the feminist-lesbian Manifa events.[11] Post-2007 was also a time of political realignment as the established parties adapted to the hardening division between Poland A and Poland B, positioning themselves for the 2011 elections. Homosexuality appeared again as a campaign focal point, creating an opening for rights activists to form alliances with parties and participate directly in electoral mobilization.

Defending the Prides

Prides are critical to movement-building because they enact sexual citizenship, making visible and concrete sexual minorities' claim to be included on equal terms in the public sphere.[12] Organizationally, they are critical because they generate internal solidarity, visibility, and provide a venue for allies to publicly endorse the movement. In Poland, the parades were also the site on which hard-right backlash—which had been building for several years but which EU leverage had largely confined to the discursive sphere—became an organized and sustained *political* backlash. Here the hard-right threat to the immediate protective surround was most visible and harsh. Thus, tracing the size and character of the marches over time offers a compelling illustration of backlash's catalyzing effects.

In June 2004, Warsaw president Lech Kaczyński (PiS) banned the city's March of Equality. The ban's timing—just months after Poland entered the EU and a year before national parliamentary and presidential elections—allowed Kaczyński to cast his party as staunch defenders of Catholic Poland against EU decadence, a mantle to which LPR also laid claim. The following year Kaczyński banned the march again. These bans dragged LGBT rights into the thick of national politics, making it a central issue in the 2005 elections, where, as one Polish political analyst noted, it all but eclipsed the traditional hot-button social issues of abortion and religious education in schools.[13] Chapter 3 showed how these moves coincided with escalating antigay rhetoric and an unprecedented increase in the salience of homosexuality in the media. My goal in this section is to describe the political side of the threat to the immediate collective surround, that is, how hard-right politicians used administrative discretion and discriminatory policies to undermine the sense of security and well-being of LGBT persons from 2004 through 2007.

Pride marches brought this political threat into sharp focus. Kaczyński's bans violated not only EU norms but also the free-speech and free-association provisions of Poland's own constitution. Kaczyński used a variety of administrative rationales—threat of violence, disruption of traffic—to justify the bans, but when these were questioned, he abandoned the pretense of equal protection under the law, announcing, "I will prohibit the parade regardless of what I find in the organizers' application. I can't see a reason for propagating gay culture."[14] When activists tried to circumvent Kaczyński's obstruction by petitioning to hold eight separate rallies along the proposed parade route (which would have addressed any traffic-related issues), the Warsaw government forbade seven of them, stating that they could not guarantee their safety.[15] A number of conservative groups—among them PiS's youth organization, LPR's All-Poland Youth, and various nationalist organizations—organized counterdemonstrations on the same day, all of which the government allowed. As described below, activists attempting to organize Prides in other cities also ran into administrative obstruction and outright bans, notably in Poznań and Cracow in 2005.[16]

The second prominent feature of the hard-right threat to the protective surround highlighted by Prides was that of violence. Of course, the threat of violence was often cited by politicians to justify parade bans; however, the logic was manifestly self-serving. Violence at Prides is a function of inadequate police presence and the signals that the authorities send to the police. Prides held after the PiS-LPR government were overwhelmingly peaceful, despite being far bigger. Prides held before PiS-LPR's tenure were, as noted earlier, also nonviolent. That violence came to mar several Prides during this period was the result of manifestly inadequate and sometimes discriminatory policing.

The first organized violence occurred at marches in Cracow and Poznań in summer 2004. An inadequate police presence was unable to prevent All-Polish Youth from pelting marchers with rocks and beating them with clubs. The attackers chanted slogans like "labor camps for lesbians," "faggots to the gas," and "pedophiles and pederasts—these are Euro-enthusiasts."[17] The 2005 Poznań march, which proceeded unofficially because it had been banned by the mayor, was the site of the greatest violence. Again, the All-Polish Youth attacked, throwing eggs and manure at an estimated 300 marchers. When the police belatedly intervened, they began arresting the rights marchers, not the attackers. As one participant described the scene:

> People were dragged away to police cars and driven away without a word of explanation. One of the boys was dragged with his head hitting the pavement. One other was dragged from the TV cameras when he was speaking to the reporters about unnecessary police brutality, which was later shown in the news. Sixty-eight people were arrested, mostly the protesters and a few of the most active members of [the All-PolishYouth].[18]

In 2006, Cracow's March of Tolerance was attacked a second time. This violence and evidently discriminatory policing occurred in an atmosphere of implicit and sometimes even explicit encouragement by national-level politicians. In its milder forms, such encouragement argued that sexual minorities should not parade their lifestyle in public.[19] Defending the bans, Prime Minister Kazimierz Marcinkiewicz (PiS) stated that if "a person tries to infect others with their homosexuality, then the state must intervene in this violation of freedom."[20] In its more explicit form, such encouragement amounted to direct incitement to violence. As LPR parliamentarian Wojciech Wierzejski declared in 2006, "The Warsaw authorities cannot allow this march! If the deviants start demonstrating, then they should be beat with clubs."[21]

The discriminatory policies of the hard right in power were at their most raw in the battle over the marches, but they were not far from the surface in other aspects of the public sphere either. The Kaczyński government's first official action was to abolish the state antidiscrimination body, thus violating Poland's implementation of EU norms. Instead, as noted in Chapter 3, it created a Plenipotentiary for Family Affairs; not only did the word "family" indicate new priorities, the office was not institutionally independent of the government, as EU directives required. With the naming of LPR leader Roman Giertych as education minister, education also became a target of "reform." Giertych attempted to reshape schools around a nationalist-Catholic conception of the citizen. His "Zero Tolerance" education agenda valorized discipline, from school uniforms to military schools for troublesome teens run by former commandos.[22] Defending the youth from "homosexual propaganda" was central to this project. A proposed Teacher's Charter would have barred persons believing that marriage could be anything other than a union between a man and a woman from teaching. As one LPR parliamentarian stated, "the aim is to prevent people from teaching who publicly declare their other sexual orientation . . . we must guard and protect our youth against deviants."[23] As mentioned earlier, the Ministry violated EU nondiscrimination rules by firing an official who had distributed a Council of Europe handbook on tolerance because it contained several paragraphs on homosexuality. As education minister, Giertych clashed with his European-level counterparts: in a meeting of EU education ministers he proposed a European "Charter of the Rights of Nations" that would ban "homosexual propaganda" and abortion.[24] Perhaps no other episode better revealed the homophobic nationalism of LPR's vision of Polish identity as Giertych's proposed revisions to the list of required readings in the school system. Witold Gombrowicz—a major figure of Polish 20th-century literature and a strong critic of nationalism—was struck from the list because his work, in Giertych's words, was "a promotion of homosexuality."[25]

The attacks on Prides and other manifestations of "homosexual propaganda" almost immediately catalyzed more collective action involving more participants and of a more political nature than ever before in Poland's movement. Within a week of the attacks on Poznań's 2005 march, solidarity rallies were organized in other cities, and even in cities outside of Poland.[26] Prides also became a site for demonstrating solidarity with the EU—and, for EU representatives and other international observers, of demonstrating solidarity with the movement. To understand how Prides changed in size and character, we should recall the Warsaw March of Equality from 2001 through 2003. As noted earlier, those had been small affairs that attracted little notice, serving primarily as a space to "come out" publicly. As Figure 6.1 shows, after 2004 the number of attendees kept increasing, including supportive allies in the NGO and political-party sphere, both domestic and international.[27]

Activists now framed Prides as *political* events. The 2004 ban was "an attack on democracy and human rights."[28] This new framing resonated with many Poles outside the movement, especially when accompanied by media images of Poznań police arresting peaceful demonstrators. Such images evoked emotion-laden memories of the Communists' crackdown on the Solidarity movement under martial law.[29] As one participant recounted, "The March became a demonstration against the ban, an attempt to protect democracy in general. . . . I think that discrimination and prejudice have one source, it doesn't matter if we're talking about gay people or those with a different skin color or ethnicity."[30] Warsaw's 2005 march (also banned) was advertised by activists as the "Polish Stonewall," becoming not just a venue for "coming out" but for claiming rights. Especially after 2006, it became common for members of center-left parties, such as the Social Democrats and Greens, to participate at Prides.

If the framing evident at Prides had become political and rights-oriented, it was also decidedly EU-oriented. This could be seen in the

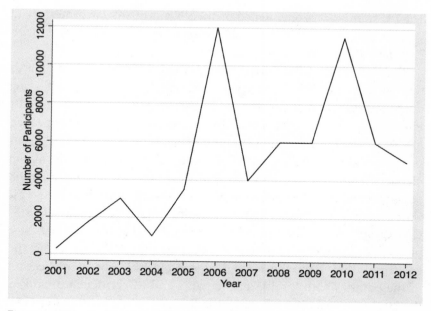

Figure 6.1. Estimated Number of Participants at Warsaw Equality Marches (2001–2012)

increasing presence of EP parliamentarians, representatives from West European parties, and other international participants. Ayoub describes the example of one Berlin-based association, the ironically titled Warschauerpakt, that arranged for Germans to participate in and donate to Warsaw Prides between 2006 and 2009.[31] Organizers explicitly identified the event with EU norms: at a parade that I attended in 2009, one parade vehicle was emblazoned with the phrase *Europa = tolerancja* (Europe = tolerance). Tomasz Bączkowski, head of the Equality Foundation, which took over organization of the Warsaw march in 2005, summed up the framing strategy thus:

> We can sell our membership [in ILGA-Europe] very well in negotiations with politicians. The truth is that nobody in Poland knows what ILGA-Europe is, but if I tell the Polish members of parliament that I am supported by an organization representing lesbians and gays in the whole EU and we are about 80 million people, then they think, "Oh, this is important."[32]

The EU framing was augmented by the slogans of antigay protestors; at Warsaw's 2004 march hecklers alternated jeers like "Gas the gays" with "Lesbians and faggots are ideal citizens of the European Union."[33]

The alignment of the Prides' rights frame with that of EU standards was aided most decisively, however, by the two EP resolutions criticizing the bans mentioned earlier. The hard right's response was furious. In the Polish parliament's debate over a formal response, the body's Speaker, Marek Jurek (PiS), declared that the EP had mistaken "moral disapproval of homosexuality" for "homophobia," thereby "promoting an ideology of homosexual communities." Zbigniew Giżyński, another PiS deputy, stated that the resolution ignored "the beautiful history of Polish tolerance" and, further, that "it seeks to counter Christian values."[34] Conservative newspapers were livid: the daily *Fakt* published front-page pictures of Polish MEPs who had voted for the resolution under the headline "They Betrayed Poland."[35] Among LPR, the identification of the parades with foreign participants and EU criticism provoked the strongest reactions of all. Just before Warsaw's 2006 march, MP Wojciech Wierzejski declared, "I do not care if some politicians from Germany are going to participate. They are not serious politicians. They are gay. . . . When they get hit in the head with a club once or twice, they will never come again."[36] As heated as the debate was, politicians outside of PiS and LPR were unwilling to attack the EU so directly. The final resolution—which rebutted the EP and stated that even using terms like homophobia was "an imposition of the language of the homosexual political movement on Europe"—was carried by government votes, while SLD opposed (54 votes) and PO abstained (101 votes).[37] Though this was tepid support for LGBT-rights activists, both the SLD and PO would gradually move closer to the movement.

As the Prides mobilized large-scale protest in a hostile political environment, they became a forum for organizational cooperation and development. As we saw previously, the organizer of the first Warsaw Equality Marches (2001–2003) had been an informally structured and primarily apolitical group, ILGCN-Poland. The challenges of responding to bans and violence prompted a whole new organizational structure. In 2005, KPH, Lambda Warszawa, and ILGCN-Poland banded together to form the Equality Foundation (Fundacja Równości), which became a member of ILGA-Europe and enjoyed ties to LGBT groups in

Germany, especially.[38] It helped coordinate the organization of Prides across Poland and mount legal challenges against bans and other obstacles.[39] These challenges proved successful, as Polish courts struck down bans in Poznań and Warsaw. Demonstrating the movement's growing professionalization, activists also took their case against the Warsaw ban to the European Court of Human Rights; it ruled in their favor in May 2007, establishing a binding precedent against future such bans in all of Europe. This verdict removed obstacles to organization and allowed activists to train their sights on specific issues such as registered partnerships, as described below.

Besides the Equality Foundation, this period saw a new wave of LGBT groups being founded, spanning the spectrum from informal/grass roots to technocratic/policy-oriented. On the former end of the spectrum was UFA, a feminist-LGBT community group based in Warsaw. Trans-Fuzja, founded in 2007, was one of the region's first specifically transgender NGOs. On the lobbying end of the spectrum, there was the Polish Society of Anti-Discrimination Law (Polskie Towarzystwo Prawa Antydyskryminacyjnego), which was formed by activists from KPH's legal team. Generally, these groups were still rather small, locally based, and lacking in direct ties to EU networks,[40] but as had been the case in the Czech movement's heyday, when SOHO had coordinated a national network of smaller groups of varying orientations and capacity, the new Polish groups were able to coordinate their efforts in service-provision, lobbying, and community-building through KPH.

KPH was rapidly increasing in professionalization and size in this period. After 2004, it set up a permanent office in Warsaw.[41] To put this in perspective, a permanent office space is a luxury not often found among East European activist groups.[42] KPH nationalized its network, establishing branches in each of the country's 16 regions. As described earlier, KPH's internal structure had been relatively informal during its first years, characterized by collective decision making, lack of internal differentiation, volunteer-based, and lacking full-time or professional staff. After 2004, this changed to suit the group's expanding network and more ambitious goals. KPH developed a functionally differentiated structure, with groups specializing in youth outreach, political lobbying, legal support and analysis, international coordination, antidiscrimination policy, and cultural/artistic projects. It also gained a formalized internal hierarchy with a Central Council of Members, a Board of Associates, a Review Committee, and even a Disciplinary Council.[43] By 2008, KPH employed four to five full-time employees and had an active membership of some 200, bigger than any of its counterparts. No other Polish LGBT group at the time had paid staff.[44] With support from the EU, ILGA-Europe, the Open Society Foundations, and others, KPH published sophisticated reports on government policy and the legal and social situation of Poland's sexual minorities. Where the government failed to live up to EU obligations, as for example in the establishment of an antidiscrimination office, KPH persistently lobbied the Commission for action. Further, KPH provided legal assistance to citizens facing discrimination, helping win at least two high-profile cases in 2007.[45]

During this period, the movement became increasingly engaged with the project of same-sex registered partnerships. To recall, this goal had long since become the Czech movement's raison d'etre. It had appeared at various points in the Polish movement's development up to this point, but it had neither resonated nor met with success. In its 2000 election campaign, SLD made vague promises about partnerships legislation—in addition to liberalizing Poland's highly restrictive abortion law—but once in power it dropped work on both. SLD's Maria Szyszkowska had unsuccessfully proposed same-sex partnerships in 2002–2004. During the 2000s, the campaign for partnerships had lived on in a kind of suspended animation in parliament. The PO-led government elected in 2007 continued its quiet avoidance of LGBT-rights issues by voting to keep the remnants of Szyszkowska's proposal from consideration by parliament. SLD continued to consider some form of registered partnerships in 2008–2009, though these halfhearted proposals did not progress beyond the discussion stage. Polish activists lacked committed political allies to support the project.[46]

Despite the established parties' foot-dragging, the period of movement-building following hard-right backlash led to renewed attention to registered partnerships by NGOs and advocacy groups. In 2009, the Initiative for Registered Partnerships (Grupa Inicjatywna ds. Związków Partnerskich) brought together representatives of KPH, Lambda Warszawa, and the Polish Greens.[47] For two years, it convened town-hall meetings throughout Poland to gather feedback on a legislative proposal. It is worth pausing here to note the differences between the Polish and

Czech campaigns for partnerships. As we saw in the previous chapter, the Czech campaign was undertaken by two rival advocacy groups and, in the absence of grassroots mobilization, took the form of persuading members of parliament. Polish activists lacked comparable connections with parliamentary parties and, therefore, made the campaign a grassroots one. Partnerships became a prominent demand at Prides, where they became imbued with the same EU resonance that characterized the parades themselves. For example, the first banner at the head of the 2010 EuroPride read "We demand a civil partnerships law."[48] The parade's main organizer, Tomasz Bączkowski of the Equality Foundation, declared registered partnerships (and improved antidiscrimination policy) the parade's policy goal.[49]

The different components of movement-building described above—internal solidarity, participation, political orientation, professionalization, and robust shows of solidarity by allies—came together most vividly in Warsaw's hosting of the 2010 EuroPride parade, the first time a postcommunist city hosted this Europe-wide event. It was organized by the Equality Foundation and drew participants estimated variously from 8,000 to 15,000.[50] The week of events leading up to the parade itself drew an estimated 30,000 people.[51] The event's very name declared the movement's EU framing, and the heavy presence of representatives from the EP, embassies, and West European activist groups strongly reinforced this frame.[52] As Ulrike Lunacek, an Austrian MEP, declared to the crowd, "Warsaw, Europe is proud of you!"[53]

While the presence of EU allies was impossible to miss, it should not obscure the significant show of support among domestic allies and the movement's pivot from demands about inclusion in the public sphere to more concrete demands about policy. Prior to the parade itself, the organizers held a week of public discussions and cultural events throughout Warsaw. These included panel discussions on EU antidiscrimination law, same-sex partnerships, and LGBT provisions in international law. A panel devoted to schools included representatives from the Polish Teachers' Union, one of the country's biggest unions.[54] As in previous years, a contingent of SLD politicians appeared on the floats alongside the organizers.[55]

As a venue for spotlighting domestic allies, EuroPride was more significant for showcasing the support of media and cultural elites than political parties, however. The country's biggest newspaper, *Gazeta Wyborcza*, lavished favorable coverage for over a week. Though the paper is considered left-leaning, even LGBT activists were surprised by its coverage. I kept an inventory of articles during the week of events surrounding EuroPride: every day the paper devoted a minimum of two solid pages—approximately five articles on average—to the parade or related topics. On the day of the parade, it printed a special four-page insert in both Polish and English, which it distributed for free. The following day, approximately 10 full pages (out of 52 total) in the paper's main sections covered the parade. One editor even joined the parade in drag, riding in the organizers' float and delivering a speech. He also contributed an article on the experience in the following day's edition.[56]

Outside the print media, EuroPride highlighted allies among cultural institutions, most notably the National Museum of Art, which opened a major exhibition coinciding with the event entitled *Ars Homo Erotica*. It is hard to overstate the significance of this exhibition, which displayed art with LGBT resonances from within the museum's collection. As the *national* museum in the *capital* city, it is Poland's central repository of canonical works celebrating the nation. In a section entitled "A Time of Struggle," the exhibition also showcased movements to expand LGBT rights in postcommunist Europe.[57] Surprisingly, there was little political outcry when the exhibition opened. The most visible exception was a PiS politician, Stanisław Pięta, who complained that "[t]he Director [of the museum] wants to turn a temple of art into a public toilet. The museum is financed from public money and cannot be a tool of demoralization in the hands of a marginal, isolated group."[58] While Pięta's comments would have been commonplace during the Kaczyński government, what was most striking about them in 2010 was that, among national-level politicians, they were limited to him. Indeed, in a public debate held at the museum on the subject "Homosexuality and Social Change," the curator Paweł Leszkowicz posed the question: "Why the silence surrounding this exhibition?"[59]

Poles had grown used to attacks like Pięta's over the previous years, and though the movement's most prominent new allies were in the cultural and media spheres, changes were also becoming evident in the political-party sphere by this time. The hyperbolically homophobic language of LPR had become rare.[60] LPR itself was no longer a political force. In the

2007 elections, LPR's support shrank to 1.3 percent, far below the minimum threshold for parliamentary representation and, even more importantly, below the minimum to receive state funding. The new government was formed by the center-right, pro-Europe PO. For PO, one lesson of the elections was that antigay politics is not a winning electoral strategy.[61] That said, PO did not take its pro-Europe platform as far as actively supporting LGBT rights; rather, it avoided saying anything at all about the issue.[62] Even though, in 2007, PiS increased its vote share by taking votes from LPR, PO's decisive victory suggested the wisdom of toning down antigay rhetoric.

Some five years after hard-right backlash had escalated from the rhetorical to the political, the movement had emerged much the stronger. It commanded territorial reach, could mobilize large-scale grassroots participation, and had a highly professionalized core. Further, it enjoyed outsized visibility in national politics, where it had come to symbolize a secularizing, European vision of Poland. It did not, however, have firm political-party allies, and in terms of policy goals, its prospects were unpromising. This too was about to change.

Forging Political Connections

Within two years of EuroPride, Poland's parliament was debating several registered-partnerships proposals, one of them authored by a party including MPs who had been leading figures in the LGBT movement. Other postcommunist LGBT movements had debated registered partnerships in parliament by this time as well, but never as representatives *in* the parliament. No other movement had elected LGBT MPs, much less on a program of greater tolerance of homosexuality. Regarding the last threshold of movement development described in Chapter 1, Poland had gone farther than any of its counterparts.

This section examines how this remarkable breakthrough occurred. Three steps were necessary for crossing this threshold in Poland. First, LGBT rights had to take on broader symbolic value as a kind of litmus test of secular, modernizing European values. As such, LGBT rights could be utilized by political entrepreneurs as a signature issue against hard-right elements espousing an exclusionary-nationalist, Euroskeptic vision of Polish identity. Second, the movement needed to be sufficiently organized to create a registered partnerships strategy that could offer political entrepreneurs and potential allies a campaign-ready issue. Third, there needed to be a political entrepreneur willing to take the risk of allying with the movement and using registered partnerships as a tool against the hard-right PiS for blocking a "modern" Poland and against the center-right PO for not standing up to PiS.

There was no small amount of contingency in all of this. Had a political entrepreneur not allied with the movement, Poland likely would have continued along the trajectory it had taken since 2007's elections. Namely, PO would have avoided LGBT issues while also condemning antigay politics. As it happened, though, two important events occurred. First, in 2009 Janusz Palikot, a self-made millionaire MP from PO, split with his party for being insufficiently liberal and too beholden to the Church, founding a new party called Your Movement (Twój Ruch, or TR). Second, on April 10, 2010, an airplane carrying President Lech Kaczyński and some 95 members of the Polish cabinet, state, and cultural institutions crashed en route to the Belarusian city of Smolensk, where they were to have participated in the commemoration of the execution of thousands of Polish officers by the Soviets during World War II. The crash left no survivors, and it triggered a new surge of defensive nationalism, especially by PiS, effectively casting the 2011 elections as a choice not between parties but between visions of Poland in the world. In this reopening of Poland's culture wars, homosexuality resonated again as an identity marker.

To say that contingency played a role in pushing the Polish movement further across the threshold of political activism than any of its regional counterparts is not to say this was a case of historical accident. Had the movement not become organized before this point and had not backlash helped frame LGBT rights in terms of European norms, Palikot would likely not have used the issue to frame his anti-PiS, anticlerical, and antinationalist outsider movement. TR's surprising electoral success in turn changed the behavior of the heretofore recalcitrant PO and SLD. Fearful of losing support to TR, they at last engaged the issue of registered partnerships, perhaps not as enthusiastic allies but as partners enabling a policy debate. As a related theoretical point, the circumstances of the LGBT movement's political breakthrough highlight again how much the diffusion of transnational norms regarding an issue like homosexuality into domestic politics differs from the conventional understanding of social learning and norm fit.[63] TR's electoral success was predicated on an intensely polarizing, and even personalized, conflict between the new party and PiS. This polarization increased the visibility and resonance of minority rights just as the hard right's conflation of anti-EU and antigay rhetoric had in the early 2000s.

This section traces out this argument in three parts. First, it describes TR's origins and its path to LGBT ally. It then describes how TR framed its campaign and the kind of voters it drew. Finally, it discusses how, following TR's electoral breakthrough, registered partnerships finally entered parliamentary politics in earnest, attracting allies among heretofore indifferent parties.

TR is best understood as a niche party built around a strong leader. Niche parties have been defined in terms of the following traits: the deemphasis of class-based politics; the espousal of unconventional issues; and a narrower issue focus than mainstream parties.[64] It was also an outsider party, whose social-movement origins stood in plain view. Unlike traditional parties, niche parties do not attempt to appeal to the widest possible swathe of voters: thus, they are less likely to compromise. Despite these features, niche parties can strongly shape traditional parties' behavior, especially if they champion issues that established parties seek to ignore.[65]

Any description of TR's history must emphasize how closely it was linked to its founder, the self-made millionaire Janusz Palikot. Indeed, he originally named the party after himself, the Palikot Movement.[66] Later, as the party became more established, the name was changed to Your Movement. However, an equally striking feature of TR was the degree to which each stage of its development occurred in opposition to the champion of socially conservative, national-Catholic Poland, PiS. This clash between worldviews—secular libertarianism vs. patriotic Christian values—is how Palikot defined the party, even if, with characteristic braggadocio, he initially named it after himself.

Curiously, Palikot's entry into politics was inconspicuous and showed little sign of the style to come later. In 2005, he used his wealth to win a seat in parliament in the Lubelski region as part of the then still-new PO. He looked like the typical PO politician—middle of the road and not someone identified with "progressive values."[67] For his first two years in parliament, Palikot's main work was on a commission to build transparency in the state administration. In 2007, however, he began his rise to prominence by criticizing the nationalism-tinged social conservatism of PiS and its coalition partners. In April 2007, he appeared at a news conference wearing a T-shirt that read "I am gay" on one side and "I am with the SLD" on the other. (The hard right equated SLD with ex-Communist.) Palikot explained that he wished to draw attention to minority rights, especially LGBT rights, which his party, PO, should be doing more to protect. These two phrases were anathema to the philosophy of the Kaczyński-led government, which defined itself as Christian nationalist and anticommunist. No politician had ever so brazenly challenged the taboos of the Polish hard right. The slogan "I am gay," while not strictly accurate, symbolized a new political identity: anticlerical, antinationalist, and iconoclastic. These became the defining elements of Palikot's movement and of a political career sustained by provoking controversy to generate publicity: it began with homosexuality.

The political bombshell of the Smolensk airline disaster was another turning point for Palikot. Among the right, accusations swirled of Russian involvement in the plane's crash, while the left suggested criminal negligence by the government in planning the flight. Palikot used the conspiracy theories and intimations that Poland's sovereignty was under attack to push his critique of PiS to new levels. Charging that Kaczyński himself was responsible for the crash—for insisting that the pilot land the plane in bad weather[68]—he established the Movement for the Support of Palikot, which was intended to represent Poles seeking an investigation of the circumstances leading to the crash. He announced in a televised interview that "the Janusz Palikot whom you all know died with Lech Kaczyński on the 10th of April."[69]

On October 2, 2010, the movement organized a founding congress. It drew over 4,000 attendees, including well-known political, cultural, and media figures. The congress launched a political initiative, "Modern Poland," which had the following core goals: reform of party-finance and electoral law; ending the immunity of parliamentarians; allowing for Internet voting; the withdrawal of religion from schools; the introduction of free contraception; and the legalization of registered partnerships.[70] Regarding partnerships, Palikot could draw on the now advanced policy groundwork laid by Poland's LGBT movement:

as mentioned earlier, since 2009 activists had been organizing town-hall meetings through the Initiative for Registered Partnerships. Within days, Palikot resigned from PO, which he accused of propagating conservatism, and launched TR as a political party for the 2011 elections. This organizing effort took the form of town-hall meetings throughout Poland, which were highly visible and well attended. Palikot increased TR's visibility by allying with and promoting controversial public figures in the campaign, not least the transgender activist Anna Grodzka; the leader of Poland's largest gay-rights NGO, Robert Biedroń; the pro-abortion campaigner Wanda Nowicka, and the editor of a prominent anticlerical journal, Roman Kotliński.[71] The campaign's tone regarding issues like homosexuality and gender was captured in this blog post by Palikot in October 2010:

> The bishops cannot threaten [us], cannot frighten [us], cannot promise excommunication. . . . Don't try to teach us parenting because you know nothing about it. Don't fight with freedom. Go back to the churches. Stop taking money for teaching religion. Listen to the people. Be humble.[72]

TR was not the first Polish party to seek secular-minded voters. SLD, successor to the Communist Party, had done so earlier, but it had also gone out of its way to avoid the charge of anticlericalism, avoiding direct criticism of and even cooperating with the Church.[73] Never had a party taken so hostile a stance toward the Church as TR.

As TR launched into the 2011 campaign, Palikot's name recognition loomed large, but the party's program was also very clearly defined.[74] Specifically, it highlighted the following positions:[75]

- tolerance of homosexuality;
- advocacy for same-sex partnerships and adoption;
- advocacy for liberal positions on family-related issues: for example, sex education, premarital sex, and contraception;
- gender equality;
- legalization of soft narcotics;
- liberal positions on the death penalty, euthanasia, abortion, and in vitro fertilization.

One would be hard put to outline a more postmaterialist political program than this, and as research by political scientists confirmed, it resonated strongly with the party's core electorate of young voters. In one study, a plurality (29 percent) of student supporters gave "worldview" as the fundamental reason for their support. A further 23 percent mentioned TR's "youth policies," and a further 15 percent the policy program as a whole. By comparison, only 10 percent mentioned Palikot's personality to justify their support.[76] As the researchers concluded, TR's appeal was "the result of its different style of communicating with the voter . . . a style accentuating those questions of world-view that in the political sphere have largely remained either taboo, unpopular, or politically incorrect."[77] Election exit polls confirmed these results among a broader swath of supporters (see Table 6.1). The largest group of voters supported TR because it represented an alternative to the established parties. About a quarter supported it because of its secularism. The third-most cited reason was its "modern and modernizing vision of Poland." These sources of support far outstrip economic program and candidate wealth, the latter of which can be seen as a proxy for anticorruption credentials.

Though TR received enormous attention during the campaign, few expected it to challenge the established political parties: PO, PiS, SLD, and the Peasant Party. In opinion polling through 2010 and 2011, it re-

TABLE 6.1. Exit Polling among TR Voters in Poland's 2011 Parliamentary Elections

Question: "Why did you vote for Your Movement?" Because . . .	Percent	Number
It offers an alternative to the parliamentary parties.	35.7	41
It has anticlerical policy positions. It is for the permanent separation of church and state.	22.6	26
It represents a modern and modernizing vision of Poland.	17.4	20
It has more free-market-oriented policy positions than other parties.	7.8	9
Janusz Palikot is wealthy. He is not in politics for material reasons.	7	8
It is for enlarging the sphere of individual values.	4.3	5
For other reasons.	5.2	6
Total	100	115

Source: Wojtasik 2012, 170.

ceived at most 1–2 percent support.[78] The elections brought a stunning result, 10.02 percent of the vote, vaulting it past the two oldest parties in the political system: the Peasant Party and SLD (see Table 6.2). Adding to the drama, the two prominent LGBT activists Robert Biedroń of KPH and Anna Grodzka of the transgender NGO Trans-Fuzja were elected on TR's list.

Once in parliament, TR was in a position to introduce a new logic into LGBT activism. The election of prominent activists conferred legitimacy by representing LGBT persons as political actors in systems in which previously they were not only frozen out, but not even recognized.[79] Second, TR's breakthrough reshaped party competition around LGBT issues, forcing the established parties—other than PiS, of course—to end their strategy of quietly ignoring the issue. Because of TR's advocacy, PO and SLD had already had to engage the issue in the election campaign: TR used the policy to appeal to voters who had previously voted PO or SLD but were disappointed by their tepid liberalism and opposition to PiS's exclusionary nationalism. Feeling this pressure, SLD presented a draft proposal in parliament during the campaign. TR had already stated that registered partnerships would be one of its first legislative items if elected. In response, PO leader Donald Tusk declared that he believed that parliament should adopt partnerships legislation.[80]

After the elections, registered partnerships, as well as LGBT issues more broadly, remained a pivotal issue of programmatic differentiation on the left and the center-left of the party spectrum. Within the next two

TABLE 6.2. Poland's 2011 Parliamentary Election Results by Party

	Vote share (%)	Seats
Civic Platform	39.2	207
Law and Justice	29.9	157
Your Movement	10.0	40
Polish People's Party	8.4	28
Democratic Left Alliance	8.2	27
German Minority Party	0.2	1
Total		460

Source: Parties and Election in Europe database, www.parties-and-elections.eu/poland.html.

years, there were three full-fledged parliamentary proposals (and votes) on the issue—more than in all the years previous. In January 2012, TR and SLD jointly submitted two draft proposals, and in April of the same year PO followed with its own version. Despite the Tusk government's imprimatur, even this last proposal failed—brought down by a mutiny within PO, with 46 party MPs voting against their leadership. The proposal failed by a narrow margin of 228–211.

As disappointing as this was to activists, they could take heart from the remarkable progress they had made from several years earlier. Where before the PM had claimed that the state had a duty to prevent homosexuals "infecting" others, now the PM was sponsoring partnerships legislation, arguing that "[y]ou can't question the existence of such people (living in homosexual partnerships) and you can't argue against the people who decide to live in such [a] way."[81] The terms and terrain of activism had changed fundamentally.

Czech Republic: Back to the State, a Movement Co-opted?

On March 15, 2006, the Czech parliament enacted registered partnerships. The law took effect on July 1, and already that summer the first couples were making their relationships official. It was the culmination of a long and draining lobbying campaign by the Czech movement, which at the time of the first parliamentary proposals in 1997 had been one of the region's best organized. It had been draining not because of hard-right opposition and public vitriol but because of the determined delaying tactics of a minority parliamentary faction and a growing schism within the movement about political goals. Just months after the law took effect, Hromada gave an interview announcing the dissolution of the most visible movement group, Gay Initiative, of which he was president. With partnerships, said Hromada, the movement had achieved the last of its goals. With the fight behind it, the movement's task now was to "maintain what has been achieved."[82]

Hromada's observation came in a December 2006 interview, but even from the perspective of 2012 (or today), one could say that in policy terms Hromada got what he wished for. The movement's signature policy gain, registered partnerships, has been preserved—and indeed has never come under threat. In terms of activism's organization, however, the gains since 1989 had largely unraveled by 2010, leaving the social-movement terrain surprisingly similar to what it had looked like in the early 1990s. First, the movement lacked a politically oriented and professionalized SMO core that could coordinate local- and service-oriented groups across territory. Less than a year after GI dissolved, its rival GLL also dissolved.[83] While cultural associations, sports clubs, service groups, and film festivals remained active, linkages among them took the form of informal, irregular, and often personalized coordination.[84] One could no longer speak of a *national* movement nor, without important qualifications, of a *political* movement. The movement's orientation toward the authorities took a very different direction than the Polish one. As we saw above, Polish activism had entered the electoral arena through building links with specific parties and representing LGBT interests to the state via institutionalized channels. In the Czech Republic, former leaders from GI and GLL were able to exploit personal connections with the government to serve as "state consultants" on LGBT issues. This occurred through the establishment of an appointed advisory committee on minority rights; however, activists served on it as individuals, not as representatives of NGOs or other organized interests. The arrangement was not very effective, and was even criticized by some as a kind of state co-optation—leading it too to fade.

On all three dimensions of movement development, this was a period of deinstitutionalization and demobilization. LGBT issues did not resonate in the public sphere with anything like their intensity in Poland. Despite manifest deficiencies in the form in which registered partnerships had been legislated, little to no progress was made in addressing them. All of these problems received tacit acknowledgment by Czech activists themselves when, in 2010–2011, a new generation of activists attempted to refound the movement. These demobilizing trends complicate generalizations about the breadth of constituencies represented in the movement at this time. While gays and lesbians remained the most visible, a more inclusive understanding of identities could be discerned in the naming of activist groups and events. For example, in 2009 the Brno-based STUD recast its annual film festival from "gay and lesbian" to "queer."[85] Likewise, local Pride events in Brno and Tabor in 2008 and 2009 used the rubric "queer." The government committee to be discussed below was the Working Group for the Issues of *Sexual*

Minorities. This more inclusive self-identification was also evident in the naming of GI and GLL's eventual replacement, PROUD (Platform for Equality, Recognition, and Diversity). After analyzing the consequences of GI and GLL's dissolution on the movement's organization, this section will close by describing the trajectory of post-2010 activism, focusing on the continuing challenges that it faces maintaining visibility and attracting participation—the twin legacies of communism that had loomed so large in the 1990s and that, in Poland, hard-right backlash had enabled activists to overcome.

The overarching political dynamics of the lobbying campaign for registered partnerships did not change appreciably after the Czech Republic became an EU member. First, the hard-right remained irrelevant; consequently, neither homosexuality nor partnerships were framed in EU terms. Parliamentary debate on partnerships often included references to their forms in other European countries, but the issue was not framed, as in Poland, as an emblem of accepting an EU identity and rejecting a nationalist one. Second, the campaign took place almost entirely in parliament and was defined by two main divides. On the one hand, there was a small faction of Christian Democrats and scattered MPs from other parties who used parliamentary procedure to block progress on the bill, and, on the other hand, there was the largely sympathetic (or indifferent) remainder, who formed the majority. The second divide was, as described earlier, within the movement itself between "pragmatists" associated with Hromada and GI and the more radical GLL, who preferred an expansive form of partnerships.

It often seemed that the sharpest language in the registered-partnerships debate occurred not in parliament but within the movement itself. Hromada and GI were adamant about leaving adoption out of the proposal—which was particularly upsetting to feminist and lesbian activists. Also contentious were Hromada's frequent statements that Czech society was essentially tolerant.[86] (This, he argued, was why it was unnecessary to march in the streets for rights.) The tensions within the movement boiled over into the mainstream press, where Hromada's critics questioned his competence in representing the movement and in lobbying for partnerships. In an article published in the widely read weekly *Respekt*, GLL member Jan Bretl wrote, "From his [Hromada's] appearances during the discussions of the proposal for a law on registered partnerships (allegedly GI's main goal), it has to be clear to everyone that he doesn't know its content." Bretl ended by saying that Hromada had "without question accomplished much for this minority in the Czech Republic. But the question is whether it wouldn't be better if he now went into a well-deserved 'gay retirement.'"[87] Another critic wrote that Hromada "didn't work together with a single lesbian woman or a single lesbian group."[88]

Despite the tensions evident in these quotes, GI and GLL both supported the partnerships proposal sponsored by a group of 11 politicians in 2005 from across the party spectrum: the Social Democrats, the center-right Freedom Union, the center-right ODS, and the Communist Party. The attitude of the more radical GLL was best captured by the following public statement: "The legislative proposal is not ideal in the opinion of GLL, but its passage by the government would be a significant step for lesbians and gays."[89] Fortunately, given the movement's internal tensions, the political environment among the parliamentary factions was accommodating. Only the Christian Democrats opposed registered partnerships in principle. The leadership of the two biggest parties, ČSSD and ODS, left it up to their individual deputies to decide, though ČSSD's leadership strongly supported the proposal. The Communists, somewhat surprisingly, took the most consistently favorable position. Both GI and GLL worked methodically to cultivate the support of individual MPs, to revise the proposal based on their feedback, and to bring it up for voting. The Social Democratic government successfully shepherded it through both the Chamber of Deputies and the Senate with support from across the party spectrum. At the final stage, President Václav Klaus (ODS) issued a surprise veto.[90] In a dramatic set of votes, his veto was overturned by a single vote.

Though it was a major accomplishment and testament to the perseverance of LGBT-rights groups, it is important to realize the legislation's limitations: it left out such important issues as inheritance, social security rights, common assets between partners, parenting rights, and adoption.[91] Due to a quirk in the law, a same-sex couple would be unable to adopt a child, whereas a single LGBT person could. Given these gaps, a government committee on minorities policy described its achievement as "mainly of symbolic value."[92] The decision of both GI and GLL to dissolve themselves after the legislation's passage was all the more significant given its weaknesses. Who would now mount a campaign to address these shortcomings?

GI and GLL's dissolution created a vacuum of political activism that lasted for at least five years. Rather than disappear entirely, however, activism changed form—thanks to the unusually accommodative nature of the Czech state. In 2007, a new cabinet post was created, the minister for human rights and national minorities (without portfolio). The post was created by the Greens, a small party with a progressive-secular program that had entered government in 2006. The Greens' appointee was Dr. Džamila Stehlíková, who as an official in the Czech Institute of Health had been a long-time collaborator with LGBT-rights activists in the area of HIV/AIDS prevention. Stehlíková established the Working Group for the Issues of Sexual Minorities within the government's advisory Council for Human Rights.[93] The Working Group comprised around 20 members, some of whom came from the activist network and others of whom represented state ministries and universities. Hromada served on the committee and as the chief of Stehlíková's team of advisors. The Working Group issued several reports and made recommendations to the government.[94]

While, in principle, the Working Group for Sexual Minorities was a potentially important tool for exercising voice in policy making, it proved to have several deep flaws. Its recommendations were nonbinding, and because Stehlíková lacked a vote in the cabinet, she was not an effective advocate there. Moreover, the Greens were a minor party within an otherwise conservative government; the Christian Democrats, whose opposition to registered partnerships we saw above, were the other junior partner. After a government reshuffling in January 2009, Dr. Stehlíková was replaced by a politician without connections to the LGBT movement and generally considered less supportive of LGBT rights. The Working Group was also problematic because it undermined the committee members' links to the grass roots. Maintaining these links put them, as state appointees, in a bind. Their role was as expert consultants, not representatives, and emphasizing the latter undermined the committee's already weak position vis-à-vis the cabinet. When the committee drew attention to the partnership law's inadequacies, it was criticized by some as an "insiders' club" and a "state lobbying group." A 2009 news article quoted an anonymous source who described its meetings "as characterized by a very familiar atmosphere (with a first-name informality among members) and the dominant role of Jiří Hromada."[95] A center-right former labor minister, Petr Nečas (ODS), said, "Rather than a government organ it is necessary to see [the committee] as an interest-group lobby, as a concrete minority interest. There is nothing illegitimate about lobbying in a democratic society, but a lobbying group ought not be represented as a state structure."[96] My interviews in 2011 elicited general feelings of disappointment with the Working Group, whose meetings had become infrequent and whose policy recommendations had not been taken up by the government.

Outside of the marginal role of the Working Group, LGBT advocates had largely withdrawn from the public sphere after GI's and GLL's dissolution. A relatively rich array of film festivals and sporting and cultural associations remained, and there were even several Prides in smaller cities around the country beginning in 2008.[97] In terms of independent political advocacy, however, there was an activism vacuum—which was most evident in the lack of further pressure aimed at addressing the partnerships law's shortcomings. In 2011, a number of younger activists, some identified with the defunct GLL, sought to reestablish the movement politically by founding two organizations. Significantly, these groups defined themselves outside of the state, framed more radical demands, and attempted to cultivate grassroots participation over professionalized lobbying. The first, Prague Pride O.S., organized the first-ever Pride in the capital, an event of great symbolic significance given earlier insistence that Prides were unnecessarily provocative and would alienate allies.[98] In May 2011, a new national-level advocacy and lobbying group was formed, PROUD (Platforma pro rovnoprávnost uznání a diverzitu, or Platform for Equality, Recognition, and Diversity).[99] It began as a group organized on Facebook. Most of the founding members knew each other from serving on the Working Group for Sexual Minorities. Neither Prague Pride nor PROUD included the earlier generation of activists, people such as Jiří Hromada, Ivo Procházka, or Džamila Stehlíková, who had married state support with political lobbying.

PROUD's mission statement challenged the perceived tolerance of Czech society, setting goals that were aspirational rather than achievable in the near term. These included same-sex marriage; adoption and parenting rights; broader education about homosexuality in schools, including support for coming out by minors; and combating transphobia.[100] Thus, it departed from the strategy-of-small-steps pragmatism of earlier Czech advocacy. Significantly, its members allied themselves with the organizers of the first Prague Pride in 2011. Compared with its Polish counterpart KPH or even earlier Czech advocacy groups, PROUD began with meager organizational resources. It had no more than 20 to 30 members. Though it had legal status, it lacked an office or paid staff. Given its underdeveloped structure, it was not positioned to seek external grants, including EU ones. PROUD's connections with politicians, state institutions like the Health Ministry, and the media were by all accounts weaker than SOHO's or GI's: journalists seeking comment on LGBT issues still tended to call Hromada for comment, not PROUD. While earlier Czech advocacy groups had prided themselves on their political connections, PROUD prized its independence.

In sum, PROUD and Prague Pride offered a more social-movement vision of activism than Czech LGBT-rights groups had pursued since the turn to policy lobbying around 2000. It was a departure from precedent, but one that was undertaken in a context where the perceived success of the movement (because of registered partnerships) and the lack of organized hard-right opposition raised again the perennial challenges of activism in postcommunist civil society: finding resonant frames and gaining visibility; mobilizing participation and maintaining internal solidarity; and bringing in outside allies. The concluding chapter will discuss the movement's record in dealing with these challenges since 2012, but the next chapter will first probe the wider scope of my argument about the interaction between external leverage and domestic backlash by exploring some additional cases that vary in terms of societal openness and the character of backlash.

Conclusion

Social movements are vulnerable and fragile creations, especially in new democracies overcoming legacies of a weak civil society. Disagreement on goals and tactics may split them into uncooperative factions. As with all collective endeavors, movements are vulnerable to free riding by their constituents, particularly if the movement's grievances appear to lose

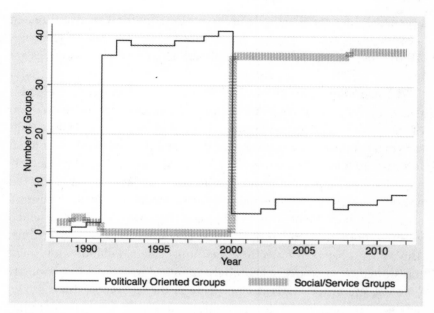

Figure 6.2. Number of Czech LGBT Groups by Primary Orientation (1988–2012)

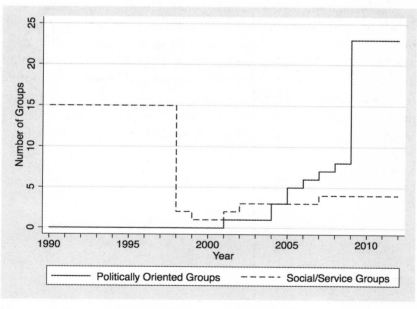

Figure 6.3. Number of Polish LGBT Groups by Primary Orientation (1990–2012)

urgency. Professionalization and institutionalization can also threaten movements if they cause the leadership to lose touch with the base. All of these vulnerabilities are amplified when financial resources are tenuous.

The demobilization of the Czech movement exemplifies these vulnerabilities: its signature policy victory was followed by the dissolution of the major rights groups. The Polish movement, by contrast, built strikingly robust organization over the same period, moving from an informal to a professional, local to national, and apolitical to electorally mobilized movement—all despite enjoying less favorable societal attitudes regarding homosexuality. Figures 6.2 and 6.3 distill the overall arcs of each movement's trajectory by creating counts of LGBT-oriented groups—both predominantly political and apolitical ones—over time. The contrast between trajectories is unmistakable. Poland's movement has shifted from an overwhelmingly apolitical orientation to a mostly political one. After nearly disappearing in the late 1990s, it has grown steadily. The number of groups comprising the Czech movement has been stable since the early 1990s, but their orientation has switched in the opposite direction, from politics to constituents.

EU leverage and links to transnational networks were critical to the Polish outcome; however, this was not a straightforward story of international norm diffusion. Both countries were equally exposed to EU leverage, but only in Poland did leverage shape the politics of homosexuality. The critical difference was the Polish hard right, whose opposition to transnational norms reframed the issue, built solidarity within the movement by threatening the "protective surround," and drew in allies for whom LGBT rights became a litmus test of Poland's place in Europe.

Exploring Alternative Trajectories

Hungary, Slovakia, and Romania

If you want your teenage son to make his first sexual experience with a bearded older man, you should vote for the SZDSZ [Socialist Party].
—Zsolt Semjén, Fidesz MP in 2005

We want to enter Europe, not Sodom and Gomorrah.
—Archbishop Bartolomeu Anania, Romanian Orthodox Church

Through a close comparison of Poland and the Czech Republic since 1989 the previous chapters have shown how hard-right backlashes spurred by transnational pressure can catalyze more organized and more influential LGBT-rights activism.[1] This comparison traced the mechanisms by which backlash in a closed society like Poland created an "EU boost" that extended even after formal EU leverage had weakened. The Czech Republic showed the decline of a movement that, although initially enjoying more favorable conditions for LGBT-rights activism, experienced no hard-right backlash with EU accession and, consequently, no "EU boost." This chapter expands the boundaries of comparison to include three additional East European applicant-states over the same time frame: Hungary, Slovakia, and Romania.

These country cases allow us to build out the argument that transnational leverage and hard-right backlash shape the trajectories of activism, enabling activists to build robust movements even in countries where legacies of weak civil society leave few resources for mobilization. Our theoretical expectations for each were summarized in Figure 1.4. While offering additional support for the main argument, these cases also allow us to explore variations in the character of backlash and its sequencing vis-à-vis the onset of transnational leverage.

In Hungary, the timing and magnitude of backlash closely followed the Polish example, producing similar results for the organization of activism. What differs in Hungary is the *character* of the backlash. Initially it is extraparliamentary, and later it is majoritarian (because one hard-right party's landslide election results obviate the need to find coalition partners). Thus, Hungary illuminates the dynamics of backlash outside the institutional logic of parliamentary politics typical of Europe.

Slovakia, by comparison, is a comparatively closed society that never experiences a hard-right threat to the "protective surround," and its movement traces out a similar trajectory to the Czech one. Slovakia highlights the point that there is no necessary link between societal openness/closure and hard-right backlash.

Romania offers the most challenging case of the three because it presents a different sequencing of transnational leverage and hard-right backlash. First, backlash occurred *before* the onset of leverage; second, when leverage was introduced, it was both stronger and longer-lasting than in the other cases. While these idiosyncrasies complicate Romania's placement within Figure 1.4, they are valuable theoretically because they highlight broader scope conditions in the argument. Romania shows that some minimum level of external leverage is necessary if backlash is to boost activism; otherwise, it suppresses it. Romania also allows us the opportunity to study the effects of higher-level and longer-lasting external leverage on the organization of activism. Romanian activists were able to exploit this leverage to broker unexpected policy gains, but not without cost to the more participatory and grassroots dimensions of movement-building.

Hungary: Backlash in the Streets

It is instructive to trace Hungary through my theoretical framework because, like the Czech Republic, it began the 1990s with a more supportive environment for LGBT activism, but, like Poland, after EU accession it experienced a strong hard-right backlash. Thus, Hungary allows us to consider an alternative branching of the Czech movement's developmental sequence: a movement that has achieved many of its long-sought goals, including registered partnerships, and *then* experiences a threat to its "immediate protective surround." At the outset, let us acknowledge that, for all its similarities, Hungary is not a perfect analogue with the Czech Republic because its society was not as open (see Figure 1.5). This relative closure imprinted itself on Hungarian activism in the 1990s insofar as it was never as organized or politically oriented as the Czech movement at that time. In the wake of postaccession backlash, the roles were reversed: Hungarian activism became broader in scope, more organizationally complex, and more politically mobilized.

Preaccession Hungary (1989–1997)

Like their Czech counterparts, Hungarian activists began the 1990s with the experience of associations established before 1989. State authorities had been comparatively supportive under the old regime, and this supportive attitude continued through the 1990s. Courts in particular stood out for their critical, if sometimes inconsistent, role as allies. Consequently, Hungary experienced unexpected policy gains regarding registered partnerships and labor market discrimination even before accession. Meanwhile, hard-right parties were fringe players in politics, and the issue of homosexuality had low salience in the public sphere. Reflecting the weak influence of the Catholic Church in politics, the predominant framing of homosexuality was not in the morality-charity mode, as in Poland.[2] It more resembled the Czech therapeutic mode, with the difference that the unusually proactive role of the courts added a legal-technocratic tone (see below). Before analyzing the organization of activism on the dimensions of professionalization, territorial reach, and political mobilization in the 1990s, this section will first describe how homosexuality was framed.

Initially, this framing was not much affected by the potential elements of a hard-right bloc. Before 1998, the Hungarian right was conservative-liberal.[3] The largest right party, the moderate Hungarian Democratic Forum (MDF), had been one of the major opposition groups in Hungary's transition from communism. It anchored the government until 1994, at which point the Socialists (MSZP) alternated into power. The MDF government included the much smaller Christian Democrats (KDNP), but their program was described by analysts as indistinguishable from

MDF's.[4] The most radical party was the Hungarian Justice and Life Party (MIÉP), which broke off from MDF in 1993. Cas Mudde classifies it as populist radical right, but it was a fringe player in the party system, similar to the Czech SPR-RSČ.[5] Conspicuously absent from the potential elements of a hard-right bloc was Fidesz, which at this time was a minor party described as a "classic liberal-cosmopolitan formation."[6] Homosexuality received little attention from any of these parties, whose attitude on the issue was "mostly passive."[7] Even Fidesz, which later became hostile to LGBT-rights activism, was "somehow supportive:" in a magazine survey of politicians about same-sex marriage, Fidesz's Viktor Orbán was the only politician *not* to respond negatively.[8] Also marginal in the framing of homosexuality during this period was the Catholic Church, which is predominant in Hungary. Though more relevant than its Czech counterpart, the Hungarian Church held relatively little political sway after 1989, especially compared to Poland.[9]

Far more consequential in modifying this legacy frame were the courts. Even beyond LGBT issues, Hungary's Constitutional Court was during the 1990s a major force "shaping politics through a strong rule of law-based jurisprudence that often opposed both legislative and public opinion."[10] In 1995, it unexpectedly ruled that the framework for common-law marriages was discriminatory and mandated that parliament grant same-sex couples the same protections. As Long observed, "Hungary became the only state in the world, outside Scandinavia and the Netherlands, to institute a form of domestic partnerships for same-sex couples."[11] In a second landmark ruling, in 1999 the Constitutional Court explicitly recognized discrimination on the basis of sexual orientation as covered by the Constitution's blanket ban on discrimination.[12] These decisions were far ahead of their time, especially by regional standards; however, it is important to put them in broader context. As Long has argued, neither decision could be said to be the result of lobbying by activists. Additionally, the Court's decisions were incomplete as part of a larger antidiscrimination agenda, and other courts' decisions sometimes cut in the opposite direction. For example, the Supreme Court rejected legal recognition of the LGBT group Rainbow Coalition during this time (see below). Even the Constitutional Court's progressive rulings contained ambiguities: the ruling on registered partnerships also upheld the definition of marriage as "the community of man and woman."[13]

For the better part of the 1990s, the Hungarian movement was concentrated in Budapest, predominantly service- and self-help oriented, and lacking in institutional complexity.[14] The Constitutional Court's pioneering rulings, while positive for LGBT individuals, had the effect of depriving the movement of the kind of mobilizing goals that had been central for its Czech counterpart. Until 1995, there were only two established groups, Homerosz and Lambda Budapest. The former was service oriented and constituency oriented. Founded under communism and receiving financial support from the National Health Care Organization for HIV/AIDS prevention, it retained an inward-looking "homophile" perspective, which in one analyst's words "confined homosexuality to the private sphere . . . without strengthening visibility and activism."[15] The second, Lambda Budapest, which broke off from Homerosz in 1991, was much smaller and less formal (as it lacked institutional support), but it offered a more outward-looking, politically oriented activism. It published a monthly journal, *Mások* (Others), with a circulation of 3,000, but it also organized public events like World AIDS Day and petitions to the authorities.[16] It was Lambda Budapest that filed the case that led to the Constitutional Court's surprising 1996 ruling on registered partnerships.[17] Yet, as one commentator notes, neither the ruling nor parliament's subsequent revision of the domestic partnerships law was "preceded by any social protests or demonstrations, nor any public 'discourse.'"[18] Parliament passed the modifications without debate, or visibility. Homerosz's passive style led it into decline, and by the mid-1990s it existed only in name, officially disbanding in 1999.[19]

As Homerosz lost vitality and Lambda Budapest focused on *Mások*, the movement struggled to build out a more politically oriented, formally structured, national-level organization. In 1994, activists petitioned the authorities to establish a national-level coordinating organization, the Rainbow Association for Gay Rights (Szivárnány Társulás a Melegek Jogaiért). In concept, the Rainbow Association closely resembled the model of the Czech SOHO. However, the authorities rejected the application, first, because the word for "gay" (*meleg*) was "improper in Hungarian" and, second, because the application lacked provisions barring minors from membership. When the Rainbow Coalition took its case to court, the decision was upheld, even on appeal to the Supreme Court. Without legal status, the Rainbow Association failed to establish itself as the political coordinator for the movement, and was defunct by the end of this period. [20]

Following this failure, in 1995 a second group, Háttér, was established; its name, which translates as "background," recalled Homerosz's incrementalist and service-oriented activism. It focused on counseling (volunteers staffed a telephone help-line) and social services such as HIV/AIDS education, and it was run on small public and private grants. As Long describes, "the purpose, for most of the thirty members, is simple, animating, and clear: community building."[21] It quickly became the most robust and most visible LGBT group in Hungary, achieving notable results in service provision and community-building. With the intensification of the EU accession process, Háttér would become more politically oriented.

Háttér's successes notwithstanding, the broader picture of Hungary's LGBT activism in the 1990s recalls the trajectory of Poland or Slovakia and contrasts with the Czech Republic. As Long writes, "Hungarian gays and lesbians have been unable to set up either a national organization or efficient, lasting local constituency groups. And this, too, seems tied to the inability to find a convincing paradigm for what the community should be or do."[22] The policy goals to which Homerosz and Rainbow Association had addressed themselves—notably, equalizing the age of consent and reforming sexual offences legislation—had not progressed.[23] The framing of homosexuality in the public discourse accorded with that in the other countries in this study besides Romania: it was a nonsalient and largely invisible issue that parties mostly ignored. Activism was in a downward drift, and the future did not look promising.

Hungary during Accession (1998–2004)

The accession period saw a major reorganization of the Hungarian right and a growing polarization between it and the social democratic and liberal elements of the political spectrum; however, it was not yet a moment of hard-right breakthrough and antigay backlash. Between 1998 and 2002 a right government of Fidesz, MDF, and the Smallholders (FKGP) was formed, but it did not include the populist radical right MIÉP, which remained a political pariah.[24] Moreover, the

Christian Democratic KDNP, which had begun articulating increasingly illiberal positions before the election, failed to clear the threshold for parliament.[25] Thus, the potential elements of a hard-right coalition (MIÉP, Fidesz, and MDF) were not cooperating. The following government (2002–2006) was comprised of the Socialists and the Liberals (SZDSZ), both of whom became increasingly supportive of LGBT rights and antidiscrimination policy. In fact, in the 2002 elections MIÉP again missed the bar for parliamentary representation, which proved a deathblow for the party. Thus, the conditions for a hard-right backlash that might threaten the "immediate protective surround" did not obtain (see Figure 7.1).

As straightforward as this characterization of a demobilized hard-right appears, it belies a more complicated set of shifts in the political system, which would later explode into full-blown hard-right mobilization after accession. These shifts were incremental enough that Hungarians themselves did not immediately appreciate their significance—and, therefore, they did not register as threats to the

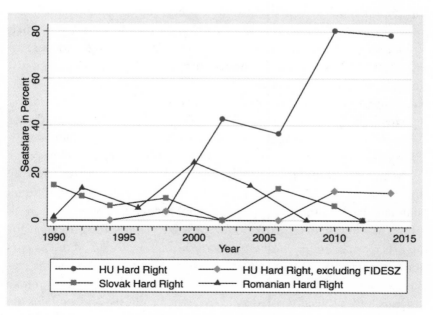

Figure 7.1. Hard-Right Seat Share in National Parliamentary Elections (Hungary, Romania, and Slovakia)

protective surround—but they are important to discuss in order to understand what happened later. The most important shift was Fidesz's redefinition from a liberal party to a Christian-nationalist-populist party in the mold of Poland's PiS.[26] Like PiS, Fidesz came to define itself in opposition to a Europeanizing liberal and social-democratic left.[27] This process culminated in the elections of 2010, but it was well under way before the 2002 ones, which Fidesz lost. Indeed, the failure of MIÉP in 2002 and KDNP in 1998 can be read not as a weakening of hard-right elements, but as the consequence of their co-optation by an increasingly illiberal Fidesz. KDNP was unofficially absorbed into Fidesz after 1998, and in the 2002 campaign Fidesz "moved ever closer to the far right to attract MIÉP voters."[28] It espoused a "second revolution"—strongly reminiscent of PiS's "Fourth Republic" in Poland—that would reconstruct the moral and cultural order around nation, family, and a state purged of lingering nomenklatura networks. Fidesz sought to reorganize and unite the right, a project that brought it into at least tacit cooperation with far-right groups. One such group was the Right-Wing Youth Community, which was established by university students in 1999 and later became the populist radical right party Jobbik. This group campaigned on behalf of a Fidesz-MIÉP coalition in 2002.[29] As a second example of such cooperation, after Fidesz lost the 2002 elections, it created a movement of "Civic Circles" to pressure the Socialist-Liberal government "not just in parliament but on the street."[30] In 2006, this "street movement" would erupt in weeks of antigovernment rioting. Prominent among the Civic Circles were the future members of Jobbik, including its leader, Gábor Vone.[31] Eventually, the more radical elements became disillusioned with Fidesz's leadership, and in 2003 established Jobbik as a competitor party.

As this summary indicates, the hard-right parties were stronger by the end of the accession period than the election results of its traditional standard-bearers and potential allies would suggest. It is better to think of this as a period of redefinition for those elements, setting the stage for an extraparliamentary hard-right breakthrough in 2006 and then a parliamentary breakthrough in 2010. One consequence of these shifts was the increasing appetite of liberal and social democratic parties to take up legislative projects favored by LGBT-rights activists. This explains the success of Háttér and its collaborators in the field of antidiscrimination legislation and registered partnerships, as described below. For potential movement allies like SZDSZ and MSZP, both issues were used to mark their opposition to Fidesz's Christian-nationalist vision.

Compared with the mixed baseline of the preaccession period, the movement experienced organizational growth as Hungary entered membership negotiations with the EU (see Figure 7.3). It became more professionalized and complex. It also became more outward-looking, branching out from service provision and community-building into engagement with the political authorities and policy. Here, activists were aided by an infusion of support from EU networks and the leverage afforded by the accession negotiations. There were two main policy achievements: equalizing the age of consent and the adoption of a comprehensive antidiscrimination law.[32] The mode of political mobilization more closely resembled the Czech rather than the Polish example, however. In his typology of European LGBT-rights activism, Ronald Holzhacker characterizes Háttér as an example of the "'incremental change' mode of interaction, involving insider, discreet lobbying." "Their ability to interact with the government," he continues, "tends to be reactive, not proactive."[33] There was, tellingly, no Hungarian equivalent of Poland's "Let Them See Us" campaign. As with Czech activism, one consequence of this style of political mobilization was a divide between activist elites and the broader movement constituency. Among the latter, there was "an increasing disillusionment on the part of many activists with more explicitly legal and political approaches to improving the situation of lesbians and gays."[34] This divide was apparent in the movement's narrow territorial reach, which remained concentrated in Budapest.[35]

In this period, Háttér consolidated its position as the leading SMO in the movement, becoming Hungary's counterpart to the Polish KPH or Czech SOHO. Besides Háttér, the other significant group was Labrisz, a lesbian organization established in 1999. Unlike Háttér, its activism was inward-looking.[36] Lambda Budapest continued to operate, though its primary activity remained publishing *Mások*. In 2001, the Rainbow Mission Foundation was established to organize the yearly Budapest Pride. Last, this period saw the development of a legal-aid society, Habeas Corpus, which, though not a LGBT-rights organization per se, cooperated closely with Háttér on its policy campaigns.

Beginning in 2000–2001, Háttér leveraged EU support to lobby parliament for comprehensive antidiscrimination legislation and the removal of Article 199 from the penal code, which established a higher age of consent for homosexual relations than for heterosexual ones.[37] It developed strong ties with the EU, "realizing early on that EU pressure would be a way to put leverage on political institutions and receive funding for their social goals."[38] Though antidiscrimination legislation would also benefit the Roma, women, and the disabled, my respondents reported that it was LGBT-rights advocates who led the lobbying effort, becoming deeply involved in authoring legislative proposals. The first legislative drafts, which appeared in April 2001, showed the clear imprint of EU models, defining, for example, the potential grounds for discrimination based on the 14 grounds defined by the EU in its own employment directive.[39] Even more striking was the addition of six more protected categories, including "gender identity." Thus, Hungary's antidiscrimination framework actually went *beyond* the requirements of the EU.[40] These additions were a strong indication of Háttér's professional capacity and behind-the-scenes lobbying of MPs. The other policy that the movement targeted in this period was equalizing the age of consent for homosexual relations, an issue that it had gotten little traction on in the 1990s. Now, however, ties to EU networks, in particular ILGA-Europe, enhanced the movement's advocacy efforts. In June 2002, the EP's foreign affairs committee recommended that Hungary eliminate Article 199 from the Penal Code. By September, the Hungarian Constitutional Court had ruled Article 199 of the Penal Code unconstitutional.

To round out this discussion of the organization of activism at this juncture, we now turn to the annual Budapest Gay Pride March, which was first held in 1997. As discussed in Chapter 1, the conduct and size of Pride marches offers a helpful shorthand for comparing postcommunist LGBT movements. The contrast between Warsaw's highly politicized march and Prague's nonexistent one (until 2011) illustrated the two movements' different organizational dynamics. This chapter will likewise compare Prides across countries. Figure 7.2 captures one important facet of this comparison, trends in size over time. As caveats, we must bear in mind that these figures are estimates and also that Budapest, Bucharest, and Bratislava differ in size and international accessibility. Budapest and Bucharest are largish European capitals, with populations of around 1.7 and 1.9 million, respectively. At just under half a million, Bratislava is considerably smaller. Budapest is also tightly linked to international channels by virtue of both geography and as the headquarters of the Open Societies Foundations and Central European University, both of which serve as a transnational hub for civil society advocacy. This makes it easier for West European activists to attend Prides when backlash politicizes them. Less than an hour's drive from Vienna, Bratislava is much more accessible to international channels than Bucharest. While these factors affect differences in participation across these countries, they likely do not account for the magnitude of differences evident in Figure 7.2, and certainly not the difference in trends over time.

Returning to the 1997 Budapest Pride, it was a small event of no more than 200 people. One scholar described it as a "dash" from a gay club to a public square and back.[41] As in Poland prior to 2004, it received little publicity.[42] In following years, it grew to some 1,000–2,000 participants, but it remained a modest affair, both in terms of media attention and atmosphere. Its purpose was primarily "bonding" rather than the public

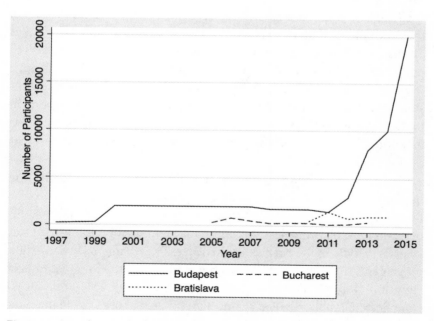

Figure 7.2. Attendance at Pride Parades in Budapest, Bucharest, and Bratislava (1997–2015)

display of political demands.[43] Few allies took part.[44] Nor, initially, did counterdemonstrators: as the ethnographer Hadley Renkin observes in his study of Budapest Pride, "What began as occasional signs and isolated catcalls in the late 1990s became organized, but still peaceful, groups of counterdemonstrators in 2003 and 2004."[45] In both character and timing, the politicization of the Budapest Pride Parade and the Warsaw Equality March are uncannily similar, reflecting the growing linkage of homosexuality and EU accession in the eyes of a newly mobilizing hard right. In Hungary the hard right's breakthrough would lag behind Poland's slightly, but its intensity would match if not surpass it.

Postaccession Hungary (since 2004)

After accession, Hungary's LGBT movement experienced a definitive transformation, from a politics of incremental pragmatism to one of openly confronting its enemies and full-scale political mobilization. It used popular protest to demand rights, forged tight links with political party allies, pressed for controversial legislation in parliament, and shed the past practice of behind-the-scenes lobbying to engage visibly in the now polarized political climate. Its organizational gains were not as extensive as Poland's; the Hungarian movement did not elect leaders to public office, as in Poland, nor could its leading SMO Háttér build out a territorial network like that of the Polish KPH's. These caveats notwithstanding, Hungary offers a clear example of organizational development in the wake of backlash and, by the same token, is a contrast to the organizational decline experienced by its Czech and Slovak counterparts during the same period.

The previous section described the Hungarian right's redefinition beginning around 2002, focusing on Fidesz's transformation from a liberal into Christian-nationalist party in the mold of Poland's PiS. Fidesz's loss in the 2002 elections and then again in 2006 intensified this transformation, as the party cultivated an extraparliamentary hard-right movement, the Civic Circles, which would spawn the populist radical right Jobbik party. Fidesz's relationship with Jobbik was (and still is) complicated. Jobbik rebelled against Fidesz's goal of organizing the right into a hegemonic majority and instead became its competitor.[46] Further complicating the trajectory of hard-right mobilization, it did not align neatly with the electoral calendar, as in Poland. A coalition of Socialists and Liberals governed from 2002 to 2010. Jobbik even failed to enter parliament in 2006, receiving just 2.2 percent of the vote. Yet both the 2002 and 2006 elections had been exceptionally close ones for an increasingly Christian-nationalist Fidesz: it won 41.1 percent of the vote to the Socialists' 42.1 percent in 2002, and 42 percent to the latter's 43.2 percent in 2006. Unlike Poland, then, we do not see a formal coalition between the populist radical right and the conservatives and Christian democrats.[47] Hungary's hard-right backlash came from the streets, and *then* it captured parliament.

The precipitating event came almost immediately after the Socialists' and Liberals' 2006 election victory. On September 17, 2006, Hungarian Radio broadcast a secret speech delivered by Prime Minister Ferenc Gyurcsány (MSZP) to members of his party earlier that year. In it, he admitted that the Socialist government had knowingly lied about the state of the economy in order to win the 2006 elections. That night and continuing through the year's end, violent street protests involving teargas, stone throwing, and tens of thousands of protestors broke out in Budapest and other cities. The right, especially Jobbik, surged, and support for the left collapsed.[48] In recent research, Béla Greskovits and Jason Wittenberg collected data on protest events in Hungary from 1989 through 2011, and their results highlight the magnitude of this hard-right mobilization.[49] Between 1990 and 2002, the number of protest events averaged around 150. Between 2002 and 2006, when Fidesz organized the Civic Circles, it climbed to 300 per year. After 2006 and the airing of Gyurcsány's speech, it climbed again, to 400 events in 2008 and 600 in 2010. Breaking these down into left- and right-initiated protests, Greskovits and Wittenberg find that "right" protests far outnumber "left" ones after 2002, even though previously the gap between the two was negligible.[50] At their peak in 2007, more than half of right-initiated protests were classified as "radical right." Though their data end in 2011, Greskovits and Wittenberg also find that after 2010 the "rise in left-initiated contention has been sharpest"—a result that comports with the backlash dynamics at the center of this book's argument.[51] The surge in protest after 2006 marked a reversal of Hungary's history of nondisruptive protest: in 2007, disruptive protests outnumbered nondisruptive ones 300 to 50, and violent protests rose from zero to approximately a dozen. During this tumult, far-right groups were especially threatening: Jobbik helped found the paramilitary Magyar Guard in 2007.[52] Much of the Guard's animus was directed against the Roma minority, but it also threatened LGBT people rhetorically and, as the 2007 Budapest Pride parade showed, physically.

Backlash against LGBT activism became one highly visible arena of the hard-right surge. It began with a violent attack on the Budapest Pride in June 2007. As mentioned earlier, in previous years the parade had elicited scant attention and at most scattered nonviolent counter-protests. The sustained and organized attack in 2007 took the approximately 2,000 participants and police by surprise. Participants endured a constant barrage of eggs, bottles, bags of sand, and even two flares.[53] They were taunted with cries of "filthy queers!" and "[Throw the] faggots into the Danube."[54] The violence continued after the parade, as 11 participants were beaten on their way home, two of whom were hospitalized. The threat of violence has continued in subsequent years, though heavy police protection has averted this scale of physical harm.[55] Hard-right counterdemonstrators have adjusted their tactics accordingly: in September 2010, they organized a "Hetero Pride Day March" in Budapest, in which Jobbik parliamentarians joined calls for a "Faggot-free Hungary!" and demanded legislation denying homosexuals the right of public assembly.[56]

In 2010 this street-level mobilization flooded into the parliamentary arena as Fidesz and Jobbik delivered crushing electoral defeats to MSZP and SZDSZ. Though Fidesz and Jobbik did not form a coalition, as PiS and LPR did in Poland, this point of divergence needs to be placed in perspective. It certainly should not be interpreted as evidence that Hungary did not experience hard-right backlash. On the contrary, it indicates that the elements of Hungary's backlash were individually so strong that they did not need to form a coalition. Fidesz won an absolute majority (52.7 percent) in the popular vote, which translated into a parliamentary supermajority—enough to amend the constitution. Had Fidesz fallen short of a majority, Jobbik would have been its likely coalition partner. It should also be emphasized that Jobbik's election results were a breakthrough that made it a political heavyweight, with almost as many seats in parliament as the second biggest party, MSZP. Finally, there was strong tacit cooperation between Fidesz and Jobbik regarding minority and values issues; to quote one description:

The governing party, Fidesz, operated in a symbiotic if ultimately silent relationship with Jobbik. When it suited them, Fidesz, [sic] could draw clear boundaries to distinguish them and Jobbik, identifying in the process what was unacceptable and what was not. On other occasions, Jobbik became the unofficial spokesperson for Fidesz, saying explicitly what Fidesz dare not say even implicitly, thus blurring the lines between politically correct and stigmatizing discourses.[57]

Homosexuality is one of the best examples of this cooperation, as Jobbik's virulently antigay rhetoric and policies have served to make Fidesz's undermining of LGBT rights appear mild by comparison. Where, for example, Jobbik sponsored legislation to ban "the promotion of sexual deviations"—under which it included homosexuality, transsexuality, transvestitism, bisexuality, and pedophile behaviors—Fidesz offered the "milder" proposal of amending the constitution to define marriage exclusively as a union between a man and a woman in 2012.[58] Jobbik's proposal failed; Fidesz's succeeded. Though the latter did not overturn registered partnerships, my interviews indicated that it raised strong doubts about their future among activists.

Bearing in mind the extent, timing, and character of the hard-right backlash, let us now turn to its effect on the organization of activism. As we have seen, by 2004 Hungary's movement had already developed strong SMOs like Háttér; however, this activist network was narrow in breadth and incrementalist and inward-looking in style. In 2004, it resembled the Czech movement, but by 2010 it looked more like the Polish one, politically mobilized, with high levels of participation and internal solidarity, claiming influential allies outside the movement, and possessing a high level of policy/professional capacity. These changes could be seen in both the evolution of Budapest Pride in the wake of the backlash and in the campaign for expanded registered partnerships.

Across my interviews with Pride participants and activists in Budapest in 2011, respondents pointed to the 2007 parade as a transformative event for the movement, particularly in terms of strengthening solidarity and mobilizing participation. As in Poland, diverse groups and goals within the movement were refocused as all felt themselves under threat. Second, homosexuality's salience as a political issue increased enormously as a result of the hard right's rhetoric. Political actors who were, at best, tangentially aware of homosexuality as a *political* issue learned to think about it in this way. Third, as in Poland, the hard right's linking of LGBT rights with the EU forged common cause among political actors opposed to the hard right.

The ethnographer Hadley Renkin describes these effects in his study of Budapest Pride, focusing in particular on the changing framing of the event. In 2008, the title was changed from "Gay Pride Day March" to "Gay Dignity March." Organizers sought to reframe the march from an inward-looking celebration of a distinctly LGBT identity to a more outward-looking campaign for human rights. As one organizer put it, "[we] intend 'dignity' to highlight the common humanity of LGBT people, their fundamental equality, rather than rights claims based on difference."[59] Concretely, they sought to "encourage coalition-building with other social minorities like Jews and Roma, as well as progressive movements . . . linking the March and LGBT rights more closely to Human Rights discourses and their associated institutional structures: NGOs and civil society groups." In particular, they highlighted EU-related networks.[60] As in Poland, this framing resonated all the more strongly for its complementarity with the hard-right's presentation of LGBT rights as an external imposition by the EU. As noted by scholars and my respondents in the field, the violence at the 2007 parade gave unprecedented visibility to the movement. This resonant framing contest drew in outside allies, most notably the governing MSZP and SZDSZ, for whom the parade symbolized larger issues of democracy, European values, and opposition to hard-right identity politics. Budapest's SZDSZ mayor decried the attacks as "in opposition to everything which the democratic countries of the world hold as normal." MSZP MP Tímea Müller declared the attacks "reminiscent of the darkest periods in human history."[61] After 2007, the number of international allies participating in the parades jumped, and the size of the parade increased markedly (see Figure 7.2).

As the Pride opened up the movement to a broader audience of grassroots constituents and outside allies, the SMO network was building its organization, technical capacity, and political engagement (see Figure 7.3). The politicization of Budapest Pride brought attempted bans, route changes, and other limitations. Háttér, the Rainbow Pride Association, and other NGOs fought these challenges in court and became adept at defeating them. In these court cases, movement SMOs found allies in

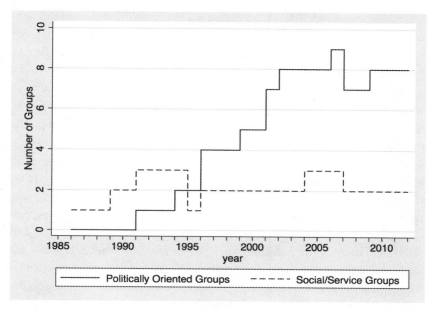

Figure 7.3. Number of Hungarian LGBT Groups by Primary Orientation (1985–2012)

the Hungarian Civil Liberties Union and the Hungarian Ombudsman for Fundamental Rights.[62] In 2011, a new SMO was founded, the Hungarian LGBT Alliance; this umbrella group organized LGBT groups into a national-level network, addressing one of the primary developmental gaps in the Hungarian movement comparatively. Háttér continued to deepen its policy capacity, developing an online system for reporting discrimination; offering legal aid; and lobbying EU and state authorities about discrimination policy.[63] In 2012, Budapest hosted the EuroGames, an international gay and lesbian athletic competition drawing thousands of participants. In terms of demonstrating organizational capacity and transnational linkages, hosting this event can be compared with Poland's EuroPride two years earlier.

The clearest demonstration of the Hungarian movement's strengthening organization, especially its growing allies among parties, was the expanded registered partnerships legislation enacted in December 2007. As described earlier, a partial partnerships framework had been enacted following the Constitutional Court's ruling in 1996, but this framework was far from satisfactory. After the attack on the 2007 Pride, parliament returned to the issue. The liberal SZDSZ had been signaling increasing support of LGBT rights since the 2002 elections, but the Pride attacks transformed them from issue advocates to champions.[64] The Socialist MSZP's sometimes inconsistent support also firmed after the attacks, as was illustrated by the public coming out of Gabor Szety, a state secretary in the prime minister's office—the first such declaration by a public official.

In fall 2007, the Liberals proposed a bill that, in defining marriage as an act between two persons over 18 years old, amounted to same-sex marriage. When it failed, the MSZP and SZDSZ partners turned to improving registered partnerships. Working closely with both parties in drafting and campaigning for the legislation was a team of some 10 different NGOs, notably Háttér. In the public debate, Fidesz joined Jobbik activists—the latter still an extraparliamentary opposition group—in vehemently opposing the proposal. With strong support from MSZP and SZDSZ, the new partnerships law was passed on December 17, 2007. Adding a further twist to the story—and underlining again the ambivalent nature of the courts in the region vis-à-vis LGBT rights—the Constitutional Court struck down the law on the grounds that allowing registered partnerships for opposite-sex couples (as well as same-sex ones) conflicted with the legal definition of marriage. This necessitated amending the law to restrict it to same-sex couples only. The amended version took effect in July 2009. This protracted legislative struggle highlighted the movement's professionalism and legal-technical proficiency. Combined with an unusually progressive antidiscrimination framework, the new partnerships law placed Hungary's LGBT-rights framework among the most progressive in Europe at the time, especially Eastern Europe. When held up against the Czech Republic, the only other case here to have passed similar legislation, one sharp contrast stands out: while Czech SMOs disbanded after achieving the law, Hungary's continued organizing and set same-sex marriage as the new goal.[65]

The glaring difference between the Czech and Hungarian movements at this juncture was that Hungary's hard-right backlash was still gathering force. In the next two years, it would metastasize from extraparliamentary mobilization to a parliamentary rout of the Socialists and Liberals. The new government would attempt to chip away at the movement's gains directly, by redefining marriage in heteronormative terms in the Constitution, and indirectly, by tightening restrictions on civil society groups. Yet these moves have only sharpened the resonance of the issue, intensifying internal solidarity (viz., the Pride parades) and attracting new allies. In 2010, for example, even as the Socialists and Liberals suffered setbacks, a new party, Politics Can Be Different, was elected as an advocate for minorities, including LGBT people.[66] Contentious politics has continued to hone the organization of activism.

Slovakia: Failure to Launch

Slovakia illustrates the trajectory of movement development in a relatively closed society that does not experience hard-right backlash against homosexuality with EU accession. We would expect its activists to struggle to sustain whatever momentum emerged from the political opening that accompanied the fall of communism in 1989 and the window of leverage for LGBT issues afforded during the accession period. We would also expect the movement to face the postcommunist obstacles of invisibility and scant resources. As we have seen, in the 1990s Czech activists were able to mitigate these drags on movement-building through the more accommodating structures of the state, especially the National Institute of Health. Such support was not on offer in Slovakia, and its movement was dwindling rapidly by the late 1990s. Unlike Poland or, later, Hungary, the onset of accession politics brought no hard-right surge, no linking of LGBT rights with the EU by antigay activists, and thus no catalyzation of an already weak movement.

Preaccession Slovakia (1989–1997)

For the better part of the 1990s, Slovak LGBT activism consisted of informally organized friendship networks; was concentrated in the capital and a couple of larger cities; and was oriented more toward constituents than the authorities. It resembled Polish activism at the time, and contrasted with that of its Czech neighbor. This contrast was all the more noteworthy given that Slovakia and the Czech Republic were part of the same federal state through January 1, 1993. Until Czechoslovakia's breakup, Slovak activists had enjoyed close connections with the Czech movement, especially SOHO. Slovakia's sexual minorities also benefited from the policy changes won by SOHO prior to 1993: equalization of the age of consent, destruction of communist-era "pink lists," and delisting homosexuality as a psychiatric disorder. Because of the association with SOHO, Slovak activism through 1993 may even be labeled political in orientation; however, all sources point to a loosely organized activist network with limited reach. After 1993, and the breakup of Czechoslovakia, the movement lost its institutional links with SOHO and became apolitical, its goal to provide a space for socializing.[67] Unlike the Czech movement, Slovakia's lacked state support in the form of links to the Ministry of Health and funding for HIV/AIDS prevention. Due to the shared history and close proximity, informal links between the two movements remained, as can be seen in the pattern of emulating the Czech movement's agenda and activities, though typically in a partial and less successful form.

The first public association for gays and lesbians, Ganymedes, was founded in March 1990. Based in the capital, Bratislava, it was a founding member of the national-level Czechoslovak SOHO organization. Thanks to these links, we can classify Ganymedes as politically oriented and possessing SMO-like attributes through its first two years. During this time it also cultivated links to transnational activism, hosting two international conferences in Bratislava with the participation of ILGA (International Lesbian, Gay, Bisexual, Trans and Intersex Association) and IGLYO (International Lesbian, Gay, Bisexual, Transgender, Queer & Intersex Youth and Student Organisation) in 1992. Ganymedes also ran a telephone help-line, but this constituted the sum of its service provision. The primary activity of Ganymedes and the various other groups that arose during the 1990s was to provide a space for association.[68] After decades of isolation and the absence of public association, such community-building was, of course, vital and counted as a necessary step to building a movement. It also reflected strong social taboos against homosexuality relative to the Czech Republic. As one telling example, when Ganymedes was first established, it took out advertisements in mainstream newspapers to announce events. At the editors' insistence, however, these advertisements could only be phrased in the vaguest terms; consequently, many early attendees mistakenly thought the meetings were mixers for women seeking single men.[69] Most Ganymedes members did not see the group in political terms, and after 1993 its more visible activities included the Gay Film Festival of Slovakia and an annual pageant, Mr. Gay.[70]

Motivated by their perceived marginalization within Ganymedes, a group of lesbians and feminists broke off to form Museion in April 1994.[71] Museion became the most visible and active group in the 1990s, yet it lacked a permanent office/meeting space, was entirely volunteer-based, primarily self-help-oriented, and claimed only 39 members after two years in existence—points underscoring the underorganized character of Slovak activism.[72] In 1997, the youth-oriented Homosexual and Bisexual Citizens (HaBiO, Homosexuálni a bisexuálni občania) was established in Bratislava: it ran a discussion club and telephone hotline, and facilitated international student exchanges. The movement was centered in Bratislava, though Ganymedes and Museion also claimed branches in the provincial cities of Košice, Handlová, and Banská Bystrica. Thus, while activist networks existed outside the capital, one could not speak of a national-level mobilizing structure. Likewise, there was no "regular, specialized periodical accessible to the public"—nothing equivalent to the Czech *SOHO revue*. Though Ganymedes, Museion, and HaBiO had legal status, their internal organization was informal in most respects: membership was anonymous, and funding was ad hoc and temporary, depending on a shifting panoply of mostly international sources.[73] Czechoslovakia's breakup, which severed links with SOHO, weakened the movement considerably.[74]

Turning now to the absence of hard-right backlash, Slovakia had strong candidates for a hard-right coalition, but enmity among them precluded any such coalition from coalescing. Thus, the LGBT community's "protective surround" remained unthreatened. The most obvious candidate for a hard-right coalition was the Slovak National Party (SNS), which Mudde classifies as populist radical right because of its antiminority and anti-EU views.[75] Its leader, Jan Slota, often described gays as "abnormal."[76] SNS's main targets, however, were ethnic minorities, notably the Roma and ethnic Hungarians, recalling its Czech counterpart SPR-RSČ. More importantly, SNS lacked allies on the right: it has always had antagonistic relations with the other Slovak party with openly intolerant views of homosexuality, the Christian Democratic Movement (KDH). Like SNS, KDH was one of the staunchest nationalist parties before Czechoslovakia's breakup. Had KDH cooperated with SNS, a formidable hard-right coalition of the populist radical right and the Christian Democrats would have formed. Instead, the parties opposed each other. This reflected the polarizing effect of the dominant party in Slovak politics in the 1990s, the Movement for a Democratic Slovakia (HZDS). SNS allied with HZDS, while KDH was its bitter opponent. HZDS might initially seem an analogue of Poland's PiS or Hungary's Fidesz; yet, though pivotal in Czechoslovakia's breakup, it was no nationalist party.[77] Instead, it was perhaps the region's purest example of a "personality party," an extension of its charismatic leader, Vladimír Mečiar, and just as programmatically inconsistent as he was.[78] Mečiar himself, not nationalism or ideology, was the dividing line that structured party politics in 1990s Slovakia. Detractors like KDH saw his corrupt rule and flouting of the rule of law as a threat to democracy. More opportunistic parties, like SNS, were willing to work with, and profit from, allying with him.[79]

Though social taboos against homosexuality were stronger in Slovakia than in the Czech Republic, reflecting religion's greater role in politics, homosexuality was not strongly politicized.[80] Certainly, the activist networks described above had not drawn much public attention to themselves. Party politics in the 1990s had a strong element of nationalism, but it was nationalism born of the country's separation from Czechoslovakia. It was not directed against transnational norms, as the popularity of EU membership among Slovak voters attested—including supporters of nationalist parties like KDH. Indeed, opinion polls reported significantly higher support for the EU in Slovakia than in the Czech Republic throughout the 1990s.[81] Further evidence of Euroskepticism's weak resonance could be found in the behavior of politicians like HZDS's Mečiar. Despite receiving strong criticism from the European Commission, Mečiar presented himself as the guarantor of Slovakia's accession to the EU: negative reports by the Commission were, in his telling, a "confirmation and not a criticism of his own national policies."[82] Meanwhile, an authentically nationalist party like KDH used EU criticism of Mečiar as a cudgel against him, a strategy that foreclosed the adoption of Euroskepticism on its part.[83] In sum, there was no negative association between the EU and homosexuality, as one saw in Romania at this time or in Poland and Hungary later.

Slovakia during Accession (1998–2004)

Scholarship on democratization and economic reform typically presents Slovakia as the paradigmatic example of how EU influence— whether it be conceptualized as external incentives,[84] passive and active leverage,[85] linkage and leverage,[86] transnational activism,[87] or geographic diffusion[88]—can tilt the playing field of domestic politics against illiberal governments and in favor of more liberal, reform-minded opposition. Other countries in the region, it may be argued, were already well on the way to democratic consolidation before EU accession: not Slovakia. Yet, as beneficial as EU influence was for Slovak democratizers and economic reformers, it did not offer much to activists struggling to build a LGBT movement. It thwarted the forging of a hard-right coalition, despite the presence of all the necessary elements for one. It prevented a framing contest over homosexuality that could generate internal solidarity and win domestic allies outside the movement. While EU advocacy of antidiscrimination norms and support for LGBT activists did spur some organizational advances, these were too modest to fundamentally alter the organization of activism. It remained primarily informal and concentrated in the capital, and though political goals emerged, providing a space for socialization remained its focus.

To understand the absence of hard-right threat to the "protective surround," it is necessary to consider the EU's overall relationship with Slovakia during the accession period. The EU's efforts to support the anti-Mečiar opposition had the effect of neutralizing the Christian-Democratic KDH as a hard-right force. EU pressure had driven Mečiar to increasingly desperate ruses to divide the opposition. One was to change the electoral law just four months before the 1998 parliamentary elections so that all parties, even those in electoral alliances, had to win at least 5 percent of the vote to enter parliament. Mečiar hoped to pick the opposition parties off in this way. In response, the latter took the even more surprising step of reconstituting themselves as a single party, the Slovak Democratic Coalition (SDK). KDH was one of the five parties constituting SDK. This gambit *formally embedded* KDH in a party that was equal parts liberal, green, and social democratic.[89] It was part of a governing party defined above all by its EU program;

despite misgivings about antidiscrimination norms, it could not politicize them as did counterparts in Poland. The second effect of EU intervention was to send HZDS and its ally SNS into sharp decline. Mečiar's governing coalition had been held together not by ideology but by patronage, and its elements fell apart once cut off from the perks of power. The populist radical right SNS was not spared these entropic tendencies: in 2001, personality conflicts led a faction calling itself the Real Slovak National Party (PSNS) to break off. In 2002's parliamentary elections, SNS and PSNS ran separately, splitting each other's vote, so that both failed to enter parliament. Slovakia's hard right, never much a force to begin with, had become irrelevant.

Turning now to Slovakia's LGBT movement, activists did lobby in favor of EU antidiscrimination norms and, following the Czech movement, registered partnerships; however, neither campaign resonated in the wider political sphere because neither catalyzed a framing contest with the hard right. As in Poland, mainstream parties avoided issues that might complicate EU membership. If anything, this calculation was even starker in Slovakia. It had, after all, come perilously close to being shut out of the first group of EU candidate states in 1998. After 1998, the new government, which included the socially conservative KDH, had to make up lost ground across a host of policy areas as a result of Mečiar's footdragging on EU reforms in the 1990s.

The mainstream party discourse around homosexuality during the years between becoming a candidate and becoming an EU member is best described as a combination of the charity and therapy discourses. This characterization does not apply to SNS or its short-lived offshoot PSNS, whose antigay rhetoric immediately recalled that of Poland's LPR and Hungary's Jobbik. SNS's Eva Slavkovská opposed EU antidiscrimination norms because, she declared in parliament, they posed a threat to schools: Slavkovská argued that if gays or lesbians could be teachers, then schools could also "employ a person with a sexual aberration such as pedophilia or necrophilia."[90] PSNS's Víťazoslav Móric described homosexuality as endangering society, likening it to the behavior of insects.[91] These were the most extreme voices in politics, and it bears emphasis that, during the accession period, the parties they represented were at their lowest ebb in Slovakia's postcommunist history, internally divided and on the verge of disappearing from parliament.

To return to the mainstream parties, KDH offered the most critical stance toward homosexuality, but compared to SNS or Poland's hard right, it was mild. For the purposes of my argument, what matters is whether hard-right mobilization is perceived as threatening the "immediate protective surround"—the kind of organized hate speech that would lead LGBT persons to feel that their taken-for-granted quotidian routines were likely to be disrupted. KDH's pronouncements, which extolled the traditional family and categorized homosexuality as a treatable psychiatric disorder, were offensive but not threatening. As one analyst observes, KDH's statements regarding homosexuality were "often worded in such a way as to evoke pity or seeming concern with [the] wellbeing of gay men and lesbians ('that life is not easy')."[92] Alojz Rakús, a prominent KDH member who served as health minister and chairman of the Slovak Psychiatric Society, publicly argued that homosexuality was a "curable aberration."[93]

Between 1998 and 2004 the LGBT movement added several new groups. These included Altera, a lesbian group established in the city of Banská Bystrica in central Slovakia in 1998.[94] Meanwhile, Bratislava-based HaBiO claimed a branch in the eastern Slovak city of Košice. Bratislava itself gained three new organizations, the Center for Communication, Cooperation, and Integration of Sexual Minorities (CKKISM, Centrum komunikácie, kooperácie a integrácie sexuálnych menšín), H-plus, and Podisea, all based on the self-help, socializing model. A library, Queer Archive (Q archív), was established in Bratislava in 2002. These groups attested to the movement's expanding territorial reach; however, the overall network remained small-scale, informal, and constituent-oriented. As one telling illustration, consider the conflicting accounts of Slovak Pride parades. There is surprising disagreement among analysts of the movement about when the first one occurred. Viera Lorencova's respondents claim that Ganymedes organized a Pride in Bratislava in 1992.[95] Paula Jójárt, however, refers to this as a "warm-up event," citing instead three Marches of Difference (Pochody Inakosti) that took place in 2001 in Bratislava, Banská Bystrica, and Košice.[96] Later analysts cite the Bratislava Pride in 2010 as Slovakia's first.[97] This lack of agreement reveals the informal, quasi-public nature of much Slovak activism. It has been difficult for activists themselves to agree on the boundaries between the public movement and the social scene. Incidentally, until

2010, none of these events provoked the kind of hard-right counterprotests that Polish marches did.

The most important developments in the movement during this time were the establishment of the first publicly available monthly magazine, *Atribút*, in 2000[98] and the launching of the Otherness Initiative (OI, Iniciatíva Inakosť), a coordinating council constituted by seven activist groups, also in 2000.[99] OI was a step toward more national-level reach, more SMO-like organization, and an orientation toward the authorities rather than to constituents. It articulated concrete policy goals including antidiscrimination protections and registered partnerships. The former showed the influence of EU norms, and the second reflected the example of the Czech movement, which was then submitting its first registered partnerships proposals. Compared to movements in neighboring countries, Slovakia's still looked weak, however. OI was informally organized and lacked legal status, unlike its Czech counterparts SOHO and GI. Remarkably, the author of OI's registered partnership proposal did not disclose her identity, instead using the pseudonym Eva Adámková.[100] Moreover, internal solidarity was comparatively weak. As in the Czech Republic, but in contrast to Poland, a palpable tension existed between lesbian and gay men's groups such as Museion and Ganymedes. The informal nature of organization left groups vulnerable to personal conflicts.[101] OI's informal structure reflected weak internal solidarity: one faction wanted an organization structured like the Czech SOHO that could organize public campaigns, while another resisted institutionalization, preferring to be flexible, "to raise questions, to annoy."[102] Moreover, even among the OI's founders there was ambivalence about taking up political goals. As one of them described the campaign for registered partnerships, "I was upset that nobody moves, so I started to move [with the project]. I thought there would be an interest in our community to join it. Well, it turned out I was wrong."[103]

Activists took up two main campaigns during the accession period. The first was registered partnerships.[104] In 1998, Ganymedes petitioned the Mečiar government regarding partnerships, only to be met with silence. In 2002, activists presented a second proposal, this time to the pro-EU SDK government. The justice minister, and KDH chief, Ján Čarnogurský, ignored it. Compared to 1998, activists were better organized this time, however. OI organized three marches in 2001 to support the proposal and, in 2002, a seminar with government representatives; during these events, it framed partnerships in terms of EU norms.[105] Because of these campaigns, LGBT issues experienced unprecedented visibility in Slovakia. As one scholar wrote, "Despite the Slovak parliament's persistent rejection of the Registered Partnership Statute (*Zákon o životnom partnerstve*) and other activist-initiated anti-discriminatory legislative proposals, members of the emerging queer community perceive the last three years to have been a gradual move up from invisibility."[106] Yet, as this quote also reveals, there were no policy gains. Except for a few social democratic deputies, the government remained wary of both registered partnerships and antidiscrimination laws with provisions regarding sexual orientation.[107] Slovakia passed the EU-mandated antidiscrimination bill in May 2004, at the last possible moment before membership. As the timing makes clear, its passage was possible only as a necessity for membership. To the end, it was strongly opposed by KDH.[108] The cabinet unanimously voted against registered partnerships in January 2002, and KDH then closed debate on the proposal.[109]

In comparative terms, opposition to antidiscrimination legislation and registered partnerships in Slovakia looks tepid, more footdragging and obfuscation than backlash. Unlike Poland, conservative politicians did not attempt to link homosexuality to the EU; after all, membership remained an overwhelmingly popular goal. On the contrary, they resisted attempts by the movement to forge a connection between LGBT rights and EU norms. As a good example, in parliamentary debate KDH MP Vladimír Palko argued that the EU did *not* require that sexual orientation be included in antidiscrimination law:

> This is not a "Euro-law." There are many myths regarding the need to adopt various laws, and this is the case of this law as well. Most EU member states do not have such a law.[110]

Yet, seen in the longer perspective, even the slight politicization of homosexuality in the public sphere had some movement-building effects. In her account of the Slovak movement, Paula Jójárt writes that "[p]aradoxically these negative responses opened up hot debates and finally helped [the] lesbian and gay community to make their claims more visible."[111] We should also remember, however, that these visibility gains occurred against the 1990s baseline of near complete marginality. The movement had virtually no political allies, and it was still unorganized compared with neighbors like Poland.

Postaccession Slovakia (since 2004)

The overwhelming majority of Slovaks saw entry into the EU on May 1, 2004 as a triumph, the ultimate validation of their new democracy's legitimacy on the European stage. It was even seen this way by parties whose positions regarding homosexuality were at odds with EU norms. As had Mečiar, such parties sought to selectively oppose or ignore EU norms on this issue while embracing the larger EU identity. At the same time, the party system underwent major reorganization after 2004 as a result of HZDS's decline, which removed the rationale holding SDK together and opened space for a new left-populist party, Smer (Direction). This flux continued to prevent the formation of a hard-right coalition of the populist radical right and the Christian democrats. Unopposed by a mobilized hard right, the campaign for same-sex registered partnerships, the Slovak movement's signature issue, engendered no major framing contest and failed to resonate publicly. Meanwhile, as a result of joining the EU, LGBT groups suffered from both the withdrawal of external aid targeted at civil society development and the loss of the role of broker between the European Commission and the Slovak government. Already discouraged by the failure of registered partnerships, the movement began to demobilize politically while the impulse to build out the territorial network and to professionalize as SMOs lost steam and even reversed itself.

Slovakia's first elections after joining the EU, which took place in 2006, brought only a marginal boost to the potential elements of a hard-right coalition even as they weakened the field of potential LGBT-rights allies. The Social Democratic Party (SDĽ), which supported registered partnerships, disbanded after failing to meet the threshold for representation. Meanwhile, the populist radical right SNS overcame its internal divisions and reentered parliament with 11.7 percent of the vote. KDH received 8.3 percent. Rather than join forces with KDH, SNS allied with the newly established Smer party, which had swept the elections and formed a new government. Smer combined social democracy with populist nationalism and anticorruption rhetoric.[112] This made for a syncretistic populism containing both socially conservative and left-sympathetic stances on LGBT issues. For example, Smer leader Robert Fico prioritized relations with the Church over registered partnerships and "other less[er] priority themes."[113] On the other hand, two prominent Smer politicians, cofounder Monika Beňová-Flašiková and Deputy Prime Minister Dušan Čaplovič, publicly supported registered partnerships.[114] The critical point regarding Smer's approach to homosexuality was that it sought to *de*politicize it as an issue—in contrast to Poland's PiS and LPR or Hungary's Jobbik and Fidesz. Smer very publicly refused opportunities to demonize homosexuality, and pressured its coalition partner SNS to do so also.[115] Thus, activists lacked sufficient allies to support the reintroduction of a registered partnerships proposal in parliament, and, in general, LGBT issues received almost no mention in the public sphere.[116]

This pattern of depoliticizing, if also marginalizing, LGBT issues prevailed through the following two governments (2010–2012 and 2012–2016). The first of these saw a coalition of liberals and KDH replace Smer's government. The 2010 elections greatly weakened the populist radical right, as SNS's vote fell to only 5.1 percent, barely enough to enter parliament. Its potential hard-right partner KDH joined the liberals. Key figures within this government—Prime Minister Iveta Radičová of the Slovak Democratic and Christian Union (SDKÚ), Richard Sulík of the libertarian SaS (Freedom and Solidarity), Rudolf Chmel of the ethnic Hungarian minority party Most-Hid—held supportive views on LGBT issues, but KDH's steadfast opposition kept them off the government's agenda. The second government (2012–2016) saw the liberal coalition unseated and Smer's return. Political scientist John Gould has noted that opinion polls at this time indicated a rise in homophobic attitudes among Smer voters, but the 2012 elections were no hard-right backlash.[117] SNS failed to enter parliament, and support for KDH remained unchanged. Smer itself did not use antigay rhetoric, and its program called for gender equality. Indeed, it continued its predecessor's strategy of defusing and co-opting LGBT issues by relegating them to government committees.

In terms of organization, the evidence describes a stalled and, until 2012, even declining movement. There was a kind of reversion to the "postcommunist mean" of thin activism, which was exacerbated by declining accession-related support. The absence of threat to the "immediate protective surround" weakened the willingness of all but the most dedicated activists to contribute to collective action. In my fieldwork, I heard similar sentiments expressed by Slovak and Czech gays and lesbians, namely that it was not difficult to lead their day-to-day lives even if, legally speaking, they lacked the same protections as in Western Europe. Even if not publicly out, they did not feel it necessary to hide their orientation. Tracing movement decline is typically more difficult than measuring growth because civil society organizations rarely pack up overnight. Instead, demobilization occurs inconspicuously, as event planning declines, fewer members attend meetings, and communication with the outside world dwindles. What follows is an assessment of the movement from 2004 through 2012 along the dimensions of breadth and territorial reach, orientation toward the authorities, and organization as SMOs.

By 2012, the first wave of activist groups had all but disappeared, and the network had largely shrunk to Bratislava. Of the eight civil society groups covered above, only two remained active, OI and Museion.[118] OI crossed the threshold from informal to formal status in 2006, when it received legal standing as a public organization, but in terms of capacity it lagged behind counterpart SMOs in neighboring countries. As one indicator, OI did not produce any significant public reports between 2004 and 2012; by comparison, Poland's KPH or Hungary's Háttér produced numerous reports. OI lacked permanent offices and staff, unlike KPH, Háttér, or Romania's ACCEPT. Following its establishment as a public organization, it filed yearly activity reports, but these ceased in 2011.[119] Likewise, Ganymedes may have existed on paper, but interviews suggested that practically speaking it was defunct, and its website was last updated in 2010.

As these first-generation activist groups declined, two new ones appeared—Queer Leaders Forum (QLF) and Duchový PRIDE Bratislava—and in doing so revealed tensions and disappointments in the movement. QLF was established in 2007, splitting off from Museion: its stated mission "to establish a functioning leadership and activist network" highlighted the movement's weakened solidarity. Recalling the Czech example of PROUD, QLF's younger members were critical of the movement's older leadership, especially its pragmatically framed project of registered partnerships. Instead, they outlined more controversial goals like same-sex marriage with adoption rights. The registered partnerships campaign had, by 2012, been languishing for several years, effectively blocked from consideration in parliament by KDH. Among analysts of Slovak politics, there is a long lull in discussion of the movement over this period; for example, the comprehensive annual reports on Slovak civil society and politics published by the Institute of Public Affairs, which had included sections and twice even chapters on LGBT issues and rights groups in the accession period, offer no mention of such rights activism after 2004.

QLF and its partner Duchový PRIDE Bratislava sought to jump-start the movement by staging a Pride in Bratislava in 2010. The absence of Prides until 2010 is further indication of organizational underdevelopment and predominantly apolitical orientation. As mentioned above, some accounts claim that Prides occurred in 1992 and 2001, but, even if we accept these dates, we must also note that Prides did not become an annual tradition, as in Poland, Hungary, and Romania.[120] Though the 2010 parade drew wider attention when it was attacked by several dozen far-right youth, it was repeated in the following four years without further incident. Here, Slovakia's experience again echoes the Czech one, where a regional parade in Brno was attacked by skinheads in 2008 but subsequent parades proceeded peacefully.

To conclude, Figure 7.4 plots the changing balance of civil society groups between 1990 and 2012, dividing them into primarily politically and apolitically oriented. For much of the 1990s, the movement was quite limited, composed of three or fewer groups. Through Ganymedes's association with the Czech movement, it could claim a political orientation; however, these early groups were primarily social and self-help oriented. The accession period was the movement's high point, as groups with both social and political orientation multiplied. This growth reflected the attention that EU accession brought to minority rights, allowing groups like OI to act as brokers between the European Commission and the Slovak government and opening up financial resources through Phare and other accession-related funds. While socially conservative parties like KDH worked quietly to obstruct policy change on LGBT issues, they strongly supported EU membership, so that no hard-right coalition formed—even if the elements were there. After 2004,

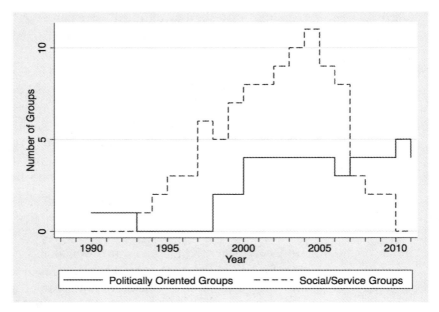

Figure 7.4. Number of Slovak LGBT Groups by Primary Orientation (1988–2012)

as accession-related funding dwindled and the possibility of brokering faded, the movement began to demobilize.

The Limits of Transnational Leverage: Romania's Arrested Development

Of the countries examined here, Romania had the harshest record of stigmatizing homosexuality before 1989, and it remained criminalized until 2001. Article 200 of the Penal Code stated that "sexual relations between same sex persons will be punished by a prison sentence of one to five years." Article 201 criminalized "acts of sexual perversion," and Article 202 banned the "sexual corruption of minors."[121] The secret police made extensive use of these laws as a pretext for jailing dissidents since Western governments were less likely to classify such actions as human rights abuses.[122] Romania is different, therefore, in that communism's legacy included both de facto and de jure repression of homosexuality. There were no therapeutic clubs, discussion groups, or other forms of public association, as in late-communist Hungary or Czechoslovakia: gay life was deeply underground.[123]

The critical factor for the development of LGBT activism in Romania was the sequencing of hard-right backlash vis-à-vis the onset of EU leverage; unlike our other cases, backlash *preceded* leverage and dropped off afterwards. As we saw in Chapter 2, the EU's framing of homosexuality in terms of minority rights did not gain traction until the late 1990s. For most of that decade, Romanian activists faced a far more forbidding POS than in our other cases: technically, LGBT activism was illegal and the hard-right parties were strong politically. Once, however, the EU clarified conditionality regarding sexual minorities, suddenly transnational leverage became decisive. Compared with the other cases, the EU's leverage was the strongest here. Romania fell so far short of membership criteria that its accession date was delayed three years, until 2007. Not only did this make elites cautious about demonizing homosexuality, it incentivized them to use comparatively progressive policy changes on LGBT issues as a signal to EU authorities of their commitment to European norms. Romanian activists were, therefore, exceptionally well positioned to act as brokers between transnational allies and the national government.

Though this sequencing complicates direct comparisons with our other cases, it is very useful theoretically. First, the weakness of 1990s activism despite the presence of a hard-right threat suggests an important scope condition regarding the benefits of backlash. Namely, some minimum level of external leverage is necessary to bound potential repression; otherwise, backlash suppresses activism. Second, the success of Romanian activists as brokers between the EU and the national government after 1998 was not without costs to movement organization, as we will see. On the positive side, it enabled surprising policy gains, but it also limited the movement's ties with its grassroots and domestic allies. After Romania gained EU membership, these weaknesses left it vulnerable to policy retrenchment.

The unusual sequencing of backlash and external leverage explains the movement's idiosyncratic developmental trajectory. In the early 1990s, it was an underground network in a very closed society: informally organized, inward-looking, apolitical, lacking in allies, not engaged with service provision, and very small. A striking, even unique, feature was the movement's transnational origins: it began largely as a project of Western expatriates living in Bucharest, who were guided by their experience in their home countries and, as foreign nationals, more willing to risk LGBT activism. Transitioning to leadership by Romanian activists proved difficult. By 2012, the movement was professionally organized, commanded stable resources, politically engaged, but it was still confined to the capital, Bucharest, still comparatively unengaged with service provision, and still lacking in domestic allies and grassroots participation. It could point to impressive policy achievements, but their implementation was questionable, and after these early gains progress stalled. This was emblematic of the movement itself: it was in a state of arrested development.

Preaccession Romania (1989–1997)

Not only did the hard right mobilize earlier than elsewhere, it enjoyed access to government power in the preaccession period. Indeed, the early success of illiberal parties was largely to blame for Romania's delayed EU membership. The following hard-right parties can be identified during this period: the Greater Romania Party (PRM) and the Romanian National Unity Party (PUNR). Scholars generally classify both as populist radical right.[124] PRM was strongly identified with its charismatic leader Vadim Tudor, an admirer of Benito Mussolini, former propagandist for Nicolae Caeusescu, and editor of an influential newspaper, *România Mare*. In his vitriolic articles Tudor skewered political elites and espoused a paranoid program of anti-Semitism, ethnic nationalism, and Christian fundamentalism.[125] If PRM's list of enemies was wide-ranging, PUNR espoused an anti-Hungarian nationalism based in historically conflictual ethnic relations in its home region of Transylvania.[126] The party system also contained a Christian Democratic party, but as in Slovakia it bitterly opposed the populist radical right because of their cooperation with ex-communists. PRM and PUNR entered government between 1992 and 1996 as coalition partners to the ex-communist Party of Social Democracy of Romania (PDSR).[127] We may also include the Romanian Orthodox Church as part of the hard right. The Church's mobilization against homosexuality strongly recalled the actions of Radio Maryja and Father Rydzyk in Poland.[128]

In 1993, Romania promised to remove Article 200 as a condition of joining the Council of Europe. The government, which included the hard right, promptly forgot the promise; after all, the CoE, unlike the EU, had only moral suasion, not conditionality, to elicit compliance.[129] In July 1995, however, Romania's Constitutional Court took up the issue, soliciting comment on Article 200 from a range of political and civil societal actors. The Church led the virtually unanimous response: Article 200 should be kept. Under Church pressure, the Senate maintained that Article 200 violated neither the constitution nor the European Convention of Human Rights. Despite this consensus, in July 1995 the Court ruled Article 200 unconstitutional "to the extent that it refers to consensual sexual relations between adults of the same sex, not taking place in public and not producing public scandal."[130] Some regarded this as a "bold move [that] paved the way for decriminalizing homosexuality,"[131] but most regarded it an obfuscation—one that, given the vaguely defined notion of "public scandal," even worsened the legal standing of LGBT people.[132] When parliament took up the Court's mandate to change the law, it became clear that the ruling's ambiguities would be exploited to the fullest. The Church waded into the debate, calling gays and lesbians "the ultimate enemy" and "Satan's army."[133] Because of entrenched resistance to homosexuality in parliament, it took almost two years and two unsuccessful votes to amend Article 200, even in an obviously flawed way.[134] The amended version removed the blanket ban on same-sex relations, but it allowed prison terms if such relations produced "public scandal." Since "public scandal" was nowhere defined, and wide open to interpretation, the amended Article 200 effectively preserved the ban on same-sex relations. As one analysis noted, "Some politicians believed that any homosexual act was potentially public because 'what is damaging and immoral on the streets cannot be permissible and moral in intimacy,' while others justified their hesitation to decriminalise homosexuality fully by pointing to opinion polls showing that Romanians regarded homosexual relations as abnormal."[135]

Thus, during the preaccession period, Romania had a clearly articulated, well-mobilized hard right that engaged with homosexuality as a political issue to a far greater extent than in Poland, Hungary, and Slovakia, our comparative referents for closed societies. Because of the debate over Article 200, homosexuality was both more visible and framed as a "European question." Why then was Romanian activism also as underdeveloped during this period as anywhere besides the Czech Republic?

The answer is straightforward: Article 200 discouraged the formation of LGBT groups of any kind. Not only was official recognition impossible, their activities could, under the law, be considered criminal. As Romania-based expatriate activist Long noted in 1997, Article 200 "can still destroy any gay group."[136] Romania's was a closed POS, which only EU leverage could open.

Let us briefly examine the organization of activism through 1997. Given both the stigma attached to homosexuality and its criminalization, these were informal networks par excellence. They were inward looking, lacked legal standing and financial resources, did not provide services, and were generally invisible.[137] Their goals were to provide space for socialization and to strategize about removing Article 200. They were also short-lived: between 1992 and 1996 four groups were established, only one of which survived.[138] As noted earlier, Western expatriates played a dominant role. The main group, ACCEPT, was founded by a combination of Romanians and (mostly American) expatriates. Also prominent among ACCEPT's founders were straight activists affiliated with the Romanian branch of the transnational minority-rights group the Helsinki Committee. In May 1995, ACCEPT hosted a conference titled "Homosexuality: A Human Right?," the first public discussion of homosexuality since 1989. In October 1996, it was registered as a human-rights NGO—not, it should be emphasized, as an LGBT group. To a much greater extent than in Poland, Hungary, or the former Czechoslovakia, ACCEPT depended on transnational actors.[139] ACCEPT comprised so many expatriates that from 1996 through 2000 it published two newsletters, in English and Romanian.

This example underlines the limits of transnational activism absent hard-edged external leverage. Outside funding and advice helped establish ACCEPT, but Romania's movement was the weakest by far during this period. To quote Long, one of ACCEPT's founders, the expatriates' outsized role revealed "the dependency on others that gay Romanians felt—to provide them with not only paradigm and discourse but also example." He gloomily concluded that "the tenuousness of this solidarity reflects an almost total lack of real community . . . [ACCEPT] will probably be unable to organize effectively against the law [Article 200]. . . . That effort must come from abroad."[140]

Romania during Accession (1998–2007)

The EP's 1998 resolution not to admit "any country that, through its legislation or policies, violates the human rights of lesbians and gay men" was more troubling for Romania than elsewhere given Article 200. This open violation of EU norms shaped the politics of homosexuality throughout this period. It made Romania a cause célèbre for transnational rights groups, which donated funding and logistical support to ACCEPT to a degree not seen with other groups in the region. This aid enabled ACCEPT to professionalize into a formidable policy broker; however, it also amplified the elitist orientation already evident in the group's expatriate origins. ACCEPT skillfully leveraged transnational pressure to make policy gains but struggled to engage its constituents and expand beyond Bucharest. Further limiting movement-building was the hard right's relative disengagement with homosexuality as an issue for contesting EU norms. Romania's hard-right parties *supported* EU integration, even though it meant moderating their antiminority rhetoric. The only actor that campaigned against EU norms was the Orthodox Church, but it found few political allies in doing so. Thus, Romania did not experience a comparable hard-right backlash to those in Poland or Hungary, the kind that threatens the "protective surround" and catalyzes framing contests between national identity and EU norms of tolerance.

As we have seen, PRM was as good an example of the populist radical right as one could find anywhere in the region. It was in opposition from 1996 to 2000, but the implosion of the Liberal-Christian Democratic coalition in 2000 put PRM in striking distance of power. Its leader reached the final round in the 2000 presidential contest, and PRM won the second largest mandate in parliament. Why did PRM's electoral success not translate into a sense of threat to the "immediate protective surround" or elevate the LGBT minority into a symbol of Romania's EU aspirations? Despite its anti-Western rhetoric PRM was, as Mudde notes, "Euro-pragmatist," one of a few such populist radical right parties that "do not believe in the underlying ideas of the European integration, but they do support the EU."[141] Political scientist Grigore Pop-Eleches even found that PRM voters were *more* supportive of the EU than the overall population in 2000.[142] The rather sedate election campaign reflected this, as parties like PRM and PDSR ran on their commitment to the

EU and democracy, despite their reputations for illiberalism.[143] On the strength of its stellar results, PRM advertised itself as a coalition partner, but PDSR rejected the offer because they now deemed it too extreme. Within a year, the PDSR government had not only repealed Article 200, it had also enacted one of the most progressive antidiscrimination frameworks of any EU applicant-state. The government's alacrity regarding antidiscrimination policy was generally seen as compensating for poor reform credentials overall by signaling commitment to EU norms in an area where reform was comparatively less financially costly.[144]

For most of the 1990s, the media's presentation of homosexuality had been sensationalist and sporadic, driven by coverage of international celebrities. The main "political" journalism on the topic was the virulently homophobic coverage of *România Mare*, the party organ of PRM. With the increasing application of EU leverage to issues regarding sexual orientation and the opening of accession negotiations in 2000, the character of media coverage changed. Coverage peaked between June and November 2000, during the parliamentary election campaign.[145] The majority of articles concerned Article 200, but as Voichita Nachescu writes, "It is remarkable that daily national newspapers avoided taking a decisive stand with regard to sexual minority rights: few opinion articles were written by stars of Romanian journalism on the matter, and even then homophobic arguments were rather masked." Nachescu notes further that "there were *no* media campaigns *either supporting or opposing* homosexual rights."[146]

If the counterframing of Romanian family values and EU antidiscrimination norms lacked resonance in the mainstream media, the same was true for the party debate. We saw earlier that even the most homophobic party, PRM, pragmatically moderated its tone on issues relating to EU membership. Other parties expressed even greater caution, refusing to be drawn into positions for or against LGBT rights, thereby thwarting the Church's attempts to politicize the issue by demanding a referendum on Article 200. Only one party declared its support for repealing Article 200, the ethnic-minority party Hungarian Democratic Union, whose support was hardly persuasive for the ethnic Romanian majority.[147] Other parties' views were a cipher. In refusing to support the Church's demand for a referendum, leaders of both the National Liberal Party and the PDSR stated that referenda should be reserved for "real laws" and "matters of principle."[148] Another feature of this confused party debate was the wildly inconsistent statements by the same politicians. One Peasant Party MP warned in 1999 that gays and lesbians "will proliferate and take over the world. And then how are we going to have children?" A year later, after voting to repeal Article 200, he stated, "The Constitution says that everybody is free to do what he wants with his life."[149]

The one actor to frame homosexuality in anti-EU terms was not a political party but the Romanian Orthodox Church. The Church used its influence with state television to support Article 200 in the strongest terms, linking homosexuality with abnormality, disease, evil, and "Westernisation."[150] To quote Archbishop Bartolomeu Anania, "We want to join Europe, not Sodom."[151] The Holy Synod implored the Senate not to repeal Article 200, and it pleaded for the president to veto any repeal should the Senate approve one. (As mentioned above, it also called for a national referendum, unsuccessfully.) It was striking how little support this campaign received from political parties, especially when compared with PiS's and LPR's cooperation with Radio Maryja in Poland. What's more, the Church's own counterframing suffered from the inconsistency between its desire to join Europe and its demand to be exempted from European norms. As Nachescu points out, the Church "claimed exceptional status for a *minority* (i.e., the Romanians) from the standards of human rights. . . . However, it would not tolerate the existence of sexual *minorities*."[152]

The combination of high transnational leverage and low resonance for EU/LGBT-rights framing contests facilitated the repeal of Article 200 and the enactment of antidiscrimination policies that far exceeded Romania's obligations for EU membership, but it sharply constrained the movement's organizational development.[153] Activism was far narrower and more inward-looking than in our other cases. After 1996, the movement consisted primarily of one organization, ACCEPT, which remained based in Bucharest. Though the infusion of transnational support eventually allowed ACCEPT to develop counseling and outreach services, the movement lacked the broader panoply of social and cultural groups—even lesbian ones—that we have noted in other countries. By its own admission, ACCEPT lacked public visibility.[154] Besides the Hungarian Democratic Union mentioned earlier, it also lacked party and media allies.

What ACCEPT lacked in domestic allies, it made up for in transnational ones. These allowed it to become an effective political lobby in short order. Through external donations it bought its own building in Bucharest, where it had office space, a community center, a library, and later, as the group began to offer services, space for counseling. ACCEPT collaborated closely with the CoE, the EP and Commission, and foreign NGOs such as ILGA-Europe and COC Netherlands. (The last deployed a Dutch project coordinator to Bucharest to help build movement infrastructure.) This lobbying was closer to the pragmatic, elite-oriented variety familiar from the Czech Republic than the more public, confrontational variety of Poland in the 2000s. ACCEPT did not mobilize the grass roots through controversial public service campaigns like "Let Them See Us" in Poland.[155] Its activities focused on "strategic lobbying."

Through the many delays in Romania's harmonization with EU norms, ACCEPT was *the* watchdog that brought every instance of failed compliance to the Commission's attention. The campaign for antidiscrimination legislation provides one of the best examples. The law mandated the establishment of an independent National Council for Combating Discrimination, but the government showed little interest in actually doing so until ACCEPT threatened to sue it. Within two weeks, an office was being set up. ACCEPT then consulted on the selection of its governing board and trained its staff.[156]

The protracted fight against official intransigence honed the group into a highly professional organization. One concrete sign of this was the significant presence of non-LGBT people in the group's leadership positions—to my knowledge a feature unique in the region's major LGBT-rights groups.[157] Numerous sources attest to this professionalization. Here is how the Romania Desk Officer for the European Commission characterized ACCEPT in 2002:

> They were the best organised lobby I've come across. . . . ACCEPT knew the system; were able to use more institutions to put pressure on. . . . If I had to give advice to any NGO in any areas, I would say that that would be a model of how to get your case across. To present your arguments and present your case successfully.[158]

ACCEPT used its influence with the EU to gain inclusion in meetings with government agencies and ministries about legal harmonization for accession. It had a reputation for toughness among Romanian politicians and was feared by them.

This intense focus on lobbying, international fund-raising, and professionalization came at a cost to ACCEPT's community-building roles: it threatened, at the very least, to stunt grassroots participation and, at worst, to split the movement's leadership and the grass roots—as happened in the Czech Republic. According to Carl Stychin, some among the grass roots wondered aloud "can ACCEPT speak for gays?"[159] After its legal victories repealing Article 200 and enacting antidiscrimination policies, it was still faced with the challenge of an inhospitable social climate for LGBT people. ACCEPT turned now to building the grass roots, but this was to prove much more difficult.

Though repealing Article 200 cleared the legal hurdles to establishing LGBT associations, few new groups have emerged. In 2002, the city of Cluj-Napoca saw the establishment of Be an Angel Romania, which has hosted an annual film festival since 2006. In 2005, ACCEPT organized Romania's first Pride parade. It had to legally challenge an attempted ban by Bucharest's mayor, but the greater hurdle proved to be mobilizing participants (see Figure 7.2). During fieldwork in Bucharest, I attended the 2011 Pride and was struck by the small number of participants and NGOs attending. The most robust presence was that of foreign embassies. Also notable was the number of participants who disguised their identities. I was told that such hesitance to publicly affiliate with an LGBT group was not unusual for participants at public events, even among ACCEPT members. In short, as successful as the movement was as a professionalized political lobby, its grass roots remained underdeveloped.

Postaccession Romania (Since 2007)

If the Romanian movement's trajectory thus far illustrates how activists can leverage transnational support to win policy gains even in a closed society, then developments since Romania joined the EU demonstrate this model's limits. Since then, the movement has remained in a state of arrested development—still concentrated in Bucharest, still lacking in domestic allies, still focused on lobbying, and still weak in grassroots participation. As the dissolution of the Czech movement's political SMOs reminds us, maintaining organizational infrastructure after policy gains is not a given. Unlike its Czech counterpart, Romania's movement did not demobilize, however. By the same token, it did not follow the Polish movement's path of heightened mobilization after accession. The chief difference was the role of the hard right during and after EU accession: whereas in Poland the end of conditionality launched the hard right politically, in Romania it marked the decline of this segment of the party spectrum. The 2008 elections pushed hard-right parties to the margins of the opposition and, in 2012, out of parliament altogether. Instead, Romania's LGBT movement experienced a disciplined, focused, lobbying campaign by social movement actors supported by a transnational social-conservative advocacy network to stop further policy change favoring LGBT people. In short, ACCEPT faced an adversary that used its own organizational model against it.

Overshadowed in the debate over Article 200 had been an idiosyncrasy in the constitution's definition of marriage as a "relationship between two 'spouses' without mentioning their gender."[160] In 2005, an informally organized group of evangelical pastors began collecting signatures to amend the constitution by referendum and define marriage as a union between a man and a woman. The campaign was supported by the Orthodox and Catholic Churches but also, crucially, by American and British conservatives. The campaign gathered 650,000 signatures and prompted ACCEPT to adopt same-sex unions as the theme for the 2006 Pride parade. Despite the grassroots politicization of homosexuality evident in this campaign, two points should be emphasized. First, Romania was still not an EU member at this point. Second, the choice of a referendum revealed the reluctance of political parties to ally with antigay mobilization—as happened earlier with the Orthodox Church's (unsuccessful) call for a referendum on Article 200. After all, going the referendum route was more difficult than working through the standard legislative process, as it required not only signatures but also validation by the Constitutional Court. ACCEPT fought the referendum campaign in the Court, which in July 2007 ruled against a referendum on technical grounds.

With the 2008 elections approaching and Romania now an EU member, the conservative campaign regrouped with additional transnational support and a new strategy. In late 2007, it became a formally recognized association, the Alliance of Families (AoF). It now pursued a strategy of lobbying parliament for smaller but interrelated policy changes that, collectively, would foreclose further LGBT legal advances. It received extensive legal advice and other support from American lobbying groups that had pioneered the US defense of marriage campaign.[161] Meanwhile, ACCEPT drew on its own transnational allies—including ILGA-Europe, the Council of Europe, the International Gay and Lesbian Human Rights Commission , and the UN—to lobby Romanian lawmakers. Even though, as mentioned above, parliament now lacked a hard-right presence, AoF was able to find votes to pass a host of smaller changes circumscribing possibilities for future registered-partnerships or marriage legislation. These were enacted over loud criticism from ACCEPT and its allies, but since none of the changes imperiled Romania's compliance with EU requirements, ACCEPT's brokering strategy was no longer effective.

Organizationally, the LGBT movement remained as professionalized as ever, and despite the setbacks it experienced regarding same-sex unions, it has prevented any rollback of its achievements regarding antidiscrimination policy. The possibility of erosion of the power of the National Council for Combatting Discrimination (CNCD) is very real. By comparison with counterpart institutions in our other countries, Romania's CNCD was established with surprisingly broad powers: it possessed political independence, its own staff, the power to impose fines, and a board whose members have ministerial status. These very strengths made it a target for political patronage soon after its establishment, and the onset of the financial crisis in 2009 increased political pressure, as the government looked for budgetary savings. Yet, even through the controversy over same-sex unions, the CNCD weathered these threats to its independence, and even existence, as it successfully prosecuted several discrimination cases regarding sexual orientation.[162] In 2013, the CNCD was active in the debate over a second proposal to amend the constitution to prevent same-sex marriage in 2013, a proposal that proved unsuccessful in parliament.[163] Thus, ACCEPT has largely been able to maintain its gains, even if it has struggled to extend them.

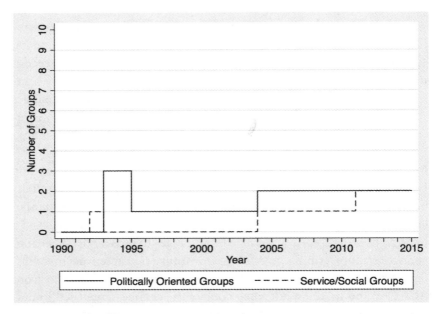

Figure 7.5. Number of Romanian LGBT Groups by Primary Orientation (1990–2012)

Clifford Bob has argued that this kind policy stalemate between progressive and conservative activism is representative of a larger pattern of transnationalized advocacy networks intervening in domestic politics.[164] My analysis here supports his assessment, but I would lay a different emphasis, from policy change to the organization of activism. The Romanian LGBT-rights movement is in many respects a great success, especially against the backdrop of Article 200 and, more broadly, the general weakness of civil society. One sign of the success of ACCEPT's model of leveraging transnational support to overcome weak mobilizing structures domestically is to be found, in fact, in its emulation by conservative counteractivists like AoF. Certainly, Romanian activists have avoided the Czech outcome of a movement that disbands itself politically. That said, to achieve further goals against an opponent like AoF, Romanian activists will need domestic allies, grassroots participation, and the wider visibility that a hard-right backlash of the kind found in Poland or Hungary generates—where threats to the "immediate protective surround" resonate outside the movement as a broader threat to democracy and EU norms. Since accession, indicators of organizational growth such as participation in Prides and the founding of new groups have been flat. As one analyst put it, "After having achieved most of its aims, the activists of ACCEPT are facing a certain agony, as the absence of harsh forms of discrimination against homosexuals have decreased both domestic mobilization as well as external assistance."[165]

Conclusion

Extending to Hungary, Slovakia, and Romania, this chapter offers further support that hard-right backlash against transnational norms builds activism even where domestic mobilizing structures are weak. At the same time, it highlights new variations—the consequences of backlash in the absence of external leverage, the possibility of extraparliamentary backlash, and the trade-off between policy gains and grassroots participation—that open up further vistas for applying the argument beyond postcommunist EU accession states and, to be bold, beyond LGBT activism. The next and final chapter begins that task.

Conclusion

Leverage, Visibility, and Movement Success

In June 2012, the Warsaw city government installed a 30-foot-tall sculpture of a rainbow arch in the public square Plac Zbawiciela (Savior Square), so named for the baroque Church of the Holiest Savior that looks out over it. The sculpture had already spent a year installed in front of the European Parliament in Brussels during Poland's term holding the EU's rotating presidency. It was transferred to Warsaw when that term ended. Its creator, Julita Wójcik, was coy about its message, calling it a symbol of tolerance, not LGBT rights per se.[1] Nevertheless, city officials, politicians, and Warsaw residents of both liberal and conservative viewpoints firmly connected the rainbow arch to LGBT rights. Stanisław Pięta, an MP from PiS, called it "a disgusting gesture, offensive to Catholics . . . a provocation."[2] Radio Maryja's Father Rydzyk decried it as a "symbol of abnormality and deviancy that should not be tolerated."[3] It was set on fire seven times during the three years that it was installed on Savior Square. The most infamous arson attack occurred on Polish National Independence Day on November 11, 2013, when far-right and nationalist groups rioted in Warsaw, attacking not only the statue but also the Russian embassy and cars parked nearby. After each arson attack, volunteers painstakingly rebuilt the sculpture, which entailed replacing the thousands of colored artificial flowers of which it was made. They felt no ambiguity about the sculpture's symbolism: as one told a journalist, "As a homosexual person, I don't feel safe in Warsaw. I became involved in the rebuilding to oppose pervasive homophobia."[4] Defending the Rainbow Arch became a highly resonant cause for allies outside the movement as well, who coined the slogan "Freedom cannot be burned" and collected signatures from over 53,000 people. Warsaw's president, Hanna Gronkiewicz-Waltz, of the liberal, pro-EU Civic Platform party, vowed that the statue would be rebuilt as many times as necessary.[5]

As a symbol, the Rainbow Arch almost perfectly encapsulates the themes of backlash, movement-building, and the reframing of homosexuality in terms of EU norms described in the preceding chapters. The saga of the arch distills several key features of the more robust instances of LGBT activism after communism: its close ties to antigay repression and the "culture of restraint" from which this homophobia springs;[6] the highly public nature of the struggle for inclusion as full citizens; and the decisive role of grassroots agency. The struggle to defend the Rainbow Arch against a persistent campaign of vandalism felt far removed from the "high politics" of policy lobbying and transnational advocacy. Both critics and supporters of the sculpture connected it with Europe, but the struggle was a deeply local engagement fought by everyday individuals to preserve their city against threatening attack. It was an enactment of the civic and participatory rights that were won in 1989—a kind of democratization after democratization.

As such, it had much in common with the larger arc of development of the LGBT movement and sexual citizenship in Britain and the US stretching from the 1960s through the enactment of same-sex partnerships in the 2000s. In Jeffrey Weeks's telling, this long revolution of democratizing everyday life played out in the West not simply as a function of economic modernization and secularization but, fundamentally, through the development of grassroots agency.[7] It was not inevitable, and opposition by various forms of fundamentalism was a central element driving the process forward. The galvanizing shocks experienced by the British and American movements—for example, Section 28, Thatcher's "new Victorianism," and the Stonewall Riot—are analogues to such episodes described in the earlier chapters as the banning of Warsaw's March of Equality, Romania's Article 200, and backlash against Directive 2000/78/EC (banning labor market discrimination on the basis of sexual orientation).

To review the argument developed in the preceding chapters, the interaction between transnational pressures associated with EU accession and the (generally unfavorable) domestic conditions in postcommunist Europe reshaped the organization of LGBT activism in the following stages. In the first stage, that is, before 1989, communism created a strong latent homophobia in society. Even if the extent of harm to sexual minorities varied by country, in all cases it was a question of harm, never progress. Also true of this period, nowhere in the communist world was homosexuality a political issue. After communism fell, high levels of societal homophobia persisted, but both homophobia and efforts to combat it remained essentially apolitical. Beginning around 2000, EU accession sparked a backlash of politicized homophobia—that is, homophobia as a tool of hard-right political mobilization. As part of this backlash, concepts like "the homosexual lobby" and the "homosexual agenda" were linked to the perceived imposition of foreign values by the EU. The association of LGBT rights with Europeanization provided the crucial impetus to previously scattered domestic LGBT-rights movements to organize themselves politically and professionally.

Backlash and political polarization drove this process. First, the backlash against homosexuality in the early to mid-2000s galvanized once moribund LGBT-rights groups to organize. Second, polarization made homosexuality a salient issue for the wider public, removing it from the invisibility of taboo. Third, backlash had the effect of bringing LGBT-rights groups to the attention of potential political allies, for whom this issue became a marker in the larger pro-Europe/Euroskeptic political cleavage. The opponents of LGBT rights were, therefore, crucial agents in the process, a process that we may even consider "Europeanization via Europeanization's enemies."

Poland is the paradigmatic case to illustrate this argument. The book has also presented close studies of four other cases that represent different constellations of the argument's core variables. Like Poland, Romania and Hungary represent closed societies that experienced hard-right backlashes, though their timing differed. The Czech Republic is an open society that did not experience a hard-right backlash. Slovakia is a mixed case, a relatively closed society that avoided a hard-right backlash. The varying fates of these LGBT-rights movements comport with the argument's expectations. Slovakia's movement is the weakest of the group. The Czech movement has experienced dramatic decline since the early 2000s. Thus, in the longer view, far from weakening the position of LGBT-rights movements in the region, the politicization of homosexuality, where it has occurred, has strengthened it.

This argument contributes to three broad literatures in comparative politics. First, it extends the growing literature on the politics of homosexuality outside of the ambit of Western Europe and the US, joining recent work on Latin America in particular. With its focus on the catalyzing role of resistance in building LGBT movements, it extends the work of Weeks and others on sexual citizenship, as discussed above.

Second, it extends the literature on Europeanization and transnational norm diffusion. It presents a theoretical framework to account for Europeanizing norm diffusion even where external leverage is weak. Further, it shows that conflict between transnational norms and entrenched domestic ones need not preclude "social learning" but instead may catalyze it. In this way, it builds on the work of scholars like Margaret Keck and Kathryn Sikkink and Phillip Ayoub on transnational activism.[8] That work described how attributes of transnational advocacy networks—for example, leverage, agenda-setting power, the embeddedness of domestic interest groups in transnational networks—could allow domestic activists to circumvent their domestic opponents. Ayoub, in particular, is sensitive to, and critical of, the tendency of Europeanization studies to focus on "'good' norm entrepreneurs and overlook contention in the domestic sphere."[9] He argues that pro- and anti-LGBT are often "mutually constitutive," especially in postcommunist Europe.[10] The importance of visibility is another common thread across Ayoub's and my productively complementary studies. As points of contrast, this book *foregrounds* the role of norm opponents, theorizing the conditions under which antigay backlash builds movements and tracing a longer historical arc with the goal of forging a processual account of the internal dynamics of social movement development and the mechanisms by which backlash helps activists overcome collective action problems. The catalyzing role of norm opponents is manifest when contrasting the organizational trajectories of movements equally exposed to transnational norms and networks but not hard-right backlash. Despite differences of analytical emphasis and (for the most part) selection of cases, the reinforcing findings of Ayoub's study and mine highlight the need for a more unified account of Europeanization that balances the push of transnational norms against the shove of domestic contention.

Third, the extension of sexual citizenship and the "democratization of everyday life" in Eastern Europe have implications not just for the study of LGBT activism but also for the study of postcommunist civil society.[11] The surprising variation in the robustness of LGBT activism—not just across countries but within the same country over time—challenges the dominant narrative of quiescent civil society as an enduring legacy of Leninist rule. The legacies literature rightly highlighted the weak appetite for participation and the paucity of mobilizing structures after communism. However, this literature also tended to study civil society from the perspective of how individuals organize to pursue collective goals, by which standards the dearth of traditional mobilizing resources spelled weak activism. This book has instead highlighted how individuals organize *in order to defend against threats to what they already have*, that is, threats to the "immediate protective surround."[12] In this way, opposition can become a resource, enabling otherwise resource-poor movements to overcome collective action problems. Thinking about civil society in this way—that is, in terms of the relations between its constituent groups rather than the overall level of resources that these groups can draw on—extends the work of Tsveta Petrova and Sidney Tarrow and opens up potentially fruitful new avenues for comparative work on civil society development in postauthoritarian settings.[13]

To close, this chapter takes up some broader questions or, more boldly, lessons from the Eastern European experience of LGBT-rights activism. My aim is to connect this experience with that of LGBT movements in other contexts; other social movements in the same contexts (i.e., the book's country cases); and ongoing debates in the broader social movement literature. At least four encouraging lessons may be drawn from the trajectories of activism traced out in this book.

First, it is important to look beyond the short term. As David Meyer has written, "The ways that movements make a difference are complex, veiled, and take far longer to manifest themselves than the news cycle that covers a single demonstration, or even a whole protest campaign."[14] By tracing LGBT activism's evolution over roughly two decades, this book confirms Meyer's insight, showing not only that mobilization's effects may be slow to manifest themselves but also that they may come in a one-step-back-two-steps-forward cycle.

Second, the examples of movement-building traced out in the previous chapters depart somewhat from the kinds of examples commonly analyzed in the literature on "moral shock," which my application of the "immediate protective surround" draws on.[15] In practice, this literature typically argues that "moral shock" catalyzes activism in rare and extreme circumstances. A good example is Mothers Against Drunk Driving, many of whose participants are motivated by the death of their child.[16] Another oft-cited example is the nuclear meltdown at Three Mile Island as a catalyst of the antinuclear movement. Hard-right electoral breakthroughs and their aftermath, while certainly dramatic and threatening, are less extreme; the LGBT activism that they catalyze differs also in that it draws on an already-defined and broader set of collective grievances. Thus, the book offers an extension of an important literature beyond its home territory.

Third, as Meyer reminds us, social movement change is only partly measured by policy gains; it is also about changing how policy is made and how participants are changed by their participation.[17] Even at the tail end of a cycle of contention, as participation ebbs, social movements leave behind institutionalized organizations that continue the task of advocacy and provide the infrastructure for subsequent movements. Likewise, participation is a formative educational experience with potentially far-reaching impact on culture and politics more broadly, even if these effects are hard to document.[18]

Fourth, transnationalization is to be embraced. It is a striking feature of the literature on transnational activism that scholars are divided as to whether transnationalization helps or hinders progressive causes such as LGBT rights. Clifford Bob and Phillip Ayoub illustrate the two poles in this debate.[19] Ayoub argues strongly that transnationalization improves policy and social attitudes on such issues. Bob, however, is skeptical of the possibility of progress. Since the opponents of progressive norms are also transnationalized, he argues, the result is policy gridlock: "[T]he joyful birth of a meaningful new policy is rare. More common is its strangulation, nonpolicy—or its evisceration, zombie policy."[20] This book cannot settle this debate regarding transnationalization and policy outcomes, but it can offer a new line of approach, first, by showing activism's broader impacts beyond policy and, second, by highlighting the connections between activism in one sphere and that in another. The transnationalization of activism increases linkages among social movements, as activists draw on a wider web of experience and resources to organize.[21] In this way, it contributes to what Tarrow describes as cycles of collective action.[22] In such cycles, sister movements may draw on common mobilizing structures built through experience as allies.[23]

One movement's breakthrough can open the POS for others, leading to spin-off movements that emulate and adapt others' tactics and framing to their own cause.[24] Thus, keeping in mind a broader metric of movement success and the potential for broader cycles of collective action leads to a more positive evaluation of transnational activism.

These points are all illustrated by postcommunist LGBT activism, but I would like to show their broader relevance by applying them to a movement frequently alluded to over the preceding chapters but, for reasons of space, not developed: the women's movement. Examining the narrative of postcommunist feminism shows how this book's argument scales not only across LGBT movements situated in different countries but also across other social movements within the same country. I focus on Poland because nowhere better illustrates the combined effect of transnational pressure and domestic backlash on social movement organization in contexts previously dismissed as inhospitable to them.

A Parallel Trajectory of Movement Development: Polish Feminism

Between 1989 and late 2016, the Polish women's movement experienced a growth in mobilizing capacity paralleling that of its LGBT movement, with which it was closely connected. This growth was also punctuated by episodes of backlash in which national identity was asserted against European encroachment.

The first three years following the fall of communism serve as one bookend to this trajectory. It was a moment of harsh disappointment for Polish women activists. In the 1980s, women had played a critical role keeping the Solidarity movement alive after the imposition of martial law and imprisonment of much of the movement's male leadership.[25] Recognizing this contribution, Solidarity formed a women's section in 1990. Yet, when Solidarity ascended to government, its male leadership embraced the agenda of a politically emboldened Polish Catholic Church. This agenda included a ban on abortion, the establishment of a national council to monitor the media (with heavy representation of Church officials), and a greatly expanded Church presence in education. By 1993, the Church had achieved all of these.[26] When Solidarity's women's section opposed the abortion ban, it was unceremoniously dissolved, its members were denied office space, and feminism was denigrated as a threat to the nation's future.[27]

Late fall 2016 furnishes a second bookend for the Polish women's movement. Once again, the central issue was abortion. The previous year had seen a revival in the hard-right's electoral fortunes, as PiS took control of both the presidency and the government. Soon after the elections, PiS undertook a campaign to further restrict Poland's already very strict abortion policies. In September, the government's proposal to ban abortion in *all* circumstances except to save the woman's life looked set to become law.[28] Women's groups organized a wave of protests, culminating in a national strike on October 3, "Black Monday." On this day, an estimated 116,000 people took part in protests organized in 90 Polish cities, and sister demonstrations took place in Europe and the United States.[29] Organizing the protests was a network of women's associations that had been organizing and professionalizing since 2000, including the centrist Polish Women's Congress and Manifa, a more radical, grassroots organization with strong links to LGBT activism. Facing widespread unrest, PiS withdrew the proposal: its sponsor, Jarosław Gowin (PiS), declared that the protests "caused us to think, and taught us humility."[30]

What factors underpinned and linked these two bookends? A survey of scholarship on the Polish women's movement reveals a developmental trajectory with strong parallels to the LGBT one described in the preceding chapters. Here, too, we can discern three broad phases that track EU accession and backlash against it. As the first bookend showed, the 1990s was a period of disappointment for women's activism. Solidarity's embrace of the Church's agenda and its suppression of its women's section crippled the movement's mobilizing structures. As one participant in a 1996 symposium of Polish feminists recalled later, "Most of the [symposium's] contributors, including myself, claimed that seven years after the dawn of democracy no feminist consciousness, and certainly no women's movement, could be detected in our culture."[31] As happened with Poland's LGBT movement, the turn of the millennium brought the refounding of a demoralized movement. As Joanna Regulska and Magda Grabowska have shown, a wave of new women's groups emerged in the early 2000s, many if not most of which drew on EU norms, funding, and recognition to fuel their activities. These groups were coordinated at both the national and transnational level.[32]

Polish women's activism thus began the postaccession period with a more solid organizational infrastructure than in the 1990s. The 2005 elections, which brought the hard-right PiS-LPR coalition to power, were perceived as a threat to the immediate protective surround as much by feminists as by LGBT-rights activists. The newly installed government signaled its hostility to gender equality by immediately dissolving the office of the Plenipotentiary for the Equal Status of Women and Men.[33] The so-called March of Life and Family, which was held to disrupt the annual Warsaw Equality March, demonstrated the symbiosis among the antigay, antifeminist, and anti-EU agenda of the hard right. Over time, these currents became rhetorically linked and reframed as the "anti-gender" movement.

Scholars date the codification of "anti-genderism" as a movement in Poland to 2012, when Justice Minister Jarosław Gowin (PiS) criticized a CoE convention preventing domestic violence as "gender ideology" and a threat to traditional family values.[34] Shortly thereafter, a Polish bishop generally considered liberal declared that "gender ideology is worse than Communism and Nazism put together."[35] With these developments, Poland became part of a broader anti-gender movement playing out in a number of European countries since the mid-2000s and broadly oriented against reproductive rights and biotechnology, sexual and equality education, and LGBT rights—all in the name of defending the family.[36] Replaying the politicization of homosexuality during the accession process, the source of gender ideology was "Europe"— from specific policies such as the domestic violence convention and EU gender-equality (or gender-mainstreaming) programs to a more broadly defined "culture of death." As homosexuality had earlier, "gender" became omnipresent in the public discourse. This word—which, because it does not have a direct equivalent in Polish, was often simply transliterated as *dżender*—was even named word of the year in 2013 by the Polish Language Foundation.[37] On the crest of this sudden visibility for gender equality (albeit in the form of a bitter framing contest), the hard right suddenly gained control of government and sought to retrench Poland's (already very limited) abortion policy. As had occurred with LGBT rights, this confluence of discursive and political backlash galvanized the network of women's groups and their domestic and transnational allies. One key difference from the earlier rollback of abortion policy in the 1990s was that a network of women's groups such as Manifa and the Congress of Women had been established during the accession process, not to mention LGBT-rights allies, who were also targeted by the anti-gender movement.[38]

In sum, the example of Polish feminism bears out the "lessons" presented in the previous section. The shared framing of the cause in terms of EU norms, the ability to mobilize participation by drawing on overlapping mobilization structures, the ability to draw on transnational networks and resources, and, above all, the common role played by hard-right backlash show that the experience of LGBT activism was not a one-off anomaly. It was part of a larger (ongoing) cycle of social contention opened up by EU integration with effects not only across countries but across movements within them. The women's movement's experience also reaffirms the importance of taking a broader metric of success than policy and, thereby, a more favorable assessment of transnational activism. A skeptic might look at Poland's Black Monday protests as a prime example of Clifford Bob's "nonpolicy": they merely blocked a proposed law. Seen in broader terms than policy alone, however, the Black Monday protests show what a social movement breakthrough looks like: the central role of international norms, the building up of an institutionalized network of advocates and allies, a transformative shift in the public discourse, and the acknowledgment of the movement by its antagonists as a valid representative of its constituency—in short, a decisive shift in the parameters of a historic social grievance. Even absent policy gains, these protests, and the larger cycle of contention of which they were a part, constitute progress. We may even push this argument further and question the temptation to write off "nonpolicy" as a failure of social change by noting that the building-out of organizational infrastructure helps prevent *future retrenchment* of extant policy achievements, a point to which I return in the penultimate section.

* * *

Having illustrated the encouraging lessons of my argument for activists in inhospitable social climates, it is equally important to consider the limitations of its reach. What, in other words, are the argument's scope conditions: How and when may backlash fail to build out social movement infrastructure? After all, as Doug McAdam cautions, collective action cycles may not render the system open to all groups.[39] The following sections break this question into three parts. The first considers the potential of transnational advocacy for progressive norms in closed societies absent matching external leverage. The second probes the relationship between backlash and social movement visibility. Specifically, what is the nature of visibility as a social movement resource? Does increased visibility have similar effects for other taboo minorities? We may speculate here by considering a comparison with the Roma movement, which in countries like Hungary experienced hard-right backlash contemporaneously with sexual minorities but differed in terms of their visibility as a minority group previously. Third, the contrasting trajectories of Czech and Polish activism—strong activism but weak progress on rights in Poland versus weak activism but comparatively bigger rights gains in the Czech Republic—provide further opportunity to consider what counts as social movement success specifically from the perspective of LGBT movements on what the political scientist Omar Encarnación has called the "gay-rights periphery."[40] Finally, I consider possible lessons for the LGBT-rights "core" at a time when hard-right backlash is also growing there.

The Limits of Transnational Advocacy and the Centrality of External Leverage

A core argument of this book is that, under the right circumstances, backlash pushes movements forward. Certainly, some will find this reading overly optimistic. They would argue that in much of the "LGBT-rights periphery" backlash has *dampened* activism and suppressed movements.[41] Perhaps the most notable example comes from the very region studied in this book, Russia. The prospects for LGBT-rights activism did not initially appear any worse in Russia than in most other postcommunist countries. True, homosexuality had been criminalized since 1960, but it was decriminalized in 1993, considerably earlier than in Romania. In the following years, Russia was increasingly exposed to transnational NGOs working in the field of HIV/AIDS and advocating tolerance of sexual minorities. At various moments, Russia came under particularly heightened international scrutiny for its treatment of LGBT persons, most recently during its hosting of the 2014 Olympics in Sochi.[42]

Yet, despite resounding international condemnation, over the last several years the Russian authorities have become increasingly repressive of LGBT-rights groups and homophobic in their public pronouncements, all the while tacitly condoning antigay violence.[43] The zenith of this repression was the passage in 2013 of a national ban on "propaganda of nontraditional sexual relations" among minors, a law whose open-ended formulation gave authorities maximum leeway to prosecute activists.[44] In addition to the threat of arrest, the law can be used preemptively to prevent public protests from taking place.[45] It is both too soon and too complicated to assess the consequences of Vladimir Putin's antigay policies for the Russian LGBT movement here, but available sources certainly do not indicate that it has yet led to more organized SMOs with broad reach beyond the big cities and new allies outside the movement. It does not seem, in short, to be heading down the Polish movement's path.

How, then, should we account for instances where movements fail to thrive, or even wither, in the wake of backlash? Explaining such cases brings us back to the three mechanisms by which backlash boosts social movements—raising visibility, building solidarity, and attracting allies—and their sensitivity to the POS, which depends critically on international monitoring and external leverage. We may expect varying levels of sensitivity to the POS for each of these mechanisms. Visibility is the least sensitive. When the hard right mobilizes by targeting a minority, that minority's visibility necessarily rises. The "solidarity effect" is more sensitive but still evident across increasing levels of backlash. After all, threats to the "protective surround" concern individuals' most basic interests; however, at some threshold of backlash, fears for safety will outweigh increased appetite for risk. Finally, we may expect the "allies effect" to be most sensitive to the POS—that is, to the costs of demonstrating support (since allies' own "protective surround" is not threatened).

Russia exemplifies a state in which the POS is largely unaffected by international pressures. If, after all, Russia can withstand an international embargo for annexing Crimea, it is too much to expect pressure from the EP to shield domestic LGBT activists. This is not to say that we cannot find some evidence of the catalyzing effects of backlash at work even in Russia. Repression has certainly boosted the issue's visibility.[46] Further, the continued existence of LGBT groups attests to the movement's internal solidarity in the face of backlash. The 2013 law even catalyzed the formation of several new LGBT *youth* groups, leading one rights activist to observe that "[e]ven as the rise of a queer rights movement provokes a backlash, the backlash undermines itself—by strengthening the resolve of the movement and by publicizing (even if through hate) the existence of a group of people who were so long invisible."[47] Even these examples of renewed internal solidarity must, however, be qualified: the youth groups mentioned consisted of a semiregular informal meeting of 20–50 Moscow youth in a park and an online chat room. This is the informal mode of organization, more social movement community than social movement. The Kremlin's targeting of LGBT activists hinders the development of more institutionalized structures, especially in a climate of general repression of protest activity.[48] Finally, and perhaps most critically, Russia's repressive POS greatly discourages potential domestic allies, illustrating their greater sensitivity to the costs of demonstrating support. The dearth of domestic allies following backlash has "forced activists to intensify their attempts to leverage *international* support via direct appeals for support or help to the *international* community."[49] Often this strategy has meant holding unsanctioned demonstrations, at which protesters are assaulted and arrested, drawing international attention.[50] Ultimately, then, Russia stands as a reminder that backlash must be "bounded" if it is to catalyze movement development and shift elite affiliations. Unbounded backlash—which includes state-sponsored backlash such as Russia's—can crush movements.

Serbia, which has experienced harsh antigay backlash coincident with Russia's, underlines the importance of external leverage in setting limits on state repression and, hence, opening the POS. Like Russia, Serb society has a strong traditionalist element and the hard right has remained a potent force since the civil wars of the 1990s; however, unlike Russia, Serbia is an EU applicant-state. Consequently, EU leverage has served to bound and contain antigay backlash, which exploded into mass violence during the 2010 Belgrade Pride. Subsequent Prides were banned in 2011, 2012, and 2013.[51] As John Gould and Edward Moe have shown, the EU's linking of minority rights with accession has emboldened allies among the Serb media and NGOs to demonstrate support.[52]

Croatia, which shares many similarities with Serbia, serves as an even more potent demonstration of surprisingly organized LGBT activism in a recent EU applicant with a closed society and a well-entrenched hard right. In 2011, Croatia made international news when, in a Pride parade in the city of Split, 200 marchers were met by some 10,000 violent counterdemonstrators; in the ensuing melee, 137 were arrested, several were hospitalized, and seven were later convicted.[53] When the country joined the EU in 2013, it almost immediately staged a referendum banning same-sex marriage. What no one expected, however, was the response by the country's LGBT movement, which had rebuilt itself following the Pride attacks in a process that closely resembled the Polish model.[54] Within a year of the referendum, it organized a successful national campaign to enact same-sex registered partnerships that offered all the major substantive entitlements to same-sex couples aside from adoption.[55]

In the global perspective, however, the EU's combination of rights promotion and hard leverage is unusual, if not unique. US assistance has had far more limited effects. In Nigeria, for example, recent US foreign aid has promoted LGBT rights through targeted funding for advocacy groups. This amounted to offering applicant NGOs financial incentives to incorporate rights programs or otherwise endorse the LGBT cause. Yet this sponsorship has been blamed for the subsequent enactment of harsh antigay legislation, which brought visibility and even some greater solidarity among LGBT people, but, as critics note, few domestic allies.[56] The key difference from the EU is that US leverage was too weak to provide a ceiling on the threat of repression, and so the domestic POS remained closed. Generally, LGBT-rights activists on the periphery face closed societies and backlash in the absence of a credible international guarantee against repression. Even if backlash may bring new visibility to LGBT rights, activists will find headwinds in building durable SMOs and attracting domestic allies. If, as Encarnación suggests, we take regime type as a proxy for the potential costs would-be allies face for endorsing LGBT rights, we find that where authoritarianism is strongest, as in much of Africa, the Middle East, and China, LGBT activism tends to be weakest.[57] In other words, outside Europe the situation faced by Russia's movement is more the rule than the exception.

The Nature of Visibility as a Resource

If external leverage over the domestic POS is a critical scope condition defining the limits of backlash's benefits, then visibility is another one. To recall its role in the book's argument, visibility is one of the core components of resonant framing contests, which are themselves the catalysts of heightened internal solidarity and sympathy from domestic allies. As shown in Chapter 3, Poland's virulent antigay backlash in the wake of EU conditionality resulted in an unprecedented amount of coverage of homosexuality in the media and public discourse. Not all of it was sympathetic, but before this point homosexuality was part of the regime of silence in Polish society's "culture of restraint."[58] Even in critical coverage, there was an important common denominator: linking homosexuality with EU norms in a context where concrete knowledge about or exposure to openly LGBT people was low. It proved far easier for Polish activists to organize when homosexuality was part of the public discussion about EU membership than when it was hidden away as a matter of individual conscience and Church teaching. As scholarship on LGBT politics has demonstrated, across a range of societies increased visibility is considered a leading cause in the broader trend of increasingly tolerant attitudes toward homosexuality.[59]

During my fieldwork in Hungary, I was struck by the frequent comparisons that LGBT-rights activists drew between their cause and that of the Roma. The Roma are the largest ethnic minority in Hungary, with a population of between 400,000 and 600,000, roughly 4–6 percent of the population.[60] They have long suffered from discriminatory stereotyping by the Hungarian majority, and the term "gypsy criminality," much used by the contemporary hard right, was familiar under communism.[61] Under communism, and before, discrimination pushed the Roma to society's margins, relegating them to certain neighborhoods, poorer jobs, and separate classes in school (often for the mentally handicapped). LGBT activists noted, however, that current Roma activism was less robust and less organized than their own. This seemed puzzling given both groups' experience of stigmatization. Musing aloud, some activists suggested that the crucial difference between the two movements was the nature of Roma visibility as compared with that of homosexuality. The Roma were a "visible minority"[62] less able to form hidden communities in majority society than sexual minorities, who may choose not to express their identity publicly and collectively—as most did under communism (and as a great many have continued to do since).[63] Contact with openly LGBT people, this argument went, tends to change attitudes, especially as heterosexuals realize that they know sexual minorities, possibly as colleagues or family members. Moreover, while homosexuality was absent from both daily experience and the public sphere under communism, the Roma minority was always quite visible. The majority of Hungarian society was far more familiar with the ethnic Roma minority than with the LGBT one, based on concrete personal experience; and, for many, prejudices were hardened by negative personal experience. Consequently, activists argued, there was less potential for new visibility to arouse sympathy for the out-group. Recent work by Aidan McGarry comparing Roma and LGBT activism in the region offers a complementary formulation: Roma have a highly visible (but highly negative) group identity, whereas LGBT group identity is less visible, since many individuals choose not to come out or "to negotiate and sustain their sexual identity online rather than through political mobilisation."[64] Thus, for Roma increased "visibility alone is not enough"; what matters is challenging negative group stereotypes controlled and perpetuated by others. For sexual minorities *invisibility* is the major issue, and increased visibility helps strengthen group identity.[65]

These intriguing hypotheses resonate with research agendas in social psychology too large to pursue here, but the twin trajectories of Hungarian LGBT and Roma activism since the early 1990s furnish an elegant comparison for speculating about the connection between backlash, visibility, issue framing, and, ultimately, movement organization. These two movements in Hungary allow an unusually tightly matched case comparison. We can rule out the POS as an explanation for differences in organization because both movements shared that POS. Moreover, as with the LGBT minority, EU accession brought new legal protections and new connections to transnational networks. The Roma received the same protections against labor market discrimination as LGBT people through Directive 2000/78 and the European Charter of Human Rights. In addition to the application of hard conditionality, transnational pressure regarding Roma rights also took the form of well-institutionalized and well-funded advocacy networks working at the EU level. In particular, the Roma received strong support from the Open Society Foundations, which were funded by Hungarian billionaire George Soros and which played an analogous role to ILGA-Europe's vis-à-vis gay-rights movements.[66] Last, the hard-right political parties instigating backlash were the same across movements, that is, Jobbik and Fidesz. Given that the POS was the same, potential movement participants and domestic allies faced largely similar calculations regarding the costs and risks of supporting the movement, allowing us to focus on visibility and framing.

A second similarity between the movements was their relatively unorganized structure at the moment that communism fell.[67] As for the Roma movement, after 1989 the expanding POS allowed for the establishment of independent civil societal organizations, and the 1990s saw the founding of a wide spectrum of groups ranging from NGOs to political parties—just as occurred with LGBT communities in Hungary. Zoltan Barany counted 18 Roma groups in 1990 and 250 by 1999.[68] According to Barany, however, the number of organizations masked—and, in fact, resulted from—a disorganized and ineffective movement: these groups "tend to be rigid and unadaptable; have simple structure and few, often ill-defined, objectives; and are marked by disunity."[69] Indeed, a distinguishing feature of the Roma movement through the 1990s and early 2000s was its lack of internal solidarity. Several fault lines ran through the different Roma groups; these not only complicated the formation of broad-based coalitions and SMOs but also created a situation of groups openly antagonistic toward one another. Groups were sharply divided between NGOs with international donors and staff but little grassroots participation, on the one hand, and local groups that, despite having grassroots participation, are generally "elite-driven and paternalistic" in organization.[70]

The consequences of this disorganization have been evident in two important areas. First, the sheer number of groups has meant that financial resources made available by international donors have been diluted and dispersed among sharply competing groups.[71] Second, it is evident in electoral mobilization. Given the Roma population's size, one would expect a sizable number of Roma MPs in parliament and even a moderately sized national-level Roma party. This has not occurred because the lack of coordination among Roma parties has led them to split the vote. According to one recent estimate, there have been 32 ethnic Roma parties established in Hungary since 1989, which is all the more remarkable given that Hungarian electoral law offers no institutional incentives to ethnically based parties. Only eight of these parties have been able to field a candidate in at least one national parliamentary election between 1990 and 2014, and none have managed to win a seat in parliament.[72]

In sum, Hungary's Roma movement rates low on the dimensions of organizational development. Groups tend to be local, elite-based, and particularistic rather than broad-based and nationally organized. Second, typically they are structured informally—often around personalized and paternalistic leadership—rather than as institutionalized SMOs. Third, although many groups have a political orientation, their attempts at electoral mobilization have been notably unsuccessful. This explains why, though the end of communism expanded the POS and the number of groups representing Hungary's Roma, it also marked a serious deterioration in their social and, especially, economic situation. The movement has found itself largely incapable of addressing soaring unemployment and the sharp curtailing of the social safety net that accompanied the transition to a market economy—both of which disproportionately affected the Roma.[73]

What is notable from the perspective of this book's argument about backlash is that Hungary's hard-right breakthrough did little to alter these dynamics—in notable contrast to its more positive effect on the organization of Hungary's LGBT activism. As described in Chapter 7, Hungarian politics lurched sharply to the right beginning in 2006 and saw a hard-right electoral breakthrough in 2010. Just as LGBT activists were experiencing violent attacks on Budapest Pride, "an unprecedented sweep of violence against the Roma community took place in Hungary."[74] The Roma experienced the hard-right mobilization in their own neighborhoods. During these marches, which sometimes included up to 3,000 participants, flags from Hungary's World War II–era fascist Arrow Cross were displayed. It was not uncommon for Jobbik politicians to take part.[75] As with the antigay backlash, there was an escalation of anti-Roma rhetoric by prominent figures in Hungarian politics.[76] For example, at a 2012 rally in a Roma section of the city of Miskolc, Jobbik MP Zsolt Egyed declared, "Those who don't work shouldn't bring children into this world. We must act now to save our future and free Hungary from gypsy crime."[77] The Roma were frequently described as welfare thieves, squatters, and a demographic threat to Hungary and its social welfare system.[78]

As with violence and hate speech against gays, this anti-Roma backlash sparked considerable coverage in both the domestic and international media.[79] Unlike the case of LGBT activism, however, it did not create a resonant framing contest pitting EU minority-rights norms against national identity. Instead, hard-right backlash was framed in well-worn clichés against a familiar target, that is, as combatting "gypsy criminality."[80] As harsh as Jobbik and other hard-right politicians' anti-Roma rhetoric was, blame for the Roma situation was also pinned on the Roma themselves. One observer noted that "[e]ven the most progressive political actors [have] come to see . . . [the Roma's] marginalization and exclusion as a result of the Roma population's own problems with morality and cultural traditions."[81] To many potential allies, this framing seemed consonant with the very visible social problems among Roma historically, as attested to by chronically bad statistics regarding employment, poverty, and educational attainment. To these abstract statistics could be added concrete incidents such as the lynching of a teacher by a group of Roma after his car struck a Roma girl in October 2006. Jobbik highlighted this incident in its 2010 election campaign.[82]

Despite the fact that at least some Roma activist groups sought to frame hard-right backlash as violating human-rights principles and EU norms, this framing failed to resonate, especially with potential liberal allies. The "Roma problem" was familiar; unlike homosexuality, it did not gain visibility coincident with the course of EU accession, and the hard right did not connect it with the EU. Analysts of Hungarian politics have noted, in fact, a decrease in support for the Roma among the established Hungarian parties in recent years.[83] Nowhere was this withholding of support better illustrated than in the case of the Alliance of Free Democrats–Hungarian Liberal Party (SZDSZ), which had included human rights as a core part of its program since their founding. Over time, SZDSZ's support for human rights shifted from policies oriented toward the Roma to those furthering LGBT rights. When Jobbik and its allies began attacking Prides in 2007, SZDSZ became the most visible ally of Hungary's LGBT, appearing prominently in Prides and making same-sex partnerships its chief legislative priority. SZDSZ leaders identified with the Roma minority issue became marginalized in the party, and past linkages with Roma NGOs dissolved.[84] What was true for SZDSZ applied in extra measure for the rest of the liberal spectrum, for whom human rights had never occupied the same central position. Thus, as one scholar gloomily noted in recent assessment of Roma activism in Hungary, "The early hopes of a burgeoning pluralistic Roma political movement, guided by a growing transnational Roma politics and undergirded by the emergent political consciousness among Romani and their progressive, liberal non-Roma allies, have been largely abandoned."[85]

Absent allies among the liberal, pro-EU parties, the task of channeling backlash into building more institutionalized SMOs proved very difficult. It also drove some Roma activists to seek compromises with more moderate elements of the hard right, greatly weakening internal solidarity. At least initially, however, the hard-right threat to the Roma's "protective surround" galvanized a defensive response, and it is not surprising that the disparate and factionalized Roma movement experienced some degree of consolidation at first. Challenging the hard right and raising public awareness became a focal point for Roma civil society groups and political parties, displacing longer-standing concerns such as housing, employment, education, and health care. Roma politicians used the issue to mobilize electorally,[86] and one prominent activist even called for the establishment of an armed "Roma Guard" to defend against the far right.[87] In 2009, a new national-level Roma party, the MCF Roma Alliance Party (MCF), was founded to compete in that year's EP elections—another first for Roma activists.

Without allies, it proved difficult to institutionalize these efforts, as Roma activists remained divided between two very different responses to the threatening political climate. One response, as described above, was confrontational and mobilized by appealing for the defense of minority rights and evoking EU norms. The other response was to seek accommodation with the less extreme elements of Hungary's hard right, namely Fidesz. This response was represented by a major Roma group, the Lungo Drom, which partnered with Fidesz despite the latter's implicit tolerance of, and even support for, anti-Roma voices.[88] Lungo Drom's behavior can be thought of as a hedge against the threat of further repression.

The results of this division within the movement could be seen most starkly in the 2009 elections to the EP. As noted above, these elections saw the attempt to form a new, more independent, more liberal Roma political party, MCF. However, Lungo Drom did not join the effort, and although the "Roma question" dominated the media, MCF's campaign was organized at the last minute and without sufficient resources. It sought to mobilize voters by invoking the hard-right threat ("We shall defend the future of our children even at the price of sacrificing our lives"), but proved unable to translate the sense of threat into votes at the polls.[89] Lungo Drom also ran in the elections—in coalition with Fidesz. It managed to win one seat. MCF did not even contest the 2010 national parliamentary elections and, in fact, was disbanded; Lungo Drom again managed to win one seat in coalition with Fidesz, an unimpressive result given the Roma electorate's size.[90]

In addition to the opportunity it provides to investigate the dynamics of visibility comparatively, the case of Hungary's Roma movement is also useful as a harbinger of ethnic minority politics within the current context of European integration. At the time of this writing, the EU is confronting a rising tide of anti-immigrant politics following the mass influx of refugees from the Middle East and Africa. Euroskepticism (even Euro-separatism) and nationalist rhetoric have accompanied the rise of hard-right parties in Western Europe. This book's framework allows us to speculate about backlash's impact on ethnic minority movements in the larger context of European integration. Postcommunist Eastern Europe offers a suggestive example in the Roma, an ethnic minority group whose situation bore unusually strong similarities with that of LGBT people in terms of stigmatization, exposure to transnational influences, and the timing of hard-right backlash. The chief point of difference was the level of group visibility prior to backlash; soberingly, from the perspective of Europe's current anti-immigrant politics, the outcomes of backlash were far less positive for the Roma movement.

Revisiting Movement Success: Policy Gains versus Building Organization

In the discussion of the Polish women's movement, we saw that social movement success should not be reduced to policy gains. Movements matter because they build organizational infrastructure, educate participants, transform the terms of public discourse, and change how policy is made. This section returns to those points with special attention to their relevance to the study of LGBT movements, especially those on the "LGBT-rights periphery." There has been a tendency to overlook these lessons based on the recent wave of policy success regarding same-sex partnerships, which has even extended to some surprising successes on the periphery. It is worth emphasizing, however, that the latter are likely to be unrepresentative: for most of the periphery, I would argue that strong organization is crucial not only to unlocking the benefits above but also to preventing rights *retrenchment.*

Social change is deepest where robust social movements reinforce rights defined in law. In looking comparatively and historically at the evolution of LGBT rights and the movements championing them scholars have noted, however, that as often as not these two levels seem to develop unevenly. Encarnación notes, for example, that despite pioneering the modern LGBT movement, the United States fell behind 19 other countries in introducing same-sex marriage at the national level. Even within the US, same-sex marriage was first legalized not in states where the movement was most organized and had the deepest historical roots, like California and New York, but in Massachusetts. In Latin America, Encarnación argues that the rights pioneer has been Argentina, not Brazil, despite the latter's more developed movement.[91] On one level, the distinction between winning rights and building organization is a false dichotomy; it is better to have both. Nevertheless, the success of movements such as Argentina's or even the Czech Republic's in making policy gains that elude similarly motivated but better organized counterparts in Brazil or Poland drives scholars such as Encarnación to suggest that the core resources identified in the "resource mobilization" school of social movement theory—SMOs, grassroots participation, connections to political actors outside the movement—have been overemphasized in the study of LGBT activism on "the periphery." In an era marked by increasingly tolerant societal attitudes toward homosexuality and the consolidation of a transnational movement capable of lending support and legitimacy to domestic movements, activists on the periphery may leapfrog organizational deficits by shrewdly choosing frames with domestic resonance—as, for instance, the highly effective strategy of framing LGBT rights as human rights in Argentina. In her work on marriage equality in Argentina, Elisabeth Jay Friedman complements these points, placing perhaps even greater emphasis on the capacity of transnational networks to foster policy change on the periphery.[92] In her telling, Argentina's enactment of same-sex marriage was largely possible due to the extensive involvement of Spanish norm entrepreneurs, who provided essential strategic and financial assistance to domestic LGBT groups. In short, strategy and transnational links may be more important than domestic organization and resources.[93]

This is a provocative insight, but we should exercise caution in extending it beyond Latin America, especially in societies where the modernizing tides of economic development and secularization have not had such far-reaching impact on attitudes toward homosexuality as in Latin America. As Figure C.1 shows, comparative attitudinal data suggest that Latin America is rather the exception when it comes to tolerance on the periphery. Of the developing world, only Asia shows comparable gains in tolerance, and it still lags behind Latin America. In postcommunist Eurasia, Africa, and the Middle East, attitudes are on average still distinctly less tolerant.

In countries where the combination of low social tolerance and an unfavorable POS makes policy gains difficult, a more appropriate measure of success may be preventing the hollowing out of rights or even their retrenchment. When we take this perspective, the advantages of organization—for example, a grassroots that can be mobilized for protest

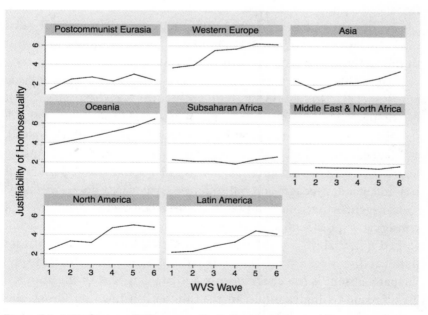

Figure C.1. Attitudes toward Homosexuality by Region (1981–2014) [Survey question: "Homosexuality is always (10)/never (0) justified."]

events, a presence outside the liberal enclave of capital cities, a network of allies outside the movement, and the resources to mount legal challenges to rights infractions—become much clearer.

Poland offers an excellent example. On the one hand, the Polish movement's policy gains have been disappointing. Since changing its labor code as a condition of accession in 2002, Poland has seen no major legal advances regarding sexual minorities. Not only did successive governments fail to broaden the scope of antidiscrimination policy, the implementation of extant labor code provisions was lackluster. Until 2010, Poland lacked legislation establishing an independent state office for antidiscrimination policy. After years of criticism, the European Commission had at last initiated legal proceedings against Poland with the European Court of Justice, which could have led to financial sanctions. As a final indication of the barebones legal framework, Poland is one of only two EU member-states to have negotiated an opt-out of the European Charter of Human Rights as a condition for signing the Lisbon Treaty.[94] The opt-out was motivated by concerns about social values, particularly fears that the Charter would undermine the traditional conception of marriage.

On the other hand, as we have also seen, the organizational gains made by Poland's movement beginning in the early 2000s allowed it to thwart sustained attacks by the hard right between 2005 and 2007 on basic rights such as freedom of expression (the overturning of Pride bans) and discrimination in employment (the Sielatycki affair).[95] It is striking that, despite the magnitude of hard-right backlash in Poland, the movement's (admittedly modest) rights gains have held up. Indeed, as Chapter 6 described, Poland came just several votes short of passing legislation recognizing same-sex unions in 2012. In 2015, its parliament passed a gender recognition bill (offering legal clarity and protections to transgender persons), only to have it vetoed by the newly elected conservative president, Andrzej Duda. Even if social attitudes have not shifted appreciably since the mid-2000s (see Table C.1), the mainstream political discourse around homosexuality has improved dramatically: virtually absent is the crude openly antigay language of the 2000s.[96] To take one telling example, in 2014 the Polish town of Słupsk, described as "a conservative city of 97,000," elected as mayor Robert Biedroń, former head of KPH and former MP of Your Movement.[97] As

TABLE C.1. Percentage of Czechs/Poles Saying That
Homosexuality Should Be Accepted

	2007	2013
Czech Republic	83%	80%
Poland	45%	42%

Source: Pew Research Center 2013.

Biedroń described the campaign, "Of course they [the voters] knew I am gay, because everyone in Poland knows that I'm gay. But it did not matter. In the campaign, none of the seven candidates tried to use it as a tool against me, not even the right-wing ones." KPH's then head Agata Chaber (now Ato Chaber) commented that "Poland has gone through a major shift in recent years in the way it views LGBT people. It can be seen in politics, in the media. Robert's election is just one of those examples."[98]

In 2015, however, Poland held presidential and parliamentary elections. An avowed social conservative, Andrzej Duda, captured the presidency and PiS returned to government, overturning PO. The 2015 elections also dealt a setback to Your Movement, which ran in coalition with the Social Democrats but failed to meet the minimum threshold for representation in parliament. During the campaign, PiS again declared its opposition to legal recognition of same-sex couples. Further, the new government took an anti-EU tone, drawing criticism for a series of constitutionally questionable moves regarding the appointment of judges, moves that have sparked a wave of mass protest and direct censure from the EU. When, in December 2017, Poland passed legislation undermining the courts' independence despite strong warnings from the EU, the European Commission took the unprecedented step of invoking Article 7. Triggered when a member state undermines the rule of law and democratic values, Article 7 could lead to Poland losing its EU voting rights.[99] As of this writing, the governing PiS party has shown little appetite for conciliation: its leader Jarosław Kaczyński recently told a Polish newspaper that "[t]he program of deep changes in our country will not slow down, on the contrary—there cannot be any talk about reaching an agreement with powers that for years treated Poland as their own private loot."[100]

Thus, Poland is entering another period of hard-right mobilization. These developments highlight a broader point about the importance of civil society in safeguarding rights, especially in new democracies whose less institutionalized party systems make them more open to populist outsider parties.[101] Maintaining strong organizations insulates rights against such swings, and it positions activists to take advantage of the next opening in the POS. As noted earlier, Andrew Reynolds has argued on the basis of a comprehensive cross-national comparison that "the presence of even a small number of openly gay legislators is associated significantly with the future passage of enhanced gay rights."[102] In the period covered in this book, Poland crossed this representation threshold, whereas the Czech Republic did not. Though TR's poor results in the last election weakened the Polish movement's political influence, the movement's network of SMOs has not scaled back. Indeed, the broader terrain of electoral mobilization looks promising: as KPH's Chaber noted after Biedroń's victory in the 2014 local elections, "In 2011, there were very few L.G.B.T. candidates in the country, maybe 10, and just two got into Parliament. In the European Parliament elections last summer, there were a few more. And during these elections, there were over 30, and Robert Biedroń was elected the mayor of Słupsk."[103]

Even when societal attitudes are more tolerant, the example of a post-communist "policy success case" like the Czech Republic should make us cautious about discounting the relevance of organization. To compare with Encarnación's study of Brazil and Argentina, the Czech case bears strong similarities to Latin America's LGBT-rights leader Argentina: both have comparatively high levels of economic development, low levels of religiosity, a weak hard right, and comparatively weakly organized rights movements.[104] Beginning with the enactment of antidiscrimination legislation in Buenos Aires in 1996, the Argentine movement began a string of legislative victories extending through the enactment of registered partnerships in 2002 and culminating with same-sex marriage in 2010. As we have seen, the Czech movement won a limited form of registered partnerships in 2006 but has achieved no major legislative victories since—despite a chorus of criticism about the limitations of the registered partnerships law. Instead, the enactment of registered partnerships served as a cue for the first wave of Czech SMOs to formally disband, reminding us that rights gains can be *demobilizing* for social movements. When a movement is weakly organized, depending on a small circle of activists to do the heavy work of lobbying for policy change, it is more vulnerable to the temptation to declare victory and demobilize. As a result, despite enjoying levels of tolerance similar to Western Europe, Czech policy gains have stalled.

The general parameters of Czech activism have changed little since 2011–2012. Political activism remains centered in PROUD, which, like its predecessors GI and GLL, comprises a small circle of Prague activists lobbying mostly out of the public's eye, and activism outside the capital is far less organized than during its heyday in the 1990s. Prague Pride O.S., the less policy-oriented element of the movement, has become the most visible and robust activist group.[105] Given the demobilization of the movement, it is perhaps unsurprising the attitudes have not improved since the enactment of registered partnerships (see Table Conclusion 1). Without a robust movement to draw on, Czech activists have thus far been ill-positioned to capitalize on their society's comparatively tolerant attitudes toward homosexuality and address the registered partnership legislation's inadequacies.[106] Czech activists have certainly not followed their Argentine counterparts in building from registered partnerships to further policy gains in same-sex marriage and family policy.

Lessons for the "LGBT-Rights Core"

These lessons from the "LGBT-rights periphery" would seem to have new relevance for the movement's geographic "core," the US and (parts of) Western Europe. In recent years, both the US and Europe have seen notable policy breakthroughs, particularly regarding same-sex marriage. Yet they are now also seeing a resurgent nationalist populism that recalls the hard-right breakthroughs analyzed in the preceding chapters. The year 2016 brought both the election of Donald Trump and the victory of Euroskeptics in the Brexit referendum; these events are emblematic of two emerging challenges for LGBT movements in current times.

First, the contemporary hard-right surge suggests a disruption of the taken-for-granted norms of mainstream American and European politics. A kind of illiberal, antiminority rhetoric has moved from the alt-right fringe to the center of the political discourse, a development nowhere more clearly illustrated than by Trump's elevation of figures such as Stephen Bannon and Jeff Sessions to his governing circle (though the former has since left his position as White House chief strategist). Meanwhile, Europe offers the specter of the National Front's Marine Le Pen's strong (but unsuccessful) bid for the French presidency in 2017, and close-call elections by far-right candidates in Austria in 2016 and the Netherlands and Germany in 2017.[107] Another Euroskeptic-populist challenge is anticipated in Italy's 2018 elections. In the US, this threat to the LGBT persons' "immediate protective surround" has already been actualized. Initial reports following the US elections have indicated an increase in bias-based attacks.[108] In terms of policy, the Trump administration has rescinded federal protections for transgender students, and was reported to have circulated an executive order that would abolish all LGBT protections put into place under President Obama.[109] Meanwhile, a wave of "religious liberty" bills directed against LGBT protections is reportedly being readied at the state level.[110]

As energizing as Trump's victory was to West European hard-right parties, it is important to acknowledge that the immediate political threat to sexual minorities, especially in terms of policy rollback, seems less imminent than in the US. Refugees, immigrants, and Muslims preoccupy the European hard right. As noted in Chapter 1, the West European populist radical right even tends to rationalize hardline policies against Muslim immigrants because of Islam's alleged homophobia.[111] Nevertheless, inasmuch as the Brexit referendum raises a question mark over the future of the EU, it signals an ominous turn for European LGBT movements.[112] Though a weakened, or even defunct, EU is unlikely to open a path for unconstrained repression of LGBT movements, it could mean the loss of critical institutional support and party allies. As we have seen, the EU provided critical institutional support to LGBT activism through a variety of pathways, from financially supporting transnational networks such as ILGA-Europe to publicly endorsing minority-rights norms. If a weakened EU scales back its commitment to potentially controversial causes like LGBT rights, why should center-left and center-right parties use LGBT issues as a signal to demonstrate their European, liberal democratic credentials—as we saw in Poland, Hungary, Slovakia, and Romania? Thus, the normalization of hard-right politics could cost the movement allies in the political center.

Naturally, it is too early to draw firm conclusions about how these developments will affect policy, but one thing seems clear from the US thus far: the hard right's electoral breakthrough has *not* deflated activism by LGBT groups and their allies in the women's movement. Quite the opposite, sexual politics became the first and most visible site of countermobilization following the presidential elections, as evidenced by the Women's March on January 21, 2017—which prominently featured LGBT issues; was estimated to be the largest public demonstration in US history; and sparked sister protests across the globe.[113] Signs of reenergized activism are also evident at the local and state level, where attempts to forestall "religious liberty" laws undermining LGBT protections have helped forge alliances between activists and corporate interests, even in conservative states such as Mississippi, North Carolina, and Indiana.[114] Attacks on transgender rights in North Carolina and Texas have had a similar countermobilizing effect.[115]

These observations are not meant to downplay the significance of differences between the US, Western Europe, and postcommunist Europe in terms of public attitudes toward homosexuality, the POS, and the extent of prior organization of the movement vis-à-vis the onset of hard-right mobilization. These will all matter to policy outcomes; nevertheless, the lesson that policy gains cannot substitute for strong organization is being borne out once again. As was true in postcommunist Europe, activists' defense of something as seemingly circumscribed as their "immediate protective surround" is actually a step with surprisingly wide-ranging consequences.

ACKNOWLEDGMENTS

A book such as this is never possible without the support and generosity of friends, family, colleagues, and institutions so numerous as to make a full accounting impossible. Nevertheless, I would like to gratefully acknowledge the contributions of the following in particular.

First, there are those to whom I owe my deepest intellectual debts. It was through conversations and collaboration with Katrina Schwartz that I first became attuned to the profound and complex changes in sexual citizenship under way in postcommunist societies. My collaboration with Kerstin Jacobsson while at the Center for Baltic and East European Studies in Stockholm was another formative moment in the gestation of this book. I am also indebted to Milada Vachudova and Valerie Sperling for their insights and inspiration.

In the course of research and writing, I have deeply benefited from the feedback, assistance, and support of Chris Ansell, Phillip Ayoub, Michael Bernhard, Michael Bosia, Arista Cirtautas, Ondřej Císař, Timothy Colton, Kevin Deegan-Krause, Jorge Dominguez, Jung Dong-Joon, Grzegorz Ekiert, Katalin Fabian, Adam Fagan, Steve Fish, Alice Freifeld, Simo Goshev, John Gould, Anna Grzymała-Busse, Peter Hall, Tim Haughton, Aida Hozic, Andrew Janos, Ann-Cathrine Jungar, Elżbieta Korolczuk, Jan Kubik, Bryon Moraski, Monika Nalepa, Ruxandra Paul, Grigore Pop-Eleches, Steven Saxonberg, Koen Slootmaeckers, Jelena Subotic, Peter Vermeersch, Ned Walker, and Meredith Weiss. I would also like to acknowledge the invaluable research assistance of Daniel Motok and Jeshow Yang, undergraduates at the University of Florida (UF).

The book's arguments and evidence greatly benefited from time spent as a Visiting Scholar at the Center for Baltic and East European Studies at Södertörn University in 2009 and the Center for European Studies at Harvard University in 2013. Financial assistance for the fieldwork and writing was made possible by the National Endowment for the Humanities, the

Center for European Studies at UF, the Center for the Humanities and the Public Sphere at UF, and UF's College of Liberal Arts and Sciences. The book includes material that appears in my article "The Benefits of Backlash: EU Accession and the Organization of LGBT Activism in Postcommunist Poland and the Czech Republic," forthcoming in *East European Politics and Societies*; I would like to thank the journal's editors for allowing me to include it here.

I am deeply grateful to my respondents for so generously sharing their time, knowledge, and experience with me, often in the midst of hectic schedules and commitments. I would also like to thank Marek Jiruše, Pavla Nováková, Andrzej Tarłowski, and Norbert Maliszewski for their help making connections and generally navigating the terrain of fieldwork across multiple countries.

Thank you to the editors and staff at New York University Press for their strong support and encouragement in preparing the manuscript, in particular Maryam Arain, Caelyn Cobb, and Amanda Ericson.

A final and especially deep word of thanks must go to my family. To them I owe the greatest debt for their unflagging patience and support over the long path of this book's making. Ingrid and Declan, I dedicate this book to you.

APPENDIX

To build off the notes on research design in Chapter 1, this book's analysis falls squarely within the multimethod tradition of comparative politics: thus, it is problem driven and guided by an eclectic and integrative use of data and methods. As David Collier and Colin Elman write, such research is *eclectic* because it draws on both qualitative and quantitative methodologies (e.g., ethnography, within-case process tracing, systematic analysis of secondary sources, content and statistical analysis), despite their sometimes differing underlying assumptions.[1] It is *integrative* because it is guided by the intuition that composite research designs can overcome the inherent limitations of relying on one kind of data, as more methodologically "pure" designs tend to do. Multimethod designs excel when seeking to extend existing theory (such as Europeanization and norm diffusion) to relatively new contexts (such as LGBT activism on the postcommunist "rights periphery"). This appendix provides supplementary notes on the various data and methodologies employed in the book, in particular the fieldwork interviews, statistical analysis in Chapter 2, categorization of hard-right parties, and measurement of trajectories of movement organization over time.

FIELDWORK INTERVIEWS

The fieldwork was conducted in the Czech Republic, Hungary, Poland, Romania, and Slovakia on multiple trips spanning from 2007 through 2015. Most respondents were activists in gay-rights groups but also included academics, policy experts, politicians, and representatives of official institutions, both domestic and international. Many respondents were interviewed over successive years. They were guaranteed anonymity unless they chose to opt out of it. Those respondents in leadership positions within established activist groups were generally willing, even eager, to opt out of anonymity, as they are public figures closely associated with LGBT activism in their respective countries and are often quoted in the domestic media.

Czech Republic

- Sylva Ficová—Activist and member of the Working Group for Sexual Minorities. Member of PROUD. August 1, 2011; Brno.
- Jiří Hromada—Activist, founding member and president of SOHO and Gay Initiative. August 4, 2011; Prague.
- Daniel Kupšovský—Activist and founding member of Prague Pride O.S. and Art for Life. July 18, 2011; Prague.
- Tereza Mikšaníková—Activist and member of L2 (eLnadruhou). July 14, 2011; Prague.
- Petr Pavlík—Academic, Gender Studies Faculty, Charles University. June 14, 2011; Prague.
- Olga Pechová—Academic, Palacký University Olomouc, member of the Working Group for Sexual Minorities. July 9, 2011; Olomouc.
- Ivo Procházka—Academic and activist, Sexological Institute, General Faculty Hospital of Prague, founding member of Socio-Therapeutic Club/Lambda and SOHO. July 15, 2011; Prague.
- Jan Seidl—Academic, historian of Czech LGBT movement. May 24, 2011, and July 24, 2015; Prague.
- Zdeněk Sloboda—Member of the Working Group for Sexual Minorities, Executive Board member of PROUD. May 26, 2011; Prague.
- Věra Sokolová—Academic, Gender Studies Faculty, Charles University. Member of the Working Group for Sexual Minorities. July 12, 2011; Prague.
- Džamila Stehlíková—Minister for Human Rights and Minorities of the Czech Government (2007–2009). July 7, 2011; Prague.
- Respondent #1—Participant in Prague-based sports association. May 20, 2011; Prague.
- Respondent #2—Participant in Prague-based sports association. May 20, 2011; Prague.
- Respondent #3—Political party consultant. June 27, 2011; Prague.

Hungary

- Adrian Balaci—Activist. Board member of Budapest Pride and member of the organizing committee of the 2012 EuroGames in Hungary. June 24, 2011; Budapest.

- Anna Borgos—Activist. Executive Board member of Labrisz Lesbian Association. June 20, 2011; Budapest.
- Tamás Dombos—Activist. Member and Executive Board member of the Háttér Society. June 17, 2011; Budapest.
- Katalin Lányi—Activist. Executive Board member of Labrisz Lesbian Association. June 20, 2011; Budapest.
- Kristófy Mária—Activist. Board member of Budapest Pride. June 20, 2011; Budapest.
- Milán Rózsa—Activist. Board member of Budapest Pride and organizer of the 2011 Budapest Pride parade. June 21, 2011; Budapest.
- Judit Takács—Academic. Institute of Sociology, Hungarian Academy of Sciences. June 23, 2011; Budapest.
- Respondent #4—Academic. Central European University. June 19, 2011; Budapest.
- Respondent #5—Former member of Fidesz and former MP. June 20, 2011; Budapest.
- Respondent #6—Activist and member of Labrisz Lesbian Association. June 18, 2011; Budapest.
- Respondent #7—Member of the Hungarian Liberal Party (SZDSZ). June 16, 2011; Budapest.
- Respondent #8—Activist and member of the political party Politics Can Be Different (Lehet Más a Politika, or LMP). June 22, 2011; Budapest.
- Respondent #9—Activist and participant in Budapest Pride. June 22, 2011; Budapest.

Poland
- Marta Abramowicz. Activist. Vice-president of KPH. June 12, 2007; July 17, 2010; Warsaw.
- Tomek Basiuk—Academic. Warsaw University. Editor of the journal *InterAlia*. June 1, 2007; July 1, 2009; July 6, 2010; June 30, 2011; Warsaw.
- Tomasz Bączkowski. Activist. President of the Equality Foundation. July 7, 2009; Warsaw.
- Robert Biedroń—Activist and politician. President of KPH and Member of Parliament (Your Movement). June 12, 2007; June 30, 2009; July 13, 2010; July 20, 2010; Warsaw.
- Adam Bodnar. Political analyst. Helsinki Foundation for Human Rights. July 8, 2009; Warsaw.

- Greg Czarnecki—Activist. Project coordinator for KPH. July 19, 2010, and June 30, 2011; Warsaw.
- Dominika Ferens—Academic. Wrocław University. Editorial board member of the journal *InterAlia*. June 9, 2007; July 3, 2009; July 11, 2010; Warsaw.
- Agnieszka Graff—Academic. Warsaw University. May 29, 2007; July 9, 2009; Warsaw.
- Anna Grodzka—Activist and politician. Vice-president of Trans-Fuzja and Member of Parliament (Your Movement). July 4, 2009; Warsaw.
- Piotr Maciej Kaczyński—Political analyst. Institute of Public Affairs and Centre for European Policy Studies. May 18, 2007, Warsaw; and June 26, 2011, Budapest.
- Yga Kostrzewa—Activist. Chairwoman of the board of Lambda Warszawa. June 5, 2007; July 1, 2009; July 20, 2010; July 1, 2011; Warsaw.
- Jacek Kucharczyk—Political analyst. Institute of Public Affairs. May 31, 2007; Warsaw.
- Paweł Leszkowicz—Curator. Curator of the exhibition *Ars Homo Erotica*. July 12, 2010; Warsaw.
- Szymon Niemiec—Activist. Founder and president of IGCLN-Poland. June 1, 2007; Warsaw.
- Tomasz Sikora—Academic. Jagiellonian University, Cracow. Editorial board member of the journal *InterAlia*. July 11, 2010; Warsaw.
- Krzysztof Śmiszek—Activist. Vice-president of the Polish Society of Anti-Discrimination Law. July 19, 2010; Warsaw.
- Tomasz Szypuła.—Activist. Vice-president (and later president) of KPH. July 7, 2009; Warsaw.
- Respondent #10—Priest. Conference of the Polish Episcopate of the Catholic Church. May 26, 2007; Warsaw.
- Respondent #11—Activist. Member of All-Poland Youth. June 15, 2007; Warsaw.
- Respondent #12—Activist. Member of All-Poland Youth. June 15, 2007; Warsaw.
- Respondent #13—Activist. Member of All-Poland Youth. June 15, 2007; Warsaw.
- Respondent #14—Politician. Member of PiS. June 15, 2007; Warsaw.
- Respondent #15—Official. Ministry of Labor and Social Policy. June 14, 2007; Warsaw.

- Respondent #16—Politician. Member of Parliament for Civic Platform. June 5, 2007; Warsaw.
- Respondent #17—Activist. Member of KPH. June 8, 2007; Warsaw.
- Respondent #18—Activist. Member of KPH. July 20, 2010; Warsaw.
- Respondent #19—Activist. Member of the Polish Society of Anti-Discrimination Law. July 3, 2009.
- Respondent #20—Regular participant in the Warsaw Pride parade and member of the Polish Green Party. May 31, 2007; June 29, 2009; July 12, 2010; Warsaw.
- Respondent #21—Regular participant in the Warsaw Pride parade. July 2, 2011; Warsaw.
- Respondent #22—Political party consultant. July 18, 2010; July 3, 2011; Warsaw.

Romania

- Florin Buhuceanu—Activist. Former president of ACCEPT. May 30, 2011; Bucharest.
- Irina Niță—Activist. Executive director of ACCEPT. May 31, 2011; Bucharest.
- Respondent #23—Former member of ACCEPT. June 2, 2011; Bucharest.
- Respondent #24—Policy expert at the reproductive rights NGO Centrul Euroregional pentru Inițiative Publice (Euroregional Center for Public Initiatives). June 3, 2011; Bucharest.
- Respondent #25—Program manager, Population Services International/Romania. June 1, 2011; Bucharest.
- Respondent #26—LGBT activist. June 4, 2011; Bucharest.
- Respondent #27—Antidiscrimination program manager, Center for Legal Resources, a Soros-supported NGO. June 1, 2011; Bucharest.
- Respondent #28—Official at the National Council for Combating Discrimination. May 30, 2011; Bucharest.
- Respondent #29—Official at the National Council for Combating Discrimination. June 2, 2011; Bucharest.

Slovakia

- Ján Benec—Activist. Chairman of the board of the Otherness Initiative. July 20, 2011; Bratislava.
- Richard Fekete—Activist. Founding member of Duchový PRIDE Bratislava. July 20, 2011; Bratislava.
- Robert Furiél—Activist. President of Charlie (Charles University LGBT Students Association) and founding member of Duchový PRIDE Bratislava. June 8, 2011; Prague.

- Roman Kollárik—Activist. Founding member of Duchový PRIDE Bratislava. July 17, 2010, Warsaw, and July 20, 2011, Bratislava.
- Martin Macko—Activist. Executive director of the Otherness Initiative. July 20, 2011; Bratislava.
- Ján Šajban—Activist. Treasurer and Advisory Board member of the Otherness Initiative. July 20, 2011; Bratislava.

EU and European-Level
- Respondent #30—Staff member. ILGA-Europe. July 18, 2010, Warsaw, and June 18, 2011, Budapest.
- Respondent #31—Official with the Political Section of the European Commission Representation in Poland. June 6, 2007; Warsaw.
- Respondent #32—Official. Office of the Council of Europe in Poland. June 14, 2007; Warsaw.
- Respondent #33—Official. US Embassy in Poland. July 9, 2009; Warsaw.
- Respondent #34—Official. US Embassy in Poland. July 9, 2009; Warsaw.
- Respondent #35—Official. US Embassy in Poland. July 9, 2009; Warsaw.

METHODOLOGICAL NOTES TO CHAPTER 2

These notes supplement the regression analysis in Chapter 2. That analysis uses panel data, with the dependent variable being a country's score on the Rainbow Index for each of the five years from 2009 through 2013. The sources and coding of the variables appear in Chapter 2. To recapitulate, the dataset includes 47 states from both Western and Eastern Europe. The categories of EU member-states and "EU outsiders" include both postcommunist and West European states. The effect of EU leverage is captured primarily cross-sectionally (as differences among states at different removes from EU membership) rather than longitudinally (as states move through the stages of accession).[2] It would be preferable to have a more substantial longitudinal component to the analysis, but unfortunately the absence of data precludes it. Table A1 provides descriptive statistics for the variables, with a separate grouping for the categorical variables. As noted in Chapter 2, the variables on tolerance of homosexuality and religiosity are constructed from waves 4 and 5 of the WVS, whichever wave was most recent (per country) before the first Rainbow Index data (2009). Waves 4 and 5 were conducted around 2000 and 2006, respectively. I would have preferred to use data from wave

TABLE A.1. Descriptive Statistics and Correlations

Variable	Mean	Standard Deviation	Min	Max	(1)	(2)	(3)	(4)
(1) Rainbow Europe Index	3.21	3.31	−2	10	1.00			
(2) Tolerance of homosexuality	4.40	2.21	1.20	8.60	0.75	1.00		
(3) Religiosity	6.46	1.61	3.60	9.40	−0.58	−0.65	1.00	
(4) GDP per capita (log)	10.13	0.93	7.76	11.87	0.68	0.76	−0.51	1.00

Categorical Variables	Number of Observations (country-years)
Communist legacy:	
• Yes	105
• No	130
Religious Tradition:	
• Orthodox	55
• Catholic	105
• Muslim	20
• Protestant	55
"EU Proximity:"	
• Outsider	51
• ENP	15
• Potential Member	33
• Member	136

5 only, but doing so cut the number of cases in half and, even worse, excluded all but two of the "potential member-states" category—that is, the variable of primary theoretical interest.[3]

Reflecting the time-invariant nature of a number of the independent variables, the analysis employs a random effects model of the form:

$$y_{it} = \beta_o + X_{it}\beta + \varepsilon_{it}$$

where $\varepsilon_{it} = \alpha_i + \mu_{it}$. This model differs from the standard OLS setup in that it includes two error terms, α_i and μ_{it}. The former captures errors common across each unit (here country), and the latter captures the error specific to each of the i,t observations. The crucial assumption in this model is that μ_i is uncorrelated with any of the independent variables. If this assumption is unwarranted, the random effects model is problematic, generating inconsistent estimates of the coefficients for the independent variables. This assumption can be probed using a Hausman test for fixed vs. random effects. If the Hausman test fails to uncover systematic variation between fixed and random effects models, then a random effects model is appropriate.[4] In this analysis, Hausman tests revealed no evidence of systematic differences between random- and fixed-effects specifications; therefore, I present random-effects GLS models.[5]

POLITICAL-PARTIES DATA

This section provides the data used to compare the mobilization of hard-right parties across countries (see Figures 3.1 and 7.1): namely, which parties were counted and what their election results were. A caveat regarding Hungary's Fidesz is necessary because it is difficult to place within conventional "party families" schema. Before 2002, Fidesz was regarded as liberal, but in 2002 it underwent a radical transformation. Since then, scholars are divided about its classification: Mudde considers it a borderline case and does not place it in the populist radical right category,[6] but others do.[7] Recognizing this divergence, Figure 7.1 shows the Hungarian hard right's electoral strength with and without Fidesz. The precise national parliamentary election results used to create Figures 3.1 and 7.1 can be found at "Parties and Elections in Europe," www.parties -and-elections.eu.

MAPPING THE ACTIVIST NETWORK (1986–2012)

This section lists the main LGBT groups in each country-case from as early as 1986 through 2012. These data went into the construction of Figures 6.2, 6.3, 7.3, 7.4, and 7.5. I drew on the work of country-based scholars, NGO and official reports, and fieldwork interviews.[8] Applying a distinction formulated by Hanspeter Kriesi, the list also categorizes groups into those that can be considered *primarily* political (i.e., oriented toward the authorities and the "'activation of commitment' for a political goal") and those that are *primarily* oriented toward the constituency (i.e., self-help groups, recreational and social groups, and service providers).[9] If the latter are formally constituted within politically

TABLE A.2. Hard-Right Parties by Country

Party Name	Period Active	Party Family
Czech Republic		
SPR-RSČ	1989–2001	Populist Radical Right
Republicans of M. Sladek (RMS)	Since 2001	Populist Radical Right
National Party (NS)	Since 1998	Populist Radical Right
Hungary		
MIÉP	Since 1993	Populist Radical Right
Jobbik	Since 2003	Populist Radical Right
Fidesz	Since 2002*	Conservative / Populist Radical Right
Poland		
National Party (SR)	Since 1989	Populist Radical Right
Party X	1990–1993	Populist Radical Right
ROP	Since 1995	Populist Radical Right
Social Movement Alternative (RSA)	1998–2001	Populist Radical Right
Confederation of Independent Poland—Fatherland (KPN-O)	Since 1999	Populist Radical Right
Alternative Party of Labor (APP)	Since 2001	Populist Radical Right
LPR	Since 2001	Populist Radical Right
PiS	Since 2001	Conservative
Romania		
PRM	Since 1991	Populist Radical Right
PUNR	Since 1990	Populist Radical Right
Slovakia		
SNS	Since 1990	Populist Radical Right
PSNS	2001–2003	Populist Radical Right

Notes: Italics indicate approximate dates.
* As noted above, 2002 was the moment when Fidesz radically transformed its programmatic profile.

oriented SMOs (e.g., SOHO), I classify them as political. The coding of each group's primary orientation depends on activists' and scholars' judgments.

As a note of caution: given the number of local, informal, and sometimes short-lived groups over this two-decade span, this list is not exhaustive. Further, it is biased toward larger, formally organized groups, and the coding of primary orientation can be subjective. However, the list does

TABLE A.3. Social-Movement Groups by Country

Name	Year Begun	Active Through	Primary Orientation
Czech Republic			
Socio-Therapeutic Club of Homosexuals	1988	1991	Social/Service
Lambda (Prague)	1988	1990	Social/Service
Hnutí tolerance (hnutí na podporu homosexuálů a boje proti AIDS)	1989	1990	Political
Činnost	1989	1990	Social/Service
Na Poříci group	1988	1989	Social/Service
HRHO	1990	1991	Political
SOHO and its associated member organizations[a]	1990	2000	Political
Gay Klub	1991	1993	Political
Logos	1992	2012	Social/Service
STUD	1995	2012	Political
Kruh A-klubu	1999	2000	Political
Transforum	1998	*2007*	Political
GI	2000	2006	Political
GLL	2003	2007	Political
Rozdilné rytmy[b]	2003	*2012*	Political
L-Platforma[c]	2003	*2012*	Political
eLnadruhou	2005	2012	Social/Service
Stejná rodina	2008	2012	Political
Art for Life	2008	2012	Social/Service
PROUD	2011	2012	Political
Prague Pride	2011	2012	Political
Hungary			
Homérosz	1986	1995[d]	Social/Service
Association for Supporting HIV-Positive People in Hungary)	1989	2012	Social/Service
Lambda Budapest Friendship Society	1991	*2007*	Political
Eötvös Loránd University "Homosexual Students Society"	1991	1995	Social/Service
Szivárvány Társulás a Melegek Jogaiért (Rainbow Association for Gay Rights)	1994	1995	Political
Háttér	1995	2012	Political
Habeas Corpus	1996	2012	Political

Name	Year Begun	Active Through	Primary Orientation
Five Loaves of Bread Community ("Öt kenyér" Christian Community for Homosexuals)	1996	2007	Social/Service
Labrisz Lesbian Association	1999	2012	Political
"DAMKÖR" Gay Association	1999	2007	Political
"Együtt Egymásért Kelet Mag-yarországon" (Together for Each Other in East-Hungary) Gay Association	2000	2007	Political
Rainbow Mission Foundation	2001	2012	Political
Szimpozion Association	2002	2012	Political
Atlasz LGBT Sport Association	2004	2012	Social/Service
Association of People Challenging Patriarchy (PATENT Egyesület)	2006	2012	Political
Magyar LMBT Szövetség (Hungarian LGBT Association)	2009	2012	Political
Poland			
All-Polish Association of Lambda Groups	1990	1997	Social/Service
Lambda Warszawa	1990	1997	Social/Service
Lambda Gdańsk	1990	1997	Social/Service
Lambda Krakow	1990	1997	Social/Service
Lambda Szczecin	1990	1997	Social/Service
Lambda Poznan	1990	1997	Social/Service
Lambda Torun	1990	1997	Social/Service
Lambda Wroclaw	1990	1997	Social/Service
Lambda Bytom	1990	1997	Social/Service
Lambda Lodz	1990	1997	Social/Service
Lambda Olsztyn	1990	1997	Social/Service
Lambda Piotrkow Trybunalski	1990	1997	Social/Service
Lambda Bydgoszcz	1990	1997	Social/Service
Lambda Lublin	1990	1997	Social/Service
Lambda Sopot	1990	1997	Social/Service
Lambola	1997	1998	Social/Service
Stowarzyszenie Lambda Warszawa	1997	2012	Social/Service
KPH	2001	2012	Political
ILGCN-Poland[e]	2001	2007	Social/Service
Queer Alliance	2002	2003	Social/Service

(*continued*)

Name	Year Begun	Active Through	Primary Orientation
Stowarzyszenie Lambda Poznań	2004	2012	Political
Stowarzyszenie Lambda Kraków	2004	2012	Political
Equality Foundation	2005	2012	Political
Poruzemienie Lesbijek	2005	2012	Political
Polskie Towarzystwo Prawa Antydyskryminacyjnego	2006	2012	Political
UFA	2007	2012	Social/Service
Foundation Anka Zet Studio	2007	2012	Social/Service
Trans-Fuzja	2007	2012	Political
Stowarzyszenie Lambda Bydgoszcz	2008	2012	Political
Stowarzyszenie Lambda Zielona Góra	2009	2012	Political
KPH-Kielce	2009	2012	Political
KPH-Lublin	2009	2012	Political
KPH-Lodz	2009	2012	Political
KPH-Olsztyn	2009	2012	Political
KPH-Opole	2009	2012	Political
KPH-Podkarpacie	2009	2012	Political
KPH-Silesia	2009	2012	Political
KPH-Szczecin	2009	2012	Political
KPH-Tri-City	2009	2012	Political
KPH-Warsaw	2009	2012	Political
KPH-Wroclaw	2009	2012	Political
KPH-Zielona Gora	2009	2012	Political
KPH-New York City	2009	2012	Political
Grupa Inicjatywna ds. Związków Partnerskich	2009	2012	Political
Romania			
Social Circle[f]	1992	1993	Social/Service
Group 200	1993	1994	Political
Gay and Lesbian Human Rights Commission	1993	1994	Political
Bucharest Acceptance Group	1993	1995	Political
ACCEPT	1996	2012	Political
PSI-Romania (later Eu Sunt! Tu?)	2004	2012	Social/Service
Be an Angel Romania	2004	2012	Political
Act-Q	2011	2012	Social/Service

Name	Year Begun	Active Through	Primary Orientation
Slovakia			
Ganymedes	1990	*2010*	• Political (1990–1992) • Social/Service (1993–1997) • Political (1998–2010)
Museion	1994	*2010*	• Social/Service (1994–1999) • Political (2000–2010)
Museion Stred	1995	1997	Social/Service
Ganymedes Košice	1997	*2010*	Social/Service
Ganymedes Handlová	1997	*2010*	Social/Service
HaBiO	1997	*2006*	Social/Service
HaBiO Košice	1998	*2006*	Social/Service
Altera	1998	2006	Political
Student Center for the Integration of the Sexual Minorities (SČISM)	*1999*	2006	Social/Service
CKKISM	1999	*2004*	Social/Service
Podisea	2002	*2006*	Social/Service
H-Plus	2000	2006	Social/Service
Otherness Initiative	2000	2011	Political
Queer Leaders Forum	2007	2011	Political
Duchový PRIDE Bratislava	2010	2011	Political

Notes:

[a] SOHO was an umbrella group organized on a national scale (originally encompassing Czechoslovakia and then, after 1993, the Czech Republic only). SOHO was estimated to include 35 member organizations originally. In Figure 4.1, I have used this number as the base, adjusting for the entry or exit of member groups each year based on historical sources (Seidl 2012; Fanel 2000; Hromada 2007). I arrived at the following estimate of the number of LGBT groups included in SOHO by year: 35 (1991), 37 (1992–1995), 38 (1996–1997), 39 (1998), and 40 (1999). Because SOHO had defined political goals, I code its members as primarily political. After SOHO's dissolution in 2000, four of its constituent groups maintained a political orientation: Gay Initiative, STUD, Transform, and Kruh A-klub. The rest generally turned to local concerns such as providing services or fora for public association. I estimate their number at 36 from 2000 through 2012, classifying them as social/service oriented.

[b] Described as an informal group by Seidl (2012).

[c] Described as an informal group by Seidl (2012).

[d] Sources indicate Homerosz was defunct by 1995, but it officially dissolved in 1999 (Riszovannij 2001).

[e] ILGCN-Poland was best known for organizing the first few Equality Marches in Warsaw, until the Equality Foundation took over organizing the march in 2005. I classify ILGCN-Poland as primarily social/service-oriented because my respondents contrasted it strongly with the Equality Foundation's pointedly outward orientation to the authorities and wider society. I would note, nevertheless, that this is a judgment call. However, classifying it instead as primarily political would not greatly affect the overall movement trends in Figure 6.3.

[f] Actual name not reported in sources (Long 1999, 246).

include informal groups, and I have cross-referenced the coding of primary orientation across sources. I am confident that the list captures the biggest and most visible LGBT groups over time, those that scholars and activists themselves would consider the most important to the movement. The purpose of Figures 6.2, 6.3, 7.3, 7.4, and 7.5 is to depict the broad trends in social movement development: growth and decline in the density of activist groups and the changing balance between the political and social/service sides of movements over time.

NOTES

CHAPTER 1. THE BENEFITS OF BACKLASH

1 The politics of sexuality comprises a broad set of identities and orientations, including lesbian, gay, bisexual, transgender, queer, intersex, and asexual. For simplicity, scholars typically use the umbrella terms "LGBT" and "sexual minorities" to "encompass people marginalized because of sexual orientation and/or gender identities that are deviant from heteronormative frameworks" (Ayoub 2016, 1n.1). This book follows that convention, recognizing that, in reality, the identities, orientations, and labels represented by the activists that it describes vary over time and space.

2 Jowitt 1992; Howard 2003.

3 Long 1999, 244.

4 Human Rights Watch 2006.

5 Long 1999, 248.

6 As Chapter 7 will describe, there was a three-year delay for Romania to enter the EU relative to the other first-wave postcommunist applicants—a lag that offers further leverage for probing the effects of external leverage. Snow et al. 1988, 5.

7 As these authors note, the concept of the "immediate protective surround" is taken from the biologists' notion of "Umwelt," that is, "the area around animals within which there is a sense of ease and safety unless signals of alarm indicate otherwise." They continue, "Extended to humans, the Umwelt can be thought of as a culturally elastic zone of privacy and control regarded as out of bounds to the uninvited, strangers, and corporate and governmental agents" (ibid., 7–8).

8 According to the World Values Survey, 75.7 percent of Poles in 1989 indicated that "homosexuality is never justifiable" compared with 25 percent of Czechs in 1991 (www.worldvaluessurvey.org). In 2013, a Pew Research Center poll found that 42 percent of Poles believed that "homosexuality should be accepted," compared with 80 percent of Czechs (Pew Research Center 2013). Systematic data on antigay violence are unavailable; however, my fieldwork and the extant literature indicate that LGBT people have felt more sense of personal threat in Polish society, especially before 2007 (Abramowicz 2007, 11–33; Beňová et al. 2007, 45–59).

9 A number of these sources are in Polish and English—in which cases quoted citations are the author's translations.

10 Encarnación 2016.

11 Ayoub 2016.

12 Ibid., 14–15.

13 The phrase is Encarnación's (2016).

14 Weeks 2007, x.

15 Ibid., 11. See also Kollman 2013; Wilson 2013.

16 Butler 2005, 69.

17 Weeks 2007, 95.

18 Gould 2009; Jasper 1997.

19 D'Emilio 1983.

20 Of course, this gradual opening was punctuated by moments of heightened discrimination, as during the HIV/AIDS epidemic in the 1980s. Given the sheer magnitude of the epidemic and inadequacy of treatment options at that time, however, we should be careful in drawing analogies for later-generation LGBT movements.

21 Badgett 2010.

22 Staggenborg 2011, 83–87.

23 Mizielińska and Kulpa 2011, 14–19.

24 Mizielińska 2011, 93. See also Binnie and Klesse 2012.

25 Bosia and Weiss 2013.

26 Ibid., 3.

27 Buechler 1990, 42.

28 The WVS includes a question asking whether "[h]omosexuality is always (10) / never (1) justified." This question is rather blunt, and there is room for diverse attitudes at this level since even tightly knit societies are never monolithic. Nevertheless, it is also clearly possible to speak about the prevailing attitudes toward homosexuality in a given society, especially in relation to other societies. In Figures 1.1 and 1.3, I use WVS data collected in wave 4 (circa 2000), which is the midpoint of the period covered and predates the construction of the ILGA-Europe rights index (www.worldvaluessurvey.org).

29 For a full description of the index and country analyses, see www.ilga-europe.org.

30 As will not surprise observers of European politics, it also reveals more fine-grained regional divides, notably between the LGBT-friendly Scandinavian countries and the generally less-so Southern European countries. Spain and Portugal are notable exceptions as both now allow same-sex marriage.

31 This difference is statistically significant with a 99 percent level of confidence.

32 The Equality Parade was the name given to Warsaw's Pride parade.

33 Quoted in Krzemiński et al. 2006, 136.

34 Ramet 2006, 128.

35 This book uses the term "registered partnerships" throughout for simplicity, though other terms are also used to describe the legal recognition of same-sex relationships.

36 Sperling 2015.

37 Reynolds 2013.

38 Lyman 2014.

39 Howard 2003.

40 Henry 2010; Sperling 1999.

41 Even under optimistic assumptions, scholars expect the participation deficit to persist for the medium term, likely longer (Pop-Eleches and Tucker 2013, 63–64).

42 Petrova and Tarrow 2007, 75.

43 Ibid., 78.

44 Snow et al. 1998, 7.

45 Ibid., 2.

46 Jasper 1997, 106, emphasis added. Both Jasper's notion of "moral shock" and prospect theory's analysis of "irrational" loss aversion resonate with Deborah Gould's work on the American group ACT UP (2009). It should also be noted that, while backlash may have movement-building effects overall, an important caveat regarding individuals on the ground is needed. Scholars have long noted that LGBT persons face a range of individual threat—from direct violence to secondary victimization, such as job loss, eviction, and loss of child custody—depending on the cultural, political, and institutional context (Berrill and Herek 1990; Herek 1990). Moreover, as Mark Ungar (2000) has noted, the global wave of democratization since the 1980s has left violence against LGBT people undiminished in many of the polities that it opened, and even increased it in some cases. State-sanctioned violence, which Ungar copiously details in Africa and Latin America, is one part of the threat from backlash. Semilegal (e.g., discriminatory policing) and extrajudicial violence (e.g., individual assault) probably constitute the greater part. Thus, backlash is a potent force that increases the potential for real harm to individuals. That is why external leverage, such as EU conditionality, is so important. It provides a ceiling on antigay repression when hard-right backlash erupts, constraining physical violence. Even where such leverage obtains and backlash boosts the overall mobilization of LGBT movements, its potential harm to individuals should never be forgotten.

47 On the expansion of EU law here, see Ayoub and Paternotte (2014, 12–14).

48 Keck and Sikkink 1998; Kollman 2013; Schimmelfennig and Sedelmeier 2005; Vachudova 2005.

49 Ayoub 2016, 34.

50 Kollman 2013, 47.

51 Keck and Sikkink 1998; Kollman 2013, 47.

52 Kollman 2013.

53 Epstein and Sedelmeier 2008, 795.

54 Ibid., 55.

55 Keck and Sikkink 1998.

56 Ayoub 2016, 4.

57 Ibid., 10.

58 Bob 2012.

59 McAdam 1996, 27.

60 On the repression of homosexuality under communism, see Gruszczynska 2009a; Long 1999; Seidl 2012.

61 Benford and Snow 2000, 615.

62 Ibid., 619.

63 Ibid., 620.

64 Chetaille 2011, 122–123; Long 2001, 258–260.

65 McCarthy 1996, 145.

66 McAdam, McCarthy, and Zald 1996, 13. See also Kriesi 1996, 152–157.

67 McCarthy 1996, 142–145.

68 Kriesi 1996, 156–157.

69 Inglehart and Welzel 2005, 25–26.

70 Using Inglehart and Welzel's data (taken from WVS, wave 4), the Czech Republic is more than one standard deviation above the postcommunist and West European averages regarding secularization. It is more survival-oriented than the West European average, but more expression-oriented than the postcommunist average (by more than a standard deviation). Poland is far less secularized than both West European and postcommunist countries (one standard deviation from the West European average and more than two from the postcommunist one). It is, however, typical of postcommunist countries regarding survival values.

71 Mudde 2007, 68.

72 Badgett 2010, 101–102; Mudde 2007, 67.

73 Brustier 2015, 22–23.

74 Slater and Ziblatt 2013.

75 The primary archives were that of the Polish rights group KPH and the Gender Studies Library of Charles University. I also made use of the archives of the archives of the Romanian rights group ACCEPT in Bucharest and its Hungarian counterpart Háttér in Budapest.

76 Where available, the case study also draws on the extant secondary literature in English, e.g., Binnie and Klesse 2011, 2012, 2013; Gruszczynska 2009a, 2009b; Holzhacker 2012; Owczarzak 2009. The English-language secondary literature is much sparser for the Czech movement.

77 See the Appendix for details on the interviews.

78 For the catalogue, see Leszkowicz 2010.

79 Russia, which will be discussed in the concluding chapter, offers an even starker example of this point.

CHAPTER 2. EU ENLARGEMENT AND LGBT RIGHTS

1 Kollman 2013, 6. As helpful as juxtaposing these vignettes is to illustrate the East-West gulf in 1989, two caveats are necessary. First, I do not mean to minimize the struggles of West European LGBT movements before 1989, which were considerable. Second, as a historical perspective shows, same-sex partnerships should not be the sole lens by which LGBT activism is measured (Adam 1995; Herzog 2011).

2 The first wave of postcommunist EU applicants comprises the Czech Republic, Poland, Slovakia, Romania, Hungary, Lithuania, Latvia, Estonia, Bulgaria, and Slovenia.

3 See, for example, Ayoub 2016; Encarnación 2016; Kollman 2013; Wilson 2013.

4 Ayoub and Paternotte 2014, 9. An even earlier antecedent can be found in the World League for Sexual Reform, established in Germany in 1928.

5 Though it lacks the same leverage as the EU, the CoE—an association of states established in 1949 for the protection of democracy and human rights—has also played an important role in the articulation of European norms protecting sexual minorities. The CoE's European Court of Human Rights has through an expanding body of decisions dating from 1981 decriminalized homosexuality in member-states, reinforced rights of public association and free speech by sexual minorities, and supported antidiscrimination policies (Bonini Baraldi and Paradis 2009, 128–130).

6 Bob 2012.

7 Ayoub and Paternotte 2014, 9; Herzog 2011.

8 Ayoub and Paternotte 2014, 9–10.

9 Clews 2013.

10 Bonini Baraldi and Paradis 2009, 127.

11 Ayoub and Paternotte 2014, 13.

12 Ibid., 10.

13 Quoted in Bonini Baraldi and Paradis 2009, 126.

14 Bell 2001, 88.

15 Bonini Baraldi and Paradis 2009, 126.

16 Swiebel 2009, 23.

17 Ayoub 2013, 285.

18 ILGA-Europe 2012.

19 When threatened with the veto of his candidacy, Buttiglione refused to back down, calling himself "the victim of a 'new totalitarianism'" (quoted in Herzog 2011, 196).

20 Hix 2008, 39.

21 Herzog 2011, 197.

22 Quoted in ibid., 197.

23 Quoted in Ayoub and Paternotte 2014, 1.

24 See rainbow-europe.org/#1/0/0.

25 Kollman 2013; Wilson 2013.

26 European Council 1993, emphasis added.

27 For example, applicants in this wave of enlargement not only had to adopt but also implement the *acquis* before accession—a requirement that earlier applicants like Greece had not faced.

28 Moravcsik and Vachudova 2003, 46.

29 O'Dwyer and Schwartz 2010, 232.

30 Börzel and Risse 2003; Epstein and Sedelmeier 2008; Grabbe 2003; Jacoby 2004; Kelley 2004; Knill and Lehmkuhl 1999; Levitz and Pop-Eleches 2010; Sasse 2008; Schimmelfennig and Scholtz 2008; Vachudova 2005.

31 Schimmelfennig and Sedelmeier 2005, 12.

32 Börzel and Risse 2003.
33 Schimmelfennig and Sedelmeier 2005, 12–17.
34 Grabbe 2003; Kelley 2004; Vachudova 2005.
35 Ayoub 2016.
36 Ayoub 2015, 307–308.
37 Börzel and Risse 2003.
38 Kelley 2004.
39 Ayoub 2015.
40 Schimmelfennig and Sedelmeier 2005, 18.
41 Ayoub 2015, 308–309.
42 Ibid., 310.
43 Ibid. 2015. The EU-15 was composed of Belgium, France, Germany, Italy, Luxembourg, and the Netherlands (joined in 1952); Britain, Denmark, and Ireland (joined 1973); Greece (joined 1981); Portugal and Spain (joined 1986); and Austria, Finland, and Sweden (joined 1995). The EU-12 include the Czech Republic, Cyprus, Estonia, Hungary, Latvia, Lithuania, Malta, Poland, Slovakia, and Slovenia (joined in 2004); and Bulgaria and Romania (joined 2007). I say "mostly" because Cyprus and Malta are not postcommunist.
44 Ayoub 2015, 293.
45 Ibid., 305–307.
46 Janos 2001; Raik 2004; Sasse 2008.
47 During the period of this analysis, the postcommunist EU members include Estonia, Latvia, Lithuania, Poland, the Czech Republic, Slovakia, Hungary, Slovenia, Romania, and Bulgaria.
48 In emphasizing this complementarity, I follow Kelley (2004) and Schimmelfennig and Sedelmeier (2005). Ayoub (2015) separates the effect of social learning and external incentives using data that he collected on organizational affiliation but, again, only for first-wave accession states.
49 Schimmelfennig and Scholtz 2008, 196.
50 Ayoub 2015, 308–309; O'Dwyer 2010.
51 For a full description and the individual country scores, see www.ilga-europe. org.publications/reports_and_other_materials/rainbow_europe_map_and _country_index_may_2010.
52 ILGA-Europe reworked its ranking criteria in 2012 to include transgender rights. Yet even this step is not uncontroversial if we take Blasius's (2013) argument that cross-national measures ought not to include rights that have not been demanded in the countries being ranked.
53 For the whole sample, the null hypothesis of no difference among rights scores can be rejected at the 0.01 level.
54 Andersen and Fetner 2008a; Inglehart and Baker 2000; Štulhofer and Rimac 2009. The literature on attitudes toward homosexuality also stresses a number of individual-level variables such as educational attainment, age, gender, and income and class (Andersen and Fetner 2008b). Since my dependent variable here is

national-level variation in the quality of legal frameworks, I focus on national-level independent variables.

55 See www.worldvaluessurvey.org and the Appendix.

56 The question wording is the same across waves.

57 See the Appendix for further details.

58 Inglehart 1997.

59 Andersen and Fetner 2008a, 943.

60 Ibid.; Wernet, Elman, and Pendleton 2005; Gerhards 2007; Štulhofer and Rimac 2009.

61 Inglehart and Baker 2000.

62 Data are from the International Monetary Fund, www.imf.org.

63 Janos 2001, 237. See also Owczarzak 2009, 423–424.

64 See Gruszczynska for a description of Operation Hyacinth (2006, 2). Amazingly, the "pink files" created during this operation seem to have gone missing, and still remain so. The police claim to have turned them over to the Polish Institute of National Remembrance, but it claims not to have them. It is rumored that the files have been used to blackmail some conservative politicians in contemporary Polish politics ("Historia homoseksualności w Polsce" [The history of homosexuality in Poland], presentation by Krzysztof Tomasik, Pride House Warsaw, July 14, 2010).

65 Grzymała-Busse 2015.

66 Norris and Inglehart 2004, 43.

67 Ibid., 43–47.

68 Inglehart and Welzel 2005; Norris and Inglehart 2004.

69 Norris and Inglehart 2004, 41. As noted earlier, this variable combines waves 4–5 of the WVS.

70 Ayoub 2015.

71 See ibid.

72 O'Dwyer 2010, 238–239.

73 Janos 2001; Raik 2004; Subotic 2009.

74 Ayoub 2015, 313.

75 Ibid., 311–312.

CHAPTER 3. HOW THE HARD RIGHT "EUROPEANIZED" HOMOSEXUALITY

1 Slogan quoted in Gruszczynska 2009a, 40. Smolar epigraph, quoted in Pankowski 2010, 169.

2 Benford and Snow 2000, 615.

3 Ibid., 619.

4 As Chapter 4 describes, even many Polish LGBT activists employed this morality-charity framing in the 1990s.

5 Ayoub 2014, 345.

6 Ayoub and Paternotte 2014, 3.

7 Benford and Snow 2000, 620.

8 As one example, the original parties in the party system collectively received only 9 percent of the vote in 2007. The comparable figure for Czech parties was 87 percent (O'Dwyer 2014, 520). See also Millard 2009.

9 O'Dwyer 2014; Ost 2006.

10 de Lange and Guerra 2009; Jasiewicz 2007 and 2008.

11 These are also called "liberal Poland" (*Polska liberalna*) and "solidarity Poland" (*Polska solidarna*). See Jasiewicz (2008) and Pankowski (2010, 163–164).

12 Blokker 2005, 371.

13 The Czech system fits the latter model (O'Dwyer 2014).

14 Grzymała-Busse and Innes 2003, 67.

15 Ibid. See also Jasiewicz (2008) and Raik (2004).

16 Grzymała-Busse and Innes 2003, 69.

17 Examples included the National Party (SR), the short-lived Party X, the Movement to Rebuild Poland (ROP), Social Movement Alternative (RSA), the Confederation of Independent Poland-Fatherland (KPN-O), and the Alternative Party of Labor (APP). See Mudde (2007).

18 Hloušek and Kopeček 2010, 149–50.

19 It was a member of the Electoral Action Solidarity (AWS) coalition.

20 Grzymała-Busse and Innes 2003.

21 These were represented in particular by the Freedom Union, with which AWS formed a coalition in 1997.

22 These included the center-right PO and center-left SLD.

23 Hloušek and Kopeček 2010, 260; Mudde 2007, 307; Pankowski 2010.

24 Hloušek and Kopeček 2010, 174–176.

25 Markowski 2007, 43.

26 Walicki 1999.

27 Chetaille 2011, 127–128.

28 The third party to enter the government after the 2005 election, Self-Defense, was also strongly Euroskeptic, but, unlike LPR, its message centered on the EU as an economic threat, especially for agriculture, not as a threat to Polishness (Jasiewicz 2008, 11). Though also an outsider-populist party, SO's position on homosexuality was muddled. On the one hand, it cultivated ties with Radio Maryja, but its leader Andrezj Lepper also stated that he did not rule out the possibility of same-sex partnerships (Pankowski 2010, 140). This inconsistency was illustrative of the larger picture: Self-Defense was not an ideologically oriented, or even ideologically coherent, party; it was organized instead around the (quixotic) personality of its leader (ibid., 14).

29 The path to PiS, LPR, and SO's coalition was not a direct one. Initially, PiS and PO were expected to form a coalition; however, talks between them collapsed almost immediately. PiS then formed a minority government with LPR and SO support. Though neither party received ministerial posts, LPR chief Roman Giertych gained a key parliamentary post in October 2005. The parties negotiated

a short-lived stabilization pact and then a formal coalition agreement (Pankowski 2010, 170–171).

30 The main predecessor was the Nationalist Party (Stronnictwo Narodowe), led by Roman Giertych. LPR's leaders were also drawn from such former nationalist-Catholic parties as the Christian National Union, the Catholic-National Movement, and Movement to Rebuild Poland (de Lange and Guerra 2009, 535; Jasiewicz 2008, 15–16; and Pankowski 2010, 112).

31 Shibata 2013, 107. The Round Table Talks referred to here were the negotiations between Solidarity and the Polish Communist Party in 1989, which paved the way for Poland's democratization.

32 Here one could point to proposals to prevent the sale of land to foreigners or of banks to foreign investors. Additionally, LPR supports state control of strategic sectors such as infrastructure and energy. While equating Catholicism with national identity is a particularly Polish twist on the populist radical right, LPR's program is standard fare for a party of this family (Mlejnek 2006, 365–370). See also Shibata (2013, 108–126).

33 de Lange and Guerra 2009, 536.

34 Balser and Foxman, quoted in Guerra 2013, 141. Another estimate counted as many as four million listeners (Jasiewicz 2008, 22).

35 Eaglin, quoted in de Lange and Guerra (2009, 536).

36 Mlejnek 2006, 368–369.

37 The original MW was established in the 1930s by Roman Giertych's grandfather Jędrzej Giertych and was chaired by the interwar theoretician of Polish nationalism Roman Dmowski. It was an anti-Semitic youth organization that attempted to forcibly Polonize the educational system and was responsible for many attacks on Jewish students. The reincarnated MW, like the LPR and its predecessors, were also characterized by strong currents of anti-Semitism. Under Giertych, MW activists developed connections with the neo-Nazi and "white power" movements, notably the rock band Twierdza (Fortress) (Pankowski 2010, 115–119).

38 Ibid., 113.

39 These included the burning of the EU flag in May 2001 in Rzeszów and in May 2002 in Kraków. MW also disrupted European meetings in Warsaw in 2001 and 2002 (Pankowski 2010, 114).

40 One example was Piotr Farfał, who had disrupted several rallies led by President Aleksander Kwaśniewski in support of EU membership in 2003 (ibid., 114).

41 Ibid., 120.

42 LPR was the most conspicuous force behind the campaign to vote "no" on EU membership in 2003. Pankowski points out that its arguments gave short shrift to the possible economic costs of membership; instead, he writes, they used "well-established cultural clichés, especially the anti-Semitic and Germanophobic conspiracy theories legitimized by the quasi-religious authority of Radio Maryja" (ibid., 123).

43 Jasiewicz 2008, 16. At times, this idea of Europe as seeking to impose homosexual lifestyles on Poland crossed the line into the absurd. For example, the Ministry of Education attempted to change the name of 2006 Council of Europe program from "All Different–All Equal" to "All Different–All in Solidarity." The reason, as explained by Minister Giertych, was to avoid any confusion with the Warsaw Equality Parade (Czarnecki 2006, 25).

44 I will draw on Shibata's analysis of the article as an example of LPR's antigay discourse (2013, 192–195).

45 Quoted in ibid. (2013, 193, emphasis in the original).

46 Ibid., 179.

47 Ibid., 194–195. To cite one example of such discourse that, despite prompting a court case, was let stand: a member of the Polish Family Association declared in a newspaper editorial in 2003 that "[h]omosexuality is an aberration and a threat to healthy families. If someone is affected by such a disease then they should be aware from the beginning that they will not be allowed to fulfil certain roles, especially if it's being a teacher that has the role of raising and shaping the conscience of children and, to a certain extent, our society's outlooks" (quoted in Czarnecki 2006, 70). KPH brought suit for defamation, but the case was dismissed.

48 Pankowski 2010, 123.

49 Art and Brown 2007, 6. Complaints brought to the Warsaw district prosecutor about Wierzejski's comments were dismissed (Amnesty International 2006, 8).

50 Quoted in Pankowski 2010, 123.

51 Wróblewski 2006.

52 Quoted in Kitlinski and Leszkowicz 2005.

53 By European standards it was abnormal and extreme, especially for governing parties—which is why it drew censure from the EP in two resolutions in 2006. By comparison with the US, such rhetoric may recall the debate over the Defense of Marriage Act in the mid-2000s. Here, too, though, it may be argued that overt homophobia helped galvanize activism, as can be seen in the ultimately successful efforts to organize against the Act.

54 Education occupied a central place in LPR's ideology, as it offered a means to shape "national culture" and the "patriotic spirit" (Shibata 2013, 120–126).

55 Again there are parallels with interwar history here. One of the major campaigns of the National Democrats and affiliated organizations like the All-Poland Youth was to separate Jewish students from Polish ones, to limit the access of Jews to education in favor of Poles, and to prevent Jews from becoming teachers. This campaign was justified in terms of protecting Polish students' morals.

56 Czarnecki 2006, 31.

57 Quoted in ibid., 27.

58 Jałowiec 2006.

59 Quoted in Amnesty International 2006, 9. Sielatycki later sued for wrongful dismissal and won. See also Kosc 2006.

60 Quoted in Amnesty International 2006, 9.
61 Quoted in ILGA-Europe (www.ilga-europe.org/content/download/6515/39986 /file/Poland%20homophobic_statements.doc), accessed July 9, 2014.
62 Quoted in Amnesty International 2006, 10.
63 The filter did not, however, block access to far-right websites such as Redwatch (Kosc 2006; Pankowski 2010, 182).
64 Quoted in Walicki 1999, 32.
65 Prazmowska 1995, 201–202.
66 Walicki 1999, 32.
67 Ibid., 35–46.
68 Walicki 1999, 44.
69 LPR's hard Euroskepticism was arguably less successful as an electoral gambit. Ultimately, its dire predictions of accession's consequences failed to materialize; indeed, there were notable improvements in indicators like unemployment and income.
70 Various Polish analysts have made this connection between anti-Semitism and homophobia (e.g., Czarnecki 2006; Graff 2006; Pankowski 2010).
71 Ostolski 2005.
72 Ibid., 164–165.
73 Quoted in Ostolski 2007, 165.
74 Pankowski 2010, 123.
75 As examples of the latter, consider the Czech Civic Democratic Party, the Slovenian Democratic Party, and Poland's Civic Platform. See Hloušek and Kopeček 2010; Mudde 2007.
76 PiS showed a willingness to ally itself with extreme elements even after 2007 and LPR's demise. In the 2007 election, members of ROP, which Mudde (2007, 307) categorizes as populist radical right, ran successfully on PiS's party list (Movement for Reconstruction of Poland, en.wikipedia.org).
77 Pankowski 2010, 154–161.
78 After all, he added, "I'm not sure if paedophilia, necrophilia and zoophilia won't simply become a 'sexual orientation' soon." Quoted in Czarnecki 2006, 75–76.
79 Quoted in ibid., 75–76.
80 Quoted in ibid., 76–77, emphasis added.
81 Quoted in Amnesty International 2006, 7.
82 Quoted in ibid., 6.
83 Millard 2006, 1011.
84 Pankowski 2010, 161.
85 Quoted in Pankowski 2010, 182.
86 Graff 2006; Gruszczynska 2009a; Millard 2006; O'Dwyer 2010.
87 Krzyżaniak-Gumowska 2005a.
88 Quoted in ibid.
89 The affiliation of PiS deputies within the EP offers another indicator of the party's stance toward the EU. Namely, PiS rejected the mainstream conservative EP

party, the European People's Party, opting instead for the Euroskeptic Alliance for Europe of the Nations.

90 Quoted in Pankowski 2010, 158.

91 Czarnecki 2006, 79; Pankowski 2010, 175.

92 These are the words of Robert Szaniawski, spokesperson for the Ministry of Foreign Affairs (quoted in Shibata 2013, 190).

93 Pankowski 2010, 167.

94 On party system institutionalization as a concept, see Mainwaring (1999) and Mair (1997). On such institutionalization in postcommunist countries, see O'Dwyer (2006) and (2014).

95 O'Dwyer 2014.

96 Hloušek and Kopeček 2010, 197.

97 Ibid.; Čakl and Wollmann 2005; Mudde 2007, 77, 87.

98 Hloušek and Kopeček 2010, 197.

99 Mudde (2007, 306) classifies two other Czech parties as populist radical right, but the first, the National Party (NS), never seriously contested national elections and, moreover, rejected the label far right (Čakl and Wollmann 2005, 37). The second, the Republicans of Miroslav Sládek (RMS), was a legal ruse to preserve the SPR-RSČ after it had been officially sanctioned (ibid., 33). In their inventory of Czech far-right groups, Čakl and Wollmann mention two other parties that, in contrast to SPR-RSČ, did support discriminatory policies against LGBT people in their programs, in addition to anti-EU ones. These were the neo-Nazi National Social Block–Right Alternative (NSB-PA) and National Unification (NS); however, they were both politically inconsequential. The former never gained more than 1 percent of the vote in elections, and since 2000 has been in a state of decay. The latter is even more marginal, with an estimated 100 members and 0.00 percent of the vote in 2002's local elections (ibid., 33–36).

100 Hloušek and Kopeček 2010, 167.

101 Ibid., 170.

102 These groups include Bohemian Hammerskins, Blood and Honor, the National Alliance, Republican Youth, the National Resistance, and the Patriotic Front (Čakl and Wollmann 2005, 42).

103 Ibid., 38.

104 Ibid., 48.

105 Ibid., 50.

106 See Ayoub and Paternotte 2014; Graff 2008; Gruszczynska 2009a, 2009b; Minałto 2007.

107 Graff (2008, 191) analyzed Poland's three largest political weeklies: *Polityka*, *Wprost*, and *Newsweek Polska*. These are mainstream, mass-market publications analogous to *Time* and *Newsweek* in the US.

108 Ibid., 192.

109 Amid such charged language, it is easy to miss a striking ambivalence at the heart of the meteoric rise in the salience of sexual politics: even the most conservative of these publications supported a "yes" vote on Poland's 2003 EU membership referendum (ibid., 192).

110 Ibid., 199.

111 Ibid.

112 *Wprost*, May 30, 2004 issue.

113 *Gazeta Wyborcza*'s archives are available at www.archiwum.wyborcza.pl/Archiwum/0,0.html.

114 At its peak in the mid-2000s, *Gazeta Wyborcza*'s circulation reached 672,000. Since 2010, it has fallen to around 200,000 and has been surpassed by the tabloid *Fakt* ("Spada sprzedaż dzienników" 2013). It remains the most influential Polish paper in terms of cachet, analogous to the *New York Times*.

115 Both papers' online search engines find all articles containing matches on requested words. I searched the entire newspapers, not just the political sections. *Gazeta Wyborcza*'s search engine can be configured to focus on specified date ranges; *Mladá fronta dnes*'s did not have this capability, obliging me to sort the search results manually. In order to guard against the possibility of editorial bias, I also ran shadow analyses of the search terms in two other Czech media sources, the weekly paper *Respekt* and Czech Radio (Český rozhlas), which also hosts a news service on its website (the archive can be found at hledani.rozhlas.cz). The results of these further analyses did not differ significantly from those of *Mladá fronta dnes*.

116 The Polish term is *homoseksualny*, the Czech *homosexuální*.

117 The same applies to "homophobia" below.

118 To probe this, I analyzed the incidence of the term "homosexual" in the archives of the newsweekly *Respekt*, which extends back to 1990. The trend was the same.

119 As a different indicator of hard-right backlash, I also tried searching the term "faggot" in both papers. In Czech, the term is *teplouš*, which is more suitable for content analysis because it has only one meaning. The Polish term *pedał* presents a challenge because its more common meaning is "pedal," as in bicycle pedal. To filter out articles using the term in this other sense, I manually went through the search results and stripped out articles about cars, cycling, pianos, and so forth. In neither newspaper did the term yield many articles in most years, though. In *Gazeta Wyborcza*, there were about eight such articles on average per year. *Mladá fronta dnes* contained even fewer. Since this term is considered offensive, it is rarely used in the print media.

120 Again, the Czech newspaper data are truncated, but evidence from my interviews supports this claim. See also Seidl 2012.

121 Besides capturing the onset of the hard-right backlash, the increasing incidence of the term "homophobia" in the Polish press may also be read as an indication of activists' success in reframing homosexuality and winning allies. Many articles using the term report criticism by foreign actors: for example, the EP's 2006

resolution warning Poland against homophobia. Others debate whether that censure was valid. Still others apply the term themselves, for example, to LPR's rhetoric.

CHAPTER 4. ACTIVISM BEFORE EU LEVERAGE

1 Rada epigraph, quoted in Seidl 2012, 18. Kliszczyński epigraph, from Kliszczyński 2001, 166.
2 Janos 2001.
3 Quoted in Pankowski 2010, 158.
4 Buechler 1990, 42; McCarthy 1996, 143.
5 Sasse 2008.
6 McAdam 1996, 27.
7 Both countries received the same score on Freedom House's civil liberties index throughout this period: they were ranked at the second highest level on a seven-point scale (see freedomhouse.org/).
8 Hloušek and Kopeček 2010, 197–198.
9 Czech president and former dissident Václav Havel endorsed LGBT-rights activists in the 1990s, in particular the various attempts at enacting registered partnerships. Movement publications such as the *Soho revue* (see below) trumpeted his favorable comments. However, in the absence of public attention to homosexuality, this endorsement had little immediate policy impact, as the torturous, drawn-out campaign for partnerships illustrated (interview with Jiří Hromada, August 4, 2011, Prague). One may further speculate that Havel's endorsement of LGBT rights, notable as it was for the time, was an evolving one and, at least initially, sounded less than full-throated. Consider his comments on the 1995 partnerships proposal: "It is a complicated problem with many diverse aspects, which I won't parse individually. But I will confess that I would welcome it if this debate were to continue or if in time it were reopened because, personally, I am inclined to think that it probably makes sense to implement registered partnerships" (quoted in Seidl 2012, 374n364).
10 To be clear, there were differences in societal openness, as we saw in Chapter 1.
11 Long 1999, 247; Seidl 2012, 305–313.
12 Long 1999, 247.
13 Seidl 2012, 306.
14 Long 1999, 247.
15 The majority were gay men.
16 Seidl 2012, 308.
17 Lambda's goals were more political than those of the Socio-Therapeutic Club, though they were initially understood more in terms of overcoming stigma and discrimination than as specific policy proposals.
18 Seidl 2012, 311–312.
19 Lambda deliberately referred to itself as a *zájmová společenská organizace* (interest group organization).

20 A representative of the Socio-Therapeutic Club also attended this conference (Seidl 2012, 310). At this time registered partnerships were presented as a means to prevent the spread of HIV/AIDS.

21 Howard (2003), for example, excludes such groups from his count of civil society organizations.

22 Quoted in Seidl 2012, 308.

23 Long 1999, 247; Sokolová 2004, 259–261.

24 Sokolová 2005, 32.

25 Seidl 2012, 342.

26 Fanel 2000, 455–46; Procházka, Janík, and Hromada 2003, 71–73.

27 Ekiert 1996.

28 Krzemiński et al. 2006, 103–107. See also Kliszczyński 2001; Zboralski 1991; Kostrzewa et al. 2009.

29 Krzemiński et al. 2006, 103.

30 See also Kliszczyński 2001, 162.

31 Krzemiński et al. 2006, 105.

32 Owczarzak 2010, 204. Kliszczyński describes the efforts of the largest such group, the Warsaw Homosexual Movement, to apply for legal status in 1988. Despite concessions, such as removing the word "homosexual" from the name (it became the "Society for Preventing and Fighting AIDS"), the Warsaw authorities "refused to register this 'dangerous' association" (2001, 162).

33 Krzemiński et al. 2006, 104.

34 Ibid., 104.

35 An example of such an individual was Professor Mikołaj Kozakiewicz from the Association of Family Planning (ibid., 104–105).

36 Ibid., 107.

37 Owczarzak 2009, 427.

38 Ibid..

39 Gruszczynska 2009a, 31; Kliszczyński 2001, 162.

40 Owczarzak 2010, 203.

41 Kliszczyński characterizes press reporting on homosexuality at the time as "sensationalistic" (2001, 162).

42 Owczarzak 2009, 422.

43 Owczarzak 2010, 204.

44 Owczarzak 2009, 437.

45 Holzhacker (2012) also describes LGBT rights in Poland as "morality politics." In contrast to my conceptualization here, Holzhacker's "morality politics" includes political activism. This reflects his focus on the post-2000 period. A broader chronology, however, reveals an earlier generation of LGBT activism that was avowedly apolitical in orientation; thus, rejecting the "morality" framing was a key part of the move to political goals.

46 Owczarzak 2009, 432.

47 Novak 1998, 62.

48 Owczarzak 2009, 434.

49 Ibid., 433.

50 Graff 2006, 434.

51 Seidl 2012, 325–329.

52 The full name was Movement for Tolerance–Movement for the Support of Homosexuals and the Fight Against AIDS (Hnutí tolerance–hnutí na podporu homosexuálů a boje proti AIDS).

53 Seidl 2012, 318.

54 Ivo Procházka explained the hesitation thus: "[The public] are not so friendly toward and familiar with the problem of homosexuality that they would evaluate our contribution very positively. And in that period it was more important to avoid discrediting the Velvet Revolution" (quoted in ibid., 318).

55 Ibid., 319.

56 Quoted in ibid., 320. See also Fanel 2000.

57 The Czech word *rovnoprávnost* is actually broader than just equality, as it incorporates the word roots for "equal" and "rights."

58 Reflecting the antipolitics spirit of the Velvet Revolution, the demonstrators carried placards with slogans such as "We want to live in truth" (Seidl 2012, 320–321). Those words quote directly from Havel's famous essay "Power of the Powerless" (1990).

59 Fanel 2000, 454.

60 Seidl 2012, 324–325.

61 The list failed to meet the 5-percent threshold for representation (Fanel 2000, 454).

62 Seidl 2012, 324–325.

63 LEGA published an erotic magazine called *Gemini* (ibid., 330).

64 Ibid., 345.

65 Ibid., 328–329.

66 Fanel 2000, 454–455.

67 Seidl 2012, 329.

68 At this time, it should be noted that the gay and lesbian press was also expanding rapidly. Besides *SOHO revue*, there was the magazine *Gemini* published by LEGA as well as Lambda Union's relaunched monthly *Lambda revue*, which had a circulation of 40,000 copies and was for sale across the country (ibid., 329).

69 Long 1999, 248. Though more critical of SOHO's tactical choices, Sokolová (2004, 259) nonetheless echoes this assessment, writing, "With the collapse of communism, [Czech] homosexuals were among the first suppressed minorities to organize into a strong political force."

70 Initially, this also included Slovakia, which was represented through its organization Ganymedes.

71 See the Appendix.

72 Long 1999, 248.

73 Ibid.

74 To give a sense of the composition of SOHO's revenue, 1.2 million Kč (out of 1.54 million Kč total revenue) came from grants in 1994. Of total revenue, 52 percent came from the Czech Ministry of Health, 2 percent from the Czech Institute of Health, 17 percent from the World Health Organization, and 8 percent from Czech-Slovak-Swiss Health Society and the Swiss government (Seidl 2012, 381–382).

75 Ibid., 339.

76 Ibid.

77 Quoted in ibid., 368.

78 Interviews with Zdeněk Sloboda, May 26, 2011, Prague, and Jan Seidl, May 24, 2011, Prague.

79 Seid 2012, 366.

80 Ibid., 362–367. Other groups to note here are Logos, a Christian-oriented group; Gales, a university student group in Prague; and Promluv, a lesbian group based in Prague.

81 Ibid., 347.

82 Quoted in ibid., 342.

83 Ibid., 342–343.

84 Long 1999, 250.

85 Sokolová 2004, 260; Sokolová 2005, 33–34.

86 For example, this period saw an annual candlelight memorial commemorating AIDS victims (Light for AIDS, Světlo pro AIDS), and in 1996 SOHO organized a "Week of the Fight Against AIDS" (Týden boje proti AIDS).

87 For example, SOHO organized an annual Gay Man contest, a kind of combination beauty/personality contest, in place of (what it saw as) the more provocative community-building Gay Pride parade familiar from Western countries (Seidl 2012, 377–378; interviews with Zdeněk Sloboda, May 26, 2011, Prague; Věra Sokolová, July 12, 2011, Prague; and Jiří Hromada, August 4, 2011, Prague).

88 Beňová et al. 2007, 17; Procházka, Janík, and Hromada 2003, 70–74.

89 Procházka, Janík, and Hromada 2003.

90 Seidl 2012: 368n340.

91 Sokolová 2005, 32. Registered partnerships had figured as an element in Hromada's program during his campaign for parliament in 1990. After that unsuccessful bid, Hromada and other members of Lambda Union discussed a registered partnerships proposal with MPs in the federal parliament, but the dissolution of Czechoslovakia in 1993 scuttled those discussions. In 1995, as the Czech government was preparing revisions to the family law, SOHO drafted a legislative proposal on partnerships, which it sent to the parliamentary factions and committee chairs. SOHO was confident that the proposal would be passed quickly, with Hromada declaring that "this year registered partnerships will be possible" (quoted in Seidl 2012, 373). As it turned out, the government rejected the proposal, saying that it did not want to create a kind of second-order marriage and that only three European countries had such partnerships, Denmark, Norway, and Sweden. With

this disappointment—the first significant setback for the movement during this period—came the realization that obtaining this goal would require considerable organization and effort. A SOHO statement from November 1995 declared, "Obviously it will take some time, but believe us, we have time and patience enough" (quoted in Seidl 2012, 374).

92 Kliszczyński 2001, 161, italics in the original.

93 Gruszczynska 2009a, 31–32; Kliszczyński 2001, 161–162.

94 This is the date of its legal registration as a civic association (Krzemiński et al. 2006, 119). For brevity's sake, I will refer to this group as the Polish Lambda Association.

95 Gruszczynska 2009a, 123n53. After 2000, this situation had reversed: now the first requirement for an activist dealing with the media was willingness to be "out" (ibid., 124).

96 Kliszczyński offers a cautionary note on this expansion, however, noting that "one of the reasons for the existence of so many Lambda Groups . . . was the fact that three people were enough to establish one" (2001, 163). This caveat calls to mind the infamous "couch parties" that characterized parliamentary politics in Poland in the early 1990s—so called because their members could all fit on a couch.

97 Gruszczynska 2009a, 33.

98 Quoted in Krzemiński et al. 2006, 119.

99 Ibid.

100 Kliszczyński mentions four gay and lesbian publications during this period: *Inaczej*, *Facet*, *Nowy Men*, and *Gejzer* (2001, 163–164).

101 Krzemiński et al. 2006, 120.

102 Ibid., 121.

103 Kliszczyński 2001, 165.

104 ILGA-Europe 2001, 53.

105 Owczarzak 2010, 204.

106 Quoted in Krzemiński et al. 2006, 122. See also Owczarzak 2010, 204–205.

107 Owczarzak 2010, 204, emphasis in the original.

108 In 2002, a conservative city government pulled funding. Lambda Warsaw's president described the decision as follows: "We asked the municipality again for the money and the new chief of this commission responsible for the HIV prevention grants answered that we, of course, are an HIV prevention organization, but she can't accept that lesbian and gay—that a gay man will do HIV prevention work among gay men because that's a kind of promotion of homosexuality. So, in case you'd like to do good HIV prevention work, you need to send straight people to the gay clubs because gay people in gay clubs promote homosexuality" (quoted in ibid., 204).

109 Ibid., 205.

110 According to Krzeminski et al. (2006, 124), the unraveling of a romantic relationship between the founders of the early 1990s group Gdańsk Initiative was the reason for that group's demise.

111 Gruszczynska 2009a, 34.

112 Owczarzak 2009, 428–432; Chetaille 2011, 122. In her study of HIV/AIDS activism in Poland, Owczarzak notes only one other group of activists, Plus, which housed five HIV-positive people in a private house in Warsaw. The only other activists were not groups, but individuals attempting to disseminate information about HIV transmission.

113 The Church's expansion into this area was part of a larger expansion of the role of faith-based organizations in providing social services in Poland after 1989 (Wilson 2013, 74).

114 Ibid., 436.

115 Ramet 2006, 122–124.

116 Owczarzak 2009, 2010.

117 Owczarzak 2009, 429.

118 Kliszczyński 2001, 165–166.

CHAPTER 5. ACTIVISM UNDER EU LEVERAGE

1 Hromada epigraph, quoted in Seidl 2012, 39; Szypuła epigraph, quoted in Ohlsen 2009, 51. Szypuła later became KPH's president (Bell 2001, 88).

2 There was no clearer example of this dynamic than the policy of the Polish Church hierarchy in the accession period: despite misgivings about EU norms regarding gender and sexuality, it remained silent about these and endorsed a "yes" vote in the accession referendum held in 2003. Obviously, the example of Father Rydzyk and Radio Maryja (as discussed in Chapter 3) departed radically from the official Church hierarchy here (Ramet 2006). Yet neither Radio Maryja nor the All-Poland Youth spoke for the mainstream Church, and while many of the clergy doubtless sympathized with them, the hierarchy found the aggressive rhetoric of these groups embarrassing.

3 Binnie and Klesse 2012, 450.

4 Ibid.; Mizielińska 2011.

5 Seidl 2012, 430n600.

6 Instead, Euroskepticism remained centered on economic policy, a small variation on the neoliberalism versus gradualism debate that had defined Czech party politics since the early 1990s. Consequently, it left elite alignments undisturbed (O'Dwyer 2014).

7 Sokolová 2005, 32.

8 The former faction tended to be gay men, and the second feminist activists (Sokolová 2004).

9 On internal framing contests, see McAdam, McCarthy, and Zald 1996, 16–17.

10 Seidl 2012, 394.

11 Owczarzak 2010.

12 Yet even with these changes, its overall mission remained primarily apolitical (Krzemiński et al. 2006, 122–123).

13 Ibid., 122.

14 Quoted in Gruszczynska 2009a, 34.

15 The following paragraphs draw closely on Krzeminski et al. (2006).

16 Ibid., 140–141.

17 Ibid., 146.

18 In the first years, there was some disagreement about what political activism meant. One camp advocated emulating the English group Outrage, which employed radical, attention-seeking tactics. A second faction favored a more culturally and identity-oriented activism (specifically a queer identity). In time, the latter group was marginalized, and the former moderated its tactics into the policy-oriented model described above (ibid., 140–143).

19 Owczarzak 2009, 204.

20 Krzemiński et al. 2006, 152.

21 Ohlsen 2009, 58.

22 Owczarzak 2010, 204.

23 Krzemiński et al. 2006, 150.

24 Ohlsen 2009.

25 Ibid.

26 O'Dwyer 2010.

27 Krzemiński et al. 2006, 133.

28 Ohlsen 2009, 43–44.

29 O'Dwyer 2010, 241–242; Ohlsen 2009, 45–46; cf. Krzemiński et al. 2006, 151.

30 Interview with Dominika Ferens, June 9, 2007, Warsaw.

31 Lang 2013.

32 KPH president Biedroń recounted how, in 2006, the Education Ministry rejected a project for training volunteers in collaboration with a Swedish NGO with the reason that "the Ministry does not accept any support for actions promoting homosexual attitudes and behaviours among young people. Moreover, it is not the role of the Ministry to support homosexual organizations or to cooperate with them" (Biedroń 2007, 55).

33 Interview with Yga Kostrzewa, June 5, 2007, Warsaw.

34 Interview with Robert Biedroń, June 12, 2007, Warsaw.

35 Warkocki 2004, 99–101.

36 Cf Krzemiński et al. 2006, 143–144.

37 Interview with Szymon Niemiec, June 1, 2007, Warsaw.

38 Graff 2006, 437.

39 Gruszczynska 2009a, 36.

40 Minałto 2007, 58.

41 Quoted in O'Dwyer 2010.

42 Interview with Szymon Niemiec, June 1, 2007, Warsaw.

43 Quoted in Krzemiński et al. 2006, 132.

44 Quoted in Ohlsen 2009, 35. See also Krzemiński et al. 2006, 134.

45 Krzemiński et al. 2006.

46 Ibid., 133.

47 Ibid., 132–133.
48 As Graff wrote, "Polish feminism did not go through a homophobic stage: it joined a rainbow coalition without ever considering identity politics. The first public appearance of a rainbow flag in Poland occurred in a feminist demonstration in Warsaw" (2003, 103).
49 Gruszczynska 2009a, 24n12.
50 Grzymała-Busse and Innes 2003; O'Dwyer 2010.
51 Interviews with Jan Seidl, May 24, 2011, Prague; Zdeněk Sloboda, May 26, 2011, Prague; and Věra Sokolová, July 12, 2011, Prague.
52 Sokolová 2004, 260–261.
53 Sokolová 2005, 34–35.
54 As Sokolová writes, "Clearly, both groups feel that they have something to lose by widening their self-presentation to include feminist politics on the one hand and gay/lesbian politics on the other. As a result, both discourses lose half their argumentative and political potential for productive critique and meaningful change in the way our society works and thinks. It is impossible to fight against sexism without reflecting and challenging homophobia and vice-versa it is impossible to fight against homophobia without understanding and analyzing the gendered foundations of social marginalization and exclusion" (2005, 30).
55 Ibid., 30.
56 Ibid., 32.
57 Quoted in ibid., 33.
58 Procházka, Janík, and Hromada 2003.
59 The grant was made through the EU's Phare program (Procházka, Janík, and Hromada 2003).
60 Ibid., 47.
61 Ibid., 39–40.
62 Seidl 2012, 380.
63 Long 1999, 259.
64 Procházka, Janík, and Hromada 2003, 74, emphasis added.
65 Seidl 2012, 381. Seidl argues that an additional factor behind the changing organization of activism in this period was the rise of the Internet, which accelerated the trend toward informal association and deinstitutionalization (380–389). While there is, no doubt, something to this argument, especially with regard to the LGBT print media, its limits are exposed through a comparison with Poland. Despite operating in an environment with similar levels of Internet penetration, Polish activism was becoming more institutionalized during this period.
66 Procházka, Janík, and Hromada 2003, 74.
67 Quoted in Sokolová 2005, 32. Bulvár is Czech term for what in English would be called tabloid journalism.
68 Quoted in Fliedr 1999, 5.
69 Seidl 2012, 388.
70 Ibid.

71 Ibid., 389.

72 Fanel 2000, 458–459.

73 Sokolová 2006.

74 There were, it should be noted, some counterbalancing trends as well. The movement was able to find other, if less financially generous, allies in the mainstream media. Beginning in September 1998, the Czech state broadcast service Radio Journal (Radiožurnál) hosted a weekly radio program, *Bona Dea*, devoted to LGBT topics. State and private TV also ran a number of documentaries and films offering sympathetic portrayals of homosexuality (Fanel 2000, 459; Sokolová 2005).

75 Sokolová 2004, 33.

76 Incidentally, this was not the first occasion on which Hromada's outsized presence provided the impulse for punning on his name. The group HRHO, which as described in Chapter 4 was the first politically oriented group after 1989, was sometimes referred to as "Hromada's Boys" (from the Czech "Hromadovi hoši," which could also be shortened to HRHO) (Fanel 2000, 454).

77 Quoted in Seidl 2012, 396.

78 See Beňová et al. 2007, 17.

79 Seidl 2012, 396; interview with Zdeněk Sloboda, May 26, 2011, Prague.

80 Sokolová 2005, 259.

81 Interviews with Jan Seidl, May 24, 2011, Prague, and Daniel Kupšovský, July 18, 2011, Prague.

82 Cooley and Ron 2002.

83 Bilić 2016; Henry 2010; Sperling 1999; Sundstrom 2006.

84 Beňová et al. 2007, 67.

85 Fanel 2000, 457.

86 Ibid.

87 Seidl writes that SOHO conceived of the Gay Man pageant and Candlelight parade as substitutes for a Pride parade (2012, 378).

88 Fanel 2000, 457.

89 Procházka, Janík, and Hromada 2003.

90 Seidl 2012, 375.

91 E.g., Sokolová 2005, 2006.

92 Beňová et al. 2007, 28–30.

93 Ibid., 23–24.

94 Procházka, Janík, and Hromada 2003; Beňová et al. 2007, 24.

95 Beňová et al. 2007, 25.

96 Kollman 2013. Hungary and Slovenia now also legally recognize same-sex partnerships—since 2009 and 2006, respectively.

97 As models for same-sex partnership legalization, Fanel cites the examples of Belgium, Denmark, Finland, Sweden, and Holland and the non-EU states Iceland, Norway, and Switzerland (2000, 464).

98 The following section draws primarily on the accounts of Seidl (2012, 419–459) and Hromada (2007).

99 Hromada 2007, 18.

100 Sokolová 2006, 259.

101 Fanel 2000, 463.

102 On this issue, MPs tended to "vote their conscience," not the party line. From the start the various parliamentary proposals were cosponsored by MPs from parties otherwise ideologically opposed: the conservative ODS, the liberal Freedom Union, the Social Democrats, and the Communists.

103 According to Fanel, these "diabolical" tactics were intended to kill the bill without publicly opposing it (2000, 463). Even if this was the case, such subtlety is not the stuff of a resonant framing contest between EU norms and national identity.

104 Quoted in ibid., 464.

105 Quoted in ibid., 465. The Christian Democrats' youth section called for Tollner's resignation.

106 Hromada 2007, 18.

107 Quoted in Sokolová 2005, 37.

108 Quoted in ibid., 37.

109 Seidl 2012, 401.

110 The conditions surrounding the vote were dramatic. After the results were announced, a ČSSD MP claimed that his vote had been miscounted, and he had actually supported the proposal. This would have decided the outcome the other way. Instead, the parliament decided to revote; this time the results were 91 for to 84 against (Fanel 2000, 465–466).

111 This strategy of "small steps" (*malé změny*) drew explicitly on the model of the Dutch LGBT-rights movement, as articulated by Kees Waaldijk. See Seidl 2012, 409–410.

112 Ibid., 413.

CHAPTER 6. ACTIVISM AFTER EU LEVERAGE

1 Pride March epigraph, quoted in Gruszczynska 2009a, 193. Lambda Warsaw epigraph, quoted in Krzemiński et al. 2006, 136. Hromada epigraph, quoted in Seidl 2012, 460.

2 Snow et al. 1998.

3 European Parliament 2006a.

4 "Commotion" 2006.

5 European Parliament 2006b.

6 "Commotion" 2006.

7 Quoted in O'Dwyer 2010, 239.

8 Quoted in ibid.

9 Quoted in ibid.

10 Kriesi calls these paths "commercialization" and "involution" (1996, 156–157).

11 See Binnie and Klesse 2011, 446–447.

12 Weeks 2007.

13 Millard 2006, 1011.

14 Quoted in Kosc 2005.

15 Krzyżaniak-Gumowska 2005b.

16 Gruszczynska 2009b.

17 Graff 2006, 439.

18 Quoted in ibid., 441.

19 Poznań's bishop justified his city's ban by saying that "[f]reedom of assembly cannot be used as a smoke screen for offending public morality and promoting homosexual behavior" (quoted in ibid., 319).

20 Quoted in Amnesty International 2006, 6.

21 Quoted in Biedroń 2007, 41.

22 Pankowski 2010, 183.

23 Quoted in Ostolski 2005.

24 Ibid., 182.

25 Quoted in ibid., 183.

26 Ferens (2006) reports rallies were held in New York, Berlin, Budapest, London, and Vienna.

27 Ayoub reports that a third of the participants in the 2006 Pride parade were foreign nationals, mostly Germans (2013, 295).

28 Dubrowska 2007.

29 Graff 2006; Gruszczynska 2009a, 186–190.

30 Quoted in Gruszczynska 2009b, 321.

31 Ayoub 2013, 295–296.

32 Quoted in Ohlsen 2009, 39.

33 Gruszczynska 2009a, 38–40.

34 "Commotion" 2006.

35 Quoted in Biedroń 2007, 38.

36 Quoted in ibid., 41.

37 Pankowski 2010, 189; "Commotion" 2006.

38 Ayoub 2013.

39 Since 2005, the Equality Foundation has organized Warsaw's march. It also belongs to the European Pride Organizations Association, which organizes Euro-Pride.

40 See Ohlsen 2009.

41 Krzemiński et al. 2006, 152.

42 Sperling 1999; Henry 2010.

43 Krzemiński 2006 et al., 144–145.

44 Ohlsen 2009, 58–59.

45 The first of these was a suit by Mirosław Sielatycki, who, as mentioned earlier, had been fired for distributing a textbook about tolerance. The second was the challenge to the Pride ban in the European Court of Human Rights.

46 "Come Along" 2010; Biedroń 2007, 42–44.

47 See www.zwiazkipartnerskie.info. The Greens were an extraparliamentary party founded in 2004.

48 "Wreszcie coś" 2010.
49 "Come Along!" 2010.
50 The former estimate was the police's, the latter the organizers' (Dubrowska and Karpieszak 2010).
51 Ibid.
52 Ayoub 2013, 300–301.
53 Quoted in Dubrowska and Karpieszak 2010.
54 Pride House Program. The participation of trade union representatives underscored a growing collaboration of KPH and Lambda Warsaw initiated in 2009 to make unions more aware of labor-market discrimination against LGBT persons (Baatzsch 2008).
55 "Geje w stolicy" 2010.
56 Pacewicz 2010.
57 Leszkowicz 2010, 1–42.
58 Quoted in "Homo-Erotic Art Exhibition" 2010.
59 "Public Debate: Homosexuality and Social Change," National Museum in Warsaw, July 11, 2010.
60 Abramowicz 2012, 101.
61 Vachudova, 2008, 875.
62 My respondents in 2009 and 2010 reported that PO was not so much tolerant as pragmatic. Its strategy was not to be drawn into politically damaging statements of any kind—that is, statements that could be seen as LGBT-friendly by a domestic audience or those that would seem homophobic to international observers. A good example was offered by Warsaw president Hanna Gronkiewicz-Waltz (PO). During EuroPride, she told an interviewer, "I am the first host-city mayor who refused [to be an honorary sponsor of EuroPride]. Everywhere in the world, city mayors open such parades. I don't have to, though" (quoted in Boniecki and Piskała 2010, 11). She further distanced herself by refusing to contribute financial or symbolic support.
63 See Kollman's review of this "norm fit" literature (2013, 55).
64 Meguid 2008, 3–4. Personality parties, by contrast, rest on their leaders' charisma and do not compete on ideological program.
65 Ibid.
66 This overview of the party's founding draws heavily on Kocur and Majczak (2013).
67 In fact, to curry support in his home district, he bought the regional Christian-nationalist weekly *Ozon* (ibid., 48).
68 Palikot even declared that Kaczyński was morally responsible for the crash—that he had the "blood of the victims on his hands." For this, Palikot was censured by parliament (ibid., 50).
69 Quoted in ibid.
70 Ibid.
71 Research by Polish sociologists found that among TR voters the most recognized figures in the party, aside from Palikot himself, were the "gender activists"

Grodzka, Biedroń, and Nowicka. In one survey, these three's names were recognized by 25 percent, 30 percent, and 4 percent of supporters, respectively. Other party figures had almost no name recognition (Baran and Sacha 2013, 90).

72 Quoted in Kocur and Majczak 2013, 52.

73 Given the repression of homosexuality in communist-era Poland, it may seem surprising that the SLD later came to support LGBT rights. This shift can be understood in terms of the SLD's transformation into a social democratic party in the early 1990s (Grzymała-Busse YEAR). A key element of this transformation was to position the party as a secular alternative to the avowedly Catholic orientation of most of the post-Solidarity parties. Thus, SLD came to support more liberal abortion law, divorce law, and in vitro fertilization in addition to same-sex partnerships (Grzymała-Busse 2015, 171–185). To the party's liberal critics, however, SLD was often too timid in its support of these issues lest it appear anti-Catholic (Biedroń 2007, 44).

74 Wojtasik 2012.

75 Piwowarczyk, Sierachan, and Stolarek 2013, 122.

76 Ibid., 123–124.

77 Ibid, 124.

78 Kocur and Majczak 2013, 52.

79 Reynolds (2013) has argued that such representation tends to presage policy gains.

80 Kawiński 2012.

81 Quoted in Borowski and Goettig 2013.

82 Quoted in Seidl 2012, 460.

83 GLL's dissolution was the more striking given its pronouncements after the enactment of registered partnerships that it would continue to lobby for provisions that had been left out of the law.

84 Seidl 2012, 460.

85 Ibid., 468.

86 See Bäumlová 2004.

87 Bretl 2004.

88 Quoted in Seidl 2012, 415.

89 Quoted in ibid., 414.

90 Klaus stated that he did not oppose the essence of registered partnerships but wanted to discuss the proposal's content. As frustrating as his veto was to activists, who refused to meet with him, it was not justified by any sort of homophobic rhetoric. Instead, it seemed a part of Klaus's general pattern of contrarian (and stubbornly held) positions, most notably regarding climate change, which he dismisses.

91 Beňová et al. 2007, 28–30.

92 Ibid., 29.

93 The latter also included working groups for Roma and ethnic minorities issues.

94 See Beňová et al. 2007.

95 Bartoš 2009.

96 Ibid.

97 Brno hosted small Prides of several hundred participants in 2008 and 2010, and Tábor held one in 2009. The 2008 parade was marred by harassment by local skinheads (Seidl 2012, 469). Unlike Pride attacks in Poland, however, Brno's were unconnected with any larger antigay backlash, and they did not recur in subsequent years.

98 It drew an estimated 5,000 participants (Konviser 2011).

99 The name is a play on words: in Czech *proud* means flow or current, suggesting movement and progress.

100 PROUD 2011.

CHAPTER 7. EXPLORING ALTERNATIVE TRAJECTORIES

1 Semjén epigraph, quoted in Buzogány 2008, 11. Anania epigraph, quoted in Nachescu 2005, 71.

2 Holzhacker 2012.

3 Hloušek and Kopeček 2010, 167.

4 When KDNP did experiment with a more populist rhetoric in the mid-1990s, it was rebuffed by MDF and the Church (ibid., 146–147).

5 Mudde 2007. MIÉP received 2 percent of the vote in the 1994 parliamentary elections; moreover, it was relatively quiet regarding homosexuality, reserving its animus for the Roma, Jews, and Slovaks (Riszovannij 2001, 157–158).

6 Hloušek and Kopeček 2010, 173.

7 Buzogány 2008, 8.

8 Ibid., 8.

9 Grzymała-Busse 2015.

10 Buzogány 2008, 8.

11 Long 1999, 250–251.

12 The Hungarian Constitution included a general ban on discrimination, but since it did not define what categories form the basis for discrimination, the provision was toothless.

13 Long 1999, 252.

14 Renkin 2009, 28.

15 Riszovannij 2001, 150.

16 Even these public events were not "gay" as such, but rather "'marked' by the presence of gays and lesbians" (Riszovannij 2001, 152–153).

17 Long 1999, 252.

18 Riszovannij 2001, 152.

19 Ibid., 153.

20 Long 1999, 252.

21 Ibid., 254.

22 Ibid., 253.

23 Buzogány 2008, 8.

24 The Smallholders were an agrarian party and do not meet our criteria as a potential hard-right coalition member (Hloušek and Kopeček 2010, 100–101).

25 Ibid., 147.
26 Ibid., 172–173.
27 Bozóki 2008, 194.
28 Ibid., 210.
29 Tóth and Grajczjár 2015, 135–136.
30 Greskovits and Wittenberg 2015, 14.
31 Tóth and Grajczjár 2015, 135.
32 Buzogány 2008, 9.
33 Holzhacker 2012, 37.
34 Renkin 2007b, 270. See also Riszovannij 2001, 153.
35 Renkin 2009, 34n14.
36 Renkin 2007b.
37 Long 1999, 251.
38 Buzogány 2008, 9.
39 See the Racial Equality Directive (2000/43) and the Employment Equality Council Directive (2000/78).
40 Employment Equality Council Directive 2000, 10.
41 Renkin 2015, 6.
42 Riszovannij 2001, 152.
43 Holzhacker 2012, 39.
44 Renkin 2015, 15.
45 Renkin 2009, 30.
46 Greskovits and Wittenberg 2015, 2.
47 It is worth mentioning again that Fidesz had by this time incorporated the Christian Democrats into its organization.
48 Tóth and Grajczjár 2015, 137.
49 Greskovits and Wittenberg 2015, 10–11. The figures quoted here are from their Appendix, 18–25.
50 The maximum divergence was in 2007: 175 right-wing protests to 25 left-wing ones (ibid., 22).
51 Ibid., 16.
52 Tóth and Grajczár 2015, 138.
53 Renkin 2009, 20.
54 Ibid., 20. This last insult had anti-Semitic resonance because, during World War II's siege of Budapest, executed Jews had been dumped in the river (ibid., 26).
55 Renkin notes that, in 2008, counterdemonstrators were even more organized and numerous than in 2007 (ibid., 20).
56 Renkin 2015, 409–410.
57 Horváth, Vidra, and Fox 2012, 318.
58 The proposed punishment was eight years in prison ("Jobbik Submits" 2012).
59 Renkin 2015, 12.
60 Ibid., 12.
61 Quoted in Renkin 2009, 21.

62 ILGA-Europe 2013.

63 ILGA-Europe 2012, 82, and 2014, 84.

64 Korkut 2012, 131–137.

65 Buzogány 2008, 12.

66 Korkut 2012, 158.

67 Jójárt 2003, 45.

68 Ibid., 28–30.

69 Ibid., 28–29.

70 Pirošík, Janišová, and Šuterová 2001, 559. Similar events were organized by the Czech movement, indicating the significance of the Czech example.

71 Lorencova 2006, 139.

72 Ibid., 140–142.

73 Daučíková, Bútorová, and Wallace-Lorencová 2003, 749.

74 Pirošík, Janišová, and Šuterová 2001, 559.

75 Mudde 2007, 307. Hloušek and Kopeček (2010, 192–194) classify it as far right.

76 Hloušek and Kopeček 2010, 193.

77 Innes 2001, 55–58.

78 Mudde 2007, 57. Hloušek and Kopeček find that HZDS is the largest case in their typology of European parties that cannot be classified within a "party family," that is, as liberal, conservative, far-right, green, social democratic, and so forth (2010, 222–223).

79 Vachudova 2005, 52.

80 Grzymała-Busse 2015, 358–359.

81 European Commission 1997, 2002.

82 Leo Mullender, Delegation of the European Commission to the Slovak Republic, quoted in Vachudova 2005, 157.

83 Ibid., 136.

84 Schimmelfennig and Sedelmeier 2005.

85 Vachudova 2005.

86 Levitsky and Way 2010.

87 Bunce and Wolchik 2011.

88 Kopstein and Reilly 2000.

89 Besides KDH, SDK consisted of the Democratic Union (liberal), the Democratic Party (liberal), the Social Democratic Party of Slovakia, and the Green Party.

90 Vališ 2001, quoted in Lorencova 2006, 188.

91 Lorencova 2006, 186.

92 Ibid., 184.

93 Ibid., 185.

94 Altera arose not only from a desire to broaden the movement's territorial reach but also from a frustration with the primarily social orientation of Museion.

95 Lorencova 2006, 131–132.

96 Jójárt 2003, 48.

97 Rohac 2014.

98 Jójárt 2003, 48.
99 These included Altera; the Center for Communication, Cooperation, and Integration of Sexual Minorities; Ganymedes; HaBiO; H-Plus; Museion; and the Student Center for the Integration of Sexual Minorities (Pirošík, Janišová, and Šuterová 2001, 562).
100 Jójárt 2003, 45.
101 Ibid., 52, 57.
102 Ibid., 58.
103 Eva Adámková, quoted in ibid., 45.
104 Ibid., 45.
105 Wallace-Lorencová 2003, 107.
106 Ibid., 104.
107 Daučíková, Bútorová, and Wallace-Lorencová 2003, 751.
108 Fialová 2005, 154.
109 Daučíková, Bútorová, and Wallace-Lorencová 2003, 752.
110 Quoted in ibid., 753.
111 Jójárt 2003, 47.
112 Gould 2015, 14.
113 Quoted in Debrecénová et al. 2009, 152.
114 Gould 2015, 17–18.
115 As an example, when Smer was threatened with expulsion from the Party of European Socialists, a faction in the European Parliament, it forced SNS to cosign a letter condemning all forms of discrimination (ibid., 18).
116 For example, Slovakia amended its antidiscrimination law in 2008 in response to EU criticism, but received virtually no public mention (Gould 2015, 19).
117 Ibid.
118 This assessment is based on the summary of LGBT NGOs provided on the website of QLF from 2013 (www.qlf.sk, accessed April 13, 2016).
119 See www.inakost.sk, accessed April 13, 2016.
120 Jójárt 2003, 29; Lorencova 2006, 155.
121 Buzogány 2008, 25n10.
122 Long 1999, 243.
123 Ibid., 243. Repression of homosexuality was only one facet of Nicolae Caeusescu's harsh gender regime (Kligman 1998). In 1966, Caeusescu criminalized abortion and removed all access to birth control. From 1984 on, women were subject to monthly medical exams asking "each one if they were pregnant and, if not, why" (Gallagher 2005, 63).
124 Borz 2012; Mudde 2008; Mungiu-Pippidi 2001.
125 Mungiu-Pippidi 2001, 235; Gallagher 2005, chap. 9.
126 Borz 2012, 179–182, 185.
127 At first, PRM and PUNR were tacit coalition partners supporting a PDSR minority government, but in January 1995 they became official coalition

partners (Pop-Eleches 2001, 161). As with Slovakia's HZDS, we do not include PDSR as part of the hard right because of its predominantly left orientation.

128 Kligman 1998; Long 1999.

129 Kelley 2004, 119, 179–182.

130 Decision no. 81 of July 15, 1995, quoted in Turcescu and Stan (2005, 293).

131 Ibid., 293.

132 Stychin 2003, 119.

133 Buzogány 2008, 13.

134 Stychin 2003, 119.

135 Turcescu and Stan 2005, 293.

136 Long 1999, 243.

137 Stychin 2003, 121.

138 The first, founded in 1992, was described only as a social circle. It was followed in 1993 by Group 200 and the Gay and Lesbian Human Rights Commission, both of which dissolved following corruption allegations against their leaders. The year 1994 brought ACCEPT, described below (Long 1999, 246).

139 Stychin 2003, 120.

140 Long 1999, 246.

141 Mudde 2007, 162. See also Gallagher 2005, 276.

142 Pop-Eleches 2001, 165.

143 Ibid.; Mungiu-Pippidi 2001, 236–238.

144 Buzogány 2008, 15. See also Nachescu 2005, 75, and Stychin 2003, 121.

145 Nachescu 2005; Turcescu and Stan 2005, 294.

146 Nachescu 2005, 63, emphasis added.

147 Ibid., 64.

148 Quoted in ibid., 63.

149 Quoted in ibid., 64.

150 Turcescu and Stan 2005, 295.

151 Quoted in Nachescu 2005, 71.

152 Ibid., 73, emphasis added.

153 Turcescu and Stan 2005, 294; Buzogány 2008, 15–16.

154 Buzogány 2008, 66.

155 Stychin 2003, 121.

156 Buzogány 2008, 17.

157 Stychin 2003, 133.

158 Quoted in Stychin 2003, 133. See also Buzogány 2008, 15.

159 Stychin 2003, 133.

160 Bob 2012, 98. The following description draws on the summaries by Bob and Buzogány (2008).

161 Bob 2012, 101–105.

162 Buzogány 2008, 17–18.

163 ILGA-Europe 2014, 135–136.

164 Bob 2012.

165 Buzogány 2008, 18.

CONCLUSION

1 Even as Wójcik denied that the sculpture endorsed LGBT rights, she linked it to them, telling the *New York Times*, "In 2011, Poland was seen as a homophobic country. I wanted to show that we're not closed but open-minded" (quoted in Kozlowska 2013).

2 Quoted in ibid.

3 Quoted in "Rydzyk o tęczy" 2013.

4 Dorota Chojna, quoted in Kozlowska 2013.

5 Sowa 2013.

6 I take this term from Weeks 2007.

7 Ibid.

8 Keck and Sikkink 1998; Ayoub 2016.

9 Ayoub 2016, 39.

10 Ibid., 40. See especially 190–196 for Ayoub's findings about the effect of anti-LGBT resistance on norm diffusion.

11 The term "democratization of everyday life" is from Weeks (2007, x).

12 Snow et al. 1998.

13 Petrova and Tarrow 2007.

14 Meyer 2003, 31.

15 For a good overview of this literature, see Jasper (1997).

16 Ibid., 95–96.

17 Meyer 2003. See also Gamson 1990; Sherkat and Blocker 1997.

18 Meyer 2003, 33–35.

19 Ayoub 2016; Bob 2012. See also Keck and Sikkink (1998) and Tarrow (2005).

20 Bob 2012, 6.

21 Ayoub 2016; Bob 2012.

22 These cycles are marked by heightened conflict, sectoral and geographic expansion of collective action, the emergence of new SMOs, the ascendancy of new master frames, and the addition of new tactics of collective action (Tarrow 1993, 284).

23 McCarthy 1996, 144.

24 McAdam 1996, 31–33.

25 Grabowska 2012, 388–389.

26 For a good description of the Church's political victories, see Grzymała-Busse (2015, 159–185).

27 Grabowska 2012, 395.

28 Previously, abortions were also allowed in cases of rape or incest, or when the fetus was irreparably damaged.

29 Berendt 2016.

30 Quoted in Osipova 2016.

31 Graff 2003, 100. For a more positive view of this period, see Grabowska (2012), who points to organized protests against the abortion ban in the early 1990s, even if they proved unsuccessful.

32 Regulska and Grabowska 2008.

33 Keinz 2009, 46.

34 Graff 2014, 432; Korolczuk 2015, 44.

35 Quoted in Graff 2014, 432.

36 See Kováts and Põim (2015), who anatomize the movement in France, Germany, Hungary, Poland, and Slovakia.

37 Sierakowski 2014a.

38 Binnie and Klesse 2012, 8–9.

39 McAdam 1996, 32–33.

40 Encarnación 2016.

41 Ibid.

42 Herszenhorn 2013.

43 Sperling 2015.

44 Gevisser 2013; Herszenhorn 2013.

45 As the director of a Russian LGBT group reported to one journalist, "The law was clearly designed to limit our activities. And in many ways it has succeeded. We cannot hold protests of more than one person. And any attempts to help young people are stifled" (Tatiana Vinnichenko, quoted in Gevisser 2013).

46 Gevisser 2013; Wilkinson 2014.

47 Gevisser 2013.

48 Sperling 2015.

49 Wilkinson 2014, 371, emphasis added.

50 Herszenhorn 2013; Wilkinson 2014, 371. Even international allies may be discouraged from showing support, as evidenced by the International Olympic Committee's only tepid support to Russia's LGBT groups during the Sochi Olympics (Longman 2013).

51 Vasilev 2016, 761.

52 Gould and Moe 2015.

53 Vasilev 2016, 760, 766.

54 See Moss 2014 and Vasilev 2016.

55 Vasilev 2016, 768.

56 Onishi 2015.

57 Encarnación 2016, 191–193.

58 Weeks 2007.

59 Andersen and Fetner 2008b; Ayoub 2016; Kollman 2013.

60 Balogh 2012, 241. The situation of the Roma has raised concerns in a number of other countries in the region as well, notably Slovakia, Romania, the Czech Republic, Bulgaria, and Albania. For an overview, see Barany 2002; Kóczé and Rövid 2012; Stewart 2012; Vermeersch 2006. I focus on Hungary because the hard-right backlash has been most extreme here.

61 Balogh 2015, 241.

62 Ibid., 242.

63 McGarry, 2016. To be clear, choosing not to publicly express one's sexual orientation does not guarantee passing as the hetero-norm, and one may still be subjected to bullying and other forms of violence and harassment.

64 Ibid., 276.

65 Ibid., 333.

66 Kóczé 2015.

67 This situation stands in contrast to minority groups that, while in conflictual relations with the majority, possessed significant political, economic, or cultural capital of their own: for example, the Russian minority in the Baltics or the Serb minority in Bosnia-Herzegovina.

68 Barany 2002, 207.

69 Barany 2005, 99.

70 The latter especially tend toward personalized, nepotistic leadership and, consequently, coordination difficulties based on personal differences (Barany 2005, 98). See also Kóczé and Rövid (2012, 119).

71 Barany 2005, 102.

72 Dobos 2014, 12.

73 Kóczé 2015, 93–98.

74 Balogh 2012, 249.

75 Balogh 2015, 246–249.

76 Horváth, Vidra, and Fox 2012, 330.

77 Quoted in "Growing Tensions" 2012. Another extreme example was Zsolt Bayer, a well-known political commentator, founding member of Fidesz, and friend of Prime Minister Victor Orban. In an article published in a far-right paper in 2013, Bayer wrote, "A significant part of the Roma are unfit for coexistence. They are not fit to live among people. These Roma are animals, and they behave like animals. . . . But one must retaliate rather than tolerate. . . . [This] needs to be solved—immediately and regardless of the method" (quoted in Kóczé 2015, 97). Jobbik's rhetoric expressed the same virulent themes.

78 Stewart 2012, 7; Zolnay 2012, 26.

79 Ahmari 2012; Dobos 2014, 12; Horváth, Vidra, and Fox 2012.

80 Tóth and Grajczár 2015, 137.

81 Kóczé 2015, 95.

82 Zolnay 2012, 25–26.

83 Horváth, Vidra, and Fox 2012; Kóczé 2015; Korkut 2012; Zolnay 2012.

84 Korkut 2012, 131–135. There were also indications that at least some in SZDSZ had joined the side of the Roma's critics. In 2009, members of the party publicly protested the dismissal of a local police chief for anti-Roma statements (Korkut 2012, 142).

85 Ibid., 106.

86 Dobos 2014, 13.

87 As one of the proposal's advocates stated, "I call on Roma society to forget about party politics and other affiliations, and join together for the interests of the Roma in Hungary, and contribute to the establishment of a self-defence movement. Let's demonstrate that we are powerful, and that we are able to defend ourselves if the situation is such!" (quoted in Balogh 2012, 248).

88 Scholars have generally been critical of Lungo Drom, seeing it as a patronage machine that undermines Roma representation in Hungarian politics. See especially Kóczé 2015.

89 Quoted in Balogh 2012, 245.

90 Ibid., 245–246.

91 Encarnación 2016.

92 Friedman 2012.

93 Encarnación 2016, 189.

94 Britain, the other country to opt out, did so for economic reasons.

95 As described in Chapter 3, the Sielatycki affair concerned the Polish education minister's illegal firing of a state official for distributing a handbook that promoted tolerance of sexual (and other) minorities in 2006.

96 Though the percentage of Poles saying that homosexuality should be accepted declined slightly between 2007 and 2013, this result should be understood with two important caveats in mind. First, as with all opinion surveys, these numbers are subject to random oscillations within the poll's standard of error. Second, it is notable that the decline in support was exactly equal to that in the Czech Republic, despite the latter not experiencing any hard-right backlash. From this perspective, Poland's numbers bespeak a surprising resilience of tolerance in the face of such backlash.

97 Lyman 2014.

98 Both quoted in ibid.

99 Santora 2018.

100 Quoted in "Poland Will Not" 2018.

101 O'Dwyer and Schwartz 2010.

102 Reynolds 2013, 259.

103 Quoted in Lyman.

104 Encarnación 2016, 77.

105 Interview with Jan Seidl, July 24, 2015, Prague.

106 As a caveat, in June 2016 the Czech Constitutional Court overturned a provision in the registered partnerships act that prevented same-sex couples from adopting children even when an individual LGBT person could. This had been one of the most obvious deficiencies in the law.

107 As of this writing, the final outcome of the German elections was still unknown. Though the hard-right Alternative for Germany's third-place finish was not enough to make it a contender for the governing coalition, it was large enough to (thus far) prevent the formation of a new government and to throw Angela Merkel's future as chancellor into question.

108 Nir 2016.
109 Peters, Becker, and Davis 2017; Thrush and Haberman 2017.
110 Boylan 2016.
111 Even in those West European countries where the so-called anti-gender movement has gained a foothold—notably, France and Germany—the major hard-
right parties like the Front National and Alternativ für Deutschland are more
anti-immigrant than anti-gender (Kováts and Põim 2015).
112 Fisher 2017; Goodwin 2017.
113 Broomfield 2017.
114 Katz and Eckholm 2016.
115 Blinder 2018.

APPENDIX
1 Collier and Elman 2008.
2 The one exception is Croatia, which switched from candidate to member between
2012 and 2013.
3 Running waves 4 and 5 separately did not much affect the results substantively,
but it wiped out the statistical significance of many variables.
4 See Muyanga, Jayne, and Burke's (2013) discussion of strategies for incorporating
time-invariant factors.
5 The one exception was Model 5 in Table 2.2, where a specification including the
economic globalization variable did not pass the Hausman test. That is why this
model includes only the social globalization variable.
6 Mudde 2007, 32, 55.
7 Jungwirth 2002; Rupnik 2002.
8 Besides the interviews, the sources were Abramowicz 2007; Beňová et al. 2007;
Buzogány 2008; Carstocea 2009; Daučíková, Bútorová, and Wallace-Lorencová
2003; Fanel 2000; Graff 2006; Gruszczynska 2009a, 2009b; Hromada 2007; ILGA-
Europe 2012–2015; Jójárt 2003; Kliszczyński 2001; Krzemiński et al. 2006; Long
1999; Lorencová 2006; Makuchowska and Pawlęga 2012; Nachescu 2005; Ohlsen
2009; Owczarzak 2009, 2010; Pirošík, Janišová, and Šuterová 2001; Procházka,
Janík, and Hromada 2003; Renkin 2007a; Riszovannij 2001; Sándor 2001; Seidl
2012; Sokolová 2005, 2006; Stychin 2003.
9 Kriesi 1996, 153.

BIBLIOGRAPHY

Abramowicz, Marta, ed. 2007. *Situation of Bisexual and Homosexual Persons in Poland.* Warsaw: Campaign Against Homophobia, www.kph.org.pl.

———. 2012. "Situation of Bisexual and Homosexual Persons in Poland: Research Analysis." In *Situation of LGBT Persons in Poland: 2010 and 2011 Report,* ed. Mirosława Makuchowska and Michał Pawlęga, 11–104. Warsaw: Campaign Against Homophobia, www.kph.org.pl.

Adam, Barry D. 1995. *The Rise of a Gay and Lesbian Movement.* Boston: Twayne.

Ahmari, Sohrab. 2012. "Dancing over Catastrophes: The Far Right and Roma in Hungary." *Dissent* (Winter): 16–21.

Amnesty International. 2006. "Lesbian, Gay, Bisexual and Transgender Rights in Poland and Latvia." www.amnesty.ie.

Andersen, Robert, and Tina Fetner. 2008a. "Economic Inequality and Intolerance: Attitudes toward Homosexuality in 35 Democracies." *American Journal of Political Science* 52 (4): 942–958.

———. 2008b. "Cohort Differences in Tolerance of Homosexuality: Attitudinal Change in Canada and the United States, 1981–2000." *Public Opinion Quarterly* 72 (2): 311–330.

Art, David, and Dana Brown. 2007. "Making and Breaking the Radical Right in Central and Eastern Europe." Paper presented at the national convention of the American Association for the Advancement of Slavic Studies, New Orleans, November 15–18.

Ayoub, Phillip M. 2013. "Cooperative Transnationalism in Contemporary Europe: Europeanization and Political Opportunities for LGBT Mobilization in the European Union." *European Political Science Review* 5 (2): 279–310.

———. 2014. "With Arms Wide Shut: Threat Perception, Norm Reception, and Mobilized Resistance to LGBT Rights." *Journal of Human Rights* 13: 337–362.

———. 2015. "Contested Norms in New Adopter States: International Determinants of LGBT Rights Legislation." *European Journal of International Relations* 21 (2): 293–322.

———. 2016. *When States Come Out: Europe's Sexual Minorities and the Politics of Visibility.* New York: Cambridge University Press.

Ayoub, Phillip M., and David Paternotte, eds. 2014. *LGBT Activism and the Making of Europe: A Rainbow Europe?* Basingstoke: Palgrave Macmillan.

Baatzsch, Achim. 2008. "LGBT Associations Are Getting Closer to Polish Trade Unions." October 7, Friedrich Ebert Stiftung, www.trade-union-rainbow-rights.org/wars-eng.pdf.

Badgett, M. V. Lee. 2010. *When Gay People Get Married: What Happens When Societies Legalize Same-Sex Marriage*. New York: New York University Press.

Balogh, Lídia. 2012. "Possible Responses to the Sweep of Right-Wing Forces and Anti-Gypsyism in Hungary." In *The Gypsy 'Menace': Populism and the New Anti-Gypsy Politics*, ed. Michael Stewart, 241–263. New York: Columbia University Press.

Baran, Julia, and Paulina Sacha. 2013. "Przywódca czy Przypadkowy Aktor? Czyli o Fenomenie i Tajemnicy Poparcia dla Janusza Palikota Słow Kilka" [Leader or accidental actor? A few words regarding the phenomenon and secret of the support for Janusz Palikot]. In *Dlaczego Palikot? Młodzi Wyborcy Ruchu Palikota: Przypadkowy czy "Twardy"Elektorat Nowej Siły a Polskiej Scenie Politycznej* [Why Palikot? Young voters of the Palikot Movement: Random or "solid" electorate of the new power on the Polish political scene], ed. Radosław Marzęcki and Łukasz Stach, 77–101. Warsaw: Elipsa.

Barany, Zoltan. 2002. *The East European Gypsies: Regime Change, Marginality, and Ethnic Politics*. New York: Cambridge University Press.

———. 2005. "Ethnic Mobilization in the Postcommunist Context: Albanians in Macedonia and the East European Roma." In *Ethnic Politics after Communism*, ed. Zoltan Barany and Robert G. Moser, 78–107. Ithaca: Cornell University Press.

Bartoš, Adam. 2009. "Homosexuálové lobbují za adopce dětí jako členové vládního výboru" [Homosexuals lobby for the adoption of children as members of a government committee]. *Mlada fronta dnes*, July 7.

Bäumlová, Barbora. 2004. "Už nás aspoň nebijí" [At least they're no longer beating us]. *Respekt* 15 (10): 4.

Bell, M. 2001. "The European Union—A New Source of Rights for Citizens in the Accession Countries?" In *Equality for Lesbians and Gay Men: A Relevant Issue in the EU Accession Process*, ed. ILGA-Europe. Brussels: ILGA-Europe.

Benford, Robert, and David Snow. 2000. "Framing Processes and Social Movements: An Overview and Assessment." *Annual Review of Sociology* 26: 611–639.

Beňová, K., et al. 2007. *Analysis of the Situation of Lesbian, Gay, Bisexual and Transgender Minority in the Czech Republic*. Prague: Working Group for the Issues of Sexual Minorities of the Minister for Human Rights and National Minorities, Office of the Government of the Czech Republic, www.vlada.cz.

Berendt, Joanna. 2016. "Protesters in Poland Rally against Proposal for Total Abortion Ban." *New York Times*, October 3.

Berrill, Kevin, and Gregory Herek. 1990. "Primary and Secondary Victimization in Anti-Gay Hate Crimes." *Journal of Interpersonal Violence* 5 (3): 401–413.

Biedroń, Robert. 2007: "How Has Discrimination against Gays and Lesbians Become a Political Issue?" In *Situation of Bisexual and Homosexual Persons in Poland*, ed. Marta Abramowicz, 37–44. Warsaw: Campaign Against Homophobia, www.kph.org.pl.

Bilić, Bojan, ed. 2016. *LGBT Activism and Europeanisation in the Post-Yugoslav Space: On the Rainbow Way to Europe*. Basingstoke: Palgrave Macmillan.

Binnie, Jon, and Christian Klesse. 2011. "Researching Transnational Activism around LGBTQ Politics in Central and Eastern Europe: Activist Solidarities and Spatial

Imaginings." In *De-centring Western Sexualities: Central and Eastern European Perspectives*, ed. Robert Kulpa and Joanna Mizielińska, 107–130. Farnham: Ashgate.

———. 2012. "Solidarities and Tensions: Feminism and Transnational LGBTQ Politics in Poland." *European Journal of Women's Studies* 19 (4): 444–459.

———. 2013. "'Like a Bomb in the Gasoline Station': East–West Migration and Transnational Activism around Lesbian, Gay, Bisexual, Transgender and Queer Politics in Poland." *Journal of Ethnic and Migration Studies* 39 (7): 1107–1124.

Blasius, Mark. 2013. "Theorizing the Politics of (Homo)Sexualities across Cultures." In *Global Homophobia: States, Movements, and the Politics of Oppression*, ed. Meredith L. Weiss and Michael J. Bosia, 218–245. Urbana: University of Illinois Press.

Blinder, Alan. 2018. "Wary, Weary, or Both, Southern Lawmakers Tone Down Culture Wars." *New York Times*, January 22.

Blokker, Paul. 2005. "Populist Nationalism, Anti-Europeanism, Postnationalism, and the East-West Distinction." *German Law Journal* 6 (2): 371–389.

Bob, Clifford. 2012. *The Global Right Wing and the Clash of World Politics*. New York: Cambridge University Press.

Boniecki, Adam, and Konrad Piskała. 2010. "Sumienie i władze" [Conscience and power: Interview with Hanna Gronkiewicz-Waltz]. *Tygodnik Powszechny*, July 18, 10–11.

Bonini Baraldi, Matteo, and Evelyne Paradis. 2009. "European Union." In *The Greenwood Encyclopedia of LGBT Issues Worldwide*, ed. Chuck Stewart, 123–145. Santa Barbara: Westport.

Borowski, Chris, and Marcin Goettig. 2013. "Polish Parliament Rejects Efforts to Legalize Gay Unions." Reuters, January 25, www.reuters.com.

Borz, Gabriela. 2012. "Extreme-Right Parties in Romania after 1990: Incumbency, Organization and Success." In *Mapping the Extreme Right in Contemporary Europe: From Local to Transnational*, ed. Andrea Mammone, Emmanuel Godin, and Brian Jenkins, 173–188. London: Routledge.

Börzel, Tanja A., and Thomas Risse. 2003. "Conceptualizing the Domestic Impact of Europe." In *The Politics of Europeanization*, ed. Kevin Featherstone and Claudio Radaelli, 57–82. Oxford: Oxford University Press.

Bosia, Michael J., and Meredith L. Weiss. 2013. "Political Homophobia in Comparative Perspective." In *Global Homophobia: States, Movements, and the Politics of Oppression*, ed. Michael J. Bosia and Meredith L. Weiss, 1–29. Urbana: University of Illinois Press.

Boylan, Jennifer Finney. 2016. "Really, You're Blaming Transgender People for Trump?" *New York Times*, December 2.

Bozóki, András. 2008. "Consolidation or Second Revolution? The Emergence of the New Right in Hungary." *Journal of Communist Studies and Transition Politics* 24 (2): 191–231.

———. 2015. "Broken Democracy, Predatory State, and Nationalist Populism?" In *The Hungarian Patient: Social Opposition to an Illiberal Democracy*, ed. Péter Krasztev and Jon Van Til, 3–36. Budapest: CEU Press.

Bretl, Jan. 2004. "Omyly pana Hromady" [Mr. Hromada's mistakes]. *Respekt* 15 (13): 20.

Broomfield, Matt. 2017. "Women's March against Donald Trump Is the Largest Day of Protests in US History, Say Political Scientists." *Independent*, January 23.

Brustier, Gaël. 2015. "France." In *Gender as Symbolic Glue: The Position and Role of Conservative and Far Right Parties in the Anti-Gender Mobilizations in Europe*, ed. Eszter Kováts and Maari Põim, 19–39. Friedrich Ebert Stiftung, library.fes.de.

Buechler, Steven. 1990. *Women's Movements in the U.S.* New Brunswick, NJ: Rutgers University Press.

Bunce, Valerie, and Sharon Wolchik. 2011. *Defeating Authoritarian Leaders in Postcommunist Countries.* New York: Cambridge University Press.

Butler, Judith. 2005. "Beside Oneself: On the Limits of Sexual Autonomy." In *Sex Rights*, ed. Nicholas Bamforth, 48–78. Oxford: Oxford University Press.

Bútora, Martin. 2010. *Slovakia 2009: Trends in Quality of Democracy.* Bratislava: Institute for Public Affairs.

Buzogány, Aron. 2008. "Joining Europe, Not Sodom: LGBT Rights and the Limits of Europeanization in Hungary and Romania." Paper presented at the national convention of the American Association for the Advancement of Slavic Studies, Philadelphia, November 20–23.

Čakl, Ondřej, and Radek Wollmann. 2005. "Czech Republic." In *Racist Extremism in Central and Eastern Europe*, ed. Cas Mudde, 28–53. London: Routledge.

Carstocea, Sinziana. 2009. "Romania." In *The Greenwood Encyclopedia of LGBT Issues Worldwide*, ed. Chuck Stewart, 347–356. Santa Barbara: Westport.

Chetaille, Agnès. 2011. "Poland: Sovereignty and Sexuality in Post-Socialist Times." In *The Lesbian and Gay Movement and the State: Comparative Insights into a Transformed Relationship*, ed. Carol Johnson, David Paternotte, and Manon Tremblay Manon, 119–133. Farnham: Ashgate.

Clews, Colin. 2013. "1984. The Squarcialupi Report: Europe Considers Homosexual Rights." April 8, www.gayinthe80s.com.

Collier, David, and Colin Elman. 2008. "Qualitative and Multimethod Research." In *The Oxford Handbook of Political Methodology*, ed. Janet Box-Steffensmeier, Henry Brady, and David Collier, 779–795. Oxford: Oxford University Press.

"Come Along!" 2010. Gazeta na EuroPride. *Gazeta Wyborcza.* July 17–18.

"Commotion over EP Resolution." 2006. *Warsaw Voice*, June 28.

Cooley, Alexander, and James Ron. 2002. "The NGO Scramble: Organizational Insecurity and the Political Economy of Transnational Action." *International Security* 27 (1): 5–39.

Czarnecki, Gregory. 2006. "'Look Who Was in the Closet with You': Comparative Experiences of Queers and Jews in Contemporary Poland." Master's thesis, Central European University.

Daučíková, Anna, Zora Bútorová, and Viera Wallace-Lorencová. 2003. "The Status of Sexual Minorities." In *Slovakia 2002: A Global Report on the State of Society*, ed. Grigorij Mesežnikov, Miroslav Kollár, and Tom Nicholson, 743–756. Bratislava: Institute for Public Affairs.

Debrecénová, Janka, et al. 2009. "Ludské pravá" [Human rights]. In *Slovensko 2008: Súhrnná sráva o stave spolčnosti* [Slovakia 2008: A global report on the state of society], ed. Miroslav Kollár, Grigorij Mesežnikov, and Martin Bútora. Bratislava: Institute for Public Affairs.

de Lange, Sarah L., and Simona Guerra. 2009. "The League of Polish Families between East and West, Past and Present," *Communist and Post-Communist Studies* 42: 527–49.

D'Emilio, John. 1983. *Sexual Politics, Sexual Communities: The Making of a Homosexual Minority in the United States, 1940–1970.* Chicago: University of Chicago Press.

Dobos, Balázs. 2014. "Roma Responses to Recent Challenges: Roma Political Parties in the Times of Crisis." Paper presented at the annual conference of the Centre for Baltic and East European Studies, Södertörn University, December 4–5.

Drabikowska, Agnieszka. 2010. "Marsz przeciwko homofobii. Radny PiS z kibolami" [March against homophobia: PiS city councilor with hooligans]. *Gazeta Wyborcza*, May 16.

Dreher, Axel, Noel Gaston, and Willem Martens. 2008. *Measuring Globalisation: Measuring Its Consequences.* New York: Springer.

Dubrowska, Magdalena. 2007. "Którędy pójdzie Parada Równości" [What route the equality march will follow]. *Gazeta Wyborcza*, May 16.

Dubrowska, Magdalena, and Wojciech Karpieszak. 2010. "W paradzie po równość" [In the parade for equality]. *Gazeta Wyborcza*, July 19.

Ekiert, Grzegorz. 1996. *The State against Society: Political Crises and Their Aftermath in East Central Europe.* Princeton: Princeton University Press.

Encarnación, Omar. 2016. *Out in the Periphery: Latin America's Gay Rights Revolution.* New York: Oxford University Press.

Epstein, Rachel, and Ulrich Sedelmeier. 2008. "Beyond Conditionality: International Institutions in Postcommunist Europe after Enlargement." *Journal of European Public Policy* 15 (6): 795–805.

European Commission. 1997. "Central and Eastern European Barometer 8." ec.europa. eu.

———. 2002. "Candidate Countries Eurobarometer 2002.2." ec.europa.eu.

European Council. 1993. "Presidency Conclusions: Copenhagen European Council, 21–22 June 1993." www.europarl.europa.eu.

European Parliament. 2006a. "European Parliament Resolution on Homophobia in Europe." January 18, www.europarl.europa.eu.

———. 2006b. "European Parliament Resolution on the Increase in Racist and Homophobic Violence in Europe." June 15, www.europarl.europa.eu.

Fanel, Jiří. 2000. *Gay historie* [Gay history]. Prague: Dauphin.

Farkas, Lilla. 2001. "Nice on Paper: The Aborted Liberalisation of Gay Rights in Hungary." In *Legal Recognition of Same-Sex Partnerships: A Study of National, European and International Law*, ed. Robert Wintemute and Mads Andenæs, 563–574. Oxford: Hart Publishing.

Ferens, Dominika. 2006. "The Equality March Goes On." *InterAlia* 1 (1), interalia.org.pl.

Fialová, Zuzana. 2005. "Human Rights." In *Slovakia 2004: A Global Report on the State of Society*, ed. Grigorij Mesežnikov and Miroslav Kollár, 149–166. Bratislava: Institute for Public Affairs.

Fisher, Max. 2017. "Europe Is Facing 4 Existential Threats. Can It Hold Together?" *New York Times*, March 13.

Fliedr, Bob. 1999. "Křest' ané z Kairos podporují RP." *Lidové noviny*, June 14.

Friedman, Elisabeth Jay. 2012. "Connecting 'the Same Rights with the Same Names': The Impact of Spanish Norm Diffusion on Marriage Equality in Argentina." *Latin American Politics and Society* 54 (4): 29–59.

Gallagher, Tom. 2005. *Theft of a Nation: Romania since Communism*. London: Hurst and Co.

Gamson, William. 1990. *The Strategy of Social Protest*. Belmont, CA: Wadsworth.

"Geje w stolicy, SLD z gejami" [Gays in the capital, SLD with the gays]. 2010. *Gazeta Wyborcza*, July 19.

Gerhards, Jürgen. 2007. "EU Policy on Equality between Homo- and Heterosexuals and Citizens' Attitudes toward Homosexuality in 26 EU Member States and Turkey." Berliner Studien zur Soziologie Europas, No. 8 (March). Berlin: Freie Universität Berlin, Institut für Soziologie.

Gevisser, Mark. 2013. "Life under Russia's 'Gay Propaganda' Ban." *International New York Times*, December 28.

Goodwin, Matthew J. 2017. "What a Le Pen Win Would Look Like." *New York Times*, March 23.

Gould, Deborah. 2009. *Moving Politics: Emotion and ACT UP's Fight against AIDS*. Chicago: University of Chicago Press.

Gould, John. 2015. "From Gay Grocer to Rainbow Activist: Uncovering Slovakia's Hidden LGBTQ Politics." Paper presented at the annual meeting of the American Political Science Association, San Francisco, September 2–6.

Gould, John, and Edward Moe. 2015. "Nationalism and the Struggle for LGBTQ Rights in Serbia, 1991–2014." *Problems of Post-Communism* 62: 273–286.

Grabbe, Heather. 2003. "Europeanization Goes East: Power and Uncertainty in the EU Accession Process." In *The Politics of Europeanization*, ed. Kevin Featherstone and Claudio Radaelli, 303–330. Oxford: Oxford University Press.

Grabowska, Magdalena. 2012. "Bringing the Second World In: Conservative Revolution(s), Socialist Legacies, and Transnational Silences in the Trajectories of Polish Feminism." *Signs* 37 (21): 385–411.

Graff, Agnieszka. 2003. "Lost between the Waves? The Paradoxes of Feminist Chronology and Activism in Contemporary Poland." *Journal of Women's Studies* 4 (2): 100–116.

———. 2006. "We Are (Not All) Homophobes: A Report from Poland." *Feminist Studies* 32 (6): 434–449.

———. 2008. "The Land of Real Men and Real Women: Gender and EU Accession in Three Polish Weeklies." In *Global Empowerment of Women: Responses to Globalization and Politicized Religions*, ed. Carolyn M. Elliott, 191–212. New York: Routledge.

———. 2010. "Looking at Pictures of Gay Men: Political Uses of Homophobia in Contemporary Poland." *Public Culture* 22 (3): 583–603.

———. 2014. "Report from the Gender Trenches: War against 'Genderism' in Poland." *European Journal of Women's Studies* 21 (4): 431–442.

Greskovits, Béla, and Jason Wittenberg. 2015. "Civil Society and Democratic Consolidation in Hungary in the 1990s and 2000s." Paper presented at the annual meeting of the American Political Science Association, San Francisco, September 3–6.

"Growing Tensions: Far-Right Protest Targets Roma in Hungary." 2012. *Spiegel Online*, October 18, www.spiegel.de.

Gruszczynska, Anna. 2006. "Living La Vida Internet: Some Notes on the Cyberization of the Polish LGBT Community." In *Beyond the Pink Curtain: Everyday Life of LGBT People in Eastern Europe*, ed. Roman Kuhar and Judit Takács, 95–115. Ljubljana: Peace Institute.

———. 2009a. "Queer Enough? Contested Terrains of Identity Deployment in the Context of Gay and Lesbian Public Activism in Poland." PhD diss., Aston University, England.

———. 2009b. "Sowing the Seeds of Solidarity in Public Space: A Case Study of the Poznan March of Equality." *Sexualities* 12 (3): 312–333.

Grzymała-Busse, Anna. 2002. *Redeeming the Communist Past: The Regeneration of Communist Parties in East Central Europe*. New York: Cambridge University Press.

———. 2015. *Nations under God: How Churches Use Moral Authority to Influence Policy.* Princeton, NJ: Princeton University Press.

Grzymała-Busse, Anna, and Abby Innes. 2003. "Great Expectations: The EU and Domestic Political Competition in East Central Europe." *East European Politics and Societies* 17 (1): 64–73.

Guerra, Simona. 2013. "Eurosceptic Allies or Euroenthusiast Friends? The Political Discourse of the Roman Catholic Church in Poland." In *Representing Religion in the European Union: Does God Matter?*, ed. Lucian Leustean, 139–151. New York: Routledge.

Henry, Laura. 2010. *Red to Green: Environmental Activism in Post-Soviet Russia*. Ithaca: Cornell University Press.

Herek, Gregory. 1990. "The Context of Anti-Gay Violence." *Journal of Interpersonal Violence* 5 (3): 316–333.

Herszenhorn, David. 2013. "Gays in Russia Find No Haven, Despite Support from the West." *New York Times*, August 11, A1.

Herzog, Dagmar. 2011. *Sexuality in Europe: A Twentieth-Century History*. New York: Cambridge University Press.

Hix, Simon. 2008. *What's Wrong with the European Union and How to Fix It*. Cambridge: Polity.

Hloušek, Vít, and Lubomír Kopeček. 2010. *Origin, Ideology, and Transformation of Political Parties: East-Central and Western Europe Compared*. Burlington, VT: Ashgate.

Holzhacker, Ronald. 2012. "National and Transnational Strategies of LGBT Civil Society Organizations in Different Political Environments: Modes of Interaction in Western and Eastern Europe for Equality." *Comparative European Politics* 10 (1): 23–47.

"Homo-erotic Art Exhibition Causes Storm in Warsaw." 2010. *Polskie Radio dla Zagranicy*, June 10, www.thenews.pl.

Horváth, Anikó, Zsuzsa Vidra, and Jon Fox. 2012. "Hungary." In *Addressing Tolerance and Diversity Discourse in Europe: A Comparative Overview of 16 European Countries*, ed. Ricard Zapata-Barrero and Anna Triandafyllidou. Barcelona: Fundació CIDOB.

Howard, Marc Morjé. 2003. *The Weakness of Civil Society in Post-Communist Europe.* New York: Cambridge University Press.

Hromada, Jiří. 2007. *Historie gay a lesbického hnutí v České Republice [History of the gay and lesbian movement in the Czech Republic].* Script for traveling exhibition under the auspices of the Minister for Human Rights, Office of the Czech Government, December.

Human Rights Watch. 2006. "'Hall of Shame' Shows Reach of Homophobia: On International Day Against Homophobia, Violations Mixed with Victories." May 17, www.hrw.org.

ILGA-Europe. 2001. "Equality for Lesbians and Gay Men. A Relevant Issue in the EU Accession Process." March, www.ilga-europe.org.

———. 2010a. "EURO-LETTER: ILGA-Europe's Monthly Electronic LGBT Political and Legal News Bulletin." No. 173 (January), www.ilga-europe.org.

———. 2010b. "Rainbow Europe Map and Country Index." May, www.ilga-europe.org.

———. 2012–2016. "Annual Review of the Human Rights Situation of Lesbian, Gay, Bisexual, Trans and Intersex People in Europe 2011." May, www.ilga-europe.org.

Inglehart, Ronald. 1997. *Modernization and Postmodernization: Cultural, Economic, and Political Change in 43 Societies.* Princeton: Princeton University Press.

Inglehart, Ronald, and Wayne E. Baker. 2000. "Modernization, Cultural Change, and the Persistence of Traditional Values." *American Sociological Review* 65 (1): 19–51.

Inglehart, Ronald, and Christian Welzel. 2005. *Modernization, Cultural Change and Democracy.* New York: Cambridge University Press.

Innes, Abby. 2001. *Czechoslovakia: The Short Goodbye.* New Haven: Yale University Press.

Jacoby, Wade. 2004. *The Enlargement of the EU and NATO: Ordering from the Menu in Central Europe.* New York: Cambridge University Press.

Jałowiec, Joanna. 2006. "Preciwnik Giertycha to gej, a gej to pedofil" [Giertych's opponents are gays, and gays are pedophiles]. *Gazeta Wyborcza*, May 15.

Janos, Andrew C. 2001. "From Eastern Empire to Western Hegemony: East Central Europe under Two International Regimes." *East European Politics and Societies* 15 (2): 221–249.

Jasiewicz, Krzysztof. 2007. "Is East-Central Europe Backsliding? The Political-Party Landscape." *Journal of Democracy* 18 (4): 26–33.

———. 2008. "The New Populism in Poland: The Usual Suspects?" *Problems of Post-Communism* 55 (3): 7–25.

Jasper, James. 1997. *The Art of Moral Protest: Culture, Creativity, and Biography in Social Movements*. Chicago: University of Chicago Press.

"Jobbik Submits Amendment Aimed at Banning 'Gay Propaganda.'" 2012. *Politics.hu*, April 12, www.politics.hu.

Jójárt, Paula. 2003. "Raising the Rainbow over Slovakia: Lesbian Women, Community and Activism in Slovakia, a Historical Perspective." Master's thesis, Central European University.

Jowitt, Ken. 1992. *New World Disorder: The Leninist Extinction*. Berkeley: University of California Press.

Jungwirth, Michael, ed. 2002. *Haider, Le Pen & Co: Europas Rechtspopulisten* [Haider, Le Pen & Co: Europe's populist right]. Graz: Styria.

Katz, Jonathan M., and Erik Eckholm. 2016. "Anti-Gay Laws Bring Backlash in Mississippi and North Carolina." *New York Times*, April 5.

Kawiński, Maciej. 2012. "PO powalczy o miłość gejów i lesbijek" [PO will fight for the love of gays and lesbians]. *Wprost*, February 17, www.wprost.pl.

Keck, Margaret E., and, Kathryn Sikkink. 1998. *Activists beyond Borders: Advocacy Networks in International Politics*. Ithaca: Cornell University Press.

Keinz, Anika. 2009. "Negotiating Democracy's Gender between Europe and the Nation." *Focaal* 53: 38–55.

Kelley, Judith. 2004. *Ethnic Politics in Europe: The Power of Norms and Incentives*. Princeton: Princeton University Press.

Kitlinski, Tomek, and Paweł Leszkowicz. 2005. "New Anti-Gay Regime in Poland." *Gully*, November 10, www.thegully.com.

Kligman, Gail. 1998. *The Politics of Duplicity: Controlling Reproduction in Caeusescu's Romania*. Berkeley: University of California Press.

Kliszczyński, Krzysztof. 2001. "A Child of a Young Democracy: The Polish Gay Movement, 1989–1999." In *Pink, Purple, Green: Women's, Religious, Environmental, and Gay/Lesbian Movements in Central Europe Today*, ed. Helena Flam, 161–168. Boulder: East European Monographs.

Knill, Christoph, and Dirk Lehmkuhl. 1999. "How Europe Matters: Different Mechanisms of Europeanization." *European Integration Online Papers* 3 (7).

Kocur, Anna, and Katarzyna Majczak. 2013. "Kim Pan Jest Panie Palikot, Czyli Krótka Biografia Wydawcy, Przedsiębiorcy i Polityka" [Who are you, Mr. Palikot? A short biography of the publisher, businessman, and politician]. In *Dlaczego Palikot? Młodzi Wyborcy Ruchu Palikota: Przypadkowy czy "Twardy"Elektorat Nowej Siły a Polskiej Scenie Politycznej* [Why Palikot? Young voters of the Palikot Movement: Random or "solid" electorate of the new power on the polish political scene], ed. Radosław Marzęcki and Łukasz Stach, 41–54. Warsaw: Elipsa.

Kóczé, Angéla. 2015. "Political Empowerment or Political Incarceration of Romani?" In *The Hungarian Patient: Social Opposition to an Illiberal Democracy*, ed. Péter Krasztev and Jon Van Til, 91–110. Budapest: CEU Press.

Kóczé, Angéla, and Márton Rövid. 2012. "Pro-Roma Global Civil Society: Acting for, with, or Instead of Roma?" In *Global Civil Society 2012: Ten Years of Critical*

Reflection, ed. Mary Kaldor, Henrietta Moore, and Sabine Selchow, 110–122. Basingstoke: Palgrave Macmillan.

Kollman, Kelly. 2013. *The Same-Sex Unions Revolution in Western Democracies: International Norms and Domestic Policy Change*. Manchester: Manchester University Press.

Konviser, Bruce I. 2011. "Czech Leader Is Isolated in Opposing Gay Parade." *New York Times*, August 15.

Kopstein, Jeffry, and David Reilly. 2000. "Geographic Diffusion and the Transformation of the Postcommunist World." *World Politics* 53 (1): 1–37.

Korkut, Umut. 2007. "The 2006 Hungarian Election: Economic Competitiveness versus Social Solidarity." *Parliamentary Affairs* 60 (4): 675–690.

———. 2012. *Liberalization Challenges in Hungary: Elitism, Progressivism, and Populism*. Basingstoke: Palgrave Macmillan.

Korolczuk, Elżbieta. 2015. "'The War on Gender' from à Transnational Perspective." In *Anti-Gender Movements on the Rise?* Heinrich Böll Foundation, Publication Series on Democracy, vol. 38, 43–53, www.boell.de.

Kosc, Wojciech. 2005. "Taking It to the Streets." *Transitions Online*, June 13, www.tol.org.

———. 2006. "Class Divisions." *Transitions Online*, September 27, www.tol.org.

Kostrzewa, Yga, et al. 2009. *Homowarszawa: Przewodnik Kulturalno-Historyczny* [Homo-Warsaw: A cultural-historical guide]. Warsaw: Lambda Warszawa.

Kováts, Eszter, and Maari Põim. 2015. *Gender as Symbolic Glue: The Position and Role of Conservative and Far Right Parties in the Anti-Gender Mobilizations in Europe*. Friedrich Ebert Stiftung, library.fes.de.

Kowalczyk, Iza. 2006. "Media Response to the Poznań Equality March." *Inter Alia* 1 (1), interalia.org.pl.

Kozlowska, Helena. 2013. "Warsaw Journal: Rainbow Becomes a Prism to View Gay Rights." *New York Times*, March 22.

Kriesi, Hanspeter. 1996. "The Organizational Structure of New Social Movements in a Political Context." In *Comparative Perspectives on Social Movements: Political Opportunities, Mobilizing Structures, and Cultural Framings*, ed. Doug McAdam, John McCarthy, and Mayer Zald, 152–184. New York: Cambridge University Press.

Krzemiński, Ireneusz, et al. 2006. *Wolność, równość, odmienność: Nowe ruchy społeczne w Polsce początku XXI wieku* [Freedom, equality, diversity: New social movements in Poland at the beginning of the 21st century]. Warsaw: Wydawnictwa Akademickie i Profesjonalne.

Krzyżaniak-Gumowska, A. 2005a. "Demonstracja przeciw Kaczyńskiemu" [Demonstration against Kaczyński]. *Gazeta Wyborcza*, June 10.

———. 2005b. "Kaczyński jednak zakazuje gejowskich wieców" [Kaczyński bans gay rallies nevertheless]. *Gazeta Wyborcza*, June 9.

Kurpios, Pawel. 2004. "Poszukiwani, Poszukiwane. Geje I Lesbijki W Rzeczywistosci PRL-u" [Wanted men and women: Gays and lesbians in the reality of the People's Republic of Poland]. www.dk.uni.wroc.pl.

Lang, Sabine. 2013. *NGOs, Civil Society, and the Public Sphere.* New York: Cambridge University Press.

Leszkowicz, Paweł. 2010. *Ars Homo Erotica: Catalogue Accompanying the Exhibition "Ars Homo Erotica" at the National Museum in Warsaw.* Warsaw: CePed.

Levitsky, Steven, and Lucan Way. 2010. *Competitive Authoritarianism: Hybrid Regimes after the Cold War.* New York: Cambridge University Press.

Levitz, Philip, and Grigore Pop-Eleches. 2010. "Why No Backsliding? The EU's Impact on Democracy and Governance before and after Accession." *Comparative Political Studies* 43: 457–485.

Long, Scott. 1999. "Gay and Lesbian Movements in Eastern Europe: Romania, Hungary, and the Czech Republic." In *The Global Emergence of Gay and Lesbian Politics: National Imprints of a Worldwide Movement,* ed. Barry D. Adam, Jan Willem Duyvendak, and André Krouwell, 242–265. Philadelphia: Temple University Press.

Longman, Jeré. 2013. "Outrage over an Antigay Law Does Not Spread to Olympic Officials." *New York Times,* August 6.

Lorencová, Viera. 2006. "Becoming Visible: Queer in Postsocialist Slovakia." PhD diss., University of Massachusetts, Amherst.

Lyman, Rick. 2014. "A Gay Mayor in Poland? No Big Deal." *New York Times,* December 2.

Lyman, Rick, and Joanna Berendt. 2016. "Poland Steps Back from Stricter Anti-Abortion Law." *New York Times,* October 6.

Mainwaring, Scott. 1999. *Rethinking Party Systems in the Third Wave of Democratization: The Case of Brazil.* Stanford: Stanford University Press.

Mair, Peter. 1997. *Party System Change: Approaches and Interpretations.* Oxford: Clarendon Press.

Makuchowska, Mirosława, and Michał Pawlęga, eds. 2012. *Situation of LGBT Persons in Poland, 2010 and 2011 Report.* Warsaw: Campaign Against Homophobia, www.kph.org.pl.

Markowski, Radoslaw. 2007. "The Party System." In *Democracy in Poland 2005–2007,* ed. Lena Kolarska-Bobińska, Jacek Kucharczyk, and Jarosław Zbieranek, 145–180. Warsaw: Instytut Spraw Publicznych.

McAdam, Doug. 1996. "Conceptual Origins, Current Problems, Future Directions." In *Comparative Perspectives on Social Movements: Political Opportunities, Mobilizing Structures, and Cultural Framings,* ed. Doug McAdam, John McCarthy, and Mayer Zald, 23–40. New York: Cambridge University Press.

McCarthy, John. 1996. "Constraints and Opportunities in Adopting, Adapting, and Inventing." In *Comparative Perspectives on Social Movements: Political Opportunities, Mobilizing Structures, and Cultural Framings,* ed. Doug McAdam, John McCarthy, and Mayer Zald, 141–151. New York: Cambridge University Press.

McGarry, Aidan. 2016. "Pride Parades and Prejudice: Visibility of Roma and LGBTI Communities in Post-socialist Europe." *Communist and Post-Communist Studies* 49: 269–277.

Meguid, Bonnie M. 2008. *Party Competition between Unequals: Strategies and Electoral Fortunes in Western Europe.* New York: Cambridge University Press.

Mesežnikov, Grigorij. 2007. "Domestic Politics and the Party System." In *Slovakia 2006: A Global Report on the State of Society*, ed. Martin Bútora, Miroslav Kollár, and Grigorij Mesežnikov, 21–90. Bratislava: Institute for Public Affairs.

Meyer, David S. 2003. "How Social Movements Matter." *Contexts* 2 (4): 30–35.

Millard, Frances. 2006. "Poland's Politics and the Travails of Transition after 2001: The 2005 Elections." *Europe-Asia Studies* 58 (7): 1007–1031.

———. 2009. "Poland: Parties without a Party System, 1991–2008." *Politics & Policy* 37 (4): 781–798.

Minałto, Michał. 2007. "Gays and Lesbians on Every Newsstand: The Explosion of the Topic of Homosexuality in the Polish Press." In *Situation of Bisexual and Homosexual Persons in Poland*, ed. Marta Abramowicz, 57–67. Warsaw: Campaign Against Homophobia, www.kph.org.pl.

Mizielińska, Joanna. 2011. "Travelling Ideas, Travelling Times: On the Temporalities of LGBT and Queer Politics in Poland and the 'West.'" In *De-Centring Western Sexualities: Central and Eastern European Perspectives*, ed. Robert Kulpa and Joanna Mizielińska, 85–106. Farnham: Ashgate.

Mizielińska, Joanna, and Robert Kulpa. 2011. "'Contemporary Peripheries': Queer Studies, Circulation of Knowledge and East/West Divide." In *De-Centring Western Sexualities: Central and Eastern European Perspectives*, ed. Robert Kulpa and Joanna Mizielińska, 11–26. Farnham: Ashgate.

Mlejnek, Josef. 2006. "Liga polských rodin—reprezentantka poražených v transformačním procesu?" [The League of Polish Families: Representative of the losers in the transformation process?]. In *III. Kongres česk ých politologů* [The Third Congress of Czech political scientists], ed. Jan Němec and Markéta Šůstková, 364–376. Prague: Česká společnost pro politické vědy.

Moravcsik, Andrew, and Milada Anna Vachudova. 2003. "National Interests, State Power and EU Enlargement." *East European Politics and Societies* 17 (1): 42–57.

Moss, Kevin. 2014. "Split Europe: Homonationalism and Homophobia in Croatia." In *LGBT Activism and the Making of Europe: A Rainbow Europe?*, ed. Phillip Ayoub and David Paternotte, 212–232. Basingstoke: Palgrave Macmillan.

Mudde, Cas. 2007. *Populist Radical Right Parties in Europe*. New York: Cambridge University Press.

Mungiu-Pippidi, Alina. 1998. "The Ruler and the Patriarch: The Romanian Eastern Orthodox Church in Transition." *East European Constitutional Review* 7 (2): 85–91.

———. 2001. "The Return of Populism—the 2000 Romanian Elections." *Government and Opposition* 36 (2): 230–252.

Muyanga, Milu, T. S. Jayne, and William J. Burke. 2013. "Pathways into and out of Poverty: A Study of Rural Household Wealth Dynamics in Kenya." *Journal of Development Studies* 49 (10): 1358–1374.

Nachescu, Voichita. 2005. "Hierarchies of Difference: National Identity, Gay and Lesbian Rights, and the Church in Postcommunist Romania." In *Sexuality and Gender in Postcommunist Eastern Europe and Russia*, ed. Aleksander Štulhofer and Theo Sandfort, 57–78. New York: Haworth Press.

Nir, Sarah Maslin. 2016. "Finding Hate Crimes on the Rise, Leaders Condemn Vicious Acts." *New York Times*, December 5.

Norris, Pippa, and Ronald Inglehart. 2004. *Sacred and Secular: Religion and Politics Worldwide*. Cambridge: Cambridge University Press.

O'Dwyer, Conor. 2006. *Runaway State-Building: Patronage Politics and Democratic Development*. Baltimore: Johns Hopkins University Press.

———. 2010. "From Conditionality to Persuasion? Europeanization and the Rights of Sexual Minorities in Postaccession Poland." *Journal of European Integration* 32 (3): 229–247.

———. 2012. "Does the EU Help or Hinder Gay-Rights Movements in Postcommunist Europe? The Case of Poland." *East European Politics* 28 (4): 332–352.

———. 2014. "What Accounts for Differences in Party System Stability? Comparing the Dimensions of Party Competition in Eastern Europe." *Europe-Asia Studies* 66 (4): 511–535.

O'Dwyer, Conor, and Katrina Z. S. Schwartz. 2010. "Minority Rights after EU Enlargement: A Comparison of Antigay Politics in Poland and Latvia." *Comparative European Politics* 8 (2): 220–243.

Ohlsen, Inga. 2009. "Non-governmental Organizations in Poland Striving for Equality of Sexual Minorities: Differential Empowerment through the EU?" Master's thesis, Free University of Berlin/Humboldt.

Onishi, Norimitsu. 2015. "U.S. Support of Gay Rights in Africa May Have Done More Harm Than Good." *New York Times*, December 20.

Osipova, Natalia. 2016. "Voices from Abortion Bill Protests." *New York Times*, October 3.

Ost, David. 2006. *The Defeat of Solidarity: Anger and Politics in Postcommunist Europe*. Cornell: Cornell University Press.

Ostolski, Adam. 2005. "Żydzie, geje i wojna cywilizacji" [Jews, gays, and the civilization war]. *op. cit.* 2 (23): 16–17.

———. 2007. "Spiskowcy i gorszyciele. Judaizowanie gejów w polskim dyskursie prawicowym" [Conspirators and offenders: The Judaization of gays in the discourse of the Polish right]. In *Co nas dzieli i co nas łaczy?* [What divides and what unites us?], ed. M. Głowacka-Grajper and E. Nowicka, 156–178. Kraków: Nomos.

Owczarzak, Jill. 2009. "Defining Democracy and the Terms of Engagement with the Postsocialist State: Insights from HIV/AIDS." *East European Politics and Societies* 23 (3): 421–445.

———. 2010. "Activism, NGOs, and HIV Prevention in Postsocialist Poland: The Role of 'Anti-Politics.'" *Human Organization* 69 (2): 200–211.

Pacewicz, Piotr. 2010. "EuroPride, heterowstyd" [EuroPride, hetero-shame]. *Gazeta Wyborcza*, July 19.

Pankowski, Rafal. 2010. *The Populist Radical Right in Poland: The Patriots*. London: Routledge.

Peters, Jeremy W., Jo Becker, and Julie Hirschfeld Davis. 2017. "Trump Rescinds Rules on Bathrooms for Transgender Students." *New York Times*, February 22.

Petrova, Tsveta, and Sidney Tarrow. 2007. "Transactional and Participatory Activism in the Emerging European Polity: The Puzzle of East Central Europe." *Comparative Political Studies* 40 (1): 74–94.

Pew Research Center. 2013. "The Global Divide on Homosexuality." June 4, www.pewglobal.org.

Pilátová, Markéta, and Matěj Stránský. 2007. "Cesta do Evropy B" [The path to Europe B]. *Respekt* 42 (October 15–21): 30–34.

Pirošík, Vladimír, Margita Janišová, and Viola Šuterová. 2001. "Marginalized Groups." In *Slovakia 2000: A Global Report on the State of Society*, ed. G. Mesežnikov, M. Kollár, and T. Nicholson, 557–577. Bratislava: Institute for Public Affairs.

Piwowarczyk, Konrad, Wojciech Sierachan, and Kamil Stolarek. 2013. "Awangarda Normatywnej Zmiany? Światopogląd Młodych Wyborców Ruchu Palikota" [The avant-garde of normative change? The worldview of young voters for the Palikot Movement]. In *Dlaczego Palikot? Młodzi Wyborcy Ruchu Palikota: Przypadkowy czy "Twardy" Elektorat Nowej Siły a Polskiej Scenie Politycznej* [Why Palikot? Young voters of the Palikot Movement: Random or "solid" electorate of the new power on the polish political scene], ed. Radosław Marzęcki and Łukasz Stach, 121–149. Warsaw: Elipsa.

"Poland Will Not Yield to EU Over Court Reforms: Kaczynski." 2018. Reuters, January 26, www.reuters.com.

Pop-Eleches, Grigore. 2001. "Romania's Politics of Dejection." *Journal of Democracy* 12 (3): 156–169.

Pop-Eleches, Grigore, and Joshua Tucker. 2013. "Associated with the Past? Communist Legacies and Civic Participation in Post-Communist Countries." *East European Politics and Societies* 27 (1): 43–66.

Prazmowska, Anita. 1995. "The New Right in Poland: Nationalism, Anti-Semitism, and Anti-Parliamentarism." In *The Far Right in Western and Eastern Europe*, 2nd ed., ed. Luciano Cheles, Ronnie Ferguson, and Michalina Vaughan, 198–214. New York: Longman.

Pride House Program. 2010. www.europride2010.eu.

Pridham, Geoffrey. 1999. "Complying with the European Union's Democratic Conditionality: Transnational Party Linkages and Regime Change in Slovakia, 1993–98." *Europe-Asia Studies* 51 (7): 1221–1244.

Procházka, Ivo. 1997. "The Czech and Slovak Republics." In *Sociolegal Control of Homosexuality: A Multi-Nation Comparison*, ed. Donald West and Richard Green, 243–254. New York: Plenum Press.

Procházka, Ivo, David Janík, and Jiří Hromada. 2003. *Social Discrimination of Lesbians, Gay Men and Bisexuals in the CR*. Prague: Gay Initiative in the CR.

PROUD. 2011. "Vznikla nová platforma proti homofobii a transfobii v ČR" [A new platform against homophobia and transphobia established in the Czech Republic]. May 16, www.proudem.cz.

Przybylska, Aleksandra. 2005. "Nie Ma Zgody Na Marsz Równości" [No agreement for the March of Equality]. *Gazeta Wyborcza*, November 18, serwisy.gazeta.pl.

Raik, Kirsti. 2004. "EU Accession of Central and Eastern European Countries: Democracy and Integration as Conflicting Logics." *East European Politics and Societies* 18 (4): 567–594.

"Rainbow Pride 2011 Event Ends with Organisers Praising Police Work." 2011. *Slovak Spectator*, June 6.

"Rainbow Pride Attracts Hundreds; No Incidents Reported This Year." 2014. *Slovak Spectator*, June 30.

"Rainbow Pride Rally Records No Major Disturbances." 2012. *Slovak Spectator*, June 11.

"Rainbow Pride Takes Place amid Hateful Campaign." 2013. *Slovak Spectator*, September 30.

"Rainbow Shines Even through Tear-gas." 2010. *Slovak Spectator*, May 24.

Ramet, Sabrina P. 2006. "Thy Will Be Done: The Catholic Church and Politics in Poland since 1989." In *Religion in an Expanding Europe*, ed. Timothy Byrnes and Peter Katzenstein, 117–147. Cambridge: Cambridge University Press.

———. 2007. *The Liberal Project and the Transformation of Democracy: The Case of East Central Europe*. College Station: Texas A&M University Press.

Regulska, Joanna, and Magda Grabowska. 2008. "Will It Make a Difference? EU Enlargement and Women's Public Discourse in Poland." In *Gender Politics in the Expanding European Union*, ed. Silke Roth. New York: Berghahn Books.

Renkin, Hadley. 2007a. "Ambiguous Identities, Ambiguous Transitions: Lesbians, Gays, and the Sexual Politics of Citizenship in Postsocialist Hungary." PhD diss., University of Michigan.

———. 2007b. "Predecessors and Pilgrims: Lesbian History-Making and Belonging in Post-socialist Hungary." In *Beyond the Pink Curtain: Everyday Life of LGBT People in Eastern Europe*, ed. Roman Kuhar and Judit Takács, 269–286. Ljubljana: Peace Institute.

———. 2009. "Homophobia and Queer Belonging in Hungary." *Focaal—European Journal of Anthropology* 53 (1): 20–37.

———. 2015. "Perverse Frictions: Pride, Dignity and the Budapest LGBT March." *Ethnos: Journal of Anthropology* 80 (3): 409–432.

Reynolds, Andrew. 2013. "Representation and Rights: The Impact of LGBT Legislators in Comparative Perspective." *American Political Science Review* 107 (2): 259–274.

Riszovannij, Mihaly. 2001. "Self-Articulation of the Gay and Lesbian Movement in Hungary after 1989." In *Pink, Purple, Green: Women's, Religious, Environmental, and Gay/Lesbian Movements in Central Europe Today*, ed. Helena Flam, 150–160. Boulder: East European Monographs.

Rohac, Dalibor. 2014. "Slovak Politics and Gay Rights." *New York Times*, December 30.

Rupnik, Jacques. 2002. "Das andere Mitteleuropa: Die neuen Populismen und die Politik mit der Vergangenheit" [The other Central Europe: The new populisms and the politics of the past]. *Transit* 23: 117–127.

"Rydzyk o tęczy: Symbole zboczeń nie powinny być tolerowane" [Rydzyk on the rainbow: A symbol of deviance should not be tolerated]. 2013. November 14, www.fakt.pl.

Sándor, B. 2001. "Report on the Discrimination of Lesbians, Gay Men and Bisexuals in Hungary." Háttér Society for Gays and Lesbians in Hungary and Labrisz Lesbian Association, Budapest, www.policy.hu/sandor/report.html.

Santora, Marc. 2018 "Poland Reshuffles Government, Hoping to Ease Tensions with E.U." *New York Times*, January 9.

Sasse, Gwendolyn. 2008. "The Politics of EU Conditionality: The Norm of Minority Protection during and beyond EU Accession." *Journal of European Public Policy* 15 (6): 842–860.

Schimmelfennig, Frank, and Hanno Scholtz. 2008. "EU Democracy Promotion in the European Neighborhood: Political Conditionality, Economic Development, and Transnational Exchange." *European Union Politics* 9 (2): 187–215.

Schimmelfennig, Frank, and Ulrich Sedelmeier. 2005. "Introduction: Conceptualizing the Europeanization of Central and Eastern Europe." In *The Europeanization of Central and Eastern Europe*, ed. Frank Schimmelfennig and Ulrich Sedelmeier, 1–28. Cornell: Cornell University Press.

Seidl, Jan. 2012. *Od žaláře k oltáři. Emancipace homosexuality v českých zemích od roku 1867 do současnosti* [From the dungeon to the altar: Homosexual emancipation in the Czech lands from 1867 to the present]. Brno: Host.

Sherkat, Darren, and T. Jean Blocker. 1997. "Explaining the Political and Personal Consequences of Protest." *Social Forces* 75 (3): 1049–1076.

Shibata, Yusako. 2013. *Discrimination for the Sake of the Nation*. Frankfurt am Mein: Peter Lang.

Siedlecka, Ewa. 2006. "Świat mowi 'rowni,' Polska—'solidarni'" [The world says "equal," Poland "solidary"]. *Gazeta Wyborcza*, February 10.

Sierakowski, Slawomir. 2014a. "The Polish Church's Gender Problem." *New York Times*, January 27.

———. 2014b. "From Pugilist to Activist." *New York Times*, October 1.

Slater, Dan, and Daniel Ziblatt. 2013. "The Enduring Indispensability of the Controlled Comparison." *Comparative Political Studies* 46 (10): 1301–1327.

Slubowski, Slawomir. 1998. "Geje Dumni Inaczej" [A different sort of gay pride]. *Super Express*, July 13.

Snow, David, Daniel Cress, Liam Downey, and Andrew Jones. 1998. "Disrupting the 'Quotidian': Reconceptualizing the Relationship between Breakdown and the Emergence of Collective Action." *Mobilization* 3 (1): 1–22.

Sokolová, Věra. 2004. "'Don't Get Pricked!': Representation and the Politics of Sexuality in the Czech Republic." In *Over the Wall/after the Fall: Post-Communist Cultures through an East-West Gaze*, ed. S. Forrester, M. Zaborowska, and E. Gapova, 251–267. Bloomington: Indiana University Press.

———. 2005. "Identity Politics and the (B)Orders of Heterosexism: Lesbians, Gays and Feminists in the Czech Media after 1989." In *Mediale Welten in Tschechien nach 1989: Genderprojektionen und Codes des Plebejismus* [Media worlds in the Czech Republic after 1989: Gender projections and codes of conventionality], ed. J. van Leuween and N. Richter, 29–44. Munich: Kubon und Sagner.

———. 2006. "Koncepční pohled na "sexuální menšiny" aneb vše je jen otázka správné orientace . . ." [A conceptual view of 'sexual minorities,' or everything is only a question of the correct orientation . . .]. In *Mnohohlasem: Vyjednávání ženských prostorů po roce 1989* [Multiple voices: Negotiating women's spaces after 1989], ed. Hana Hašková, Alena Křížková, and Marcela Linková, 253–266. Prague: SoÚ.

Sowa, Agnieszka. 2013. "Polityczna historia tęczy z placu Zbawiciela" [A political history of the rainbow on Savior Square]. *Polityka*, November 19, www.polityka.pl.

"Spada sprzedaż dzienników, 'Gazeta Wyborcza' poniżej 190 tys. egz." [Sales of *Gazeta Wyborcza fall* below 190,000 copies]. 2013. Wirtualnemedia.pl, April 9, www.wirtu alnemedia.pl.

Sperling, Valerie. 1999. *Organizing Women in Contemporary Russia: Engendering Transition*. New York: Cambridge University Press.

———. 2015. *Sex, Politics, and Putin: Political Legitimacy in Russia*. New York: Oxford University Press.

Spiegel Online International. 2012. "Growing Tensions: Far-Right Protest Targets Roma in Hungary." October 18, www.spiegel.de.

Staggenborg, Suzanne. 2011. *Social Movements*. New York: Oxford University Press.

Stewart, Michael. 2012. "Populism, Roma, and the European Politics of Cultural Difference." In *The Gypsy 'Menace': Populism and the New Anti-Gypsy Politics*, ed. Michael Stewart, 3–23. New York: Columbia University Press.

Stokes, Gale. 2012. "Purposes of the Past." In *The End and the Beginning: The Revolutions of 1989 and the Resurgence of History*, ed. Vladimir Tismaneanu and Bogdan C. Iacob, 35–53. Budapest: CEU Press.

Štulhofer, Aleksander, and Ivan Rimac. 2009. "Determinants of Homonegativity in Europe." *Journal of Sex Research* 46 (1): 24–32.

Stychin, Carl. 2003. *Governing Sexuality: The Changing Politics of Citizenship and Law Reform*. Oxford: Hart Publishing.

Subotic, Jelena. 2009. *Hijacked Justice: Dealing with the Past in the Balkans*. Ithaca: Cornell University Press.

Sundstrom, Lisa. 2006. *Funding Civil Society: Foreign Assistance and NGO Development*. Stanford: Stanford University Press.

Swiebel, Joke. 2009. "Lesbian, Gay, Bisexual and Trans Human Rights: The Search for an International Strategy." *Contemporary Politics* 15 (1): 19–35.

Takács, Judit. 2007. *How to Put Equality into Practice? Anti-discrimination and Equal Treatment Policymaking and LGBT People*. Budapest: Új Mandátum.

Takács, Judit, and Ivett Szalma. 2011. "Homophobia and Same-Sex Partnership Legislation in Europe." *Equality, Diversity and Inclusion* 30 (5): 356–78.

Tarrow, Sidney. 1993. "Cycles of Collective Action: Between Moments of Madness and the Repertoire of Contention." *Social Science History* 17 (2): 281–307.

———. 2005. *The New Transnational Activism*. New York: Cambridge University Press.

Tóth, András, and István Grajczjár. 2015. "The Rise of the Radical Right in Hungary." In *The Hungarian Patient: Social Opposition to an Illiberal Democracy*, ed. Péter Krasztev and Jon Van Til, 133–163. Budapest: CEU Press.

Thrush, Glenn, and Maggie Haberman. 2017. "Ivanka Trump and Jared Kushner Said to Have Helped Thwart L.G.B.T. Rights Rollback." *New York Times*, February 3.

Turcescu, Lucian, and Lavinia Stan. 2005. "Religion, Politics and Sexuality in Romania." *Europe-Asia Studies* 57 (2): 291–310.

Ungar, Mark. 2000. "State Violence and Lesbian, Gay, Bisexual and Transgender (lgbt) Rights." *New Political Science* 22 (1): 61–75.

Vachudova, Milada. 2005. *Europe Undivided: Democracy, Leverage, and Integration after Communism.* New York: Oxford University Press.

———. 2008. "Tempered by the EU? Political Parties and Party Systems before and after Accession." *Journal of European Public Policy* 15 (6): 861–879.

Vališ, Oliver. 2001. "Národniari lesbičkám neprajú: Eva Slavkovská brojí proti homosexuálizm učiteľom" [Nationalists do not support lesbians: Eva Slavkovská argues against homosexual teachers]. *Praca*, June 9.

van der Vleuten, Anna. 2014. "Transnational LGBTI Activism and the European Courts." In *LGBT Activism and the Making of Europe: A Rainbow Europe?*, ed. Phillip M. Ayoub and David Paternotte, 119–144. Basingstoke: Palgrave Macmillan.

Vasilev, George. 2016. "LGBT Recognition in EU Accession States: How Identification with Europe Enhances the Transformative Power of Discourse." *Review of International Studies* 42 (4) (October): 748–772.

Vermeersch, Peter. 2006. *The Romani Movement: Minority Politics and Ethnic Mobilization in Contemporary Central Europe.* New York: Berghahn Books.

Walicki, Andrzej. 1999. "The Troubling Legacy of Roman Dmowski." *East European Politics and Societies* 14 (1): 12–46.

Wallace-Lorencová, Viera. 2003. "Queering Civil Society in Postsocialist Slovakia." *Anthropology of East Europe Review* 21 (2): 103–112.

Warkocki, B. 2004. "Biedni Polacy patrzą na homosekualistów" [Poor Poles look at homosexuals]. In *Homofobia po polsku* [Homophobia in Polish], ed. Zbyszek Sypniewski and Błażej Warkocki, 97–119. Warsaw: Sic!

Warsaw Voice. 2006. "Commotion over EP Resolution." June 28, www.warsawvoice.pl.

Weeks, Jeffrey. 2007. *The World We Have Won: The Remaking of Erotic and Intimate Life.* London: Routledge.

Wernet, Christine, Cheryl Elman, and Brian Pendleton. 2005. "The Postmodern Individual: Structural Determinants of Attitudes." *Comparative Sociology* 4 (3): 339–364.

Wilkinson, Cai. 2014. "Putting 'Traditional Values' into Practice: The Rise and Contestation of Anti-Homopropaganda Laws in Russia." *Journal of Human Rights* 13 (3): 363–379.

Wilson, Angelia. 2013. *Why Europe Is Lesbian and Gay Friendly (and Why America Never Will Be).* Albany: SUNY Press.

Wojtasik, Waldemar. 2012. "Sukces Ruchu Palikota w Świetle Czynników Możliwego Sukcesu Politycznego" [The success of the Palikot Movement in light of the political opportunity structure model]. *Preferencje Polityczne* 3: 159–174.

World Values Survey (WVS). 2008. World Values Survey 1999–2008. www.worldvaluessurvey.org.

"Wreszcie coś się dzieje" [At last something is happening]. 2010. *Gazeta Wyborcza*, July 19.

Wróblewski, Bogdan. 2006. "Polscy politycy chcą szukać wsparcia w Europie dla kary śmierci" [Polish politicians seek support in Europe for death penalty]. *Gazeta Wyborcza*, July 27.

Zablocki, Krzysztof. 2007. "Surviving under Pressure: Working for 'Days of Tolerance' in Poland." In *Challenging Homophobia: Teaching about Sexual Diversity*, ed. Lutz van Dijk and Barry Van Driel, 139–148. Stoke on Trent: Trentham Books.

Zalewski, Igor. 2004. "Dyktatura równości" [The dictatorship of equality]. *Wprost*, June 13, www.wprost.pl.

Zboralski, Waldemar. 1991. "Wspomnienia weterana" [Memories of a veteran]. *Inaczej* 9 (February): 3–5.

Zolnay, János. 2012. "Abusive Language and Discriminatory Measures in Hungarian Local Policy." In *The Gypsy 'Menace': Populism and the New Anti-Gypsy Politics*, ed. Michael Stewart, 25–41. New York: Columbia University Press.

INDEX

abortion, 72, 145, 224, 292n123, 294n28; banning of, 148, 295n31; restrictions on, 123; retrenchment of policy on, 225–26

ACCEPT, 206–15, 266n75, 293n138

accession, EU, 77–78, 142; blocking of, 36; candidates for, 43; consequences of, 273n69; of Czech Republic, 138; as disruptive, 42; domestic politics of homosexuality shaped by, 3–4; homosexuality shaped by, 3–4; of Hungary, 179; Hungary during, 176–82; party competition weakened by, 62; of Poland, 65, 138–39; policy change after, 54–56; preaccession, postaccession and, 30, 34; pressures of, 109; proximity to, as variable, 46, 47, 54; requirements for, 38–41; of Romania, 203; Romania during, 207–11; of Slovakia, 192; Slovakia during, 193–98; timing and implementation of, 28–29; transnational pressures associated with, 218

acquis communautaire, 38–41, 113

activism: after communism, 218; Czech compared to Polish, 16, 29–30, 60–64, 86, 109–10, 227; demobilization of, 200; linking the transnational and domestic determinants of, 17–23; national reach of, 128–29; perennial challenges of, 168; robustness of, 220–21; in Romania, 203–4, 209; self-help as, 104; in terms of citizenship, 8; trajectories of, 171–72; transnational pressures boosting, 23; variations in, 5–6. *See also* apolitical activism; feminist activism; local activism; organization of activism; queer activism; transnational activism

activist groups, 30–31; cooperation between, 113, 121, 141; educational funds access blocked for, 68; financial resources of, 45, 98–99, 104–7, 110; naming of, 115; rivalry between, 122; self-help as orientation of, 22, 88–90

activists: allies for, 19–20; framing by, 101–2; institutional structures built by, 85–86; interviews with, 29; mapping network of, 256–62; solidarity among, 5

adoption, 167, 297n106; Hromada's position regarding, 136–37, 164–65; by same-sex partnerships, 38

age, of consent for sex, 90, 96, 176, 179–80

Alexandrowicz, Przemyslaw, 71

Alliance of Families (AoF), 213–14

Alliance of Free Democrats-Hungarian Liberals Party (SZDSZ), 177, 183, 186, 188, 235, 296n84

alliances: beteeen LGBT and feminist groups, 122; building of, 97; of hard right, 25–26

allies, 114, 179, 236; of activists, 19–20; attracting of, 4, 57; availability of, 141; at highest levels of national politics, 36–37; mobilizing structures built through experience as, 222; resonance, solidarity and, 22; visibility, solidarity and, 58, 145, 228

All-Poland Association of Lambda Groups (Ogólnopolskie Stowarzyszenie Grup Lambda), 104–9

ABOUT THE AUTHOR

Conor O'Dwyer is Associate Professor of Political Science at the University of Florida. He specializes in comparative politics, with a regional emphasis on East Central Europe and the EU. In addition to his work on LGBT politics, he has published on democratization, comparative political parties, and postcommunist state-building.